Lecture Notes in Computer Science

Vol. 1: GI-Gesellschaft für Informatik e.V. 3. Jahrestagung, Hamburg, 8.–10. Oktober 1973. Herausgegeben im Auftrag der Gesellschaft für Informatik von W. Brauer. XI, 508 Seiten. 1973.

Vol. 2: GI-Gesellschaft für Informatik e.V. 1. Fachtagung über Automatentheorie und Formale Sprachen, Bonn, 9.–12. Juli 1973. Herausgegeben im Auftrag der Gesellschaft für Informatik von K.-H. Böhling und K. Indermark. VII, 322 Seiten. 1973.

Vol. 3: 5th Conference on Optimization Techniques, Part I. (Series: I.F.I.P. TC7 Optimization Conferences.) Edited by R. Conti and A. Ruberti. XIII, 565 pages. 1973.

Vol. 4: 5th Conference on Optimization Techniques, Part II. (Series: I.F.I.P. TC7 Optimization Conferences.) Edited by R. Conti and A. Ruberti. XIII, 389 pages. 1973.

Vol. 5: International Symposium on Theoretical Programming. Edited by A. Ershov and V. A. Nepomniaschy. VI, 407 pages. 1974.

Vol. 6: B. T. Smith, J. M. Boyle, J. J. Dongarra, B. S. Garbow, Y. Ikebe, V. C. Klema, and C. B. Moler, Matrix Eigensystem Routines – EISPACK Guide. XI, 551 pages. 2nd Edition 1974. 1976.

Vol. 7: 3. Fachtagung über Programmiersprachen, Kiel, 5.–7. März 1974. Herausgegeben von B. Schlender und W. Frielinghaus. VI, 225 Seiten. 1974.

Vol. 8: GI-NTG Fachtagung über Struktur und Betrieb von Rechensystemen, Braunschweig, 20.–22. März 1974. Herausgegeben im Auftrag der GI und der NTG von H.-O. Leilich. VI, 340 Seiten. 1974.

Vol. 9: GI-BIFOA Internationale Fachtagung: Informationszentren in Wirtschaft und Verwaltung. Köln, 17./18. Sept. 1973. Herausgegeben im Auftrag der GI und dem BIFOA von P. Schmitz. VI, 259 Seiten. 1974.

Vol. 10: Computing Methods in Applied Sciences and Engineering, Part 1. International Symposium, Versailles, December 17–21, 1973. Edited by R. Glowinski and J. L. Lions. X, 497 pages. 1974.

Vol. 11: Computing Methods in Applied Sciences and Engineering, Part 2. International Symposium, Versailles, December 17–21, 1973. Edited by R. Glowinski and J. L. Lions. X, 434 pages. 1974.

Vol. 12: GFK-GI-GMR Fachtagung Prozessrechner 1974. Karlsruhe, 10.–11. Juni 1974. Herausgegeben von G. Krüger und R. Friehmelt. XI, 620 Seiten. 1974.

Vol. 13: Rechnerstrukturen und Betriebsprogrammierung, Erlangen, 1970. (GI-Gesellschaft für Informatik e.V.) Herausgegeben von W. Händler und P. P. Spies. VII, 333 Seiten. 1974.

Vol. 14: Automata, Languages and Programming – 2nd Colloquium, University of Saarbrücken, July 29–August 2, 1974. Edited by J. Loeckx. VIII, 611 pages. 1974.

Vol. 15: L Systems. Edited by A. Salomaa and G. Rozenberg. VI, 338 pages. 1974.

Vol. 16: Operating Systems, International Symposium, Rocquencourt 1974. Edited by E. Gelenbe and C. Kaiser. VIII, 310 pages. 1974.

Vol. 17: Rechner-Gestützter Unterricht RGU '74, Fachtagung, Hamburg, 12.–14. August 1974, ACU-Arbeitskreis Computer-Unterstützter Unterricht. Herausgegeben im Auftrag der GI von K. Brunnstein, K. Haefner und W. Händler. X, 417 Seiten. 1974.

Vol. 18: K. Jensen and N. E. Wirth, PASCAL – User Manual and Report. VII, 170 pages. Corrected Reprint of the 2nd Edition 1976.

Vol. 19: Programming Symposium. Proceedings 1974. V, 425 pages. 1974.

Vol. 20: J. Engelfriet, Simple Program Schemes and Formal Languages. VII, 254 pages. 1974.

Vol. 21: Compiler Construction, An Advanced Course. Edited by F. L. Bauer and J. Eickel. XIV. 621 pages. 1974.

Vol. 22: Formal Aspects of Cognitive Processes. Proceedings 1972. Edited by T. Storer and D. Winter. V, 214 pages. 1975.

Vol. 23: Programming Methodology. 4th Informatik Symposium, IBM Germany Wildbad, September 25–27, 1974. Edited by C. E. Hackl. VI, 501 pages. 1975.

Vol. 24: Parallel Processing. Proceedings 1974. Edited by T. Feng. VI, 433 pages. 1975.

Vol. 25: Category Theory Applied to Computation and Control. Proceedings 1974. Edited by E. G. Manes. X, 245 pages. 1975.

Vol. 26: GI-4. Jahrestagung, Berlin, 9.–12. Oktober 1974. Herausgegeben im Auftrag der GI von D. Siefkes. IX, 748 Seiten. 1975.

Vol. 27: Optimization Techniques. IFIP Technical Conference. Novosibirsk, July 1–7, 1974. (Series: I.F.I.P. TC7 Optimization Conferences.) Edited by G. I. Marchuk. VIII, 507 pages. 1975.

Vol. 28: Mathematical Foundations of Computer Science. 3rd Symposium at Jadwisin near Warsaw, June 17–22, 1974. Edited by A. Blikle. VII, 484 pages. 1975.

Vol. 29: Interval Mathematics. Procedings 1975. Edited by K. Nickel. VI, 331 pages. 1975.

Vol. 30: Software Engineering. An Advanced Course. Edited by F. L. Bauer. (Formerly published 1973 as Lecture Notes in Economics and Mathematical Systems, Vol. 81) XII, 545 pages. 1975.

Vol. 31: S. H. Fuller, Analysis of Drum and Disk Storage Units. IX, 283 pages. 1975.

Vol. 32: Mathematical Foundations of Computer Science 1975. Proceedings 1975. Edited by J. Bečvář. X, 476 pages. 1975.

Vol. 33: Automata Theory and Formal Languages, Kaiserslautern, May 20–23, 1975. Edited by H. Brakhage on behalf of GI. VIII, 292 Seiten. 1975.

Vol. 34: GI – 5. Jahrestagung, Dortmund 8.–10. Oktober 1975. Herausgegeben im Auftrag der GI von J. Mühlbacher. X, 755 Seiten. 1975.

Vol. 35: W. Everling, Exercises in Computer Systems Analysis. (Formerly published 1972 as Lecture Notes in Economics and Mathematical Systems, Vol. 65) VIII, 184 pages. 1975.

Vol. 36: S. A. Greibach, Theory of Program Structures: Schemes, Semantics, Verification. XV, 364 pages. 1975.

Vol. 37: C. Böhm, λ-Calculus and Computer Science Theory. Proceedings 1975. XII, 370 pages. 1975.

Vol. 38: P. Branquart, J.-P. Cardinael, J. Lewi, J.-P. Delescaille, M. Vanbegin. An Optimized Translation Process and Its Application to ALGOL 68. IX, 334 pages. 1976.

Vol. 39: Data Base Systems. Proceedings 1975. Edited by H. Hasselmeier and W. Spruth. VI, 386 pages. 1976.

Vol. 40: Optimization Techniques. Modeling and Optimization in the Service of Man. Part 1. Proceedings 1975. Edited by J. Cea. XIV, 854 pages. 1976.

Vol. 41: Optimization Techniques. Modeling and Optimization in the Service of Man. Part 2. Proceedings 1975. Edited by J. Cea. XIII, 852 pages. 1976.

Vol. 42: James E. Donahue, Complementary Definitions of Programming Language Semantics. VII, 172 pages. 1976.

Vol. 43: E. Specker und V. Strassen, Komplexität von Entscheidungsproblemen. Ein Seminar. V, 217 Seiten. 1976.

Vol. 44: ECI Conference 1976. Proceedings 1976. Edited by K. Samelson. VIII, 322 pages. 1976.

Vol. 45: Mathematical Foundations of Computer Science 1976. Proceedings 1976. Edited by A. Mazurkiewicz. XI, 601 pages. 1976.

Vol. 46: Language Hierarchies and Interfaces. Edited by F. L. Bauer and K. Samelson. X, 428 pages. 1976.

Vol. 47: Methods of Algorithmic Language Implementation. Edited by A. Ershov and C. H. A. Koster. VIII, 351 pages. 1977.

Vol. 48: Theoretical Computer Science, Darmstadt, March 1977. Edited by H. Tzschach, H. Waldschmidt and H. K.-G. Walter on behalf of GI. VIII, 418 pages. 1977.

Lecture Notes in Computer Science

Edited by G. Goos and J. Hartmanis

93

Anton Nijholt

Context-Free Grammars: Covers, Normal Forms, and Parsing

Springer-Verlag
Berlin Heidelberg New York 1980

Author

Anton Nijholt
Vrije Universiteit
Wiskundig Seminarium
De Boelelaan 1081
Postbus 7161
1007 MC Amsterdam
The Netherlands

AMS Subject Classifications (1979): 68F05, 68F25
CR Subject Classifications (1974): 4.12, 5.23

ISBN 3-540-10245-0 Springer-Verlag Berlin Heidelberg New York
ISBN 0-387-10245-0 Springer-Verlag New York Heidelberg Berlin

Library of Congress Cataloging in Publication Data. Nijholt, Anton, 1946-
Context-free grammars. (Lecture notes in computer science; 93) Bibliography: p.
Includes index. 1. Formal languages. I. Title. II. Series.
QA267.3.N54. 511.3. 80-21378

Printing and binding: Beltz Offsetdruck, Hemsbach/Bergstr.
2145/3140-543210

PREFACE

This monograph develops a theory of grammatical covers, normal forms and parsing. Covers, formally defined in 1969, describe a relation between the sets of parses of two context-free grammars. If this relation exists then in a formal model of parsing it is possible to have, except for the output, for both grammars the same parser.

Questions concerning the possibility to cover a certain grammar with grammars that conform to some requirements on the productions or the derivations will be raised and answered. Answers to these cover problems will be obtained by introducing algorithms that describe a transformation of an input grammar into an output grammar which satisfies the requirements.

The main emphasis in this monograph is on transformations of context-free grammars to context-free grammars in some normal form. However, not only transformations of this kind will be discussed, but also transformations which yield grammars which have useful parsing properties.

Organization of the monograph

This monograph can be viewed as consisting of four parts.

The first part, Chapters 1 through 3, introduces the cover concept, the motivation of our research, the problems and, moreover, it reviews previous research.

The second part, Chapters 4 through 7, provides cover results for normal form transformations of context-free and regular grammars.

The third part, Chapters 8 through 10, is devoted to cover results for three classes of deterministically parsable grammars, viz. LL(k), strict deterministic and LR(k) grammars. In this part, a discussion of some syntactic aspects of compiler writing systems is included.

The fourth and final part of this monograph consists of Chapters 11 and 12. Chapter 11 contains a detailed discussion on simple chain grammars. Chapter 12 surveys parsing strategies for context-free grammars. In this chapter cover properties of transformations to LL(k) and some other classes of grammars are considered.

A Bibliography and an Index appear at the end of the monograph.

A few sections and notes in this monograph are marked with a star. These starred sections and notes can be skipped without loss of continuity. Some of these starred sections and notes deal with syntax categories and grammar functors. Others deal with technical arguments on parsing at a moment that a reader who is not acquainted with some less conventional ideas of parsing will not grasp their significance.

The sections and notes on syntax categories are included to give the interested reader and the reader who is familiar with these concepts a notion of the differences and the similarities between these concepts and the grammar cover concept.

Moreover, it will become clear that in our grammar cover framework of Chapter 2 we have borrowed from ideas of the grammar functor approach.

We have tried to give full and formal proofs for most of the results which appear in this monograph. Only in those cases that proofs are available in publications elsewhere or in cases that *we* had the idea that a certain result should be clear because of its simplicity or because of what has been proven in the foregoing parts of the monograph, we have omitted a proof or formal detail.

Acknowledgements

Several people have helped me prepare this monograph. I should like to mention particularly Michael A. Harrison of the University of California at Berkeley and Jaco W. de Bakker of the Vrije Universiteit and the Mathematical Centre in Amsterdam for providing time, confidence and for their comments on a first handwritten version of the manuscript. Although not all their suggestions have been incorporated many improvements are due to their comments.

Other people, maybe sometimes unknowingly, did encourage me. Especially I want to mention Derick Wood of McMaster's University at Hamilton.

This monograph was prepared during my stay with the Vakgroep Informatica of the Department of Mathematics of the Vrije Universiteit in Amsterdam. I want to express my gratitude to Marja H., Marja V., Betty and Carla for being there and helping me. Carla Reuvecamp did an excellent job of typing the lengthy manuscript.

Anton Nijholt
April 1980.

CONTENTS

1. INTRODUCTION AND PRELIMINARIES 1

1.1. Introduction 1
1.2. Overview of the contents 4
1.3. Preliminaries 5
  1.3.1. Grammars, automata and transducers 5
  1.3.2*. Syntax categories 12

2. GRAMMAR COVERS AND RELATED CONCEPTS 14

2.1. Grammar covers 14
2.2. Restrictions on parse relations 20
  2.2.1*. Some notes on parsing 22
  2.2.2. Production directed parses 24
2.3*. Grammar functors 28
2.4. Related concepts 29

3. COVERS, PARSING AND NORMAL FORMS 32

3.1. Covers and parsing 32
3.2. Covers and normal forms: Historical notes 34
3.3. Covers and normal forms: An introduction 35

4. PROPERTIES OF COVERS AND PRELIMINARY TRANSFORMATIONS 38

4.1. Properties of covers 38
4.2. Preliminary transformations 41

5. NORMAL FORM COVERS FOR CONTEXT-FREE GRAMMARS 48

5.1. From proper grammars to non-left-recursive grammars 48
5.2. From non-left-recursive to Greibach normal form grammars 51
5.2.1. The 'substitution' transformation 51
5.2.2. The left part transformation 55
5.3. Transformations on Greibach normal form grammars 76

6. THE COVER-TABLE FOR CONTEXT-FREE GRAMMARS 80

7. NORMAL FORM COVERS FOR REGULAR GRAMMARS 85

8. DETERMINISTICALLY PARSABLE GRAMMARS 98

8.1. Introduction 98
8.2. Preliminaries 105

9. COVERS AND DETERMINISTICALLY PARSABLE GRAMMARS 111

9.1. Deterministically parsable grammars 111
9.2. On the covering of deterministically parsable grammars 117

10. NORMAL FORM COVERS FOR DETERMINISTICALLY PARSABLE GRAMMARS 127

10.1. Normal form covers for LL(k) grammars 127
10.2. Normal form covers for strict deterministic grammars 141
10.3. Normal form covers for LR(k) grammars 164

11. COVER PROPERTIES OF SIMPLE CHAIN GRAMMARS 171

11.1. Simple chain grammars 172
11.2. Relationships between simple chain grammars and other classes of grammars 180
11.3. Simple chain languages 184
11.4. A left part theorem for simple chain grammars 189
11.5. Left part parsing and covering of simple chain grammars 196

12. TRANSFORMATIONS AND PARSING STRATEGIES: A CONCRETE APPROACH 205

12.1. Introduction 205
12.2. From LL(k) to LR(k) grammars: Parsing strategies 207
12.3. Transformations to LL(k) grammars 210
12.4. Parsing strategies revisited: A survey of recent research 230

BIBLIOGRAPHY 239

INDEX 248

CHAPTER 1

INTRODUCTIONS AND PRELIMINARIES

1.1. INTRODUCTION

Two context-free grammars which generate the same language are said to be weakly equivalent. Weak equivalence can be considered as a relation of grammatical similarity of context-free grammars. If two grammars G_1 and G_2 are weakly equivalent, then for each parse tree T_1 of G_1 there exists a parse tree T_2 of G_2 which has the same frontier, and conversely. Clearly, this relation of weak equivalence does not necessarily say that the shapes of the trees are closely related. Grammatical similarity relations have been introduced which describe relationships between the parse trees of the two grammars.

These relations sometimes but not always presuppose weak equivalence. For example, there exists the relation of structural equivalence. In that case we demand that, except for a relabeling of the internal nodes, the parse trees of the two grammars are the same.

Many other relations have been defined. Only a few will be considered here and only one of them, the grammar cover, will be treated in detail.

In many cases of interest it is quite natural to have weak equivalence between two grammars. For example, a grammar can be changed to an other grammar which generates the same language. Such a transformation on a grammar may be done for several reasons.

By definition, each context-free language is generated by a context-free grammar. Instead of arbitrary context-free grammars one can consider context-free grammars which conform to some requirements on, for example, the productions or the derivations of the grammar. Then it is natural to ask whether each context-free language has a context-free grammar of this form and, if so, how to transform a grammar to this (normal) form.

One reason for considering normal forms may be the inherent mathematical interest in how to generate a family of context-free languages with a grammatical description as simple as possible. Moreover, normal forms can simplify proofs and descriptions in the field of formal languages and parsing. However, in 1975 it still could be remarked (Hotz[65]):

"*Resultate über die strukturelle Verwandschaft verschiedener Sprachen existieren kaum. Selbst bei der Herleitung von Normalformentheoremen für Grammatiken hat man sich mit der Feststellung der schwachen Äquivalenz begnügt*".

Some normal form descriptions for context-free grammars, or for grammars belonging to the various subclasses of the class of context-free grammars, can be particularly amenable for parsing, and this can be a strong motivation to transform grammars.

Transforming grammars into normal forms or to grammars which have other parsing properties can sometimes lead to faster or more compact parsers for these grammars. However, in these cases it is desirable to have a stronger relation than weak equivalence between the original grammar and the newly obtained grammar. This can be seen as follows.

Consider a very practical situation in which we want to build a compiler for a given programming language. We are interested in the part of the compiler which performs the syntactic analysis. We can consider this analysis as a translation from a sentence to a string which consists of procedure calls to perform the code generation.

One now can try to find a 'better' grammar (from the point of view of parsing) such that this translation is preserved. If this is possible, then parsing can be done with respect to the new grammar. The concept of grammar cover which is studied in this monograph describes a preservation of this translation.

We confine ourselves to a model of parsing in which each sentence is given a 'description' of each of its parse trees by means of a string of productions of the grammar. The correspondence of two grammars which is described by the grammar cover is the relation between the parse tree descriptions for a given sentence. In Chapter 8 we have a short discussion on the limitations of this model.

Often a description of a parse tree of a sentence w is given by means of a left or right parse, that is, a string of productions which are used in a derivation (leftmost or rightmost) of the sentence w. Although we will also allow other descriptions of parse trees, it will be clear that we are interested in the relationships among the derivations of sentences of the grammars which we want to relate. This idea can be recognized in many concepts.

In the older literature one can find ideas and examples which come close to later formal concepts. Transformations on context-free grammars have been defined in practically oriented situations of compiler construction. In those cases no general definition of the relation between the grammars was presented.

Grammar covers, in the sense that we will use them here, were introduced about 1969 by Gray and Harrison [48]. Their interest in this concept was based on its applications in the field of parsing.
The product of the syntactic analysis, the parse, can be considered as the argument of a semantic mapping. In the case that a context-free grammar G' covers a context-free grammar G, then each parse with respect to G' of a sentence w can be mapped by a homomorphism on a parse with respect to G of w. Hence, we can parse with respect to G' and use the original semantic mapping.

Other examples of grammatical similarity relations are grammar functors and grammar forms. Grammar functors (X-functors) were introduced by Hotz [63,64] as special functors on categories associated with (general) phrase structure grammars. These categories originate from work on switching circuits. The objects of a syntax category are strings over the grammar alphabet. The derivations are then considered as morphisms. The main concern has been to find an algebraic framework for describing general properties of phrase structure grammars. Later, functors have been considered from a more practical point of view and topics related to parsing have been discussed within this framework. See, for example, Bertsch [14], Benson [13] and Hotz and Ross [68].

In the case of grammar forms (Cremers and Ginsburg [21]) the starting point is a (master) grammar from which by means of substitutions of the nonterminal and terminal symbols other grammars are obtained. Observations on the parsing properties of the master grammar can be valid for all the grammars in the grammatical family which is obtained by these substitutions (cf. Ginsburg, Leong, Mayer and Wotschke [44]).

There are other examples of grammatical similarity relations. In Hunt and Rosenkrantz [69] many of them are discussed from the point of view of complexity.

In this monograph we will discuss the concept of grammar cover and its usefulness for parsing.

At this point we should mention two approaches which could have been followed and which will not be discussed further.

Firstly, it would be possible to consider transformations on attribute grammars (Knuth [78]). Here, attributes are associated with the nodes of a parse tree. These attributes (which contain the necessary information for the code generation) are obtained from attributes associated with the symbols which appear in the productions and from attribute evaluation rules. If an attribute grammar is transformed to, for example, some normal form attribute grammar, then we have not only the question of language equivalence, but also, explicitly, the question of 'semantic' equivalence. Such an equivalence is explored in Bochmann [15] and Anderson [5].

Secondly, it would have been possible to discuss translation grammars (Brosgol [18]) and transformations on translation grammars.

There is a third remark which we want to make at this point. We consider transformations of grammars. If they are applied with a view to obtain faster or compacter parsing methods then, instead of transforming the grammar, one can build a parser for the grammar and then change (optimize) this parser. This is, for instance, a very common method if an LR-parser is constructed. For example, instead of eliminating single productions from the grammar, single reductions can be eliminated from the parser (cf. e.g. Anderson, Eve and Horning [6]).

Answers to questions on the existence of a covering grammar can be answers to questions whether or not a parser for a given grammar can be modified in certain advantageous ways.

1.2. OVERVIEW OF THE CONTENTS

In Chapters 1 to 6 of this monograph we will be concerned with transformations of arbitrary context-free grammars to context-free grammars in some normal form representation. The main normal forms which will be considered are the non-left-recursive form and the Greibach normal form. Cover results for these normal forms will be presented.

Throughout this monograph we will pay much attention to what has been said before by various authors on these transformations. However, hardly any attention will be paid to grammar functors. Grammar covers are much more amenable than grammar functors and we think this is shown fairly convincingly.

This section will be followed by a section in which we review some basic terminology concerning formal grammars, automata and syntax categories.

In Chapter 2 grammar covers and functors are introduced. The framework for grammar covers which is presented is very general. Partly this is done to obtain an analogy with the grammar functor approach. The second reason, however, is that we need this generality to include various definitions of covers which have been introduced before and to be able to describe practical situations which appear in the field of compiler building.

Chapter 3 shows the efforts which have been made by other authors to grasp some of the 'structure' or 'semantic' preserving properties of transformations of context-free grammars.

In Chapter 4 some general properties of grammar covers are shown and a few preliminary transformations are introduced.

Chapter 5 contains the main transformations of this monograph. It is shown, among others, that any context-free grammar can be covered with a context-free grammar in Greibach normal form. In Chapter 6 we have collected the cover results for normal forms of context-free grammars. Chapter 7 is devoted to some similar results for the class of regular grammars.

In Chapter 8, 9 and 10 we will be concerned with classes of grammars for which there exist parsing methods which can be implemented by a deterministic pushdown transducer. Especially in these chapters we will pay attention to the usefulness of grammar covers for compiler writing systems. Both general cover results and results for normal forms for LL(k), strict deterministic and LR(k) grammars will be presented.

Finally, in Chapter 11 and 12 we discuss a few subclasses of LR(k) grammars in the light of the results which were obtained in the preceeding chapters. In Chapter 11 a variety of results are shown for the class of simple chain grammars. Cover properties, parsing properties and properties of the parse trees of simple chain grammars will be introduced. In Chapter 12 we consider generalizations of the class of simple chain grammars.

1.3. PRELIMINARIES

We review some basic definitions and concepts of formal language theory. Most of the notation used in this monograph is presented in this section. It is assumed that the reader is familiar with the basic results concerning context-free grammars and parsing, otherwise, see Aho and Ullman [3,4], Lewis, Rosenkrantz and Stearns [100] and Harrison [58]. Notations concerning grammars and automata and notations concerning categories follow closely those of Aho and Ullman [3] and Benson [13], respectively.

An *alphabet* is a finite set of *symbols* (equivalently, *letters*). The set of all strings (or *words*) over an alphabet V is denoted by V^*. If $\alpha \in V^*$, then $|\alpha|$, the *length* of α, is the number of occurrences of symbols in α. The *empty* string (the string with length zero) is denoted by ε. If $\alpha \in V^*$, then α^R denotes the *reverse* of α.

The set of non-negative integers is denoted by $\mathbb{N}$. If Q is a set, then $|Q|$ stands for the number of its elements. The *empty set* is denoted by $\emptyset$. If Q and R are sets, then $Q\backslash R$ or $Q-R$ denotes the set $\{x \mid x \in Q \text{ and } x \notin R\}$. V^* is the *free monoid* finitely generated by V. $V^+ = V^*\backslash\{\varepsilon\}$. A (monoid) *homomorphism* is a mapping between monoids with *concatenation* as operation. If V^* and W^* are two free monoids and $h : V^* \to W^*$ is a homomorphism between them, then $h(\varepsilon) = \varepsilon$ and $h(\alpha\beta) = h(\alpha)h(\beta)$ for all $\alpha, \beta \in V^*$.

1.3.1. GRAMMARS, AUTOMATA AND TRANSDUCERS

DEFINITION 1.1. A *context-free grammar* G is a four-tuple $G = (N,\Sigma,P,S)$, where

(i) N and Σ are alphabets, $N \cap \Sigma = \emptyset$ and $S \in N$. The elements of N are called *nonterminals* and those of Σ *terminals*. S is called the *start symbol*.

(ii) P is a finite set of ordered pairs (A,α) such that $A \in N$ and α is a word over the vocabulary $V = N \cup \Sigma$. Elements (A,α) of P are called *productions* and are written $A \to \alpha$.

Context-free grammar will be abbreviated to CFG. Elements of N will generally be denoted by the Roman capitals A, B, C,...; elements of Σ by the smalls a, b, c,... from the first part of the Roman alphabet; X, Y and Z will usually stand for elements of V; elements of Σ^* will be denoted by u, v, w, x, y and z and Greek smalls α, β, γ,... will usually stand for elements of V^*

It will be convenient to provide the productions in P with a *label*. In general these labels will be in a set Δ_G (or Δ if G is understood) and we always take $\Delta_G = \{i \mid 1 \le i \le |P|\}$; we often identify P and Δ_G.

We write $i.A \to \alpha$ if production $A \to \alpha$ has label (or number) i. A is called the *lefthand side* of this production; α is the *righthand side* of the production and α is a *rule alternative* of A. If A has rule alternatives $\alpha_1, \alpha_2, \ldots, \alpha_n$, we write

$$A \to \alpha_1 \mid \alpha_2 \mid \ldots \mid \alpha_n$$

hence, '|', a symbol not in V, is used to separate rule alternatives. If these productions have labels $i_1, i_2, \ldots, i_n$, then we use the notation

$$i_1/i_2/\ldots/i_n.\ A \to \alpha_1|\alpha_2|\ldots\ldots|\alpha_n.$$

If $A \in N$, then $rhs(A) = \{\alpha \mid A \to \alpha \text{ is in } P\}$.

DEFINITION 1.2. Let $G = (N,\Sigma,P,S)$ be a CFG. For $\alpha,\beta \in V^*$ we say that α *directly derives* β, written $\alpha \Rightarrow_G \beta$, if there exist $\alpha_1,\alpha_2 \in V^*$ and $A \to \gamma$ in P such that $\alpha = \alpha_1 A \alpha_2$ and $\beta = \alpha_1 \gamma \alpha_2$.
If $\alpha_1 \in \Sigma^*$ we say that α *left derives* β, written $\alpha \underset{L}{\Rightarrow}_G \beta$. If $\alpha_2 \in \Sigma^*$ we say that α *right derives* β, written $\alpha \underset{R}{\Rightarrow}_G \beta$.

The subscript G denoting the grammar in question is omitted whenever the identity of this grammar is clear from context. The *transitive-reflexive* closures of these relations are denoted by $\overset{*}{\Rightarrow}$, $\overset{*}{\underset{L}{\Rightarrow}}$ and $\overset{*}{\underset{R}{\Rightarrow}}$, respectively. The *transitive-irreflexive* closures are denoted by $\overset{+}{\Rightarrow}$, $\overset{+}{\underset{L}{\Rightarrow}}$ and $\overset{+}{\underset{R}{\Rightarrow}}$, respectively.

A sequence $\alpha_0 \Rightarrow \alpha_1 \Rightarrow \ldots\ldots \Rightarrow \alpha_n$ is called a *derivation* of α_n from α_0. A sequence $\alpha_0 \underset{L}{\Rightarrow} \alpha_1 \underset{L}{\Rightarrow} \ldots\ldots \underset{L}{\Rightarrow} \alpha_n$ ($\alpha_0 \underset{R}{\Rightarrow} \alpha_1 \underset{R}{\Rightarrow} \ldots\ldots \underset{R}{\Rightarrow} \alpha_n$) is called a *leftmost (rightmost)* derivation of α_n from α_0.

If we want to indicate a derivation using a specific sequence π of productions, we write $\overset{\pi}{\Rightarrow}$ ($\overset{\pi}{\underset{L}{\Rightarrow}}$, $\overset{\pi}{\underset{R}{\Rightarrow}}$), hence, $\pi \in P^*$ or $\pi \in \Delta^*$. In some cases we will use the notation $\alpha \overset{n}{\Rightarrow} \beta$ ($\alpha \overset{n}{\underset{L}{\Rightarrow}} \beta$, $\alpha \overset{n}{\underset{R}{\Rightarrow}} \beta$) to indicate that the derivation in question is such that α derives β in n steps, that is, $(\alpha,\beta) \in (\Rightarrow)^n$.

DEFINITION 1.3. Let $G = (N,\Sigma,P,S)$ be a CFG. The *language* of G is the set $L(G) = \{w \in \Sigma^* \mid S \overset{*}{\Rightarrow} w\}$. For any $\alpha \in V^*$, $L(\alpha) = \{w \in \Sigma^* \mid \alpha \overset{*}{\Rightarrow} w\}$. CFG G is said to be *unambiguous* if there does not exist $w \in \Sigma^*$ and $\pi, \pi' \in \Delta^*$ such that $S \overset{\pi}{\underset{L}{\Rightarrow}} w$ and $S \overset{\pi'}{\underset{L}{\Rightarrow}} w$, where $\pi \neq \pi'$. Otherwise, G is said to be *ambiguous*. Let $w \in L(G)$, then w is called a sentence of G. L(G) is said to be a *context-free language* (CFL for short).

DEFINITION 1.4. Let $G = (N,\Sigma,P,S)$ be a CFG. Let $\alpha \in V^*$.

a. $k : \alpha$ is the *prefix* of α with length k if $|\alpha| \geq k$, otherwise $k : \alpha = \alpha$.

b. $\alpha : k$ is the *suffix* of α with length k if $|\alpha| \geq k$, otherwise $\alpha : k = \alpha$.

c. $FIRST_k(\alpha) = \{k : w \in \Sigma^* \mid \alpha \overset{*}{\Rightarrow} w\}$.

Index k of $FIRST_k$ will be omitted when $k = 1$.

NOTATION 1.1. Let Σ and Δ be disjoint alphabets. Homomorphism $h_\Sigma : (\Sigma \cup \Delta)^* \to \Delta^*$ is defined by

$$h_\Sigma(X) = X \text{ if } X \in \Delta, \text{ and}$$

$$h_\Sigma(X) = \varepsilon \text{ if } X \in \Sigma.$$

Homomorphism h_Σ will be called the *Σ-erasing homomorphism.*

The number of different leftmost derivations from S to w is called the *degree of ambiguity* of w (with respect to G), written $\langle w,G\rangle$. By convention, if $w \notin L(G)$, then $\langle w,G\rangle = 0$. We say that $\alpha \in V^*$ is a *sentential form, a left sentential form* or a *right sentential form,* if $S \overset{*}{\Rightarrow} \alpha$, $S \overset{*}{\underset{L}{\Rightarrow}} \alpha$ and $S \overset{*}{\underset{R}{\Rightarrow}} \alpha$, respectively.

Derivations (or rather, equivalence classes of derivations) can be represented by *trees*. We distinguish between *derivation trees* and *parse trees*.

DEFINITION 1.5. A *derivation tree* is recursively defined by

(i) A single node labeled S is a derivation tree.

(ii) For every derivation tree, let D, labeled $A \in N$, be a leaf of the tree. If $A \rightarrow X_1X_2\ldots X_n$ ($X_i \in V$, $1 \leq i \leq n$) is in P, the tree obtained by appending to D n sons with labels $X_1,X_2,\ldots,X_n$ in order from the left, is a derivation tree. If $A \rightarrow \varepsilon$ is in P, the tree obtained by appending to D one son with label ε is a derivation tree.

The set PTR(G), the set of *parse trees* of G, consists of all derivation trees where each leaf is labeled with a terminal or with ε. The *frontier* of a derivation tree is the string obtained by concatenating the labels of the leaves from left to right. If T is a derivation tree, then $fr(T)$ denotes the frontier of T.

DEFINITION 1.6.

a. Let $G = (N,\Sigma,P,S)$ be a CFG. Define $P' = \{A \rightarrow [\alpha] \mid A \rightarrow \alpha \in P\}$, where '[' and ']' are special brackets that are not terminal symbols of G. $[G] = (N,\Sigma \cup \{[,]\},P',S)$, the *parenthesized version* of G, is called a *parenthesis grammar* (McNaughton[107]).

b. Let $G = (N,\Sigma,P,S)$ be a CFG. Define $P' = \{A \rightarrow [_i\alpha]_i \mid i.A \rightarrow \alpha \in P\}$, where '$[_i$' and '$]_i$' are special brackets that are not terminal symbols of G. Grammar G_B = $= (N,\Sigma \cup \{[_i \mid i \in \Delta_G\} \cup \{]_i \mid i \in \Delta_G\}, P', S)$, the *bracketed version* of G, is called a *bracketed grammar* (Ginsburg and Harrison [43]).

DEFINITION 1.7.

a. CFG G and CFG H are said to be *weakly equivalent* if $L(G) = L(H)$.

b. CFG G and CFG H are said to be *strongly equivalent* if $PTR(G) = PTR(H)$.

c. CFG G and CFG H are said to be *structurally equivalent* if $L([G]) = L([H])$.

A symbol $X \in V$ is *useless* in a CFG $G = (N,\Sigma,P,S)$ with $P \neq \emptyset$, if there does not exist a derivation $S \overset{*}{\Rightarrow} wXy \overset{*}{\Rightarrow} wxy$, where $wxy \in \Sigma^*$. There exists a simple algorithm to remove all useless symbols from a CFG (Aho and Ullman [3]). Throughout this monograph we assume that the grammars under consideration have no useless symbols. Any production of the form $A \rightarrow \alpha$ with $\alpha \in N$ is called a *single production*.

DEFINITION 1.8. A CFG $G = (N,\Sigma,P,S)$ is

a. *reduced*, if it has no useless symbols or if $P = \emptyset$.
b. *ε-free*, if $P \subseteq N \times V^+$ or $P \subseteq N \times (V\setminus\{S\})^+ \cup \{S \to \varepsilon\}$.
c. *cycle-free*, if, for any $A \in N$, a derivation $A \stackrel{+}{\Rightarrow} A$ is not possible.
d. *proper*, if G has no useless symbols, G is ε-free and G is cycle-free.

DEFINITION 1.9. Let $G = (N,\Sigma,P,S)$ be a CFG. A nonterminal $A \in N$ is said to be *left recursive* if there exists $\alpha \in V^*$ such that $A \stackrel{+}{\Rightarrow} A\alpha$. Grammar G is said to be *left recursive* if there exists a left recursive nonterminal in N. Otherwise, G is said to be *non-left-recursive* (NLR).

For any CFG $G = (N,\Sigma,P,S)$ define $G^R = (N,\Sigma,P^R,S)$ with $P^R = \{A \to \alpha^R \mid A \to \alpha \in P\}$. A CFG G is said to be *non-right-recursive* (NRR) if G^R is NLR.

DEFINITION 1.10. A CFG $G = (N,\Sigma,P,S)$ is

a. in *Greibach normal form* (GNF) if

$$P \subseteq N \times \Sigma N^* \text{ or } P \subseteq N \times \Sigma(N\setminus\{S\})^* \cup \{S \to \varepsilon\}.$$

b. in *quasi Greibach normal form* (quasi-GNF) if

$$P \subseteq N \times \Sigma V^* \text{ or } P \subseteq N \times \Sigma(V\setminus\{S\})^* \cup \{S \to \varepsilon\}.$$

c. *left factored* if P does not contain distinct productions of the form $A \to \alpha\beta_1$ and $A \to \alpha\beta_2$ with $\alpha \neq \varepsilon$.

We say that G is in $\overline{\text{GNF}}$ if grammar G^R is in GNF. For each CFL one can find a CFG which is in one of the forms defined in the Definitions 1.8 to 1.10. Greibach normal form is also called *standard form*. A grammar is said to be in *standard 2-form* if it is in GNF and each righthand side of a production contains at most two nonterminals.

DEFINITION 1.11. A CFG $G = (N,\Sigma,P,S)$ is said to be

a. *right regular*, if each production in P is of the form $A \to aB$ or $A \to a$, where $A,B \in N$ and $a \in \Sigma$.
b. *left regular*, if each production in P is of the form $A \to Ba$ or $A \to a$, where $A,B \in N$ and $a \in \Sigma$.

A *regular* grammar is a grammar which is either left regular or right regular. A set L is said to be regular if there exists a regular grammar G such that $L = L(G)$.

Now we will generalize grammars to (simple) syntax directed translation schemes.

DEFINITION 1.12. A *simple syntax directed translation scheme* (simple SDTS) is a five-tuple $T = (N,\Sigma,\Sigma',R,S)$, where

(i) N,Σ and Σ' are alphabets, $S \in N$, $N \cap \Sigma = \emptyset$ and $N \cap \Sigma' = \emptyset$. Let $V = N \cup \Sigma$ and $V' = N \cup \Sigma'$. The elements of N are called *nonterminals* and those of Σ and Σ' *input symbols* and *output symbols*, respectively. S is called the *start symbol*.

(ii) R is a finite set of *rules* of the form $A \to \alpha,\beta$, where $\alpha \in V^*$, $\beta \in V'^*$ and $h_\Sigma(\alpha) = h_{\Sigma'}(\beta)$.

We write $(\alpha,\beta) \Rightarrow (\gamma,\delta)$ if there exist $\alpha_1,\alpha_2 \in V^*$, $\beta_1,\beta_2 \in V'^*$ and $A \to \varphi,\varphi'$ in R such that $(\alpha,\beta) = (\alpha_1 A\alpha_2, \beta_1 A\beta_2)$, $h_\Sigma(\alpha_1) = h_{\Sigma'}(\beta_1)$, $h_\Sigma(\alpha_2) = h_{\Sigma'}(\beta_2)$ and $(\gamma,\delta) = (\alpha_1\varphi\alpha_2, \beta_1\varphi'\beta_2)$. Closures of "$\Rightarrow$" are defined analogous to those for a CFG.

The *(syntax directed) translation* defined by T, denoted $\tau(T)$, is the set of pairs $\{(w,w') \mid (S,S) \overset{*}{\Rightarrow} (w,w'),\ w \in \Sigma^* \text{ and } w' \in \Sigma'^*\}$. Grammar $G_1 = (N,\Sigma,P,S)$ with

$$P = \{A \to \alpha \mid A \to \alpha,\alpha' \text{ is in R for some } \alpha' \in (N \cup \Sigma'^*)\},$$

is said to be the *input grammar* of T. Similarly, the *output grammar* $G_0 = (N,\Sigma',P_0,S)$ is defined by the set of productions

$$P_0 = \{A \to \alpha' \mid A \to \alpha,\alpha' \text{ is in R for some } \alpha \in (N \cup \Sigma)^*\}.$$

Frequently we will start with a CFG $G = (N,\Sigma,P,S)$ and generalize it to a simple SDTS $T = (N,\Sigma,\Delta_G,R,S)$, where Δ_G contains the production numbers and R contains rules of the form $A \to \alpha,\alpha'$, where $A \to \alpha$ is in P and α' is a word over $(N \cup \Delta_G)^*$ which satisfies $h_\Delta(\alpha') = h_\Sigma(\alpha)$.
In such a case we say that simple SDTS T is defined on CFG G.

DEFINITION 1.13. A simple SDTS is *semantically unambiguous* if there are not two distinct rules of the form $A \to \alpha,\beta$ and $A \to \alpha,\gamma$.

The final definitions (again from Aho and Ullman [3]) in this subsection deal with automata.

DEFINITION 1.14. A *pushdown automaton* (PDA for short) is a seven-tuple $P = (Q,\Sigma,\Gamma,\delta,q_0,Z_0,F)$, where

(i) Q is a finite set of *state symbols*, Σ and Γ are alphabets of *input symbols* and *pushdown list symbols*, respectively; $q_0 \in Q$ is the *initial state*, $Z_0 \in \Gamma$ is the *start symbol* and $F \subseteq Q$ is the set of *final states*.

(ii) δ is a mapping from $Q \times (\Sigma \cup \{\varepsilon\}) \times \Gamma$ to the finite subsets of $Q \times \Gamma^*$.

A *configuration* of a PDA P is a triple (q,w,α) in $Q \times \Sigma^* \times \Gamma^*$. The binary relation $\vdash$ ('*move*') on configurations is defined by:

$$(q,aw,Z\alpha) \vdash (r,w,\gamma\alpha)$$

if and only if

$\delta(q,a,Z)$ contains (r,γ), for any $q,r \in Q$, $a \in \Sigma \cup \{\varepsilon\}$, $w \in \Sigma^*$, $Z \in \Gamma$ and $\alpha,\gamma \in \Gamma^*$.

If $a = \varepsilon$, then such a move is called an ε-*move*. An *initial* configuration of P is a configuration of the form (q_0,w,Z_0) for some $w \in \Sigma^*$.
The *language* defined by P is

$$L(P) = \{w \in \Sigma^* \mid (q_0,w,Z_0) \overset{*}{\vdash} (q,\varepsilon,\alpha) \text{ for some } q \in F \text{ and } \alpha \in \Gamma^*\}.$$

The *language accepted with empty pushdown list* is the set

$$L_e(P) = \{w \in \Sigma^* \mid (q_0,w,Z_0) \overset{*}{\vdash} (q,\varepsilon,\varepsilon) \text{ for some } q \in Q\}.$$

It can be shown that each PDA P can be transformed to a PDA P' such that $L_e(P') = L(P)$, and conversely. This PDA P' can be constructed in such a way that emptiness of the pushdown list is always achieved in the same state. That is, there exists a state $q_e \in Q$ such that $L_e(P) = \{w \in \Sigma^* \mid (q_0,w,Z_0) \overset{*}{\vdash} (q_e,\varepsilon,\varepsilon)\}$.

Any PDA $P = (Q,\Sigma,\Gamma,\delta,q_0,Z_0,F)$ can be converted to a CFG $G = (N,\Sigma,P,S)$ such that $L(G) = L_e(P)$ and such that any leftmost derivation of w in G directly corresponds to a sequence of moves made by P in processing w (cf. Lemma 2.26 in Aho and Ullman [3]).

One of the basic results in the theory of formal languages and automata is the following.

THEOREM 1.1. The following two statements are equivalent:

1. L is L(G) for a CFG G.
2. L is $L_e(P)$ for a PDA P.

We will be concerned with pushdown automata which can produce output.

DEFINITION 1.15. A *pushdown transducer* (PDT) is an eight-tuple $P = (Q,\Sigma,\Gamma,\Sigma',\delta,q_0,Z_0,F)$, where all symbols have the same meaning as for a PDA except that Σ' is an alphabet of *output symbols* and δ is a mapping from $Q \times (\Sigma \cup \{\varepsilon\}) \times \Gamma$ to finite subsets of $Q \times \Gamma^* \times \Sigma'^*$.

A *configuration* of P is a quadruple (q,w,α,w') in $Q \times \Sigma^* \times \Gamma^* \times \Sigma'^*$. The *move* $\vdash$ is now defined by:

$$(q,aw,Z\gamma,w') \vdash (r,w,\alpha\gamma,w'v)$$

if $\delta(q,a,Z)$ contains (r,α,v), for any $q,r \in Q$, $a \in \Sigma \cup \{\varepsilon\}$, $w \in \Sigma^*$, $Z \in \Gamma$, $\alpha,\gamma \in \Gamma^*$

and $w'v \in \Sigma'^*$.

The *(syntax directed) translation* defined by P is

$$\tau(P) = \{(w,w') \mid (q_0,w,Z_0,\varepsilon) \overset{*}{\vdash} (q,\varepsilon,\alpha,w') \text{ for some } q \in F \text{ and } \alpha \in \Gamma^*\},$$

and

$$\tau_e(P) = \{(w,w') \mid (q_0,w,Z_0,\varepsilon) \overset{*}{\vdash} (q,\varepsilon,\varepsilon,w') \text{ for some } q \in Q\}.$$

It can be shown that each PDT P can be transformed to a PDT P' such that $\tau_e(P') = \tau(P)$, and conversely. Also in this case PDT P' can be constructed in such a way that emptiness of the pushdown list is always achieved in the same state.

Theorem 1.1 has an analogue for simple SDTS's and PDT's.

THEOREM 1.2. The following two statements are equivalent:

1. L is $\tau(T)$ for a simple SDTS T.
2. L is $\tau_e(P)$ for a PDT P.

The following construction shows how to transform a PDT P to a simple SDTS T such that $\tau(T) = \tau_e(P)$. We start with a PDT with one final state.

STANDARD CONSTRUCTION

Let $P = (Q,\Sigma,\Gamma,\Sigma',\delta,q_0,Z_0,\{q_e\})$ be a pushdown transducer which accepts with empty pushdown list in state q_e. We define a simple SDTS $T = (N,\Sigma,\Sigma',R,S)$ such that $\tau(T) = \tau_e(P)$.

(1) $N = \{[pAq] \mid p,q \in Q,\ A \in \Gamma\}$, $S = [q_0Z_0q_e]$.

(2) R is defined as follows.

If $\delta(p,a,A)$ contains $(r,X_1X_2\ldots X_k,y)$, where $a \in \Sigma \cup \{\varepsilon\}$ and $y \in \Sigma'^*$, then if $k > 0$, R contains rules

$$[pAq_k] \to a[rX_1q_1][q_1X_2q_2]\ldots.[q_{k-1}X_kq_k],$$
$$y[rX_1q_1][q_1X_2q_2]\ldots.[q_{k-1}X_kq_k]$$

for all sequences $q_1,q_2,\ldots,q_k$ of states in Q.

If $k = 0$, then the rule is $[pAr] \to a,y$. □

Semantical unambiguity can be defined for a PDT in the following way.

DEFINITION 1.16. A PDT $P = (Q,\Sigma,\Gamma,\Sigma',\delta,q_0,Z_0,F)$ is *semantically unambiguous* if, for any $q,r \in Q$, $a \in \Sigma \cup \{\varepsilon\}$, $Z \in \Gamma$, $\gamma \in \Gamma^*$ and $\pi_1, \pi_2 \in \Sigma'^*$,

$$(r,\gamma,\pi_1) \text{ and } (r,\gamma,\pi_2) \text{ in } \delta(q,a,Z)$$

implies $\pi_1 = \pi_2$.

If a PDT P is semantically unambiguous, then the simple SDTS T which is obtained from the standard construction is semantically unambiguous.

As in the case of context-free grammars, we assume that the rules of a simple SDTS T are labeled with labels from an alphabet $\Delta_T = \{i \mid 1 \leq i \leq |R|\}$.

Let $P = (Q,\Sigma,\Gamma,\Sigma',\delta,q_0,Z_0,\{q_e\})$ be a semantically unambiguous PDT which translates with empty pushdown list in a final state q_e. Simple SDTS $T = (N,\Sigma,\Sigma',R,S)$ is obtained from P by the standard construction. Define a homomorphism $\psi : \Delta_T^* \rightarrow \Sigma'^*$ in the following way:

If $i.A \rightarrow a\alpha, y\alpha'$ in R, where $a \in \Sigma \cup \{\varepsilon\}$, $y \in \Sigma'^*$, $\alpha \in N^*$ and $\alpha' = \alpha$, then $\psi(i) = y$. In this situation we have the following observation.

STANDARD OBSERVATION

Let PDT P, simple SDTS T and homomorphism $\psi : \Delta_T^* \rightarrow \Sigma'^*$ be defined as above. Then

$$(w,x) \in \tau_e(P) \text{ if and only if } (S,S) \overset{\pi}{\underset{L}{\Rightarrow}} (w,x)$$

in T, with $\psi(\pi) = x$.

1.3.2*. SYNTAX CATEGORIES

Category theory has found wide applications in theoretical computer science. For the general theory the reader can consult MacLane [103] and Arbib and Manes [7]. Some of the applications in computer science can be found, among others, in the ADJ-papers (see Goguen, Thatcher, Wright and Wagner [45]). For our purposes, the categorical treatment of grammars, Hotz and Claus [67], Benson [12] and Schnorr [151] contain useful material. For concepts and terminology we follow Benson [13].
The characterization of Chomsky-type grammars with categories is due to Hotz [63,64] and finds its origin in work on switching circuits. Grammar functors will be defined as certain types of functors between categories associated to grammars.

For the simple reason that grammar functors give too easily occasion to negative results when one tries to describe the preserving of structure under certain transformations on grammars, our main interest will be in grammar covers. Therefore, we confine ourselves to a few notes on (syntax) categories and, in section 2.3, on grammar functors.

For the concept of syntax category we follow Benson [13]. Let $G = (N,\Sigma,P,S)$ be a CFG. Then (V^*,P) generates the *(free strict monoidal) category* S(G), which will be called the *syntax category* of G. Here, *objects* are elements of V^* and *morphisms* are derivations (or, in fact, equivalence classes of similar derivations) from one object to the other. Clearly, one can take as representative of such an equivalence class a certain type of derivation, for example a leftmost derivation.

Two operations are defined on the morphisms. Firstly, *composition* of morphisms, that is, if $f_1 : \alpha \to \beta$ and $f_2 : \beta \to \gamma$, then $f_1 \circ f_2 : \alpha \to \gamma$ is defined to be the composition

$$\alpha \xrightarrow{f_1} \beta \xrightarrow{f_2} \gamma$$

Secondly, *concatenation* of morphisms, that is if $f_1 : \alpha_1 \to \beta_1$ and $f_2 : \alpha_2 \to \beta_2$, then $f_1 + f_2 : \alpha_1\alpha_2 \to \beta_1\beta_2$ is (equivalently) described by

$$\alpha_1\alpha_2 \xrightarrow{\text{applying } f_1} \beta_1\alpha_2 \xrightarrow{\text{applying } f_2} \beta_1\beta_2$$

and

$$\alpha_1\alpha_2 \xrightarrow{\text{applying } f_2} \alpha_1\beta_2 \xrightarrow{\text{applying } f_1} \beta_1\beta_2,$$

respectively.

A well-known relation for morphisms is the following

$$(f_1 \circ g_1) + (f_2 \circ g_2) = (f_1 + f_2) \circ (g_1 + g_2)$$

illustrated in Figure 1.1.

$$\begin{pmatrix} f_1 \\ \circ \\ g_1 \end{pmatrix} + \begin{pmatrix} f_2 \\ \circ \\ g_2 \end{pmatrix} = \begin{pmatrix} f_1 + f_2 \\ \circ \\ g_1 + g_2 \end{pmatrix}$$

Figure 1.1. Operations on morphisms.

For each object α the *categorical identity* at α is denoted by $id_\alpha : \alpha \to \alpha$.

CHAPTER 2

GRAMMAR COVERS AND RELATED CONCEPTS

2.1. GRAMMAR COVERS

This section introduces the framework for grammar covers. This framework is built up in a rather formal and general way. Ideas of the grammar functor approach (cf. section 2.3) will be used. We think this general setting is useful because of the following reasons.

- Existing grammar cover definitions can be obtained from the framework by introducing natural restrictions.
- The framework shows the freedom to choose parses for covers different from the left and right parses.
- The role of ambiguity is made apparent. The framework is such that special properties of covers can easily be formulated. A possible comparison with the grammar functor approach is made more simple.

Each of the features of the framework will either be given an application in this monograph or we will refer to a (possible) application elsewhere.

Let $G = (N,\Sigma,P,S)$ be a CFG with production numbers in Δ_G. The following definition is also in Brosgol [18]. However, we distinguish between parse relations and proper parse relations. Recall that $<w,G>$ denotes the degree of ambiguity of w.

<u>DEFINITION 2.1.</u>

a. A relation $f_G \subseteq \Sigma^* \times \Delta_G^*$ is said to be a *proper parse relation* for G provided that

(i) if $(w,\pi) \in f_G$ and $(w',\pi) \in f_G$ then $w = w'$, and
(ii) for each $w \in \Sigma^*$

$$|\{\pi \mid (w,\pi) \in f_G\}| = <w,G>.$$

b. A relation $f_G \subseteq \Sigma^* \times \Delta_G^*$ is said to be a *parse relation* for G provided that

(i) for each $w \in L(G)$ there exists at least one element $(w,\pi) \in f_G$, and
(ii) for each $w \in \Sigma^*$

$$|\{\pi \mid (w,\pi) \in f_G\}| \leq <w,G>.$$

If f_G is a parse relation and $(w,\pi) \in f_G$ then π is said to be an f_G-parse of w. It follows from the definition that if f_G is a proper parse relation, then for each f_G-parse there is a unique sentence and for each sentence the number of parse trees is equal to the number of different f_G-parses for this sentence.

Index G of f_G will be omitted whenever it is clear from the context.

Our following definitions will be based on parse relations. Clearly, every proper parse relation is a parse relation.

DEFINITION 2.2. Let $G' = (N',\Sigma',P',S')$ and $G = (N,\Sigma,P,S)$ be CFG's. Let $f_{G'} \subseteq \Sigma'^* \times \Delta_{G'}^*$ and $h_G \subseteq \Sigma^* \times \Delta_G^*$ be parse relations. If $f \subseteq f_{G'}$ then a *partial parse homomorphism* $g_f : f_{G'} \to h_G$ is defined by two homomorphisms $\varphi : \Sigma'^* \to \Sigma^*$ and $\psi : \Delta_{G'}^* \to \Delta_G^*$ such that $(w,\pi) \in f$ implies $(\varphi(w), \psi(\pi)) \in h_G$.

Throughout this section f, $f_{G'}$ and h_G refer to the relations in this definition. The notation $g_f = \langle\varphi,\psi\rangle$ will be used to denote that g_f is defined by the two homomorphisms φ and ψ. We say that g_f is a total parse homomorphism or simply a parse homomorphism whenever $f = f_{G'}$. In this case we omit index f from g_f.
If $(w,\pi) \in f$ then $g_f(w,\pi)$ denotes $(\varphi(w), \psi(\pi))$. For any $f' \subseteq f$ we use $g_f(f')$ to denote the set $\{g_f(w,\pi) \mid (w,\pi) \in f'\}$.

We can now describe various properties of (partial) parse homomorphisms.

DEFINITION 2.3. A partial parse homomorphism $g_f : f_{G'} \to h_G$ is said to be *injective* if for any $(w_1,\pi_1) \in f$ and $(w_2,\pi_2) \in f$, if $g_f(w_1,\pi_1) = g_f(w_2,\pi_2)$ then $(w_1,\pi_1) = (w_2,\pi_2)$.

Notice that if a partial parse homomorphism is injective then this does not exclude the possibility that two different sentences in L(G') will be mapped on the same sentence in L(G).
To describe such a property of a partial parse homomorphism we use the following definition.

DEFINITION 2.4. A partial parse homomorphism $g_f : f_{G'} \to h_G$ is said to be *properly injective* if its restrictions to Σ'^* and $\Delta_{G'}^*$ are *injective*, that is, if $g_f = \langle\varphi,\psi\rangle$ then, for any $(w_1,\pi_1) \in f$ and $(w_2,\pi_2) \in f$,

(i) $\varphi(w_1) = \varphi(w_2)$ implies $w_1 = w_2$, and
(ii) $\psi(\pi_1) = \psi(\pi_2)$ implies $\pi_1 = \pi_2$.

Our next definition deals with surjectivity of partial parse homomorphisms

DEFINITION 2.5. A partial parse homomorphism $g_f : f_{G'} \to h_G$ is said to be *surjective* if for all $(w,\pi) \in h_G$ there exists $(w',\pi') \in f$ such that $g_f(w',\pi') = (w,\pi)$.

Hence, g_f is surjective if $g_f(f) = h_G$. In analogy with Definition 2.4 we can introduce the notion of proper surjectivity.

DEFINITION 2.6. A partial parse homomorphism $g_f : f_{G'} \to h_G$ is said to be *properly surjective* if for all $(w,\pi) \in h_G$ there exists

(i) $(w',\pi') \in f$ such that $\varphi(w') = w$, and

(ii) $(w',\pi') \in f$ such that $\psi(\pi') = \pi$.

However, if h_G is a proper parse relation, then there is no difference between surjective partial parse homomorphisms and properly surjective partial parse homomorphisms.

THEOREM 2.1.

a. Any properly injective partial parse homomorphism is injective.

b. Let h_G be a proper parse relation. A partial parse homomorphism from a parse relation $f_{G'}$ to h_G is properly surjective if and only if it is surjective.

Proof. Part a. of this theorem is trivial. Consider part b. Assume that a partial parse homomorphism $g_f = \langle\varphi,\psi\rangle$ is properly surjective. From condition (ii) of Definition 2.6 it follows that for any $(w,\pi) \in h_G$ there exists $(w',\pi') \in f$ such that $\psi(\pi') = \pi$. Thus, we have $(\varphi(w'),\pi)$ and (w,π) in h_G. From Definition 2.1 (a) it follows that $\varphi(w') = w$. Hence, g_f is surjective. If g_f is surjective then, trivially, g_f is properly surjective. □

Note that if G is unambiguous and h_G is a proper parse relation, then any injective partial parse homomorphism $g_f : f_{G'} \to h_G$ is also a proper injective partial parse homomorphism. Also in the case that $\Sigma' = \Sigma$, φ is the identity homomorphism and h_G is a proper parse relation, both notions coincide.

Next we introduce (partial) cover homomorphisms.

DEFINITION 2.7. A partial parse homomorphism (a total parse homomorphism) $g_f : f_{G'} \to h_G$ is said to be a *partial cover homomorphism (a total cover homomorphism)* if it is surjective.

Any partial cover homomorphism g_f which is an injection is called *faithful*. If the partial cover homomorphism g_f is a proper injection then it is called a *proper partial cover homomorphism*. Clearly, in analogy with the remarks above, if G is unambiguous and h_G is a proper parse relation, then the notions of faithfulness and properness coincide. The same holds if $\Sigma' = \Sigma$, φ is the identity homomorphism and h_G is a proper parse relation.

Whenever we speak of a cover homomorphism then a *total* cover homomorphism is meant. Notice that in general in the case of a cover homomorphism, without knowledge of the specific grammars, we are not able to compare $\langle w,G'\rangle$ and $\langle\varphi(w),G\rangle$. However, if φ is the identity homomorphism and h_G is a proper parse relation, then $L(G') = L(G)$

and $\langle w,G'\rangle \geq \langle \varphi(w),G\rangle$.

EXAMPLE 2.1.

Let G' be defined † by

$$\begin{array}{lll} 1./2. & S \to aA & \mid cB \\ 3./4. & A \to aA & \mid b \\ 5./6. & B \to cB & \mid d \end{array}$$

and G by

$$\begin{array}{lll} 1./2. & S \to Ab & \mid Bb \\ 3./4. & A \to Aa & \mid a \\ 5./6. & B \to Ba & \mid a \end{array}$$

Define

$$f_{G'} = \{(a^{n+1}b, 13^n4) \mid n \geq 0\} \cup \{(c^{n+1}d, 25^n6) \mid n \geq 0\}$$

and

$$h_G = \{(a^{n+1}b, 43^n1) \mid n \geq 0\} \cup \{(a^{n+1}b, 65^n2) \mid n \geq 0\}.$$

We can define a parse homomorphism $g = \langle \varphi,\psi\rangle$ by

$$\begin{array}{lllll} \varphi(a) = a & \varphi(c) = a & \psi(1) = 4 & \psi(3) = 3 & \psi(5) = 5 \\ \varphi(b) = b & \varphi(d) = b & \psi(2) = 6 & \psi(4) = 1 & \psi(6) = 2 \end{array}$$

Parse homomorphism g is surjective, therefore, g is a cover homomorphism. Although homomorphism g is injective, g is not properly injective. Hence, g is a faithful but not a proper cover homomorphism.

The results in the following table are immediate consequences of the definitions. We compare the degrees of ambiguity and the languages of two grammars G' and G with proper parse relations between which a parse homomorphism $g = \langle \varphi,\psi\rangle$ has been defined.

PARSE HOMOMORPHISM	DEGREE OF AMBIGUITY	LANGUAGES
cover (surjection)	-	$\varphi(L(G')) = L(G)$
proper injection	$\langle w,G'\rangle \leq \langle \varphi(w),G\rangle$	$\varphi(L(G')) \subseteq L(G)$
faithful cover	$\langle w,G'\rangle \leq \langle \varphi(w),G\rangle$	$\varphi(L(G')) = L(G)$
proper cover	$\langle w,G'\rangle = \langle \varphi(w),G\rangle$	$\varphi(L(G')) = L(G)$

Table I. Properties of parse homomorphisms.

†In our example grammars we only list the productions. From our conventions it will be clear how to distinguish terminal and nonterminal symbols.

If $\Sigma' = \Sigma$ and φ is the identity homomorphism then the notions of faithful cover and proper cover coincide. In this case we have the situation depicted in Table II (Again for proper parse relations).

PARSE HOMOMORPHISM	DEGREE OF AMBIGUITY	LANGUAGES
cover (surjection)	$<w,G'> \geq <w,G>$	$L(G') = L(G)$
proper injection	$<w,G'> \leq <w,G>$	$L(G') \subseteq L(G)$
faithful cover	$<w,G'> = <w,G>$	$L(G') = L(G)$

Table II. $\Sigma' = \Sigma$ and φ is the identity homomorphism.

In the following diagram the definition of a parse homomorphism is illustrated.

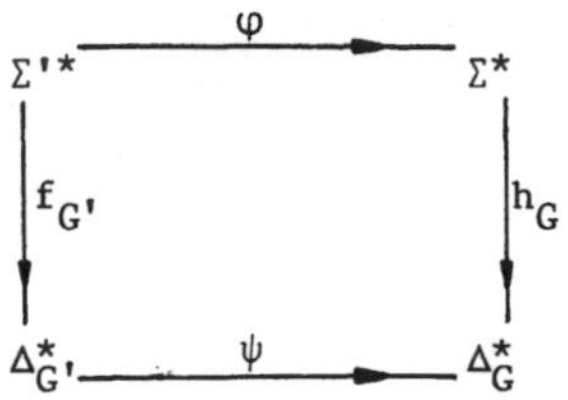

Figure 2.1. Diagram for the parse homomorphism.

Now we are sufficiently prepared to define when a grammar G' covers a grammar G.

<u>DEFINITION 2.8.</u> Let $G' = (N',\Sigma',P',S')$ and $G = (N,\Sigma,P,S)$ be CFG's. Let $f_{G'} \subseteq \Sigma'^* \times \Delta^*_{G'}$ and $h_G \subseteq \Sigma^* \times \Delta^*_G$ be parse relations. Grammar G' is said to *f-to-h cover* grammar G if there exists a cover homomorphism $g : f_{G'} \rightarrow h_G$.

In an obvious way the notions of partial, faithful (partial) and proper (partial) cover are defined.

Let us start to clarify Definition 2.8. For most of our applications it will be sufficient to consider a homomorphism $g_f = <\varphi,\psi>$ where $\Sigma' = \Sigma$ and φ is the identity homomorphism. In such cases there is only one homomorphism to consider, namely $\psi : \Delta^*_{G'} \rightarrow \Delta^*_G$ and we will simply speak of partial cover homomorphism ψ.

Two well-known examples of proper parse relations are the left parse relation and the right parse relation. They are defined as follows. Let $G = (N,\Sigma,P,S)$ be a CFG. The *left parse relation* of G is the set

$$\ell_G = \{(w,\pi) \mid S \overset{\pi}{\underset{L}{\Rightarrow}} w\}.$$

The *right parse relation* of G is the set

$\bar{r}_G = \{(w,\pi^R) \mid S \underset{R}{\overset{\pi}{\Rightarrow}} w\}$.

Now we consider a few aspects of our cover framework. If $\Sigma \subseteq \Sigma'$, φ is the identity homomorphism, $g_f = \langle\varphi,\psi\rangle$ is a partial cover homomorphism which satisfies $f = \{(w,\pi) \in f_{G'} \mid w \in L(G)\}$ and, moreover, the parse relations are restricted to the left and right parse relations then we have the notion of *weak cover* which is used in Ukkonen [164] to show the nonexistence of certain covers.

There are examples of transformations on context-free grammars for which it is useful to have a cover definition with the possibility that φ is not the identity homomorphism. For example, there are classes of CFG's for which a two-pass no-backtracking parsing algorithm has been defined. One pass translates a sentence w of L(G) to a sentence w' of L(G'), where G' is a grammar which can be constructed from G and the device which performs the first pass (for example, a sequential machine). In the second pass w' is parsed with respect to G'. The reader is referred to Culik and Cohen [23] and Nijholt [114,126] for possible applications. In Figure 2.2 such an application is displayed.

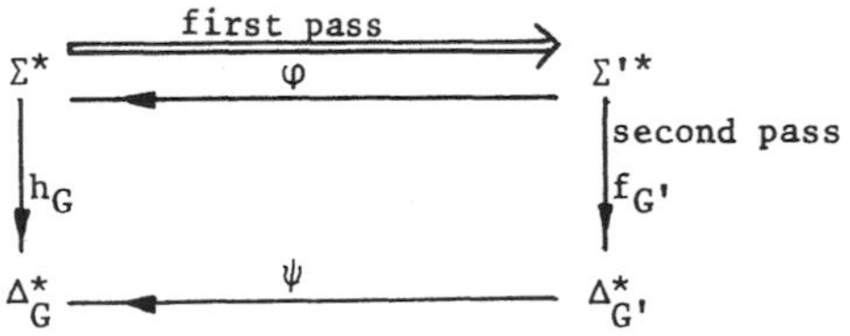

Figure 2.2. Two pass parsing algorithm.

For the applications in this monograph the full generality of Definition 2.1 is not needed. Before we introduce restrictions on this definition we will mention examples for which the general definition is necessary.

One might think, for example, of the parses which are obtained with the parsing methods for the subclasses of the context-free grammars described in Colmerauer [20], Szymanski and Williams [159] and Williams [169]. These methods are also called non-canonical parsing methods and the parses which are obtained differ from the usual (canonical) left and right parses.

As a second example we discuss how the definition of cover as it was presented in Gray and Harrison [48, 49] might be dealt with in our formalism. Gray and Harrison distinguish between productions of a CFG $G = (N,\Sigma,P,S)$ which do have or do not have semantic significance. The idea is that if a production does not have semantic significance then it can be omitted from the parses. (In [49] the programming language 'Euler' is used as example.) In this way, if we let $H \subseteq P$ be the set of productions with semantic significance, we can talk about H-*sparse derivations* and *parses*.

DEFINITION 2.9. Let $G = (N,\Sigma,P,S)$ be a CFG with a proper parse relation h_G and a set $\Omega_H \subseteq \Delta_G$ of productions with semantic significance. Define a homomorphism $\delta_H : \Delta_G^* \to \Omega_H^*$ by $\delta_H(p) = p$ if $p \in \Omega_H$ and $\delta_H(p) = \varepsilon$ otherwise. The H-*sparse parse relation* $h_G(H)$ is defined by

$$h_G(H) = \{(w,\delta_H(\pi)) \mid (w,\pi) \in h_G\}.$$

Clearly, if h_G is a proper parse relation, then $h_G(H)$ is a parse relation. In [49] there is no further discussion on this point. One may choose H in such a way that two otherwise different sentences obtain the same H-sparse parse. Another possibility is that H reduces the number of parses of a sentence. A 'cover' in the sense of Gray and Harrison is then defined between pairs (G',H') and (G,H) if there exists a 'cover' homomorphism $g : f_{G'} \to h_G(H)$, where $g = \langle\varphi,\psi\rangle$ satisfies $\psi(p) = \varepsilon$ if $p \in \Delta_{G'} - \Omega_{H'}$.
If H = P then G' is said to 'completely cover' grammar G.

There are a few restrictions in [49] which should be mentioned. Firstly, only right parses are considered. In the second place, $\Sigma' = \Sigma$ and a homomorphism $\varphi : \Sigma'^* \to \Sigma^*$ is not considered. More interesting, however, is the condition $\psi(p) \in \Omega_H$ for any $p \in \Omega_{H'}$. This leads to the following definition.

DEFINITION 2.10. A partial parse homomorphism $g_f = \langle\varphi,\psi\rangle$ is said to be *fine* if ψ satisfies $\psi(p) \in \Delta_G \cup \{\varepsilon\}$, for any $p \in \Delta_{G'}$. It is said to be *very fine* if $\psi(p) \in \Delta_G$ for any $p \in \Delta_{G'}$.

Hence, one can say that the homomorphism which is used in [49] is fine. We shall usually consider parse homomorphisms without restrictions on ψ. That is, we allow each production p to be mapped on a, possibly empty, string of productions. For some of the transformations on context-free grammars which will be presented in the forthcoming sections it will be shown that the existence of a cover homomorphism depends on the way ψ is defined.

In Hunt, Rosenkrantz and Szymanski [71] a fine cover homomorphism is called a *production map*. Aho and Ullman [3] mention the possibility of using transducer mappings for ψ. In Chapter 9 we consider the use of a deterministic finite transducer to define covers for a subclass of the context-free grammars.

2.2. RESTRICTIONS ON PARSE RELATIONS

We will now introduce restrictions on the class of parse relations and their parses.

DEFINITION 2.11. Let $G = (N,\Sigma,P,S)$ be a CFG. A parse relation $f \subseteq \Sigma^* \times \Delta^*$ is said to be a *syntax directed parse relation* of G if there exists a simple SDTS $T = (N,\Sigma,\Delta,R,S)$, defined on G, such that $\tau(T) = f$.

EXAMPLE 2.2.
Let $G = (N,\Sigma,P,S)$ be a CFG with P defined by

1./2.	$S \to BAb \mid CAc$	5.	$B \to a$
3./4.	$A \to BA \mid a$	6.	$C \to a$

Define a parse relation f by

$$f = \{(aab,154),(aaab,13545),(aac,264),(aaac,23645)\}$$
$$\cup\ \{(a^{n+4}b,15(35)^{n+2}4) \mid n \geq 0\}$$
$$\cup\ \{(a^{n+4}c,26(35)^{n+2}4) \mid n \geq 0\}.$$

It can be verified that f is not a syntax directed parse relation of CFG G.

With our following definition a more amenable class of parse relations is singled out. We use the Σ-erasing homomorphism $h_\Sigma : (N \cup \Sigma \cup \Delta)^* \to (N \cup \Delta)^*$.

DEFINITION 2.12. Let $G = (N,\Sigma,P,S)$ be a CFG. A relation $f_G \subseteq \Sigma^* \times \Delta_G^*$ is said to be a *production directed parse relation* of G if there exists a simple SDTS $T = (N,\Sigma,\Delta_G,R,S)$ such that $\tau(T) = f_G$ and where R satisfies the following condition. If $A \to \alpha$ is the ith production in P then R contains exactly one rule of the form $A \to \alpha$, $h_\Sigma(\alpha_1 i\alpha_2)$, where $\alpha_1\alpha_2 = \alpha$ and R does not contain other rules.

It will be clear that if each rule of this simple SDTS T has the form $A \to \alpha$, $h_\Sigma(i\alpha)$ then each pair of the translation defined by T consists of a sentence of L(G) and a left parse of this sentence. Similarly, if each rule has the form $A \to \alpha$, $h_\Sigma(\alpha i)$ then each sentence is associated with a right parse.

In these both cases $\tau(T)$ satisfies the conditions of a proper parse relation. Unfortunately, this is not necessarily the case for relations $\tau(T)$ which are obtained by inserting the symbols of Δ_G at arbitrary places in the righthand sides of the rules. This has also been observed by Brosgol [17]. The following grammar illustrates this phenomenon. Consider ambiguous grammar G_0 with productions

1. $S \to aS$
2. $S \to Sb$
3. $S \to c$

We define R, the set of rules of a simple SDTS T as follows

$S \to aS, 1S$

$S \to Sb, S2$

$S \to c, 3$

It follows that $\tau(T_0) = \{(a^n cb^m, 1^n 32^m) \mid n,m \geq 0\}$. The parses of the form $1^n 32^m$ are the so-called *left corner parses* ([3,p.278], cf. also Table III in this section). Hence, although G_0 is ambiguous each sentence has exactly one left corner parse. Therefore, $\tau(T_0)$ is not a proper parse relation of grammar G_0.

In the following subsection, which can be skipped on a first reading, we shall discuss a few consequences of this observation for parsing.

2.2.1*. SOME NOTES ON PARSING

In this subsection we slightly anticipate on forthcoming sections.

A parse can be considered as a sequence of productions which are 'recognized' during the parsing process. In situations of practical interest parsing should provide the information which makes it possible to perform error-recovery and code generation for a program which has been given as input to a compiler. However, there exist 'parsing' methods which can produce the same parse for different sentences (programs) and for different parse trees.

Left corner parsing is a well-known parsing technique. Deterministic left corner parsing has been defined for LC(k) grammars (Rosenkrantz and Lewis [143]), generalized left corner parsing was introduced by Demers [24] and a nondeterministic left corner parser can be found in [3]. If one considers parsing as the process which yields for each parse tree a unique parse, that is, no two different trees have the same parse, then one should not call the nondeterministic left corner parser of [3] a parser.

The following example will be convincing. Consider the grammar G_1 with productions

1. $S \to aSa$
2. $S \to Ab$
3. $A \to S$
4. $S \to c$

One can verify that grammar G_1 is an LC(1) grammar. This means that grammar G_1 can be parsed with a deterministic left corner parsing method with one symbol of look-ahead. With this method each sentence of $L(G_1)$ is translated to its left corner parse. These parses are defined with the following simple SDTS T_1 with rules

$S \to aSa,\ 1S$	$A \to S,\ S3$
$S \to Ab,\ A2$	$S \to c,\ 4$

Now it is simple to verify that different sentences of G_1 may have the same left corner parse. In Figure 2.3 we have displayed two parse trees which have the same left corner parse.

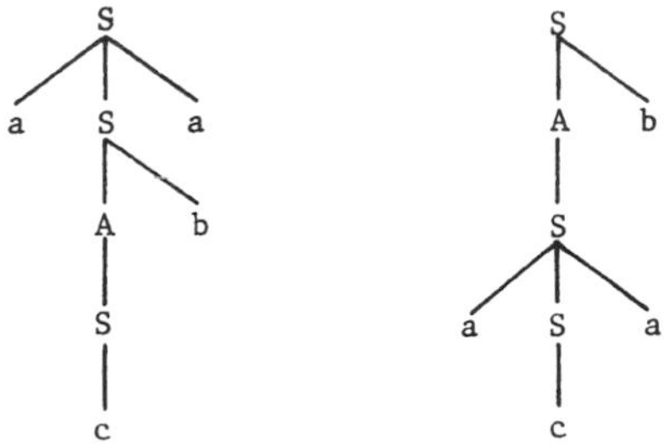

Figure 2.3. Two trees with left corner parse 1432.

The following example refers to a *simple chain grammar*. In Chapter 11 of this monograph the class of simple chain grammars will be treated in more detail. The underlying grammar G_2 of the following simple SDTS T_2 is a simple chain grammar.

$S \to aSa,\ S1$
$S \to aSb,\ S2$
$S \to A,\ \ 3A$
$A \to bS,\ \ 4S$
$S \to c,\ \ 5$

T_2 defines the left part parses (cf. Table III) of grammar G_2. Different sentences of G_2 can have the same left part parse, e.g. the string 34521 is a left part parse for aabcba and for baacba.
One can strictly adhere to the point of view that parsing should always be done with respect to a proper parse relation. We take a more practical point of view and consider the (generalized) left corner parsing methods as parsing methods. Clearly, it remains useful to distinguish the subclass of the proper parse relations from the arbitrary parse relations.

The following theorem gives a necessary and sufficient condition for a production directed parse relation to be proper.

THEOREM 2.2. A production directed parse relation $\tau(T)$ of a simple SDTS T is a proper parse relation if and only if the output grammar of T is unambiguous.

Proof. Let CFG G and simple SDTS T be as in Definition 2.12. The output grammar of T, denoted by G_0, is defined by the set of productions

$$P_0 = \{i.A \to h_\Sigma(\alpha_1 i\alpha_2) \mid A \to \alpha, h_\Sigma(\alpha_1 i\alpha_2) \text{ is in } R\}.$$

Assume that G_0 is unambiguous. Then each $x \in L(G_0)$ has exactly one left parse. Now, assume that $(w_1,x) \in \tau(T)$ and $(w_2,x) \in \tau(T)$ with $w_1 \neq w_2$. Clearly, there exist $\pi_1 \in \Delta_G^*$ and $\pi_2 \in \Delta_G^*$ such that $(w_1,\pi_1) \in \ell_G$ (the left parse relation of G) and $(w_2,\pi_2) \in \ell_G$ and, necessarily, $\pi_1 \neq \pi_2$. But then there exist also $(x,\pi_1) \in \ell_{G_0}$ and $(x,\pi_2) \in \ell_{G_0}$ which is impossible since G_0 is unambiguous. We conclude that condition (i) of Definition 2.1 is satisfied.

Next we show the existence of an one-to-one mapping between ℓ_G and $\tau(T)$. This mapping, together with the trivial property that, for any $w \in \Sigma^*$,

$$\langle w,G\rangle = |\{\pi \mid (w,\pi) \in \ell_G\}|$$

is sufficient to conclude that condition (ii) of Definition 2.1 is also satisfied. Firstly, notice that trivially, for any $(w,x) \in \tau(T)$ there exists $\pi \in \Delta_G^*$ such that $(w,\pi) \in \ell_G$. Now, assume that $(w,\pi_1) \in \ell_G$ and $(w,\pi_2) \in \ell_G$ for some $\pi_1 \neq \pi_2$. In general, if $(w,\pi_1) \in \ell_G$ then there exists exactly one $x \in L(G_0)$ which satisfies $(w,x) \in \tau(T)$ and $(x,\pi_1) \in \ell_{G_0}$. Otherwise we would have a situation in which two different sentences in $L(G_0)$ would have the same left parse, which is clearly impossible. Hence, if $(w,\pi_1) \in \ell_G$ and $(w,\pi_2) \in \ell_G$ then there exist $(w,x) \in \tau(T)$ and $(w,y) \in \tau(T)$ with $x \neq y$. This concludes the proof that $\tau(T)$ is a proper parse relation.

Now assume that $\tau(T)$ is a proper parse relation while G_0 is ambiguous. In this case there exists at least one $x \in L(G_0)$ with left parses π_1 and π_2, $\pi_1 \neq \pi_2$. From the existence of π_1 and π_2 we may conclude the existence of pairs (w_1,π_1) and (w_2,π_2) in ℓ_G and pairs (w_1,x) and (w_2,x) in $\tau(T)$. Since $\tau(T)$ is a proper parse relation we have that $w_1 = w_2$. Hence, in general, each pair $(w,x) \in \tau(T)$ with $\langle x,G_0\rangle = n$ gives rise to n elements $(w,\pi_1),\ldots(w,\pi_n)$ in ℓ_G. Thus, a one-to-one mapping between ℓ_G and $\tau(T)$ can not be defined and consequently $\tau(T)$ is not a proper parse relation. This concludes the proof. □

2.2.2. PRODUCTION DIRECTED PARSES

We briefly describe various ways in which production directed parses appear in the literature.

It is a well-known trick to insert special symbols (standing for production numbers or, generally , marking the place for semantical information) in the right-hand sides of productions to obtain special parses or to activate semantic actions (for example, Aho and Ullman [3,4]). In fact, this has also been done by Kurki-Suonio [89] who adds a symbol to the right of the righthand sides of the productions and Kuno [87] who adds a symbol to the left of the righthand sides. A related idea is in the definition of parenthesis and bracketed grammars (cf. McNaughton [107] and Ginsburg and Harrison [43]). The special symbols are sometimes handled as lefthand sides of ε-productions. For example, this is done by Demers [24] to define generalized left corner parsing. Following Demers, all production directed parses should be called generalized left corner parses. In this terminology, if we have a rule $A \to \alpha$, $h_\Sigma(\alpha_1 i \alpha_2)$ then α_1 is called the generalized left corner† of the rule and α_2 is its trailing part.

The following table lists a few names of parses which have been introduced before.

SIMPLE SDTS	NAME
$i.A \to \alpha,\ h_\Sigma(i\alpha)$	left parses
$i.A \to \alpha,\ h_\Sigma(\alpha i)$	right parses
$i.A \to \alpha,\ h_\Sigma(\alpha_1 i \alpha_2)$ $\alpha_1\alpha_2 = \alpha$ and $\lvert\alpha_1\rvert = 1$	left corner parses (Rosenkrantz and Lewis [143])
$i.A \to \alpha,\ h_\Sigma(\alpha_1 i \alpha_2)$ $\alpha_1\alpha_2 = \alpha$, $\alpha \in \Sigma^*$ or $\alpha_1 \in \Sigma^* N$	extended left corner parses (Brosgol [17])
$i.A \to \alpha,\ h_\Sigma(\alpha_1 i \alpha_2)$ $\alpha_1\alpha_2 = \alpha$ and $\lvert\alpha_2\rvert = 1$	left part parses (Nijholt [118])

Table III. Types of parses

It is usual to associate left parses with top-down parsing. In deterministic top-down parsing (LL-parsing) each production is recognized before reading its yield, that is, at position 1 of the righthand side. In deterministic bottom-up parsing (LR-parsing) the recognition is at position n + 1. The right parses are associated with bottom-up parsing. In (deterministic) generalized left corner parsing each production is recognized immediately after its generalized left corner†. Generalized left corner parses are associated with generalized left corner parsing. Note that left part parses are defined as the 'opposite' of left corner parses. Because we want to associate left part parses with left parts (cf.Chapter 11) we have not chosen the name right corner parse. Moreover *left* part parses are a special case of generalized *left* corner parses. Consider the following example.

In Figure 2.4 we display a grammatical tree T and a particular way in which this tree is constructed. The tree is built up with partial subtrees by considering the next terminal symbol, reading from left to right.

† The *left corner* of a production is the leftmost symbol of its righthand side. A *generalized left corner* of a production is a prefix of its righthand side.

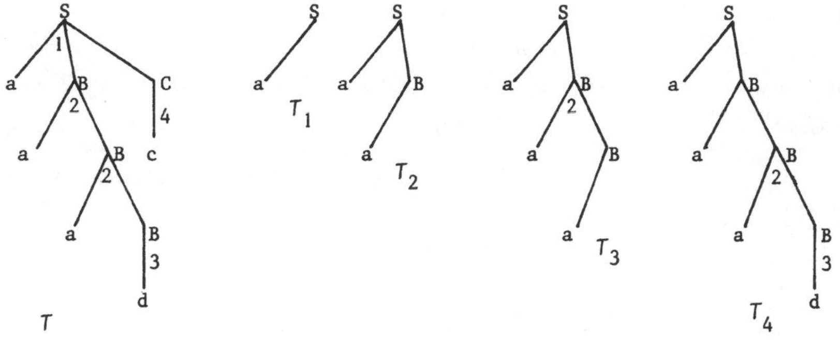

Figure 2.4. Tree T and its partial subtrees.

After reading the first terminal symbol we construct tree T_1. The second terminal symbol gives rise to tree T_2. After reading the third terminal symbol we have obtained tree T_3 and we notice that a production with label 2 is now complete. The fourth terminal symbol gives us tree T_4 and two more productions, 2 and 3, are now complete. The last terminal symbol which is read makes tree T and the productions 1 and 4 complete.

The string 22314 of productions, which is obtained in this way is the formally defined left part parse for sentence aaadc of a corresponding context-free grammar. We will return to these partial trees and the left part parses in the forthcoming sections.

We conclude this section with some notational remarks. In the following table some frequently used names and notations are displayed. We use ℓ to denote left parses (and left parse relations) and $\bar{r}$ to denote the right parses. In general, if f denotes a parse relation then $\bar{f}$ denotes the parse relation $\{(w,\pi) \mid (w,\pi^R) \in f\}$. Apart from $\ell, \bar{r}, \bar{\ell}$ and r the abbreviations ℓp, standing for left part parses, and ℓc, standing for left corner parses, will sometimes be used.

PARSE RELATION		NOTATION	NAME
f	f	G'[f/h]G	f-to-h cover
left	left	$G'[\ell/\ell]G$	left cover
left	right	$G'[\ell/\bar{r}]G$	left-to-right cover
right	left	$G'[\bar{r}/\ell]G$	right-to-left cover
right	right	$G'[\bar{r}/\bar{r}]G$	right cover

Table IV. Covers

In algorithms and examples it is often convenient to use the notations $A \to \alpha\ \langle\pi\rangle$ or $i.A \to \alpha\ \langle\pi\rangle$ to denote that a production $i.A \to \alpha$ of a CFG G' is mapped by a parse homomorphism on a (possibly empty) string of productions $\pi \in \Delta_G^*$ of a CFG G.

We will need a notation to refer to positions in the righthand sides of the productions.

NOTATION 2.1. Let $j.A \to X_1X_2 \ldots X_n$ be a production of a CFG G. The positions in the righthand side are numbered according to the following scheme:

$$j.A \to [1]X_1[2]X_2 \ldots [n]X_n[n+1]$$

For a given production directed parse relation each production has a fixed position in which its number is inserted, conform Definition 2.12. We use $\Gamma_G(j)$, or simply $\Gamma(j)$ to denote this position, i.e., $\Gamma_G : \Delta_G \to \mathbb{N}$. By definition, $\Gamma_G(j) = 1$ if $j.A \to \varepsilon$ is a production of G.

It is convenient to introduce an order relation $\leq$ on the parse relations of a CFG G. If $\Gamma_G^x : \Delta_G \to \mathbb{N}$ induces a production directed parse relation $x \subseteq \Sigma^* \times \Delta_G^*$ and $\Gamma_G^y : \Delta_G \to \mathbb{N}$ induces a production directed parse relation $y \subseteq \Sigma^* \times \Delta_G^*$, then we define

$$x \leq y$$

if and only if

$$\forall j \in \Delta_G : \Gamma_G^x(j) \leq \Gamma_G^y(j).$$

In this way the production directed parse relations of a grammar G induce a finite lattice with order $\leq$.

EXAMPLE 2.3.
Consider CFG G with productions 1. $S \to AB$, 2. $A \to AB$, 3. $A \to a$ and 4. $B \to b$. For G we can define nine production directed parse relations. In Table V it is shown how they can be obtained if we insert production numbers in the righthand sides.

x_0	x_1	x_2	x_3	x_4	x_5	x_6	x_7	x_8
1AB	A1B	1AB	A1B	AB1	1AB	AB1	A1B	AB1
2AB	2AB	A2B	A2B	2AB	AB2	A2B	AB2	AB2
3	3	3	3	3	3	3	3	3
4	4	4	4	4	4	4	4	4

Table V. Production directed parse relations.

The corresponding finite lattice is pictured below.

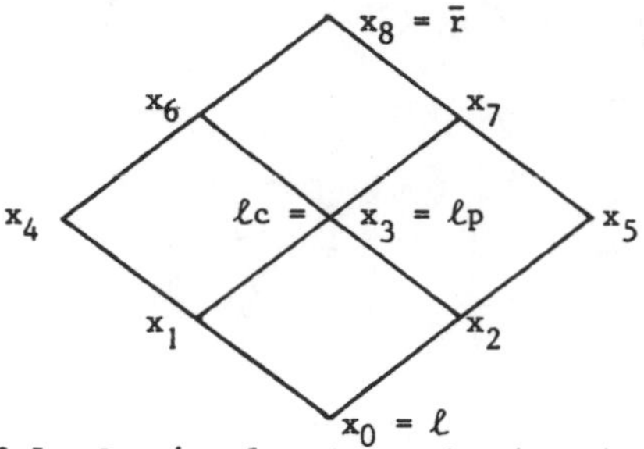

Figure 2.5. Lattice for the production directed parse relations.

2.3* GRAMMAR FUNCTORS

The concept of grammar functor is one of the well-known grammatical similarity relations. This section is devoted to a short discussion on grammar functors in order to make it possible to compare functors and covers. In later sections examples of the use of grammar functors will be given.
Having introduced syntax categories in section 1.3.2 we will now define functors between syntax categories. We use a slightly adapted version of the definition in Benson [13].

<u>DEFINITION 2.13.</u> Let $G' = (N',\Sigma',P',S')$ and $G = (N,\Sigma,P,S)$ be CFG's. A *grammar functor*

$$F : S(G') \to S(G)$$

is a functor which preserves concatenation (for both objects and morphisms) and the empty string, and which satisfies

(i) $F(A) \in V^*$ for all $A \in N'$,
(ii) $F(a) \in \Sigma^*$ for all $a \in \Sigma'$, and
(iii) $F(S') = S$.

F is said to be *externally fixed* if $\Sigma' = \Sigma$ and $F(a) = a$ for each $a \in \Sigma'$.

In Benson [13], instead of S and S', start strings in N^* and N'^*, respectively, are used. Moreover, we have $F(A) \in V^*$ instead of $F(A) \in N^*$. With our definition it becomes possible to define a functor in a situation as portrayed in Figure 2.6.

To define a grammar functor $F : S(G') \to S(G)$ it is sufficient to define F on $V' = N' \cup \Sigma'$ and on P'. Free generation takes care of the rest. From Definition 2.13 it follows that $F(L(G')) \subseteq L(G)$.

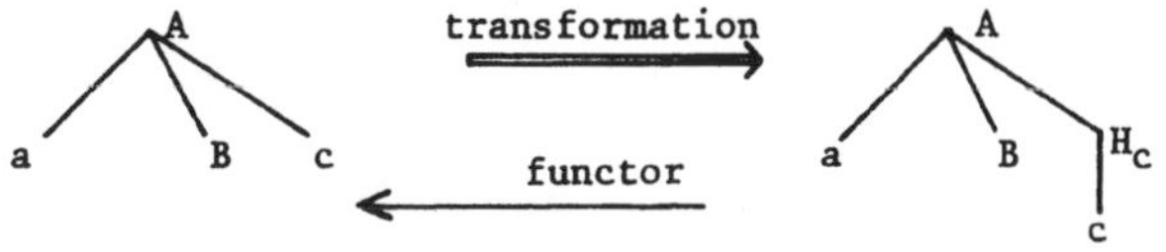

Figure 2.6. Functor F, $F(H_c \to c) = id_c$ and $F(H_c) = c$.

Without further restrictions on F we can not, without further knowledge of G and G', compare $\langle w,G'\rangle$ and $\langle F(w),G\rangle$. Grammar functor F can be restricted to the HOM-sets of S(G'). Let $\alpha,\beta \in V'^*$ then the HOM-set of (α,β) is denoted by $S(G')(\alpha,\beta)$ and the restriction of F to this HOM-set is denoted by

$$F(\alpha,\beta) : S(G')(\alpha,\beta) \to S(G)(F(\alpha), F(\beta)).$$

It is fairly easy to compare grammar functors and covers. In the case of a cover we are only interested in the relation between the parse relations of G' and G. That is, in the functor terminology, in the relation between $S(G')(S',w')$ and $S(G)(S,F(w'))$ for each $w' \in \Sigma'^*$. Except for S', S, w' and $F(w')$ domains and codomains of derivations are not compared when covers are considered.

A cover homomorphism can now be compared with a grammar functor F which has the property that for each $w \in \Sigma'^*$ the restriction $F(S',w)$ is a surjection. In this case $F(L(G')) = L(G)$ and if F is externally fixed then $\langle w,G'\rangle \geq \langle w,G\rangle$.

Clearly, for grammar functors we can go into more details. A grammar functor is said to be *full* if for each pair of objects α, $\beta \in V'^*$, $F(\alpha,\beta)$ is surjective; it is said to be *externally full* if for each pair of objects $\alpha \in V'^*$ and $w \in \Sigma'^*$, $F(\alpha,w)$ is surjective. A grammar functor is *faithful* if for each pair of objects α, $\beta \in V'^*$, $F(\alpha,\beta)$ is injective. If one wishes to incorporate these concepts in the cover approach a further refinement of the cover framework is necessary.

Obviously, covers say less about the preserving of syntactic structure than grammar functors. However, the definition of cover is much more flexible, cover results can be obtained more easily than grammar functor results and from the point of view of parsing one can say that covers describe a natural and sufficient representation of a parse tree and its changes under a transformation of the grammar.

2.4. RELATED CONCEPTS

We mention a few other concepts which have been introduced to express grammatical similarity. In Gray and Harrison [49], Ginsburg and Harrison [43], Hunt and Rosenkrantz [69] and Reynolds and Haskell [141] definitions and results are given for *grammar homomorphisms, grammar isomorphisms, weak Reynolds covers* and *Reynolds covers*. In these definitions the emphasis is on the sets of the productions of the grammars and not, as in the case of grammar covers, on the sets of derivations or parses.

Structural equivalence was introduced by Paull and Unger [129] (cf.Definition 1.7. c.).

DEFINITION 2.14. Two trees are *structurally isomorphic* if by relabeling their nodes they may be made the same. Let $w \in L(G_i)$ and let $T_i(w)$ be a parse tree for CFG G_i, $i = 1,2$. CFG G_1 is *structurally equivalent* to CFG G_2 if for every tree $T_1(w)$ there exists a tree $T_2(w)$ such that $T_1(w)$ is structurally isomorphic with $T_2(w)$ and, conversely, for each tree $T_2(w)$ there is at least one tree $T_1(w)$ such that $T_1(w)$ is structurally isomorphic with $T_2(w)$.

Notice that with this definition $L(G_1) = L(G_2)$, while in general, without further knowledge of G_1 and G_2, we can not compare $\langle w,G_1\rangle$ and $\langle w,G_2\rangle$. Definition 2.14 is equivalent to Definition 1.7. c.

Structural equivalence is decidable, that is, there exists an algorithm for determining whether or not two arbitrary CFG's are structurally equivalent (cf. Paull and Unger [129], McNaughton [107] and Knuth [77]). Paull and Unger [129] present an algorithm for generating structurally equivalent simple deterministic grammars corresponding to a given CFG. If no such grammar exists the algorithm terminates with an indication of this fact. In Paull and Unger [130] this result is extended to ε-free LL(1) grammars. Other results on structural equivalence appear in Prather [134] and in Taniguchi and Kasami [160], who present transformations from a CFG G_1 to a structurally equivalent CFG G_2 which has either a minimal number of nonterminal symbols or a minimal number of productions. Some decidability results on the existence of certain grammar functors appear, for example, in Schnorr [151] and Bertsch [14].

The notion of weak equivalence of grammars is an equivalence relation (in the algebraic sense). Much effort has been made to subclassify weak equivalence by equivalence relations which are defined with the help of grammar functors (cf. Hotz and Claus [67], Schnorr [151] and Schepen [146]).

Decidability results for covers are extensively discussed in Hunt, Rosenkrantz and Szymanski [72] and in Hunt and Rosenkrantz [69]. In the latter paper grammatical similarity relations are used to generalize the grammar form definition of Cremers and Ginsburg [21].

Finally, we mention Kuroda [91] who introduces topologies on grammatical trees and who defines strong and weak structural homeomorphisms between context-free grammars to subclassify weak equivalence.

Our main motivation in mentioning the literature listed above is to show the existence of problems which may again become interesting if the concept of cover is used as grammatical similarity relation.

Attribute grammars (cf. Knuth [78]) are not dealt with in this monograph. However, if we take the point of view that a practical reason to consider covers concerns compiler construction then attribute grammars should also be discussed. In the case of covers we consider a parse as the argument of a semantic mapping. In case

CFG G' covers CFG G then we can use the original semantic mapping, corresponding to G. In section 3.1 more details are given. Attribute grammars form an alternative method. Here, attributes (which contain semantic information) are associated with the nodes of a parse tree. These attributes are obtained from attributes associated with the symbols which appear in the productions and from attribute evaluation rules. If an attribute grammar is transformed to, for example, some normal form attribute grammar, then we have not only the question of language equivalence, but also that of semantic equivalence. Grammar transformations which yield positive cover results should be the first to apply (obviously in an adapted form) for attribute grammars. Bochman [15] explores this semantic equivalence of attribute grammars.

CHAPTER 3

COVERS, PARSING AND NORMAL FORMS

This chapter contains the motivation of our investigations on grammar covers. The first section deals with the grammar cover concept and its use for parsing. In section 3.2 we try to give a historical overview of covers and normal forms. Finally, in section 3.3 we start our investigations on covers, normal forms and parsing.

3.1. COVERS AND PARSING

Apart from the theoretical interest in covers one can view the cover concept as a possible tool in the field of parsing. To analyze or to parse a given potential sentence is the process of determining whether it is indeed an element of the language defined by the grammar under consideration and to make the syntactic structure of the sentence explicit. This can be the analysis of natural language sentences or of sentences (programs) of a formal language such as a programming language. In the latter case parsing can be a phase in the structure of a compiler which follows lexical analysis and which precedes the code generation and optimization.

Parses can then be considered as a type of intermediate code from which the code generation can be done. It should be observed that with our use of simple SDTS's only one possible way of translation (from language to intermediate code) is considered. Other translations make use of more powerful devices such as, for example, (not necessarily simple) SDTS's, generalized SDTS's or nondeterministic generalized SDTS's (cf. Baker [9]).

In the case of parsing, the following two figures will clarify the intended use of covers. Figure 3.1 can be considered as a more practically oriented version of Figure 2.1.

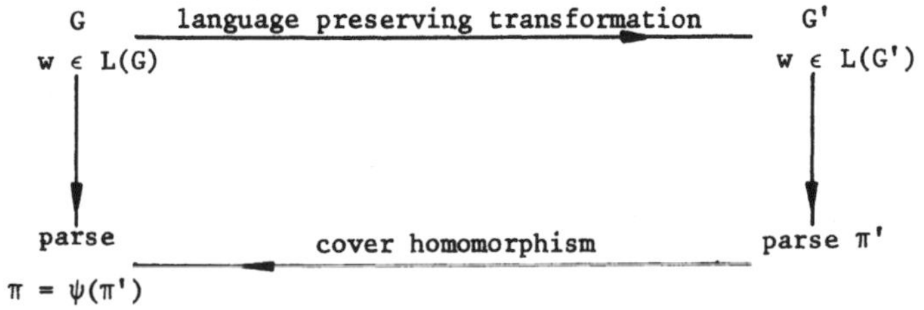

Figure 3.1. Covers and parsing

The idea is that a CFG G which is hard to parse is transformed to a CFG G' which is easier to parse. Parsing is then done with respect to G' and afterwards the parse is mapped by the cover homomorphism on the corresponding parse of G.

Numerous parsing methods for subclasses of the context-free grammars appear in the literature. In Chapter 1 we already mentioned (cf.section 1.3.1) that any simple syntax directed translation can be obtained by means of a PDT. Therefore, any of the syntax directed parse relations can be obtained as a translation defined by a PDT.

Several important subclasses of the context-free grammars which are based on a specific parsing method have been introduced. For example, the bounded context grammars (Floyd [33], Graham [46]), precedence grammars (Floyd [32], Wirth and Weber [170]), LR(k) grammars (Knuth [76], DeRemer [25], Geller and Harrison [40]) and LL(k) grammars (Rosenkrantz and Stearns [144], Lewis and Stearns [101]). Most of these parsing methods can be 'implemented' by a DPDT. Other parsing methods make use of a device which uses two stacks (e.g., Colmerauer [20] and Williams [169]). In Chapter 9 cover results will be obtained from DPDT's (deterministic pushdown transducers).

A class of grammars with attractive parsing properties is the class of LL(k) grammars. It has been the aim of many authors to transform grammars to LL(k) grammars. As we mentioned before this has been the goal in Paull and Unger [129,130]. In Hunt and Rosenkrantz [69] such a transformation for a 'Reynolds cover' is considered. It is worth noting that in the latter case the newly obtained grammar is not necessarily weakly equivalent with the original grammar. Other methods to obtain LL(k) grammars make use of more or less refined techniques of left factoring.

Both in Soisalon-Soininen [155] and Hammer [55] transformations are discussed from 'bottom-up' parsable grammars (restricted LR(k) grammars) to 'top-down' parsable grammars (LL(k) grammars). In these cases left-to-right covers can be defined.

In Figure 3.2, which appears also in a slightly different form in both Kuno [87] and Gray and Harrison [49], the situation for parsing is made more explicit.

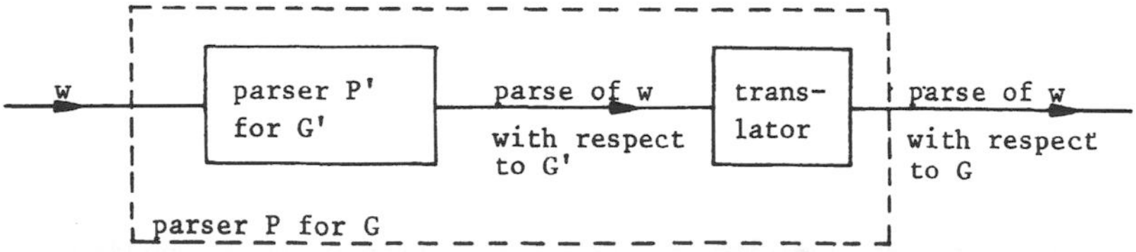

Figure 3.2. A parser for CFG G.

For the parser P' in Figure 3.2 one may think of one of the parsing methods mentioned above. In the case of covers, the translator is simply a homomorphism. Then it is not necessary to consider it as a separate device. Of course, more general devices may be chosen.

3.2. COVERS AND NORMAL FORMS: HISTORICAL NOTES

The aim of this section is to show that although not always presented in a formal way, the idea of grammar covers for transformations to grammars in some normal form has attracted attention from several authors. It should be observed that when the grammar cover concept was introduced systematically (see Gray and Harrison [48,49]), this link with the older literature was not exposed. Therefore we think it is useful to do so. The formal idea of a cover is also due to J.C.Reynolds.

The original transformation to Greibach normal form (GNF) is due to Greibach [50]. Her algorithm transforms an ε-free CFG without single productions to a CFG in this normal form. In Rosenkrantz [142] another transformation is presented to obtain this normal form.

In the following quotations *'standard form'* stands for GNF. Griffiths and Petrick [53] comment on Greibach's paper:

"We have already observed that Greibach has shown that for any CF grammar without cyclic nonterminals an equivalent standard form can be constructed. To date, no efficient procedure for relating the structural descriptions of standard form grammars to the CF grammars from which they were constructed has been found".

In Griffiths and Petrick [54] further remarks can be found.

The next in line is Kurki-Suonio [89] who comments on Griffiths and Petrick's paper:

"One way to avoid left recursion is to transform the grammar into standard form, but the desired structural descriptions are then lost as the authors point out".

However, this can be repaired. Kurki-Suonio considers a method to eliminate left recursion for applying top-down parsing to any context-free language. His method coincides with, what we call now, the usual method for eliminating left recursion (Aho and Ullman's Algorithm 2.12, [3]). The method appeared before in some informal settings, for example, Greibach [51]. Kurki-Suonio remarks:

"The above removal of left recursion distorts the phrase structure of sentences. Information on the original phrase boundaries is preserved, however, if a marker is attached to the end of each right-hand side of the original rules, and the markers are then carried along in the transformation".

This is a useful observation. In fact, Foster [35] and Kuno [87] have the same idea. Foster [34], presenting earlier work, describes a program that, given a CFG attempts to transform this grammar into an equivalent CFG which can be parsed by a simple one-pass parsing algorithm. Also in this case, the objective is that semantic routines which are associated with the original rules remain unchanged, that is:

"Any transformations on the syntax which would produce an equivalent grammar if the routines were all ordinary basis symbols, will give a recognizer which will produce the same translation as the original".

One of the transformations which is used in this *'Syntax Improving Device'*-program is the elimination of left recursion. In Foster [34] more details are given. The method is also described in Wood [171].

Kuno [87] converts a given CFG into an 'augmented' standard form grammar, each of whose rules is in standard form, supplemented by additional information describing its derivation from the original context-free grammar. Contrary to Kurki-Suonio who supplies this information in a marker at the end of each righthand side of the original rules, Kuno supplies this information at the beginning of each righthand side. Kuno's method to transform a non-left-recursive grammar to a GNF grammar coincides with the usual method (Aho and Ullman's Algorithm 2.14, [3]). In this case the technique for performing the conversion of the structural descriptions is simple. However, as soon as this idea is used for the transformation of an arbitrary grammar to a non-left-recursive grammar then the method for undistorting the structural description back to the original description becomes very complicated.

Stearns [158] is another source where we can find similar ideas as were presented by Foster.

After we are able to give a fairly complete overview of cover results for context-free grammars in some normal forms we will (informally) evaluate them in view of the remarks presented in this section (cf. Chapter 6). In Chapter 8, where we shortly discuss the use of grammar covers for compilers and compiler writing systems, we will return to some of the notes of this section.

3.3. COVERS AND NORMAL FORMS: AN INTRODUCTION

In this monograph, from now on, unless stated otherwise, we assume that whenever we define a cover homomorphism $g = \langle\varphi,\psi\rangle$ between grammars $G = (N,\Sigma,P,S)$ and $G' = (N',\Sigma',P',S')$ then $\Sigma = \Sigma'$ and φ is the identity homomorphism. Hence we only consider homomorphism ψ. Both in Gray and Harrison [49] and in Aho and Ullman [3] results and remarks are presented on the existence and nonexistence of certain covers of grammars with grammars in some normal form. Some of these remarks are not correct. In some case a negative result is caused by the fact that the cover homomorphism is assumed to be fine. The following observation shows that if we consider a transformation to GNF a fine cover homomorphism is too restrictive.

<u>OBSERVATION 3.1.</u> Let $G = (N,\Sigma,P,S)$ be a proper (cf. Definition 1.8. d.) and unambiguous CFG such that there exist $w \in L(G)$ and $S \overset{\pi}{\Rightarrow} w$ with $|\pi| > |w|$. CFG G can not be

covered by a CFG in GNF under a fine cover homomorphism.

It should be noted (cf. Chapter 5) that any proper CFG G can be transformed to a NLR grammar G' such that $G'[\bar{r}/\bar{r}]G$ under a fine cover homomorphism. In Gray and Harrison [49] a grammar G_0 with productions

$$1./2. \quad S \to S0 \mid S1$$
$$3./4. \quad S \to 0 \mid 1$$

is used to show that not every CFG can be right covered by a CFG in GNF (under a fine cover homomorphism). The proof of this result is somewhat difficult to read because some details are missing. In J.N.Gray's Ph.D.Thesis a more detailed proof can be found. In Chapter 7 we will introduce algorithms for transforming regular grammars into grammars in GNF.

It is simple to find for G_0 a grammar G such that $G[\bar{r}/\bar{r}]G_0$ and G is non-left-recursive. Consider, for example, grammar G_1 defined by

1.	$S \to C$	$\langle\varepsilon\rangle$	5.	$D \to 0$	$\langle 1\rangle$
2.	$S \to CS'$	$\langle\varepsilon\rangle$	6.	$D \to 1$	$\langle 2\rangle$
3.	$S' \to D$	$\langle\varepsilon\rangle$	7.	$C \to 0$	$\langle 3\rangle$
4.	$S' \to DS'$	$\langle\varepsilon\rangle$	8.	$C \to 1$	$\langle 4\rangle$

According to the terminology of Gray and Harrison [49], one can say that the productions 1. until 4. do not have semantic significance.

As was first shown in Nijholt [117], one can find a grammar G' in GNF which satisfies both $G'[\ell/\bar{r}]G_0$ and $G'[\bar{r}/\bar{r}]G_0$ (under the same cover homomorphism). This grammar is listed in Table VI. Symbol S' is the new start symbol.

$S' \to 0H_{15}S$	$\langle\varepsilon\rangle$	$S' \to 1H_{27}$	$\langle\varepsilon\rangle$	$S \to 0H_{58}$	$\langle\varepsilon\rangle$
$H_{15} \to 0$	$\langle 31\rangle$	$H_{27} \to 0$	$\langle 41\rangle$	$H_{58} \to 1$	$\langle 12\rangle$
$S' \to 0H_{16}S$	$\langle\varepsilon\rangle$	$S' \to 1H_{28}$	$\langle\varepsilon\rangle$	$S \to 1H_{65}S$	$\langle\varepsilon\rangle$
$H_{16} \to 1$	$\langle 32\rangle$	$H_{28} \to 1$	$\langle 42\rangle$	$H_{65} \to 0$	$\langle 21\rangle$
$S' \to 0H_{17}$	$\langle\varepsilon\rangle$	$S' \to 0$	$\langle 3\rangle$	$S \to 1H_{66}S$	$\langle\varepsilon\rangle$
$H_{17} \to 0$	$\langle 31\rangle$	$S' \to 1$	$\langle 4\rangle$	$H_{66} \to 1$	$\langle 22\rangle$
$S' \to 0H_{18}$	$\langle\varepsilon\rangle$	$S \to 0H_{55}S$	$\langle\varepsilon\rangle$	$S \to 1H_{67}$	$\langle\varepsilon\rangle$
$H_{18} \to 1$	$\langle 32\rangle$	$H_{55} \to 0$	$\langle 11\rangle$	$H_{67} \to 0$	$\langle 21\rangle$
$S' \to 1H_{25}S$	$\langle\varepsilon\rangle$	$S \to 0H_{56}S$	$\langle\varepsilon\rangle$	$S \to 1H_{68}$	$\langle\varepsilon\rangle$
$H_{25} \to 0$	$\langle 41\rangle$	$H_{56} \to 1$	$\langle 12\rangle$	$H_{68} \to 1$	$\langle 22\rangle$
$S' \to 1H_{26}S$	$\langle\varepsilon\rangle$	$S \to 0H_{57}$	$\langle\varepsilon\rangle$	$S \to 0$	$\langle 1\rangle$
$H_{26} \to 1$	$\langle 42\rangle$	$H_{57} \to 0$	$\langle 11\rangle$	$S \to 1$	$\langle 2\rangle$

Table VI. Productions of grammar G'.

Our aim in the forthcoming sections is to study the existence and nonexistence of grammar covers for some normal forms for context-free grammars. That is, we consider problems in which we ask: Given classes of grammars Γ_1 and Γ_2, can we find for each grammar G in Γ_1 a grammar G' in Γ_2 such that G' covers G ? At some places we will also discuss the question of the existence of grammar functors.

The examples which we gave above will be referred to in the following sections. For Γ_1 we will consider arbitrary context-free grammars and by introducing conditions which should be satisfied we consider also some subclasses of the context-free grammars. For Γ_2 we will concentrate on the ε-free, the non-left-recursive and the Greibach normal form grammars.

The next chapter will be devoted to some general results and observations on covers. In Chapter 5 transformations to obtain non-left-recursive and Greibach normal form grammars are considered. In Chapter 6 we present a cover-table which gives yes and no answers for various cover existence questions. In Chapter 7 we have a short discussion on regular grammars.

CHAPTER 4

PROPERTIES OF COVERS AND PRELIMINARY TRANSFORMATIONS

4.1. PROPERTIES OF COVERS

It is useful to put forward a few general properties of grammar covers. The most frequently used property will be the transitivity of covers, that is, if grammar G_2 covers grammar G_1 and grammar G_3 covers grammar G_2, then grammar G_3 covers G_1. More formally (we assume the parse relations to be understood from the notation):

<u>LEMMA 4.1.</u> If $G_3[f/g]G_2$ and $G_2[g/h]G_1$ then $G_3[f/h]G_1$.

Proof. Trivial. □

For future applications we generalize the idea of transitivity.

<u>DEFINITION 4.1.</u> Let G and G' be CFG's such that G'[f/h]G for some parse relations $f_{G'}$ and h_G and a cover homomorphism ψ. A partition π_t of $\Delta_{G'}$ is said to be a *transitivity partition* of $\Delta_{G'}$ if, for each block $B \in \pi_t$, i and j in B implies $\psi(i) = \psi(j)$.

Clearly, there is always a minimal partition $\{\{i\} \mid i \in \Delta_{G}'\}$ and a maximal partition $\{B \mid i,j \in B \text{ iff } \psi(i) = \psi(j)\}$. We introduce a homomorphism $\delta_t : \Delta_{G'}^* \to \pi_t^*$ by defining, for any $i \in \Delta_{G'}$, if $i \in B$ then $\delta_t(i) = B$.

<u>OBSERVATION 4.1.</u> Let the three CFG's, G_1, G_2 and G_3 have parse relations f_{G_1}, g_{G_2} and h_{G_3}, respectively. Suppose $G_2[g/f]G_1$. Let π_t be a transitivity partition of Δ_{G_2}. Define a *transitivity relation* $\tilde{g}_{G_2} \subseteq \Sigma^* \times \pi_t^*$ by

$$\tilde{g}_{G_2} = \{(w,\pi) \mid (w,\pi') \in g_{G_2} \text{ and } \delta_t(\pi') = \pi\}.$$

Now we may conclude that $G_3[h/f]G_1$ if there exists a homomorphism $\psi_t : \Delta_{G_3}^* \to \pi_t^*$, which satisfies

(i) if $(w,\pi) \in h_{G_3}$ then $(w,\psi_t(\pi)) \in \tilde{g}_{G_2}$, and

(ii) for each $(w,\pi) \in \tilde{g}_{G_2}$ there exists $(w,\pi') \in h_{G_3}$ such that $\psi_t(\pi') = \pi$.

End of Observation 4.1.

This observation is illustrated in Figure 4.1. Although we do not necessarily have that G_3 covers G_2 we may conclude that G_3 covers G_1 because of the existence of the homomorphism ψ_t.

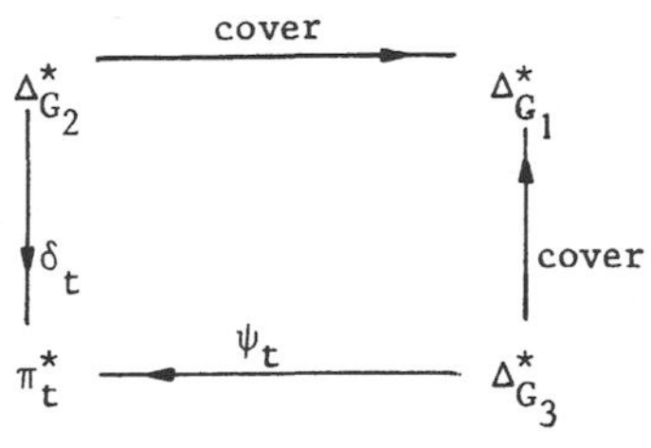

Figure 4.1. Observation 4.1.

The notation in the following lemma was explained in section 2.2.

<u>LEMMA 4.2.</u> Let $f_{G'}$ and h_G be parse relations for grammars G' and G, respectively. If G'[f/h]G then G'[$\bar{f}/\bar{h}$]G.

Proof. Let ψ be the cover homomorphism under which G'[f/h]G. Define $\psi^R : \Delta^*_{G'} \to \Delta^*_G$ such that, for any $i \in \Delta_{G'}$, $\psi^R(i) = \pi^R$ if $\psi(i) = \pi$. Then G'[$\bar{f}/\bar{h}$]G under cover homomorphism ψ^R. □

Note, if the cover homomorphism ψ is fine then ψ^R and ψ are identical on $\Delta_{G'}$. Rather loosely formulated one can say that if a cover is supported† by rules of the form $A \to a$ or $A \to \varepsilon$ only, then we can treat left and right parses of the covering grammar as being identical. This is formalized in the following way.

<u>LEMMA 4.3.</u> Consider two CFG's, $G' = (N',\Sigma,P',S')$ and $G = (N,\Sigma,P,S)$. Assume that h_G is a parse relation of G. If, for each production $i.A \to \alpha$ in P', homomorphism $\psi : \Delta^*_{G'} \to \Delta^*_G$ satisfies $\psi(i) = \varepsilon$ if $\alpha \notin \Sigma \cup \{\varepsilon\}$, then G'[$\ell$/h]G if and only if G'[$\bar{r}$/h]G.

Proof. Observe that for any parse tree $T \in PTR(G')$ there are unique pairs $(w,\pi_1) \in \bar{r}_{G'}$ and $(w,\pi_2) \in \ell_{G'}$. Define $\Omega = \{i \in \Delta_{G'} \mid i.A \to \alpha \text{ in } P' \text{ and } \alpha \notin \Sigma \cup \{\varepsilon\}\}$. Now observe that $h_\Omega(\pi_1) = h_\Omega(\pi_2)$ and therefore, for any cover homomorphism ψ,

$$\psi(\pi_1) = \psi(h_\Omega(\pi_1)) = \psi(h_\Omega(\pi_2)) = \psi(\pi_2).$$ □

As the following result shows, it is fairly simple to convert the problem of finding a covering grammar G_3 for a CFG G_1 such that G_3[f/h]G_1 to the problem of

† We say that a production rule supports the cover when its homomorphic image is not empty, hence, when it has semantic significance.

finding a grammar G_3 which satisfies $G_3[f/\ell]G_2$ or $G_3[f/\bar{r}]G_2$. Here, G_2 is an intermediate grammar which satisfies both $G_2[\ell/h]G_1$ and $G_2[\bar{r}/h]G_1$.

LEMMA 4.4. For any CFG G and production directed parse relation h_G there exists a CFG G' such that both $G'[\ell/h]G$ and $G'[\bar{r}/h]G$.

Proof. Let $G = (N,\Sigma,P,S)$ be the CFG. Define $G' = (N',\Sigma,P',S)$ by the sets N' and P' in the following way. We use an auxiliary set P_0.

(i) Initially, set $N' = N$ and $P' = P_0$, where

$$P_0 = \{i.A \to \alpha \ \langle i\rangle \mid \alpha \in \Sigma \cup \{\varepsilon\}\}.$$

(ii) For any $i.A \to \alpha$ in $P - P_0$, if $\Gamma_G(i) = k$, where $\Gamma_G : \Delta_G \to \mathbb{N}$ is the mapping which defines h_G, then

a. Add $A \to \alpha_1 H_i \alpha_2 \ \langle\varepsilon\rangle$ and $H_i \to \varepsilon \ \langle i\rangle$ to P', where $\alpha_1\alpha_2 = \alpha$ and $|\alpha_1| = k - 1$.

b. Add H_i to N'. It is easily seen that both $G'[\ell/h]G$ and $G'[\bar{r}/h]G$. □

OBSERVATION 4.2. If CFG G in Lemma 4.4 is non-left-recursive, then CFG G' is also non-left-recursive.

It should be noted that in Lemma 4.4 we have restricted ourselves to production directed parse relations. This will also be done in the following observation on the symmetry of production directed parse relations. We will frequently refer to this symmetry in the cover-table construction of Chapter 6. First we need the following definition.

DEFINITION 4.2. Let h_G be a production directed parse relation for a grammar $G = (N,\Sigma,P,S)$. Assume that h_G is defined by the mapping $\Gamma_G : \Delta_G \to \mathbb{N}$. Define the production directed parse relation h^s_G by a mapping $\Gamma^s_G : \Delta_G \to \mathbb{N}$, which is defined, for any production $i.A \to \alpha$ in P, by

$$\Gamma^s_G(i) = |\alpha| + 2 - \Gamma_G(i).$$

Notice, that due to this definition $\ell^s_G = \bar{r}_G$, $\bar{r}^s_G = \ell_G$ and $\ell p^s_G = \ell c_G$ (the left corner parse relation of G is denoted by ℓc_G; the left part parse relation of G is denoted by ℓp_G).

OBSERVATION 4.3. *('SYMMETRY')*
Let $G = (N,\Sigma,P,S)$ be a CFG. Define $G^R = (N,\Sigma,P^R,S)$ by defining $P^R = \{A \to \alpha^R \mid A \to \alpha \text{ is in } P\}$. Notice that, for example, a leftmost derivation of $w \in L(G)$ coincides with a rightmost derivation of $w^R \in L(G^R)$. More generally, any production directed parse

relation h_G of G coincides with a production directed parse relation $h^s_{G^R}$ of G^R, where, for example, h is chosen from $\{\ell, \bar{r}, \ell p, \ell c\}$.
Hence if a grammar G can not be left covered by an ε-free grammar, then G^R can not be right covered by an ε-free grammar (Use Lemma 4.2). Another example is the situation in which a grammar G does not have a left-to-right covering grammar in GNF. It follows that grammar G^R does not have a right-to-left covering grammar in $\overline{\text{GNF}}$ (Use again Lemma 4.2). End of Observation 4.3.

4.2. PRELIMINARY TRANSFORMATIONS

Whenever context-free grammars are involved, the discussion on ε-productions and, to a lesser extent, single productions (sometimes called unit productions) consumes a disproportionate amount of space. In this section we single out two transformations which deal with these types of productions. In the following lemma, two trivial cases are considered.

<u>LEMMA 4.5.</u> Let h_G be a parse relation for a CFG G = (N,Σ,P,S).

a. If $(\varepsilon,\pi_1) \in h_G$ and $(\varepsilon,\pi_2) \in h_G$, with $\pi_1 \neq \pi_2$, then G can not be covered by an ε-free grammar.

b. For any $a \in \Sigma$, if $(a,\pi_1) \in h_G$ and $(a,\pi_2) \in h_G$, with $\pi_1 \neq \pi_2$, then G can not be covered by a grammar in GNF.

Proof.

a. A CFG G' = (N',Σ,P',S') which is ε-free has at most one element (ε,π) in any parse relation of G'. Therefore, a surjective parse homomorphism can not be defined.

b. Similarly. There is at most one element (a,π) in any parse relation of a CFG G' in GNF. □

In what follows we tacitly assume that each CFG under consideration is reduced, cycle-free and it does not have different leftmost derivations of the empty word.

We continue with some remarks on the elimination of single productions, that is, productions of the form A → B, with both A and B nónterminal symbols.

<u>LEMMA 4.6.</u> Let G = (N,Σ,P.S) be an ε-free grammar which, for each $a \in \Sigma$, does not have different leftmost derivations from S to a.
There exists an ε-free CFG G' = (N',Σ,P',S') without single productions such that both $G'[\ell/\ell]G$ and $G'[\bar{r}/\bar{r}]G$.

Proof. We show how the elimination of single productions can be done. We use auxiliary sets P_0, P_1 and P_2. The set P_0 is the set of all the single productions in P. Initially , $P_1 = \{A \to \alpha <i> \mid i.A \to \alpha \text{ is in } P - P_0\}$, $N' = N$ and $P_2 = \emptyset$.

(i) For any $A \in N$, if $A \overset{\delta}{\Rightarrow} B \overset{i}{\Rightarrow} \gamma$ is a derivation in G such that $\delta \neq \varepsilon$ and either $|\gamma| \geq 2$ or $\gamma \in \Sigma$, then add $[A\delta i] \to \gamma <\pi>$ to P_1 and $[A\delta i]$ to N'. To obtain a left cover, define $\pi = \delta i$. To obtain a right cover, define $\pi = i\delta^R$. Notice that since G is cycle-free there are finitely many derivations to consider.

(ii) Define a homomorphism $h : (N' \cup \Sigma)^* \to (N \cup \Sigma)^*$ by defining $h(X) = X$ for any $X \in N \cup \Sigma \cup \{\varepsilon\}$ and $h([A\delta]) = A$ for each $[A\delta] \in N' - N$. For each production $H \to \gamma <\pi>$ in P_1 add the productions in the set

$$\{H \to \gamma' <\pi> \mid H \to \gamma <\pi> \text{ is in } P_1,\ h(\gamma') = \gamma \text{ and } \gamma' \in (N' \cup \Sigma)^*\}$$

to P_2.

(iii) Initially set $P' = P_2$. For any $\alpha \in (N' \cup \Sigma)^*$ such that $[S\delta_1] \to \alpha, .., [S\delta_n] \to \alpha$ are all the productions in P_2 with a lefthand side of the form $[S\delta]$, $\delta \in \Delta_G^+$ and with the same righthand side α, the following is done.

(a) Assume $\alpha = c\beta$ for some $c \in \Sigma$ and $\beta \in (N' \cup \Sigma)^+$. Add the productions $S' \to H_i\beta <\pi_i>$ and $H_i \to c <\varepsilon>$ to P', $1 \leq i \leq n$. Here, H_i is a newly introduced nonterminal symbol which is added to N' and $\pi_i = \delta_i$ in the case of a left cover and $\pi_i = \delta_i^R$ in the case of a right cover, $1 \leq i \leq n$. Symbol S' will be the start symbol of the newly obtained grammar G' without single productions.

(b) Assume $\alpha = C\beta$, for some $C \in N'$ and $\beta \in (N' \cup \Sigma)^+$. Add the productions $S' \to C_{\delta_i}\beta <\pi_i>$ to P', $1 \leq i \leq n$, with $\pi_i = \delta_i$ in the case of a left cover and $\pi_i = \delta_i^R$ in the case of a right cover. The newly introduced nonterminal symbols C_{δ_i}, $1 \leq i \leq n$, are added to N'. Moreover, for each $\gamma \in \text{rhs}(C)$, if $C \to \gamma <\pi>$ is in P', add the productions $C_{\delta_i} \to <\pi>$, $1 \leq i \leq n$, to P'.

(c) Assume $\alpha = c$, $c \in \Sigma$. Since there are no different leftmost derivations from S to c, we have that $n = 1$. Add $S' \to c <\pi_1>$ to P', with $\pi_1 = \delta_1$ in the case of a left cover and $\pi_1 = \delta_1^R$ in the case of a right cover.

(iv) For each production $S \to \alpha <\pi>$ in P_2 add the production $S' \to \alpha <\pi>$ to P'.

(v) Remove the useless symbols. The newly obtained grammar will be referred to as $G' = (N',\Sigma,P',S')$.

Clearly grammar G' does not have single productions. Grammar G' left covers G. Let ψ be the cover homomorphism which is defined in the steps above. After step (ii) has been performed the following properties hold.

a. If $A \overset{\pi'}{\underset{L}{\Rightarrow}} w$ in G' then $A \overset{\pi}{\underset{L}{\Rightarrow}} w$ in G, with $\psi(\pi') = \pi$.

b. If $[A\delta] \overset{\pi'}{\underset{L}{\Rightarrow}} w$ in G' then $A \overset{\pi}{\underset{L}{\Rightarrow}} w$ in G, with $\psi(\pi') = \pi$.

c. If $A \overset{\pi}{\underset{L}{\Rightarrow}} w$ in G then there exists π' such that either $A \overset{\pi'}{\underset{L}{\Rightarrow}} w$ in G' or $[A\delta] \overset{\pi'}{\underset{L}{\Rightarrow}} w$ in G', for some $\delta \in \Delta_G^+$ and with $\psi(\pi') = \pi$.

These properties can formally be proved by induction on the lengths of the derivations. Similar properties hold for rightmost derivations.
In step (iii) and (iv) the new start symbol S' is introduced and the productions with lefthand side S' are created in such a way that from S' we can derive 'everything' which could be derived from the symbols of the form S and $[S\delta]$. From a, b, c and simple observations on the definition of ψ in steps (iii) and (iv) it follows that $G'[\ell/\ell]G$ (and $G'[\bar{r}/\bar{r}]G$). □

<u>EXAMPLE 4.1.</u>
Let G be the CFG with productions

S → aA	aB	<1,2>
A → B	a	<3,4>
B → C		<5>
C → aA	a	<6,7>

We define a cover homomorphism for a left cover. The productions 3 and 5 are removed from P in order to obtain set P_1. In step (i) the following productions are added to P_1.

[A357] → a	<357>	[A356] → aA	<356>
[B57] → a	<57>	[B56] → aA	<56>

In step (ii) the following productions are created.

S → a[A357]	<1>	[A356] → a[A356]	<356>	C → a[A356]	<6>
S → a[A356]	<1>	[A356] → a[A357]	<356>	C → a[A357]	<6>
S → a[B57]	<2>	[B56] → a[A356]	<56>		
S → a[B56]	<2>	[B56] → a[A357]	<56>		

Now define S' = S and remove nonterminal C and the productions C → a, C → aA C → a[A356} and C → a[A357] from the grammar.

It will be clear that the cover which is defined in Lemma 4.6 is faithful. If we allow endmarkers for sentences then the condition mentioned in Lemma 4.5 and in Lemma 4.6 does not play a role.

<u>LEMMA 4.7.</u> For any ε-free CFG $G = (N,\Sigma,P,S)$ there exists a CFG G' without single productions such that both $G'[\ell/\ell]G$ and $G'[\bar{r}/\bar{r}]G$.

Proof. If $L(G) = \{\varepsilon\}$, then $G' = G$. Otherwise, define $G_0 = (N \cup \{S_0\}, \Sigma \cup \{\bot\}, P_0, S_0)$ such that

$$P_0 = P \cup \{S_0 \to S \bot \langle\varepsilon\rangle\}$$

if $S \to \varepsilon \notin P$, and

$$P_0 = (P - \{S \to \varepsilon\}) \cup \{S_0 \to S\bot \langle\varepsilon\rangle, S_0 \to \bot \langle i\rangle\}$$

if $i.S \to \varepsilon \in P$.

Here $\bot$ is an endmarker and S_0 will be treated as the new start symbol.

Perform steps (i) and (ii) of the method used in the proof of Lemma 4.6. Then remove the useless symbols. Clearly, instead of including $S_0 \to \bot \langle i\rangle$ in P_0 it is possible to include $S_0 \to \varepsilon \langle i\rangle$. □

OBSERVATION 4.4. If CFG G in Lemma 4.6 is non-left-recursive then CFG G' is also non-left-recursive.

A note on grammar functors*.

With some simple observations we show the existence of an externally fixed and externally full grammar functor $H : S(G') \to S(G)$, where G' and G are as in Lemma 4.6. Consider the method which is used in this lemma and assume that a left cover is defined. Notice that for any production $C \to \gamma \langle\pi\rangle$ which is in P_2 after steps (i) and (ii) have been performed, π stands for a leftmost derivation from $h(C)$ to $h(\gamma)$. This leftmost derivation will be the image morphism of production $C \to \gamma$ under H. We use $\tilde{\pi}$ to denote this morphism. For example, a leftmost derivation

$$A \overset{1}{\underset{L}{\Rightarrow}} BD \overset{2}{\underset{L}{\Rightarrow}} CcD \overset{3}{\underset{L}{\Rightarrow}} bcD$$

for a CFG G has a corresponding left parse 123, while the corresponding morphism of S(G) is

$$1 \circ (2 + id_D) \circ (3 + id_{cD}).$$

This morphism uniquely follows from the string 123.

LEMMA 4.8. Let G' and G be CFG's under the same conditions as in Lemma 4.6. There exists an externally fixed, externally full and faithful grammar functor $H : S(G') \to S(G)$.

Proof. We confine ourselves to the definition of $H : S(G') \to S(G)$. Faithfulness and external fullness will be clear from the definition of H and the method which is used in Lemma 4.6.

For the objects it is sufficient to define H on $V' = N' \cup \Sigma$, which is done by defining:

(i) $H(X) = X$ for each $X \in V$.

(ii) $H([A\delta]) = A$ for each nonterminal of the form $[A\delta]$ which is introduced in step (i) of the method.

(iii) $H(S') = S$.

(iv) $H(H_i) = c$ for each nonterminal H_i introduced in step (iii) (a) of the method, with corresponding production $H_i \to c$.

(v) $H(C_{\delta_i}) = C$ for each newly introduced nonterminal symbol C_{δ_i} in step (iii) (b) of the method.

For the morphisms it is sufficient to define H on P' which is done as follows.

(i)' $H(A \to \alpha <\pi>) = \tilde{\pi}$, for each production $A \to \alpha$ created in step (ii) of the method.

(ii)' $H(S' \to \alpha <\pi>) = \tilde{\pi}$, where α is either of the form $H_i\beta$ or of the form $C_{\delta_i}\beta$,
$H(H_i \to c <\varepsilon>) = id_c$, and
$H(C_{\delta_i} \to \gamma <\pi>) = \tilde{\pi}$, for the productions created in step (iii) of the method.

(iii)' $H(S' \to \alpha <\pi>) = \tilde{\pi}$ for each production $S' \to \alpha <\pi>$ created in step (iv) of the method. Notice that in this case $\tilde{\pi}$ coincides with $S \to \alpha$. □

End of note.

Now consider the possibility of eliminating ε-productions from a CFG in such a way that covers can be defined. The following method is due to Ukkonen [163]. It eliminates ε-productions from a CFG in such a way that the resulting grammar right covers the original grammar.

<u>DEFINITION 4.3.</u> Let $G = (N,\Sigma,P,S)$ be a CFG. If $A \in N$, $\alpha \in rhs(A)$ and $L(\alpha) \neq \{\varepsilon\}$ then a *representation* of α is a factorization $\alpha = \alpha_0X_1\alpha_1X_2\ldots\alpha_{n-1}X_n\alpha_n$, $n > 0$ which satisfies

(i) $X_i \in N \cup \Sigma$ and $L(X_i) \neq \{\varepsilon\}$, $1 \leq i \leq n$.

(ii) $\alpha_i \in N^*$ and $\varepsilon \in L(\alpha_i)$, $0 \leq i \leq n$.

Notice that, in general, a righthand side α may have different representations.

<u>ALGORITHM 4.1.</u>

Input. A CFG $G = (N,\Sigma,P,S)$ such that there is at most one π such that $S \overset{\pi}{\underset{R}{\Rightarrow}} \varepsilon$ and there is in G no derivation of the form $A \overset{*}{\Rightarrow} \alpha A\beta$, where $\alpha \overset{+}{\Rightarrow} \varepsilon$.

Output. An ε-free CFG $G' = (N',\Sigma,P',S')$ such that $G'[\bar{r}/\bar{r}]G$.
Method. Initially $P' = \emptyset$ and $N' = \{S'\}$. If $S \overset{\pi}{\underset{R}{\Rightarrow}} \varepsilon$, add $S' \to \varepsilon$ $\langle\pi^R\rangle$ to P'. If $L(G) = \{\varepsilon\}$ then we are done. Otherwise add $S' \to [\underline{S}]$ $\langle\varepsilon\rangle$ to P' and $[\underline{S}]$ to N'. Repeat steps (1) and (2) until no changes are possible.

(1) For each element $[\gamma\underline{A}]$ in N' and for each production $j.A \to \alpha$ in P such that $L(\alpha) \neq \{\varepsilon\}$ add to P', for any representation $\alpha = \alpha_0X_1\alpha_1X_2\ldots\alpha_{n-1}X_n\alpha_n$, $n > 0$ the production $[\gamma\underline{A}] \to Z_1Z_2\ldots Z_n$ $\langle j\rangle$, where

  (i) $Z_1 = [\gamma\alpha_0\underline{X_1}\alpha_1]$, if $\gamma\alpha_0\alpha_1 \neq \varepsilon$ or $X_1 \in N$, and $Z_1 = X_1$, otherwise.

  (ii) For $2 \leq i \leq n$, $Z_i = [\underline{X_i}\alpha_i]$, if $\alpha_i \neq \varepsilon$ or $X_i \in N$ and $Z_i = X_i$, otherwise.

Add to N' all newly created nonterminal symbols.

(2) Let $j.B \to \beta$ be a production of G such that $\varepsilon \in L(\beta)$. For each nonterminal $[\gamma\underline{X}\alpha B]$ in N' where $\alpha,\gamma \in N^*$ and $X \in N \cup \Sigma$, the following is done.

  (i) If $\gamma\alpha\beta \neq \varepsilon$ or $X \in N$, add the production $[\gamma\underline{X}\alpha B] \to [\gamma\underline{X}\alpha\beta]$ $\langle j\rangle$ to P' and $[\gamma\underline{X}\alpha\beta]$ to N'.

  (ii) If $\gamma\alpha\beta = \varepsilon$ and $X \in \Sigma$, add to P' the production $[\gamma\underline{X}\alpha B] \to X$ $\langle j\rangle$.

Similarly, for each nonterminal $[\gamma B\underline{X}]$ in N' where $X \in \Sigma$ and $\gamma \in N^*$, if $\gamma\beta \neq \varepsilon$, add the production $[\gamma B\underline{X}] \to [\gamma\beta\underline{X}]$ $\langle j\rangle$ to P' and the nonterminal $[\gamma\beta\underline{X}]$ to N', and otherwise, add the production $[\gamma B\underline{X}] \to X$ $\langle j\rangle$ to P'. □

In this algorithm it is demanded that G has no derivations of the form $A \overset{*}{\Rightarrow} \alpha A\beta$, where $\alpha \overset{+}{\Rightarrow} \varepsilon$. This condition ensures termination of the method. Notice that if G is NLR, then this condition is satisfied.

A detailed proof for a symmetric version of this algorithm can be found in Ukkonen [165]. The proof is basedon the following properties. Let $[\gamma\underline{X}\delta]$ be in N'.

(a) If $[\gamma\underline{X}\delta] \overset{\pi}{\underset{R}{\Rightarrow}} w$ for some nonempty w in Σ^*, then $\gamma X\delta \overset{\rho^R}{\underset{R}{\Rightarrow}} w$, where $X \overset{*}{\underset{R}{\Rightarrow}} w$ and $\rho = \psi(\pi^R)$.

(b) If $\gamma X\delta \overset{\pi}{\underset{R}{\Rightarrow}} w$, where X derives w, then there is a unique derivation $[\gamma\underline{X}\delta] \overset{\rho}{\underset{R}{\Rightarrow}} w$, with $\psi(\rho^R) = \pi^R$.

The cover which is defined in this way is faithful and, moreover, if G is non-left-recursive, then G' is non-left-recursive. Notice that except for a possible production $S' \to \varepsilon$, the cover homomorphism is very fine. It should also be observed that the ε-productions are in fact replaced by single productions.

<u>COROLLARY 4.1.</u> Any NLR grammar $G = (N,\Sigma, P,S)$, which satisfies the condition that there is at most one π such that $S \overset{\pi}{\underset{R}{\Rightarrow}} \varepsilon$, has an ε-free NLR grammar G' such that $G'[\bar{r}/\bar{r}]G$.

Algorithm 4.1 will be used at various places in this monograph. In Chapter 6 negative results concerning the possibility to find ε-free covering grammars will be shown.†

Before concluding this chapter we want to make one final remark. Not only in this chapter but also in the forthcoming chapters transformations will be introduced and discussed. For each of these methods it is interesting and useful to investigate the efficiency of the method. However, this will not be done in this monograph. The interested reader should consult Chapter 4 in Harrison [58] where the appropriate notions can be found.

† (Added in proof) Laufkötter [177] has independently found the conditions which guarantee that elimination of ε-productions can be done in such a way that a right covering grammar will be obtained. In his 'Diplomarbeit' many other results concerning ε-free covers can be found.

CHAPTER 5

NORMAL FORM COVERS FOR CONTEXT-FREE GRAMMARS

In this chapter we will present results on the existence and nonexistence of certain covers for some normal forms. The emphasis will be on the non-left-recursive grammars and the grammars in Greibach normal form. Except for a few notes the existence of grammar functors will not be discussed. In, e.g., Hotz [66], Benson [13] and Reichardt [139] grammar functor results for these normal forms can be found.

Any CFG can be transformed to a weakly equivalent CFG in GNF. Transformations to obtain grammars in GNF are in Greibach [50,52], Rosenkrantz [142] and Hotz [66]. Sometimes the transformation is performed in two steps. In the first step a NLR grammar is constructed, in the second step this grammar is transformed to a GNF grammar (cf. Aho and Ullman [3] and Wood [171]).

We investigate transformations which lead to Greibach normal form grammars. It should be noted that in the definition of an ε-free grammar and in the definition of a Greibach normal form grammar we have allowed a production $S \to \varepsilon$ (cf. section 1.3). Since this production, if it is in the grammar, remains unchanged under all forthcoming transformations we omit mentioning it.

The organization of this chapter is as follows. In section 5.1 transformations to non-left-recursive grammars are considered. Section 5.2 deals with transformations from non-left-recursive to grammars in GNF. Section 5.3 discusses transformations on grammars which are already in GNF or in $\overline{\text{GNF}}$.

5.1. FROM PROPER GRAMMARS TO NON-LEFT-RECURSIVE GRAMMARS

There are several methods to obtain non-left-recursive grammars from proper context-free grammars. The most wellknown method which is described in e.g. Aho and Ullman [3] (Algorithm 2.13) will be referred to as the standard method for eliminating left recursion. It appeared before, in different versions, in e.g. Greibach [51], Kurki-Suonio [89] and in Kuno [87]. Another method is due to Foster [34,35]. This method was used in Wood [171]. A similar method was used in Anderson [5] to eliminate left recursion from attribute grammars. Other transformations are in Rosenkrantz, Lewis and Stearns [100] (cf. Appendix C7, the 'goal corner transformation'), Soisalon-Soininen and Ukkonen [157], Soisalon-Soininen [155,156], Ukkonen [162] and Nijholt [115].

Our investigations on the existence of non-left-recursive covering grammars for proper context-free grammars started with the observation that some remarks concerning this problem in Gray and Harrison [49] and in Aho and Ullman [3] were not correct (cf. Nijholt [115]). That is, we showed that for any proper CFG G there exists a

CFG G' which is NLR and $G'[\bar{r}/\bar{r}]G$. Moreover, the existence of a NLR grammar G' such that $G'[\ell/\bar{r}]G$ was verified (cf. Lemma 4.4.). In both cases the cover can be defined in such a way that the cover homomorphism is fine.

In the case of direct left recursion, that is, if $A \overset{\pi}{\Rightarrow} A\alpha$, with $|\pi| = 1$, these results can easily be shown. For general left recursion, if we follow the method of [115], the generalization becomes rather complicated. A simpler method, based on a trick of Kurki-Suonio [89], is presented in Soisalon-Soininen [156].

Similar 'tricks' are in Foster [35] and in Kuno [87]. We illustrate the method with the following example.

EXAMPLE 5.1. (Foster)
Let G_F be the grammar with productions

$$S \to T \mid S + T \quad \langle p,q\rangle$$
$$T \to id \mid T \times id \quad \langle r,s\rangle$$

Add to the right of each righthand side a new 'terminal' symbol. For convenience we use the labels p, q, r and s. In this way we obtain

$$S \to Tp \mid S + Tq$$
$$T \to idr \mid T \times ids$$

The new grammar can be considered as a translation grammar (Brosgol [17]); the new symbols can then be considered as semantic actions.
If the standard method for eliminating left recursion is applied to this grammar, we obtain the NLR grammar

$$S \to Tp \mid TpX$$
$$X \to + Tq \mid + TqX$$
$$T \to idr \mid idrY$$
$$Y \to \times\, ids \mid \times\, idsY$$

Now define a grammar $G' = (N',\Sigma,P',S)$ as follows. The set N' consists of the symbols

S, T, X, Y, p, q, r and s,

and the set P' of the productions

$$S \to Tp \mid TpX \quad \langle\varepsilon,\varepsilon\rangle \qquad p \to \varepsilon \quad \langle p\rangle$$
$$X \to + Tq \mid + TqX \quad \langle\varepsilon,\varepsilon\rangle \qquad q \to \varepsilon \quad \langle q\rangle$$
$$T \to idr \mid idrY \quad \langle\varepsilon,\varepsilon\rangle \qquad r \to \varepsilon \quad \langle r\rangle$$
$$Y \to \times\, ids \mid \times\, idsY \quad \langle\varepsilon,\varepsilon\rangle \qquad s \to \varepsilon \quad \langle s\rangle$$

It is straightforward to verify that $G'[\bar{r}/\bar{r}]G_F$, and (with the help of Lemma 4.3)

$G'\,[\ell/\bar{r}]G_F$. This example will be continued later in this section.

The argument in this example can be formalized (cf. [156]) and, obviously, this idea of adding special symbols to the right of the righthand sides is independent of the method which is used to eliminate left recursion. Therefore, also methods different from the standard method may be used to obtain the same cover results. This 'trick' always yields a faithful cover and a fine cover homomorphism.

<u>COROLLARY 5.1.</u> Any proper CFG G can be given a NLR grammar G' such that $G'[\bar{r}/\bar{r}]G$ and $G'[\ell/\bar{r}]G$ under a fine and faithful cover homomorphism.

Notice that this method introduces ε-productions. With Algorithm 4.1 they can be eliminated in such a way that the right cover is preserved. Unfortunately the left-to-right cover can not be preserved (cf. Chapter 6).

<u>EXAMPLE 5.1.</u> (continued)
If Algorithm 4.1 is applied to G', then we obtain the grammar with productions

$$S' \to [\underline{S}] \quad \langle\varepsilon\rangle$$

$$
\begin{array}{llll}
[\underline{S}] \to [\underline{T}p] & \langle\varepsilon\rangle & [\underline{T}p] \to [\underline{T}] & \langle p\rangle \\
[\underline{S}] \to [\underline{T}p][\underline{X}] & \langle\varepsilon\rangle & [\underline{T}q] \to [\underline{T}] & \langle q\rangle \\
[\underline{X}] \to +\,[\underline{T}q] & \langle\varepsilon\rangle & & \\
[\underline{X}] \to +\,[\underline{T}q][\underline{X}] & \langle\varepsilon\rangle & &
\end{array}
$$

$$
\begin{array}{llll}
[\underline{T}] \to [\underline{id}r] & \langle\varepsilon\rangle & [\underline{id}r] \to id & \langle r\rangle \\
[\underline{T}] \to [\underline{id}r][\underline{Y}] & \langle\varepsilon\rangle & [\underline{id}s] \to id & \langle s\rangle \\
[\underline{Y}] \to \times\,[\underline{id}s] & \langle\varepsilon\rangle & & \\
[\underline{Y}] \to \times\,[\underline{id}s][\underline{Y}] & \langle\varepsilon\rangle & &
\end{array}
$$

If the single productions are eliminated from this grammar (Lemma 4.6), we delete some superfluous productions and we rename the nonterminal symbols, then we obtain

$$
\begin{array}{ll}
S \to AB \mid DC \mid id & \langle\varepsilon,p,rp\rangle \\
A \to DC \mid id & \langle p,rp\rangle \\
B \to +\,E \mid +\,EB & \langle\varepsilon,\varepsilon\rangle \\
E \to DC \mid id & \langle q,rq\rangle \\
C \to \times\,F \mid \times\,FC & \langle\varepsilon,\varepsilon\rangle \\
D \to id & \langle r\rangle \\
F \to id & \langle s\rangle
\end{array}
$$

This grammar right covers grammar G_F. In section 5.2.2 we will return to this grammar.
End of Example 5.1.

5.2. FROM NON-LEFT-RECURSIVE TO GREIBACH NORMAL FORM GRAMMARS

Each GNF grammar is NLR. In this section transformations from NLR to GNF grammars are considered. There are numerous instances of this transformation. Clearly, any transformation to GNF which is defined for proper context-free grammars can be used for proper NLR grammars as well.

Algorithm 2.14 in Aho and Ullman [3] (attributed by them to M.Paul) has become known as the standard method for transforming NLR grammars to GNF grammars. Other methods are sometimes defined for special subclasses of the (non-left-recursive) context-free grammars. E.g., the strict deterministic grammars (Geller, Harrison and Havel [42]), the simple chain grammars (Nijholt [122]) and the LL(k) grammars (Rosenkrantz and Stearns [144], Aho and Ullman [3]).

In section 5.2.1 we use an adaptation of the standard method to obtain covering context-free grammars in GNF. In section 5.2.2 transformations are described which are based on the concept of 'chain'.

5.2.1. THE 'SUBSTITUTION' TRANSFORMATION

The standard method to produce a GNF grammar from a proper NLR grammar consists of repeated substitutions in the righthand sides of the productions. This process does not preserve ambiguity. More precisely, there is the possibility that there exists $w \in L(G')$ such that $\langle w,G'\rangle < \langle w,G\rangle$, where G' is the GNF grammar which is obtained from grammar G. It follows that due to the surjectivity condition of the cover definition a cover can not be defined.

This 'loss' of ambiguity which is caused by the process of substitution is simply illustrated in Figure 5.1. In this figure we use a CFG G with productions

1. $S \to AC$
2. $S \to BC$
3. $A \to a$
4. $B \to a$
5. $C \to c$

The transformation to GNF of this grammar with the standard method is portrayed in Figure 5.1. a. Our adaptation of this method gives the situation of Figure 5.1. b.

The standard method is also used in Benson [13]. There it is said that the transformation depicted in Figure 5.1. a is ambiguity preserving by providing the production $S \to aC$ with two different indexes. In this way we obtain the situation of Figure 5.1. c. One may say that in this way syntactical ambiguity is replaced by semantical ambiguity. With our adaptation of the standard method this replacement of ambiguity is not necessary.

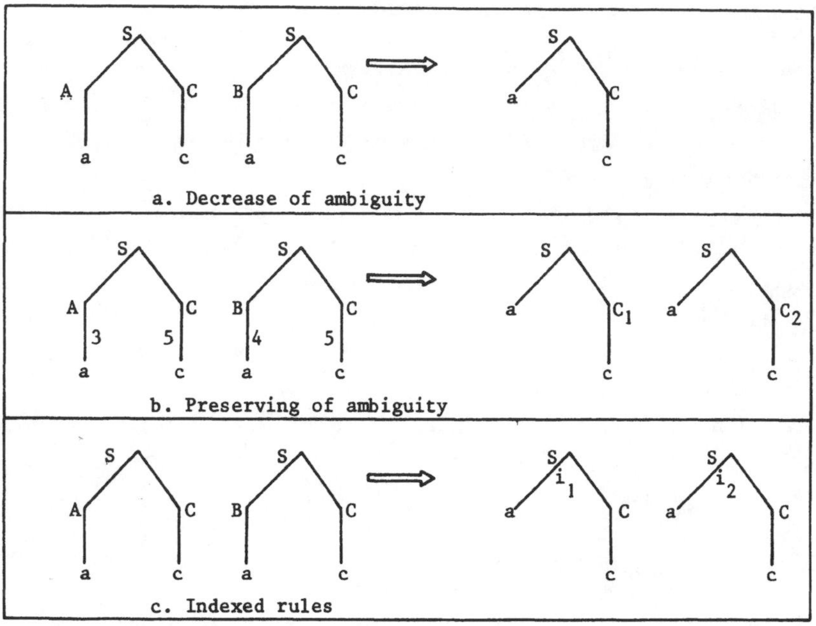

Figure 5.1. Transformations to Greibach normal form.

The following algorithm will produce a left covering grammar in GNF for a proper NLR grammar. We may assume (cf. Chapter 4) that the input grammar has no single productions. Moreover, it is assumed that in the righthand sides of the productions of the input grammar a terminal symbol can only occur in the leftmost position. This can be done without loss of generality; for example, a production $i.A \to \alpha a\beta$, $\alpha \neq \varepsilon$, can be replaced by productions $A \to \alpha H_a\beta$ $\langle i\rangle$ and $H_a \to a$ $\langle\varepsilon\rangle$.

ALGORITHM 5.1.

Input. A proper NLR grammar $G = (N,\Sigma,P,S)$ such that each production is of the form $A \to \alpha$, $\alpha \in \Sigma N^* \cup NN^+$.

Output. A CFG $G' = (N',\Sigma,P',S)$ in GNF, $G'[\ell/\ell]G$ and the cover is faithful.

Method. Let P_0 be the subset of P which consists of all the productions of the form $A \to a\alpha$ with $a \in \Sigma$ and $\alpha \in N^*$. Initially, set $P_1 = P_0$ and $N' = N$. There are three steps.

(i) For each $A \in N$ and $a \in \Sigma$, if

$$A \overset{\pi'}{\underset{L}{\Rightarrow}} C\alpha' \overset{i}{\underset{L}{\Rightarrow}} a\alpha$$

G with $C \in N$, $\alpha,\alpha' \in N^+$ and $\pi' \neq \varepsilon$, then add

$$A \to a[(1:\alpha)\pi]\beta \ \langle\pi\rangle$$

to P_1. Here, $\beta = \alpha:(r-1)$, $r = |\alpha|$, $\pi = \pi' i$ and $[(1:\alpha)\pi]$ is a newly created nonterminal which is added to N'.

(ii) Set $P' = P_1$. For each newly created nonterminal symbol $[A\pi]$ do the following. If $\gamma \in \Sigma N'$ such that $A \to \gamma \ \langle\rho\rangle$ is in P_1, then add the production $[A\pi] \to \gamma \ \langle\rho\rangle$ to P'.

(iii) Remove the useless symbols. □

<u>EXAMPLE 5.2.</u>
Let G be the CFG with productions

$$S \to AS \mid BS \mid c \quad \langle 1,2,3\rangle$$
$$A \to a \quad \langle 4\rangle$$
$$B \to a \quad \langle 5\rangle$$

For example $\langle aac,G\rangle = 4$. The standard method produces a CFG G_1 with $\langle aac,G_1\rangle = 1$. Algorithm 5.1 yields a CFG G' in GNF with $\langle aac,G'\rangle = 4$. Initially $P_1 = \{S \to c\langle 3\rangle, A \to a\langle 4\rangle, B \to a\langle 5\rangle\}$. In step (i) the productions $S \to a[S14]\ \langle 14\rangle$ and $S \to a[S25]\ \langle 25\rangle$ are obtained from the derivations

$$S \overset{1}{\underset{L}{\Rightarrow}} AS \overset{4}{\underset{L}{\Rightarrow}} aS$$

and

$$S \overset{2}{\underset{L}{\Rightarrow}} BS \overset{5}{\underset{L}{\Rightarrow}} aS,$$

respectively.
In step (ii) the following productions are obtained.

$[S14] \to a[S14]$	$\langle 14\rangle$	$[S25] \to a[S14]$	$\langle 14\rangle$
$[S14] \to a[S25]$	$\langle 25\rangle$	$[S25] \to a[S25]$	$\langle 25\rangle$
$[S14] \to c$	$\langle 3\rangle$	$[S25] \to c$	$\langle 3\rangle$

In step (iii) the nonterminals A and B and the productions $A \to a$ and $B \to a$ are removed from the grammar.

<u>LEMMA 5.1.</u> Algorithm 5.1, when applied to a proper NLR grammar $G = (N,\Sigma,P,S)$ without single productions, yields a GNF grammar $G' = (N',\Sigma,P',S)$ such that $G'[\ell/\ell]G$ under a faithful cover homomorphism.

Proof. Let ψ be the homomorphism which is defined in the algorithm. The proof is based on the following observations. Both of them can be proved by induction on the lengths of the derivations.

Assume that $X \in N'$, $X = A$ or $X = [A\gamma]$ for some $A \in N$ and $\gamma \in \Delta_G^*$. If $X \overset{\pi'}{\underset{L}{\Rightarrow}} w$ in G', then there exists $\pi \in \Delta_G^*$ such that $A \overset{\pi}{\underset{L}{\Rightarrow}} w$ and $\psi(\pi') = \pi$.

Conversely, consider the grammar which is obtained before step (iii) is executed. If $A \overset{\pi}{\underset{L}{\Rightarrow}} w$ in G, then there exists (a unique) $\pi' \in \Delta_{G'}^*$, such that $X \overset{\pi'}{\underset{L}{\Rightarrow}} w$ and $\psi(\pi') = \pi$. □

Second note on grammar functors*

This note is a continuation of the note on grammar functors in section 4.2. As mentioned above, using the standard method for producing a GNF grammar does not necessarily lead to a cover. Neither do we have that, if $F : S(G') \to S(G)$ is a grammar functor, $F(S',w)$ is surjective, where S' is the start symbol of G'.

If we use the idea illustrated in Figure 5.1. c, then, as is shown in Benson [13] an externally fixed grammar functor can be defined which is faithful and externally full. However, here we will use Algorithm 5.1 (hence, Figure 5.1. b) to obtain this result.

Notice that faithfulness and external fullness are preserved under functor composition. Therefore, if we have a proper NLR grammar G, we may first eliminate the single productions (cf. the note in section 4.2) and then, as presently will be shown, apply Algorithm 5.1 to obtain a grammar G' in GNF such that a faithful and external full grammar functor $H : S(G') \to S(G)$ can be defined.

Notice that the condition mentioned before Algorithm 5.1 can also be handled functorially. For example, for the given example the functor H should satisfy $H(H_a) = a$, $H(A \to \alpha H_a \beta) = A \to \alpha a \beta$ and $H(H_a \to a) = id_a$. This can be generalized in an obvious way, and clearly, such a functor is faithful and externally full.

LEMMA 5.2. Algorithm 5.1, when applied to a proper NLR grammar G without single productions, yields a GNF grammar G' such that there exists an externally fixed, externally full and faithful grammar functor $H : S(G') \to S(G)$.

Proof. The method which is used in Algorithm 5.1 is functorial as well. We confine ourselves again to the definition of $H : S(G') \to S(G)$.

For each newly created nonterminal symbol of the form $[A\pi]$ define $H([A\pi]) = A$. Furthermore, define for each newly created production $A \to a[B\pi]\beta$ $\langle\pi\rangle$ in step (i), $H(A \to a[B\pi]\beta) = \tilde{\pi}$. For each newly created production $[A\pi] \to \gamma$ $\langle\rho\rangle$ in step (ii), define $H([A\pi] \to \gamma) = \tilde{\rho}$. For all the other nonterminals and productions H is the identity functor. □

End of note.

5.2.2. THE LEFT PART TRANSFORMATION

The key concept in the left part transformation is that of a 'chain'. Chains were first used in the definition of simple chain grammars (cf. [119,122]).

DEFINITION 5.1. Let $G = (N,\Sigma,P,S)$ be a proper CFG. Define a relation $CH \subseteq V \times N^*\Sigma$ as follows. If $X_0 \in N$ then $CH(X_0)$, the set of *chains* of X_0 is defined by
$CH(X_0) = \{X_0X_1\ldots X_n \in N^*\Sigma \mid X_0 \underset{L}{\Rightarrow} X_1\psi_1 \underset{L}{\Rightarrow}\ldots\underset{L}{\Rightarrow} X_n\psi_n,\ \psi_i \in V^*,\ 1 \leq i \leq n\}$,
and for $c \in \Sigma$,
$CH(c) = \{c\}$.

In the following theorem some properties of chains are listed. Quasi-GNF was defined in Definition 1.10. b.

THEOREM 5.1. Let $G = (N,\Sigma,P,S)$ be a proper CFG.

(i) For each $X \in V$, $CH(X)$ is a regular set.

(ii) Grammar G is NLR if and only if, for all $X \in V$, $CH(X)$ is a finite set.

(iii) Grammar G is in quasi-GNF if and only if, for each $X \in V$ and for each $\omega \in CH(X)$, $|\omega| \leq 2$.

Proof. (i) If $X \in \Sigma$ then $CH(X) = \{X\}$, which is a regular set. Assume $X \in N$. We construct a (right) regular grammar $G_X = (N_X,\Sigma_X,P_X,[X])$ such that $L(G_X) = CH(X)$. Three auxiliary sets, N',Σ' and P', are used. Define

(1) $N' = \{[Z] \mid Z \in V\}$

(2) $\Sigma' = V$

(3) $P' = \{[a] \to a \mid a \in \Sigma\}$
$\cup$
$\{[C] \to C[Z] \mid C \to Z\alpha \text{ in } P,\ Z \in V,\ \alpha \in V^*\}$.

For each $X \in N$, grammar $G_X = (N_X,\Sigma_X,P_X,[X])$, which is right regular and which satisfies $L(G_X) = CH(X)$, is obtained by removing the useless symbols from $G'_X = (N',\Sigma',P',[X])$.

Properties (ii) and (iii) follow immediately from the definitions. □

Chains will be used for the construction of the righthand sides of productions of a grammar in GNF. Before discussing the 'structure preserving' left part transformation we present a simpler version which preserves the original language. The degree of ambiguity for each sentence is not necessarily preserved.

To avoid a possible complication we demand that the set of productions of the original grammar is prefix-free, that is, if $A \to \alpha$ and $A \to \alpha\beta$ are in P then $\beta = \varepsilon$.

Obviously, this can be done without loss of generality. For example, if both $A \to \alpha$ and $A \to \alpha\beta$ are in P then replace them by $A \to \alpha$, $A \to H_\alpha\beta$ and $H_\alpha \to \alpha$.

The righthand sides of the newly obtained productions will now be finite length strings which are obtained with a homomorphism ξ from $\Sigma[N]^*$. Homomorphism ξ and alphabet [N] are defined below.

DEFINITION 5.2. Let $G = (N,\Sigma,P,S)$ be a proper CFG. Assume that P is prefix-free. Define

$$[N] = \{[A\alpha] \mid A \in N,\ \alpha \in V^* \text{ and } A \to \alpha\beta \text{ in } P \text{ for some } \beta \in V^*\}$$

and define homomorphism $\xi : [N]^* \to [N]^*$ by

(i) $\xi([A\alpha]) = \varepsilon$ if $A \to \alpha$ is in P, and

(ii) $\xi([A\alpha]) = [A\alpha]$ if $A \to \alpha\beta$ is in P, $\beta \neq \varepsilon$.

Now we are sufficiently prepared to present the algorithm.

ALGORITHM 5.2. *(Left part transformation)*

Input. A proper NLR grammar $G = (N,\Sigma,P,S)$ such that P is prefix-free.

Output. A weakly equivalent CFG $G' = (N',\Sigma,P',[S])$ in GNF.

Method. Initially, $N' = P' = \emptyset$. N' will consist of all the symbols of [N] which appear in the productions introduced below.

(i) For each $SX_1 \ldots X_n \in CH(S)$, add

$$[S] \to X_n\xi([X_{n-1}X_n][X_{n-2}X_{n-1}]\ldots[SX_1])$$

to P'.

(ii) For each $A \to \alpha X_0\varphi$ in P, where $\alpha \neq \varepsilon$ and $X_0X_1\ldots X_n \in CH(X_0)$, add

$$[A\alpha] \to X_n\xi([X_{n-1}X_n]\ldots[X_0X_1][A\alpha X_0])$$

to P'. □

In Figure 5.2, which we hope is self-explanatory we have illustrated in (a) and (b) the algorithm for productions $S \to A\alpha_1$, $A \to B\alpha_2$ and $B \to a\alpha_3$. The arcs of chain SABa can be considered as the new nonterminals. In (c) and (d) the situation is portrayed for productions $A \to BC\beta_0$, $C \to D\beta_1$ and $D \to c\beta_2$.

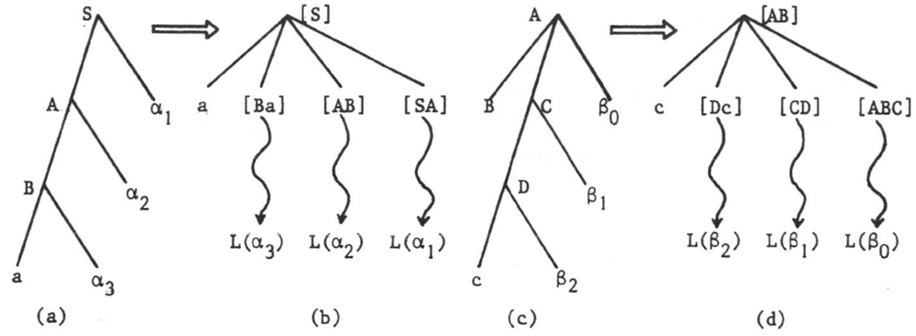

Figure 5.2. Transformation to Greibach normal form.

The proof that $L(G') = L(G)$ is based on the following lemma. We omit the proof since similar proofs will be given for other versions of the transformation.

<u>LEMMA 5.3.</u>

a. If $[A\alpha] \overset{m}{\Rightarrow} w$ then $A \overset{*}{\Rightarrow} \alpha w$.

b. Let $A \rightarrow \alpha X_0 \varphi$ be a production in P such that if $A \neq S$ then $\alpha \neq \varepsilon$. Assume that $X_0 X_1 \ldots X_n \in CH(X_0)$, $n \geq 0$. Then, for each X_i, $0 \leq i \leq n$, if $X_i \overset{m}{\underset{L}{\Rightarrow}} y$, where $y \in \Sigma^*$, then $[A\alpha] \overset{*}{\Rightarrow} y\xi([X_{i-1}X_i] \ldots [A\alpha X_0])$.

Proof. Straightforward induction on the length m of the derivations. □

Note. It is possible to drop in Algorithm 5.2 the input condition that P is prefix-free. In that case ξ should be taken as a substitution which satisfies

(i) $\xi([A\alpha])$ contains ε if $A \rightarrow \alpha$ is in P, and

(ii) $\xi([A\alpha])$ contains $[A\alpha]$ if $A \rightarrow \alpha\beta$ is in P, $\beta \neq \varepsilon$.

Hence, ξ maps $[A\alpha]$ to a subset of $\{\varepsilon, [A\alpha]\}$ and Algorithm 5.2 should be adapted in such a way that sets of productions are added to P'.
End of the note.

Consider the following property of this left part transformation, which is valid for less simple versions as well.

If Algorithm 5.2 is applied to a CFG G which satisfies the input conditions then a CFG G' in GNF is obtained. Subsequently, apply Algorithm 5.2 to grammar G'. The newly obtained grammar G" is again in GNF and, moreover, each production is of the form $A \rightarrow a\gamma$, with $|\gamma| \leq 2$ (standard 2-form).

A second property of the left part transformation which will only be mentioned here is the following. Suppose G is a proper CFG. For each $X \in V$ we have that CH(X) is a regular set. Therefore, we can adapt Algorithm 5.2 in such a way that the righthand sides of the productions of G' will become regular expressions (or equivalently, regular sets or finite automata).

In this way we obtain an extented CFG (cf. e.g. Heilbrunner [62]). Each extended CFG can be transformed to a CFG by replacing each righthand side by a subgrammar which generates the regular set represented by the righthand side. If we use the straightforward method which is described in Heilbrunner [62], then the newly obtained grammar is proper NLR. A second application of the left part transformation yields a grammar in GNF. Hence, the left part transformation can be used, in an adapted version, for arbitrary proper CFG's as well.

Both the special alphabet [N] and the algorithm to obtain a GNF grammar will become slightly more complicated in the 'structure preserving' case. It is assumed that, if necessary, first the single productions of the input grammar are eliminated. Due to the special alphabet [N] we do not have to bother about P being prefix-free.

The transformation which is described is such that the new grammar G' in GNF left-to-x covers grammar G, where, informally, x may 'run' from left to left part. That is, if $G = (N,\Sigma,P,S)$ then, for each production $i.A \to \alpha$ in P, Γ_G satisfies $1 \le \Gamma_G(i) \le |\alpha|$. In accordance with the notation introduced in section 2.2 we write $\ell \le x \le \ell p$. Hence, x is the production directed parse relation induced by Γ_G.

Unfortunately, the algorithm does not yield a left-to-right cover. Surprisingly, this is not a 'shortcoming' of the algorithm but, as will be shown in Chapter 6, this is a general negative result.

<u>DEFINITION 5.3.</u> Let $G = (N,\Sigma,P,S)$ be a CFG. Define

$$[N] = \{[Ai\alpha] \mid i.A \to \alpha\beta \text{ is in P for some } \beta \in V^*\}$$

and define a homomorphism $\xi : [N]^* \to [N]^*$ by

(i) $\xi([Ai\alpha]) = \varepsilon$ if $i.A \to \alpha$ is in P, and

(ii) $\xi([Ai\alpha]) = [Ai\alpha]$ if $i.A \to \alpha\beta$ is in P, $\beta \neq \varepsilon$.

<u>DEFINITION 5.4.</u> Let $G = (N,\Sigma,P,S)$ be a CFG. Define a relation $LP \subseteq N^*\Sigma \times \Delta_G^*$ as follows:

Let $\omega = X_0X_1\ldots X_n \in N^+\Sigma$. LP($\omega$), the set of left production chains of ω, is defined by

$$LP(\omega) = \{i_0i_1\ldots i_{n-1} \in \Delta_G^* \mid X_0 \overset{i_0}{\underset{L}{\Rightarrow}} X_1\psi_1 \overset{i_1}{\underset{L}{\Rightarrow}} \ldots \overset{i_{n-1}}{\underset{L}{\Rightarrow}} X_n\psi_n,\ \psi_j \in V^*,\ 1 \le j \le n\}.$$

If $\omega \in \Sigma$ then $LP(\omega) = \{\varepsilon\}$.

ALGORITHM 5.3.

Input. A proper NLR grammar $G = (N,\Sigma,P,S)$ without single productions.

Output. A weakly equivalent CFG $G' = (N',\Sigma,P',[S])$ in GNF.

Method. Initially, $N' = \{[S]\}$ and $P' = \emptyset$.

All the elements of [N], which appear in the productions introduced below, will be added to N'.

(i) For each pair (ω,ρ), $\omega = SX_1\dots X_n \in CH(S)$ and $\rho = i_0 i_1 \dots i_{n-1} \in LP(\omega)$, add

$$[S] \to X_n \xi([X_{n-1} i_{n-1} X_n]\dots[S i_0 X_1])$$

to P'.

(ii) For any production $i.A \to \alpha X_0 \varphi$ in P, $\alpha \neq \varepsilon$, and for each pair (ω,ρ), $\omega = X_0 X_1 \dots X_n \in CH(X_0)$ and $\rho = i_0 i_1 \dots i_{n-1} \in LP(\omega)$, add

$$[Ai\alpha] \to X_n \xi([X_{n-1} i_{n-1} X_n]\dots[X_0 i_0 X_1][Ai\alpha X_0])$$

to P'. □

Notice that for this algorithm the condition that the input grammar G does not have single productions is not a necessary condition. To obtain the cover result of Theorem 5.2 it would have been sufficient to demand that, for any $A \in N$ and $X \in V$, if $A \overset{\pi}{\Rightarrow} X$ and $A \overset{\pi'}{\Rightarrow} X$, then $\pi = \pi'$. Clearly, this condition is satisfied for any unambiguous grammar G.

As we have shown, the single productions can be eliminated in a simple way and we can avoid the introduction of new conditions.

THEOREM 5.2. Let $G = (N,\Sigma,P,S)$ be a proper and NLR grammar. There exists a CFG G' in GNF such that, for any production directed parse relation x, $\ell \le x \le \ell p$, $G'[\ell/x]G$.

Proof. We assume that the single productions have been eliminated. Use Algorithm 5.3 to transform the proper and NLR grammar G to a grammar $G' = (N',\Sigma,P',[S])$ which is in GNF.

Let $T = (N,\Sigma,\Delta_G,R,S)$ be the simple SDTS, defined on $G = (N,\Sigma,P,S)$, which performs the translation x.

Define $T' = (N',\Sigma,\Delta_G,R',[S])$ on G' by the rules:

(i) $[S] \to X_n \xi([X_{n-1} i_{n-1} X_n]\dots[S i_0 X_1])$,

$$j_0 j_1 \dots j_{n-1} \xi([X_{n-1} i_{n-1} X_n]\dots[S i_0 X_1])$$

for each corresponding production introduced in step (i) of the algorithm. The j_k's are defined by, for $0 \le k \le n-1$, $j_k = i_k$ if $\Gamma_G(i_k) = 1$ and $j_k = \varepsilon$, otherwise. Here, $\Gamma_G : \Delta_G \to \mathbb{N}$ is as in Notation 2.1.

(ii) $[Ai\alpha] \to X_n\xi([X_{n-1}i_{n-1}X_n]\ldots[X_0i_0X_1][A_i\alpha X_0])$,

$jj_0j_1\ldots j_{n-1}\xi([X_{n-1}i_{n-1}X_n]\ldots[X_0i_0X_1][Ai\alpha X_0])$

for each corresponding production introduced in step (ii) of the algorithm. The j_k's and j are defined by, for $0 \le k \le n-1$,

$j_k = i_k$ if $\Gamma_G(i_k) = 1$ and $j_k = \varepsilon$, otherwise, and

$j = i$ if $|\alpha X_0| = \Gamma_G(i)$ and $j = \varepsilon$, otherwise.

Cover homomorphism ψ is defined by mapping each production of P' on the string $j_0j_1\ldots j_{n-1}$ or $jj_0j_1\ldots j_{n-1}$ of its corresponding rule in R', obtained in (i) or (ii), respectively. Clearly, T' is semantically unambiguous (cf. also the note immediately preceeding this theorem) and therefore ψ is well-defined.

The main task is now to prove that $\tau(T') = \tau(T)$. Then, if $(w,\pi') \in \ell_{G'}$ it follows immediately that $(w,\psi(\pi')) \in x_G$. Moreover, from the definitions of T' and ψ it follows also that if $(w,\pi) \in x_G = \tau(T)$ then there exists $(w,\pi') \in \ell_{G'}$ such that $(w,\psi(\pi')) = (w,\pi)$. In fact, this π' is unique and therefore cover homomorphism ψ is faithful. Thus we may conclude that $G'[\ell/x]G$. Two claims are used in the proof that $\tau(T') = \tau(T)$. The following notation will be useful.

<u>NOTATION 5.1.</u> Let $G = (N,\Sigma,P,S)$ be a CFG. For any string $\alpha \in V^*$ the notation $\delta_k(\alpha)$, where $k \in \Delta_G$, is used as follows. (It is assumed that $\Delta_G \cap V = \emptyset$.)

(a) If $1 \le \Gamma_G(k) \le |\alpha| + 1$ then $\delta_k(\alpha)$ denotes the string $\alpha_1k\alpha_2$, where $\alpha_1\alpha_2 = \alpha$ and $|\alpha_1| = \Gamma_G(k) - 1$.

(b) If $\Gamma_G(k) > |\alpha| + 1$ then $\delta_k(\alpha)$ denotes α.

<u>CLAIM 1.</u> Consider a production $p.A \to \alpha X_0\varphi$ in P with $\alpha\varphi \in V^*$, $X_0 \in V$ and if $\alpha = \varepsilon$ then $A = S$. Let $\rho = X_0X_1\ldots X_{n-1}X_n \in CH(X_0)$, $n \ge 0$. Then, for each X_i, $0 \le i \le n$, the existence of a derivation

$$(X_i,h_\Sigma(X_i)) \overset{m}{\underset{L}{\Rightarrow}} (y,\pi),$$

for some $m \ge 0$, $y \in \Sigma^*$ and $\pi \in \Delta_G^*$, implies that there exists $p_0p_1\ldots p_{i-1} \in LP(\rho)$ such that either

(a) if $\alpha = \varepsilon$, then

$([S],[S])$

$\overset{*}{\Rightarrow}$

$(y\xi([X_{i-1}p_{i-1}X_i]\ldots[X_0p_0X_1][SpX_0])$,

$jj_0\ldots j_{i-1}\pi\xi([X_{i-1}p_{i-1}X_i]\ldots[X_0p_0X_1][SpX_0]))$, or

(b) if $\alpha \neq \varepsilon$, then

$$([Ap\alpha],[Ap\alpha])$$
$$\overset{*}{\Rightarrow}$$
$$(y\xi([X_{i-1}p_{i-1}X_i]\ldots[X_0p_0X_1][Ap\alpha X_0]),$$
$$jj_0\ldots j_{i-1}\pi\xi([X_{i-1}p_{i-1}X_i]\ldots[X_0p_0X_1][Ap\alpha X_0])).$$

Here, j and j_k, $0 \leq k \leq i-1$ are defined as in (i) and (ii).

Proof of Claim 1. The proof proceeds by induction on m. Suppose m = 0, then $y = X_i \in \Sigma$ and $\pi = \varepsilon$.

In case (a), with $\alpha = \varepsilon$, we have $p.S \to X_0\varphi$ in P and

$$X_0 \overset{p_0}{\underset{L}{\Rightarrow}} X_1\gamma_1 \underset{L}{\Rightarrow}\ldots\underset{L}{\Rightarrow} X_{i-1}\gamma_{i-1} \overset{p_{i-1}}{\underset{L}{\Rightarrow}} X_i\gamma_i,$$

for some $p_0p_1\ldots p_{i-1} \in LP(\rho)$ and $\gamma_k \in V^*$, $1 \leq k \leq i$.
From the construction of P' it follows that

$$[S] \to X_i\xi([X_{i-1}p_{i-1}X_i]\ldots[X_0p_0X_1][SpX_0])$$

and from the construction of R' the desired result follows.

Case (b) with $\alpha \neq \varepsilon$ follows in an analogous way. Now let m > 0 and assume the claim holds for all m' < m (induction hypothesis). Let

$$k.\ Y \to Y_1Y_2\ldots Y_q,\ h_\Sigma(\delta_k(Y_1Y_2\ldots Y_q))$$

be the first of the m rules which are used in the leftmost derivation

$$(X_i,h_\Sigma(X_i)) \overset{m}{\underset{L}{\Rightarrow}} (y,\pi).$$

Thus, we have

$$Y = X_i,\ Y_1 = X_{i+1} \text{ and } h_\Sigma(X_i) = X_i$$

and we have the derivation

$$(Y,Y) \underset{L}{\Rightarrow} (Y_1Y_2\ldots Y_q,\ h_\Sigma(\delta_k(Y_1Y_2\ldots Y_q))) \overset{*}{\underset{L}{\Rightarrow}}$$
$$\overset{*}{\underset{L}{\Rightarrow}} (y_1y_2\ldots y_q,\ \pi_1\pi_2\ldots\pi_{\Gamma(k)-1}k\pi_{\Gamma(k)}\ldots\pi_q),$$

where $y_1y_2\ldots y_q = y$, $\pi_1\pi_2\ldots\pi_{\Gamma(k)-1}k\pi_{\Gamma(k)}\ldots\pi_q = \pi$ and where

$$(Y_r,h_\Sigma(Y_r)) \overset{m_r}{\underset{L}{\Rightarrow}} (y_r,\pi_r),$$

where $1 \leq r \leq q$, $y_r \in \Sigma^*$, $\pi_r \in \Delta_G^*$ and $m_r < m$.

We confine ourselves with a proof of the induction step for case (b). Case (a) follows along similar lines and therefore its proof is omitted.

For the derivation

$$(Y_1, h_\Sigma(Y_1)) \overset{m_1}{\underset{L}{\Rightarrow}} (y_1, \pi_1)$$

we can use the induction hypothesis to obtain

$$([Ap\alpha],[Ap\alpha])$$
$$\overset{*}{\Rightarrow}$$
$$(y_1\xi([YkY_1][X_{i-1}p_{i-1}X_i]\ldots[X_0p_0X_1][Ap\alpha X_0]),$$
$$jj_0\ldots j_{i-1}k_1\pi_1\xi([YkY_1][X_{i-1}p_{i-1}X_i]\ldots[X_0p_0X_1][Ap\alpha X_0])),$$

where $k_1 = k$ if $\Gamma_G(k) = 1$ and $k_1 = \varepsilon$, otherwise.

Analogously, for

$$(Y_r, h_\Sigma(Y_r)) \overset{m_r}{\underset{L}{\Rightarrow}} (y_r, \pi_r),\ r > 1$$

we obtain from the induction hypothesis that

$$([YkY_1\ldots Y_{r-1}],\ [YkY_1\ldots Y_{r-1}])$$
$$\overset{*}{\Rightarrow}$$
$$(y_r\xi([YkY_1\ldots Y_r]),\ k_r\pi_r\xi([YkY_1\ldots Y_r])),$$

where $k_r = k$ if $\Gamma_G(k) = |Y_1Y_2\ldots Y_r|$ and $k_r = \varepsilon$ otherwise, $1 < r \leq q$.

Combining these results yields

$$([Ap\alpha],[Ap\alpha])$$
$$\overset{*}{\Rightarrow}$$
$$(y_1y_2\ldots y_q\xi([X_{i-1}p_{i-1}X_i]\ldots[X_0p_0X_1][Ap\alpha X_0]),$$
$$jj_0\ldots j_{i-1}k_1\pi_1k_2\pi_2\ldots k_{q-1}\pi_{q-1}k_q\pi_q\xi([X_{i-1}p_{i-1}X_i]\ldots[X_0p_0X_1][Ap\alpha X_0])).$$

Notice that only $k_{\Gamma(k)} = k$ and all other k_r's, $r \neq \Gamma(k)$, are equal to ε. This concludes the induction proof of part (b) and therefore the proof of Claim 1. □

Now let $(S,S) \overset{*}{\Rightarrow} (w,\pi)$ and assume that $k.S \to Z_1Z_2\ldots Z_n$, $h_\Sigma(\delta_k(Z_1Z_2\ldots Z_n))$ is the first rule which is used in this derivation. Hence, $k.S \to Z_1Z_2\ldots Z_n$ is in P. If we use a similar partition of w and π as in the induction proof of Claim 1, we obtain from this claim

$([S],[S])$

$\overset{*}{\Rightarrow}$

$(w_1\xi([SkZ_1],k_1\pi_1\xi([SkZ_1]))$

$\overset{*}{\Rightarrow}$

$(w_1w_2\cdots w_n,\pi_1\pi_2\cdots\pi_{\Gamma(k)-1}k\pi_{\Gamma(k)}\cdots\pi_n) = (w,\pi).$

Consequently, $\tau(T) \subseteq \tau(T')$.

For the converse, the following claim is used.

CLAIM 2. Suppose that $([Ap\alpha X],[Ap\alpha X]) \overset{m}{\underset{L}{\Rightarrow}} (w,j\pi)$, where $j = p$ if $|\alpha X| = \Gamma_G(p)-1$ and $j = \varepsilon$, otherwise. Then $(A,A) \overset{*}{\Rightarrow} (\alpha Xw,h_\Sigma(\delta_p(\alpha X))\pi)$.

Proof of Claim 2. Notice that in this claim α may be the empty word. Write $w = av$, hence, $a \in \Sigma$ and $v \in \Sigma^*$. If $m = 1$, then $v = \varepsilon$ and $w = a$. In this case we have a rule

$[Ap\alpha X] \to a,j\pi$

in T', where

$j = p$ if $|\alpha X| = \Gamma_G(p)-1$, and
$j = \varepsilon$, otherwise.

This rule is obtained from either a production

$p.A \to \alpha Xa$ (*)

in P, hence, $\pi = \varepsilon$, or from productions

$p.A \to \alpha XX_0$, and
$p_0.\ X_0 \to a$ (**)

in P such that $\pi = p_0$.

Therefore, in the case of (*) we have, according to the definition of T, $A \to \alpha Xa$, $h_\Sigma(\delta_p(\alpha Xa))$ in R, that is, we have

$(A,A) \Rightarrow (\alpha Xa,h_\Sigma(\delta_p(\alpha X))\pi)$,

as desired.

In the case of (**) we have in R,

$A \to \alpha XX_0,h_\Sigma(\delta_p(\alpha XX_0))$, and
$X_0 \to a,p_0$

that is, we have

$$(A,A) \Rightarrow (\alpha XX_0, h_\Sigma(\delta_p(\alpha XX_0))) \Rightarrow (\alpha Xa, h_\Sigma(\delta_p(\alpha Xp_0))),$$

where $h_\Sigma(\delta_p(\alpha Xp_0)) = h_\Sigma(\delta_p(\alpha X))\pi$, as desired.

This concludes the basis of the induction proof. Induction. Assume $m > 1$ and assume that the claim holds for all $m' < m$. Let the first rule which is used in the derivation be

$$([Ap\alpha X],[Ap\alpha X])$$
$$\Rightarrow$$
$$(a\xi([X_{n-1}p_{n-1}X_n]\ldots[X_0p_0X_1][Ap\alpha XX_0]),$$
$$jj_0j_1\ldots j_{n-1}\xi([X_{n-1}p_{n-1}X_n]\ldots[X_0p_0X_1][Ap\alpha XX_0])),$$

under the assumption that w is written as av, $a \in \Sigma$ and $v \in \Sigma^*$. Notice that by construction of T' the rules of R' are of this form.

Here, $j,j_0,\ldots,j_{n-1}$ are again as previously defined. In this case we have the leftmost derivation

$$([Ap\alpha X],[Ap\alpha X])$$
$$\overset{1}{\underset{L}{\Rightarrow}}$$
$$(a\xi([X_{n-1}p_{n-1}X_n]\ldots[X_0p_0X_1][Ap\alpha XX_0]),$$
$$jj_0j_1\ldots j_{n-1}\xi([X_{n-1}p_{n-1}X_n]\ldots[X_0p_0X_1][Ap\alpha XX_0]))$$
$$\overset{m-1}{\underset{L}{\Rightarrow}}$$
$$(av,j\pi).$$

Write $j\pi = jj_0j_1\ldots j_{n-1}\pi'$. Obviously, there exist $v_\ell \in \Sigma^*$ and $\pi_\ell \in \Delta_G^*$, $0 \le \ell \le n$, such that

(i) $v = v_nv_{n-1}\ldots v_1v_0$ and $\pi' = \pi'_n\pi'_{n-1}\ldots\pi'_1\pi'_0$.

(ii) $v_n = \pi'_n = \varepsilon$, if $\xi([X_{n-1}p_{n-1}X_n]) = \varepsilon$

and

$v_0 = \pi'_0 = \varepsilon$, if $\xi([Ap\alpha XX_0]) = \varepsilon$.

(iii) for each ℓ, $1 \le \ell \le n$ and $\xi([X_{\ell-1}p_{\ell-1}X_\ell]) \ne \varepsilon$

we have

$$([X_{\ell-1}p_{\ell-1}X_\ell],[X_{\ell-1}p_{\ell-1}X_\ell])$$
$$\overset{t_\ell}{\underset{L}{\Rightarrow}}$$
$$(v_\ell,k_{\ell-1}\pi_\ell),$$

where $t_\ell < m$, $k_{\ell-1}\pi_\ell = \pi'_\ell$ and $k_{\ell-1} = p_{\ell-1}$ if $|X_\ell| = \Gamma_G(p_{\ell-1})-1$ and $k_{\ell-1} = \varepsilon$, otherwise.

(iv) if $\xi([Ap\alpha XX_0]) \neq \varepsilon$, then

$$([Ap\alpha XX_0],[Ap\alpha XX_0]) \overset{t_0}{\underset{L}{\Rightarrow}} (v_0,k\pi_0),$$

where $t_0 < m$, $k\pi_0 = \pi_0'$ and $k = p$ if $|\alpha XX_0| = \Gamma_G(p)-1$ and $k = \varepsilon$ otherwise.

If $\xi([X_{\ell-1}p_{\ell-1}X_\ell]) \neq \varepsilon$, $1 \leq \ell \leq n$, then, since $t_\ell < m$, we obtain from the induction hypothesis

$$(X_{\ell-1},X_{\ell-1}) \overset{*}{\Rightarrow} (X_\ell v_\ell, h_\Sigma(\delta_{p_{\ell-1}}(X_\ell))\pi_\ell)$$

and otherwise, in which case $\ell = n$, it follows from the construction of T' that

$$(X_{n-1},X_{n-1}) \Rightarrow (X_n,h_\Sigma(\delta_{p_{n-1}}(X_n))).$$

Analogously, if $\xi([Ap\alpha XX_0]) \neq \varepsilon$, then, since $t_0 < m$, we obtain

$$(A,A) \overset{*}{\Rightarrow} (\alpha XX_0v_0,h_\Sigma(\delta_p(\alpha XX_0))\pi_0)$$

and otherwise, it follows that

$$(A,A) \Rightarrow (\alpha XX_0,h_\Sigma(\delta_p(\alpha XX_0))).$$

If we combine these results the desired result follows. Notice that due to our notations we have

$$\delta_{p_{\ell-1}}(X_\ell) = j_{\ell-1}X_\ell k_{\ell-1}, \quad 1 \leq \ell \leq n,$$

and

$$\delta_p(\alpha XX_0) = \delta_p(\alpha X)X_0k.$$

Therefore,

$$\begin{aligned}
(A,A) &\overset{*}{\Rightarrow} (\alpha XX_0v_0,h_\Sigma(\delta_p(\alpha XX_0))\pi_0)\\
&= (\alpha XX_0v_0,h_\Sigma(\delta_p(\alpha X)X_0k)\pi_0)\\
&\overset{*}{\Rightarrow} (\alpha XX_1v_1v_0,h_\Sigma(\delta_p(\alpha X)h_\Sigma(\delta_{p_0}(X_1))\pi_1k)\pi_0)\\
&= (\alpha XX_1v_1v_0,h_\Sigma(\delta_p(\alpha X)h_\Sigma(j_0X_1k_0)\pi_1k)\pi_0)\\
&\overset{*}{\Rightarrow} \ldots\ldots\\
&\overset{*}{\Rightarrow} (\alpha XX_\ell v_\ell\ldots v_0,h_\Sigma(\delta_p(\alpha X)h_\Sigma(j_0\ldots h_\Sigma(j_{\ell-1}X_\ell k_{\ell-1})\pi_\ell k_{\ell-2}\ldots\pi_1k)\pi_0)\\
&\overset{*}{\Rightarrow} \ldots\ldots
\end{aligned}$$

$$\overset{*}{\Rightarrow} (\alpha X a v_n \ldots v_0, h_\Sigma(\delta_p(\alpha X)) j_0 \ldots j_{n-1} k_{n-1} \pi_n k_{n-2} \ldots k_0 \pi_1 k \pi_0)$$
$$= (\alpha X w, h_\Sigma(\delta_p(\alpha X)) \pi),$$

which had to be proved. This completes the proof of Claim 2. □

Let $([S],[S]) \overset{*}{\Rightarrow} (w,\pi)$ in T'. Let w = av and assume that the first step of this derivation is done with a rule

$$([S],[S]) \Rightarrow (a\xi([X_{n-1}p_{n-1}X_n]\ldots[X_0p_0X_1][SpX_0]),$$
$$jj_0\ldots j_{n-1}\xi([X_{n-1}p_{n-1}X_n]\ldots[X_0p_0X_1][SpX_0]),$$

where again X_n = a and the other notations are as usual. Strings v and π can again be partitioned in $v_nv_{n-1}\ldots v_1v_0 = v$ and $jj_0j_1\ldots j_{n-1}\pi'_n\pi'_{n-1}\ldots\pi'_1\pi'_0 = \pi$, respectively, as we did in the proof of Claim 2. Application of this claim then gives the result $(S,S) \overset{*}{\Rightarrow} (w,\pi)$.

This completes the proof that $\tau(T) = \tau(T')$ and therefore the proof of the theorem. □

The algorithm is illustrated with the following example.

<u>EXAMPLE 5.3.</u>

Let G = (N,Σ,P,S) be the CFG with productions

1.S → AaB, 2.A → cB, 3.B → AB and 4.B → b.

Define

$$\Gamma_G(1) = 1,\ \Gamma_G(2) = 2,\ \Gamma_G(3) = 2 \text{ and } \Gamma_G(4) = 1.$$

Step (i) of the algorithm yields

[S] → cξ([A2c][S1A]),

and from step (ii) we obtain

[A2c] → cξ([A2c][B3A][A2cB]),
[A2c] → bξ([B4b][A2cB]),

and

[B3A] → cξ([A2c][B3A][B3AB]),
[B3A] → bξ([B4b][B3AB]),

and

$[S1A] \rightarrow a\xi([S1Aa])$,
$[S1Aa] \rightarrow c\xi([A2c][B3A][S1AaB])$,
$[S1Aa] \rightarrow b\xi([B4b][S1AaB])$.

Performing ξ and listing the image of each production under the cover homomorphism ψ (such that $G'[\ell/x]G$, where x is defined by Γ_G) after each production, we obtain the following productions

$[S] \rightarrow c[A2c][S1A]$ <1>
$[A2c] \rightarrow c[A2c][B3A]$ <2>
$[A2c] \rightarrow b$ <24
$[B3A] \rightarrow c[A2c][B3A]$ <3>
$[B3A] \rightarrow b$ <34>
$[S1A] \rightarrow a[S1Aa]$ <ε>
$[S1Aa] \rightarrow c[A2c][B3A]$ <ε>
$[S1Aa] \rightarrow b$ <ε>

End of Example 5.3.

Before we turn our attention to right covers we have a final remark on the theorem. It is demanded that, for each production $i.A \rightarrow \alpha$ in P, Γ_G satisfies $\Gamma_G(i) \leq |\alpha|$. We can slightly weaken this condition by letting $\Gamma_G(i) \leq |\alpha|$ if $\alpha : 1 \in N$ and $\Gamma_G(i) \leq |\alpha| + 1$ if $\alpha : 1 \in \Sigma$.

In section 5.3 and in Chapter 6 we will return to the problem of finding left-to-right covers.

Next we consider the possibility of obtaining a CFG in GNF which right covers the ε-free NLR grammar. We use two transformations. We transform ε-free NLR grammars to grammars which are *almost*-GNF. For convenience of description we assume that the input grammar is such that terminal symbols in the righthand sides of the productions can only appear at the leftmost positions of the righthand sides.

This can be done without loss of generality. For example, if a grammar has a production $i.A \rightarrow \alpha a\beta$, with $\alpha \neq \varepsilon$, then we can replace this production by $A \rightarrow \alpha H_a\beta$ <i> and $H_a \rightarrow a$ <ε> and the new grammar right covers the original grammar.

The second transformation will produce GNF grammars from almost-GNF grammars.

<u>DEFINITION 5.5.</u> A CFG $G = (N,\Sigma,P,S)$ is said to be an *almost*-GNF grammar if for any production $A \rightarrow \alpha$ in P either

(i) $\alpha \in \Sigma$, or
(ii) $\alpha \in NN^+$ and $rhs(1:\alpha) \subseteq \Sigma$.

ALGORITHM 5.4.

Input. A NLR grammar $G = (N,\Sigma,P,S)$ such that $P \subseteq N \times (\Sigma N^* \cup NN^+)$.

Output. An almost-GNF grammar $G' = (N',\Sigma,P',[S])$, such that $G'[\bar{r}/\bar{r}]G$.

Method. The set P' will contain all productions introduced below. The set N' will contain [S], all symbols of [N] which appear in the productions and some special indexed symbols H. Initially set $P' = \emptyset$.

(i) For each production of the form $i.S \to a$ in P with $a \in \Sigma$, add $[S] \to a \langle i\rangle$ to P'.

(ii) For each pair (ω,ρ), $\omega = SX_1\ldots X_n \in CH(S)$ and $\rho = i_0i_1\ldots i_{n-1} \in LP(\omega)$, $n > 1$, add

$$[S] \to H_{i_{n-1}}\xi([X_{n-1}i_{n-1}X_n]\ldots[Si_0X_1]) \quad \langle\varepsilon\rangle$$

and

$$H_{i_{n-1}} \to X_n \quad \langle p\rangle$$

to P'. Here, $p = i_{n-1}$ if $i_{n-1}.X_{n-1} \to X_n \in P$ and $p = \varepsilon$ otherwise.

(iii) Let $i.A \to \alpha X_0\varphi$ be in P, $\alpha \neq \varepsilon$. For each pair (ω,ρ), $\omega = X_0X_1\ldots X_n \in CH(X_0)$ and $\rho = i_0i_1\ldots i_{n-1} \in LP(\omega)$, the following two cases are distinguished: (Notice that always $n > 0$.)

(1) $n = 1$, $\varphi = \varepsilon$ and $i_0.X_0 \to X_1$ is in P; add $[Ai\alpha] \to X_1 \langle i_0i\rangle$ to P'

(2) otherwise, add

$$[Ai\alpha] \to H_{i_{n-1}}\xi([X_{n-1}i_{n-1}X_n]\ldots[X_0i_0X_1][Ai\alpha X_0]) \quad \langle p\rangle$$

and

$$H_{i_{n-1}} \to X_n \quad \langle q\rangle$$

to P', where $p = i$ if $i.A \to \alpha X_0$ is in P and $p = \varepsilon$ otherwise, and $q = i_{n-1}$ if $i_{n-1}.X_{n-1} \to X_n \in P$ and $q = \varepsilon$ otherwise. □

LEMMA 5.4. Any ε-free NLR grammar G can be transformed to an almost-GNF grammar G' such that $G'[\bar{r}/\bar{r}]G$.

Proof. Without loss of generality we may assume that G does not have single productions. We use Algorithm 5.4 to transform G to a grammar G'. By construction G' is almost-GNF.

CLAIM 1. The cover homomorphism ψ, implicitly defined in the algorithm, is well defined.

Proof of Claim 1. To verify that for any pair p and p' of productions in P' it follows that if $\psi(p) = \pi$ and $\psi(p') = \pi'$, with $\pi \neq \pi'$, then $p \neq p'$. This is straightforward to verify and therefore it is omitted. □

In the following claims $\varphi : \Delta_{G'}^* \to \Delta_G^*$ is defined by letting, for any $p \in \Delta_{G'}$, $\varphi(p) = \pi^R$ if and only if $\psi(p) = \pi$.

<u>CLAIM 2.</u> If $[Ai\alpha] \overset{\pi'}{\underset{R}{\Rightarrow}} w$ then $A \overset{\varphi(\pi')}{\underset{R}{\Longrightarrow}} \alpha w$.

Proof of Claim 2. The proof is by induction on $|\pi'|$.
Basis. If $|\pi'| = 1$ then $\pi' = [Ai\alpha] \to a$ <ji>. In this case there is a derivation $A \overset{i}{\underset{R}{\Rightarrow}} \alpha X_0 \overset{j}{\underset{R}{\Rightarrow}} \alpha a$, for $X_0 \in N$.
Induction. Assume $|\pi'| = m$, $m > 1$ and assume the property holds for all rightmost derivations with length less than m. Let $p'.[Ai\alpha] \to H_{i_{n-1}}\ \xi([X_{n-1}i_{n-1}X_n]\ldots[X_0i_0X_1][Ai\alpha X_0])$ be the first production which is used in the derivation $[Ai\alpha] \overset{\pi'}{\underset{R}{\Rightarrow}} w$. Hence, we may write $w = X_n x$ and $\pi' = p'\gamma q'$, where $q' = H_{i_{n-1}} \to X_n$. Then we have

$$[Ai\alpha] \overset{p'}{\underset{R}{\Rightarrow}} H_{i_{n-1}}\ \xi([X_{n-1}i_{n-1}X_n]\ldots[X_0i_0X_1][Ai\alpha X_0]) \overset{\gamma}{\underset{R}{\Rightarrow}} \ldots$$

$$\ldots \overset{\gamma}{\underset{R}{\Rightarrow}} H_{i_{n-1}} x_n x_{n-1}\ldots x_1 x_0 \overset{q'}{\underset{R}{\Rightarrow}} X_n x_n x_{n-1}\ldots x_1 x_0 = w,$$

such that

(a) if $\xi([Ai\alpha X_0]) \neq \varepsilon$ then $[Ai\alpha X_0] \overset{\pi_0}{\underset{R}{\Rightarrow}} x_0$, otherwise $x_0 = \pi_0 = \varepsilon$,

(b) $[X_{k-1}i_{k-1}X_k] \overset{\pi_k}{\underset{R}{\Rightarrow}} x_k$, $1 \le k \le n-1$,

(c) if $\xi([X_{n-1}i_{n-1}X_n]) \neq \varepsilon$ then $[X_{n-1}i_{n-1}X_n] \overset{\pi_n}{\underset{R}{\Rightarrow}} x_n$, otherwise $\pi_n = x_n = \varepsilon$, and

(d) $q'.H_{i_{n-1}} \to X_n$ with $p'\pi_0\pi_1\ldots\pi_n q' = p'\gamma q' = \pi'$.

It follows from the induction hypothesis that

(a)' $A \overset{\varphi(p'\pi_0)}{\underset{R}{\Longrightarrow}} \alpha X_0 x_0$, with either $\varphi(p') = \varepsilon$ or $\pi_0 = x_0 = \varepsilon$,

(b)' $X_{k-1} \overset{\varphi(\pi_k)}{\underset{R}{\Longrightarrow}} X_k x_k$, $1 \le k \le n-1$, and

(c)' $X_{n-1} \overset{\varphi(\pi_n q')}{\underset{R}{\Longrightarrow}} X_n x_n$, with either $\varphi(q') = \varepsilon$ or $\pi_n = x_n = \varepsilon$.

Thus, $A \overset{\varphi(\pi')}{\underset{R}{\Longrightarrow}} \alpha w$. □

<u>CLAIM 3.</u> Assume that $i.A \to \alpha X_0 \varphi$ is in P and $A \overset{i\pi}{\underset{R}{\Rightarrow}} \alpha w$. Then there exists $\pi' \in \Delta_{G'}^*$ such that $[Ai\alpha] \overset{\pi'}{\underset{R}{\Rightarrow}} w$ and $\varphi(\pi') = i\pi$.

Proof of Claim 3. The proof is by induction on $|\pi|$.
Basis. If $|\pi| = 1$ then, with $\pi.X_0 \to w$ in P, $w \in \Sigma$, we have

$$A \underset{R}{\overset{i}{\Rightarrow}} \alpha X_0 \underset{R}{\overset{\pi}{\Rightarrow}} \alpha w$$

in G, and by construction of G'

$$[Ai\alpha] \underset{R}{\overset{i'}{\Rightarrow}} w,$$

with $\varphi(i') = i\pi$.

Induction. Assume $|\pi| > 1$. We factorize

$$A \underset{R}{\overset{i}{\Rightarrow}} \alpha X_0\varphi \underset{R}{\overset{\pi}{\Rightarrow}} \alpha w$$

into

$$A \underset{R}{\overset{i}{\Rightarrow}} \alpha X_0\varphi,$$

$$\varphi \underset{R}{\overset{\rho_1}{\Rightarrow}} v_1, \text{ and}$$

$$X_0 \underset{R}{\overset{\rho_0}{\Rightarrow}} av_0,$$

where $av_0v_1 = w$. Since $X_0 \in N$ we have $|\rho_1| < |\pi|$ and from the induction hypothesis we obtain, if $\varphi \neq \varepsilon$,

$$[Ai\alpha X_0] \underset{R}{\overset{\rho_1'}{\Rightarrow}} v_1, \text{ with } \varphi(\rho_1') = i\rho_1.$$

Moreover, there exist productions $i_k.X_k \to X_{k+1}\varphi_k$, $0 \leq k \leq n-1$ and $X_n = a$, such that

(i) $$X_k \underset{R}{\overset{i_k}{\Rightarrow}} X_{k+1}\varphi_k \underset{R}{\overset{\pi_k}{\Rightarrow}} X_{k+1}w_k,$$

with $0 \leq k \leq n-1$ and such that $|\pi_k| < |\pi|$, hence

$$[X_k i_k X_{k+1}] \underset{R}{\overset{\pi_k'}{\Rightarrow}} w_k$$

and $\varphi(\pi_k') = i_k\pi_k$

(ii) $$X_{n-1} \xrightarrow[R]{i_{n-1}} a\varphi_n \xrightarrow[R]{\pi_{n-1}} aw_{n-1},$$

such that $|\pi_{n-1}| < |\pi|$, hence, if $\varphi_n \neq \varepsilon$,

$$[X_{n-1}i_{n-1}a] \xrightarrow[R]{\pi_{n-1}'} w_{n-1},$$

and $\varphi(\pi_{n-1}') = i_{n-1}\pi_{n-1}$

(iii) $w_{n-1}\dots w_1 w_0 = v_0$ and $i_0\pi_0 i_1\pi_1\dots i_{n-1}\pi_{n-1} = \rho_0$.

It follows that in P' there exists a production

$$p'.[Ai\alpha] \rightarrow H_{i_{n-1}}\xi([X_{n-1}i_{n-1}a]\dots[X_0 i_0 X_0][Ai\alpha X_0])$$

and a derivation

$$[Ai\alpha] \overset{\pi'}{\underset{R}{\Rightarrow}} w,$$

such that

(a) $w = av_0v_1$, $\pi' = p'\rho_1'\pi_0'\dots\pi_{n-1}'q'$, with q' is $H_{i_{n-1}} \rightarrow a$.

(b) $\varphi(p'\rho_1') = i\rho_1$,

$\varphi(\pi_0'\dots\pi_{n-1}') = i_0\pi_0 i_1\dots i_{n-2}\pi_{n-2}$,

$\varphi(\pi_{n-1}'q') = i_{n-1}\pi_{n-1}$, and

$i_0\pi_0 i_1\dots i_{n-2}\pi_{n-2}i_{n-1}\pi_{n-1} = \rho_0$.

Hence, $\varphi(\pi') = i\rho_1\rho_0 = i\pi$. □

Now it is not difficult to verify that $G'[\bar{r}/\bar{r}]G$. Therefore we omit the details and only mention that if $[S] \overset{\pi'}{\underset{R}{\Rightarrow}} w$ then one should distinguish the first production from the remainder of the derivation. A similar argument can be used to show the surjectivity of the cover homomorphism. This concludes the proof of Lemma 5.4. □

Next we show that any almost-GNF grammar can be transformed to a GNF grammar. This is done in the following algorithm. The newly obtained grammar will right cover the original grammar.

<u>ALGORITHM 5.5.</u>

Input. An almost-GNF grammar $G = (N,\Sigma,P,S)$.

Output. A GNF grammar $G' = (N',\Sigma,P',S)$ such that $G'[\bar{r}/\bar{r}]G$.

Method. We use two auxiliary sets, N_0 and P_0. Initially set $N' = N$, $N_0 = \emptyset$ and

$$P_0 = \{A \rightarrow \alpha\ \langle i\rangle \mid i.A \rightarrow \alpha \text{ is in } P \text{ and } \alpha \in \Sigma\}.$$

Step 1. For each production $i.A \rightarrow BC\alpha$ in P (with $B,C \in N$ and $\alpha \in N^*$) the following is done.

(i) If $j.C \to D\beta E$ is in P (with $D,E \in N$ and $\beta \in N^*$) then, for any pair of productions $k.B \to a$ and $\ell.D \to b$ in P add

$$A \to aH_{k\ell}\beta[Ej]\alpha \ \langle i\rangle$$

and

$$H_{k\ell} \to b \ \langle kl\rangle$$

to P_0. Add [Ej] to N_0 and [Ej] and $H_{k\ell}$ to N'.

(ii) If $j.C \to b$ is in P, then, for any production $k.B \to a$ add

$$A \to aH_{kj}\alpha \ \langle i\rangle$$

and

$$H_{kj} \to b \ \langle kj\rangle$$

to P_0. Add H_{kj} to N'.

Step 2. Set $P' = P_0$. For each [Ej] in N_0 add $[Ej] \to \alpha \ \langle ij\rangle$ to P' for each production $E \to \alpha \ \langle i\rangle$ in P_0.

Step 3. Remove the useless symbols. □

The general idea of the transformation is displayed in Figure 5.3.

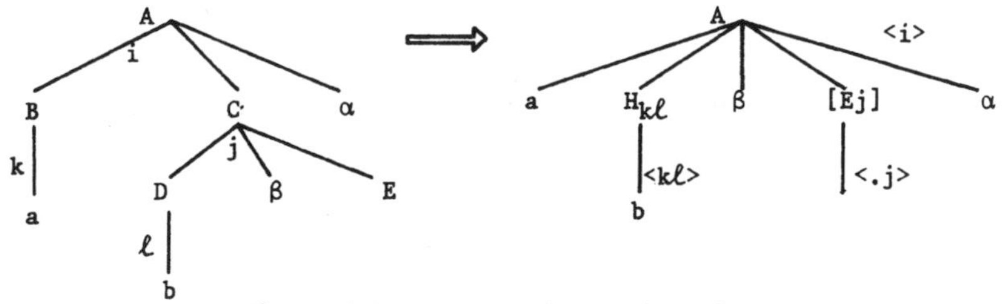

Figure 5.3. Step 1 of Algorithm 5.5.

<u>LEMMA 5.5.</u> Any almost-GNF grammar G can be transformed to a GNF grammar G' such that $G'[\bar{r}/\bar{r}]G$.

Proof. Let $\psi : \Delta_{G'}^* \to \Delta_G^*$ be the cover homomorphism which is defined in the algorithm. As we did in the proof of Lemma 5.4 we will use homomorphism φ instead of ψ. Two claims are used in the proof of Lemma 5.5. For any triple of strings α, β and γ with $\alpha = \beta\gamma$ we have that α/β denotes γ.

CLAIM 1. Assume $A \in N$.

(i) If $A \overset{\pi'}{\underset{R}{\Rightarrow}} w$ in G' then $A \overset{\varphi(\pi')}{\underset{R}{\Longrightarrow}} w$ in G.

(ii) If $[Ak] \overset{\pi'}{\underset{R}{\Rightarrow}} w$ in G' then $A \overset{\delta}{\underset{R}{\Rightarrow}} w$ in G, with $\delta = \varphi(\pi')/k$.

Proof of Claim 1. The proof is by induction on $|\pi'|$.

Basis. If $|\pi'| = 1$ then we have

(i) Production $A \to w$ is both in P and P', hence the claim is trivially satisfied.

(ii) Production $\pi'.[Ak] \to w$ is in P'. From step 2 of the algorithm it follows that $\varphi(\pi') = ki$, where $i.A \to w$ is in P. Therefore $A \overset{\delta}{\underset{R}{\Rightarrow}} w$ in G, with $\delta = \varphi(\pi')/k$.

Induction. Consider case (i). Assume $A \overset{\pi'}{\underset{R}{\Rightarrow}} w$ in G', with $|\pi'| > 1$. The first production which is used in this derivation is either of the form $i'.A \to aH_{k\ell}\beta[Ej]\alpha$ <i> or $i'.A \to aH_{kj}\alpha$ <i>. Notice that in both cases we can completely determine from which two productions of P such a production has been constructed. We continue with the former case. The case in which $A \to aH_{kj}\alpha$ is the first production can be treated similarly and is therefore omitted. Now we can factorize the derivation in the following way:

(a) $i'.A \to aH_{k\ell}\beta[Ej]\alpha$, with $\varphi(i') = i.A \to BC\alpha$, where B is the lefthand side of production k in P and C is the lefthand side of production j in P.

(b) $\alpha \overset{\pi_0'}{\underset{R}{\Longrightarrow}} w_0$, and from the induction hypothesis it follows that $\alpha \overset{\pi_0}{\underset{R}{\Longrightarrow}} w_0$ in G, where $\pi_0 = \varphi(\pi_0')$.

(c) $[Ej] \overset{\pi_1'}{\underset{R}{\Longrightarrow}} w_1$, and from the induction hypothesis it follows that $E \overset{\pi_1}{\underset{R}{\Longrightarrow}} w_1$ in G, where $\pi_1 = \varphi(\pi_1')/j$.

(d) $\beta \overset{\pi_2'}{\underset{R}{\Longrightarrow}} w_2$, and from the induction hypothesis it follows that $\beta \overset{\pi_2}{\underset{R}{\Longrightarrow}} w_2$ in G, where $\pi_2 = \varphi(\pi_2')$.

(e) $q'.H_{k\ell} \to b$, where we assume that $b \in \Sigma$ is the righthand side of production ℓ in P. Moreover, $\varphi(q') = \ell k$.

It follows that $i'\pi_0'\pi_1'\pi_2'q' = \pi'$, $abw_2w_1w_0 = w$ and $\varphi(\pi') = i\pi_0 j\pi_1\pi_2\ell k$, such that (if we assume that D is the lefthand side of production ℓ)

$$A \overset{i}{\underset{R}{\Rightarrow}} BC\alpha \overset{\pi_0}{\underset{R}{\Rightarrow}} BCw_0 \overset{j}{\underset{R}{\Rightarrow}} BD\beta Ew_0 \overset{\pi_1}{\underset{R}{\Rightarrow}} BD\beta w_1w_0 \overset{\pi_2}{\underset{R}{\Rightarrow}} BDw_2w_1w_0 \overset{\ell}{\underset{R}{\Rightarrow}} Bbw_2w_1w_0 \overset{k}{\underset{R}{\Rightarrow}} abw_2w_1w_0 = w$$

This concludes the verification of case (i). Case (ii) can be verified along similar lines and therefore this case is omitted. This concludes the induction part of the proof and therefore the claim is proved. □

CLAIM 2. Consider CFG G' before step 3 of the algorithm is executed. If $A \overset{\pi}{\underset{R}{\Rightarrow}} w$ in G then there exists $\pi' \in \Delta_{G'}^*$, such that $A \overset{\pi'}{\underset{R}{\Rightarrow}} w$ in G' and $\varphi(\pi') = \pi$.

Proof of Claim 2. In the proof which may proceed by induction on $|\pi|$ one should distinguish that $A \overset{\pi}{\underset{R}{\Rightarrow}} w$ in G can also imply $[Ak] \overset{\pi'}{\underset{R}{\Rightarrow}} w$, for some $k \in \Delta_G$ and with $\varphi(\pi')/k = \pi$. We omit the proof since it proceeds along the same lines as the proof of Claim 1. □

From these two claims it is now clear that $G'[\bar{r}/\bar{r}]G$.

The next theorem follows from the previous results.

<u>THEOREM 5.3.</u> Any ε-free CFG G can be transformed to a CFG G' in GNF such that $G'[\bar{r}/\bar{r}]G$.

Proof. For any ε-free CFG G we can find an ε-free NLR grammar G_0 (Corollary 5.1) such that $G_0[\bar{r}/\bar{r}]G$. The single productions of G_0 can be eliminated in such a way that the right cover is preserved (Lemma 4.6) and the new grammar, which is also non-left-recursive (Observation 4.4) can be transformed with Algorithm 5.4 followed by Algorithm 5.5 to a grammar G' which is in GNF and which has the property $G'[\bar{r}/\bar{r}]G$. □

Now that we have seen this positive cover result one can ask for an anologous result for left covers. Unfortunately, as we will see in Chapter 6, this is not possible.

We conclude this section with an example.

<u>EXAMPLE 5.4.</u>

In Example 5.1 we introduced grammar G_F and we transformed it to a proper NLR grammar without single productions. Hence, we can transform it to an almost-GNF grammar. Assume that the productions are numbered from 1 to 13 (cf. p.49).

In step (i) and (ii) of Algorithm 5.4 we obtain

$[S] \rightarrow id \quad \langle rp\rangle$
$[S] \rightarrow H_{12}[A4D][S1A] \quad \langle \varepsilon\rangle$
$[S] \rightarrow H_5[S1A] \quad \langle \varepsilon\rangle$
$[S] \rightarrow H_{12}[S2D] \quad \langle \varepsilon\rangle$
$H_{12} \rightarrow id \quad \langle r\rangle$
$H_5 \rightarrow id \quad \langle rp\rangle$

In step (iii) the following productions are obtained:

$[A4D] \rightarrow H_{10}[C10\times] \quad \langle p\rangle$
$[A4D] \rightarrow H_{11}[C11\times] \quad \langle p\rangle$
$H_{10} \rightarrow \times \quad \langle \varepsilon\rangle$
$H_{11} \rightarrow \times \quad \langle \varepsilon\rangle$

$[S1A] \rightarrow H_6[B6+] \quad \langle\varepsilon\rangle$
$[S1A] \rightarrow H_7[B7+] \quad \langle\varepsilon\rangle$
$H_6 \rightarrow + \quad \langle\varepsilon\rangle$
$H_7 \rightarrow + \quad \langle\varepsilon\rangle$

$[S2D] \rightarrow H_{10}[C10\times] \quad \langle p\rangle$
$[S2D] \rightarrow H_{11}[C11\times] \quad \langle p\rangle$

$[C10\times] \rightarrow \mathit{id} \quad \langle s\rangle$
$[C11\times] \rightarrow H_{13}[C11\times F] \quad \langle\varepsilon\rangle$
$H_{13} \rightarrow \mathit{id} \quad \langle s\rangle$
$[C11\times F] \rightarrow H_{10}[C10\times] \quad \langle\varepsilon\rangle$
$[C11\times F] \rightarrow H_{11}[C11\times] \quad \langle\varepsilon\rangle$

$[B6+] \rightarrow H_{12}[E8D] \quad \langle\varepsilon\rangle$
$[B6+] \rightarrow \mathit{id} \quad \langle rq\rangle$

$[B7+] \rightarrow H_{12}[E8D][B7+E] \quad \langle\varepsilon\rangle$
$[B7+] \rightarrow H_9[B7+E] \quad \langle\varepsilon\rangle$
$H_9 \rightarrow \mathit{id} \quad \langle rq\rangle$

$[E8D] \rightarrow H_{10}[C10\times] \quad \langle q\rangle$
$[E8D] \rightarrow H_{11}[C11\times] \quad \langle q\rangle$

$[B7+E] \rightarrow H_6[B6+] \quad \langle\varepsilon\rangle$
$[B7+E] \rightarrow H_7[B7+] \quad \langle\varepsilon\rangle$

Clearly, this grammar is in almost-GNF. Moreover, it right covers G_F under the cover homomorphism which is indicated after each production displayed above.

Since it is already sufficiently clear that our methods will transform the four productions of the example grammar G_F to an unattractively long list of productions for a right covering grammar in GNF, we will not bother the reader with the transformation from almost-GNF to GNF for this example. Instead we consider a more simple example.

<u>EXAMPLE 5.5.</u>
Consider CFG G with productions

1. $S \rightarrow AS$, 2. $S \rightarrow b$, 3. $A \rightarrow a$.

Grammar G is in almost-GNF. Therefore it can be transformed to a CFG G' in GNF such that $G'[\bar{r}/\bar{r}]G$.

In step 1 of Algorithm 5.5 the following productions are added to $P_0 =$ $= \{S \to b \quad \langle 2\rangle,\ A \to a \quad \langle 3\rangle\}$:

$$S \to aH_{33}[S1] \quad \langle 1\rangle$$
$$H_{33} \to a \quad \langle 33\rangle$$
$$S \to aH_{32} \quad \langle 1\rangle$$
$$H_{32} \to b \quad \langle 32\rangle$$

In step 2 the following productions are added in order to obtain P'.

$$[S1] \to aH_{33}[S1] \quad \langle 11\rangle$$
$$[S1] \to aH_{32} \quad \langle 11\rangle$$
$$[S1] \to b \quad \langle 21\rangle$$

In step 3 production $A \to a$ is removed from P' and A is removed from N'.

5.3. TRANSFORMATIONS ON GREIBACH NORMAL FORM GRAMMARS

In this section we consider transformations on context-free grammars which are in GNF or in $\overline{\text{GNF}}$.

As we already mentioned in section 5.2, if we apply the left part transformation (Algorithm 5.2 or Algorithm 5.3) to a CFG which is already in GNF then the newly created grammar is in standard 2-form.

Once we have a CFG in GNF we can use the following algorithm to convert left parses into right parses. This algorithm is a slight generalization of a method which was first used in [121].

ALGORITHM 5.6.

Input. A CFG $G = (N,\Sigma,P,S)$ in GNF.

Output. A CFG $G' = (N',\Sigma,P',S)$ in GNF such that $G'[\bar{r}/\ell]G$.

Method. Initially, $P' = \{A \to a \quad \langle i\rangle \mid i.A \to a \in P,\ a \in \Sigma\}$ and $N' = N$. The indexed symbols H which are created below are added to N'. Each newly created production is followed by its image under the cover homomorphism ψ.

(i) For each production of the form $i.A \to a\alpha$ in P, $\alpha \neq \varepsilon$, the following is done. Assume $\alpha = B\gamma$, $\gamma \in N^*$. For any $j_k.\ B \to b_k\gamma_k$ in P, $1 \le k \le |rhs(B)|$ add

$$A \to aH_{ij_k}\gamma_k\gamma \quad \langle \varepsilon\rangle$$

and

$$H_{ij_k} \to b_k \quad \langle ij_k\rangle$$

to P'. □

(ii) Remove all useless symbols.

THEOREM 5.4. Any CFG G in GNF can be transformed to a CFG G' in GNF such that $G'[\bar{r}/\ell]G$.

Proof. Two claims are used to prove the theorem. Homomorphism $\varphi : \Delta^*_{G'} \to \Delta^*_G$ is defined by letting, for any $p \in \Delta_G$, $\varphi(p) = \pi^R$ iff $\psi(p) = \pi$, where ψ is as in Algorithm 5.6.

CLAIM 1. If $A \overset{\pi'}{\underset{R}{\Rightarrow}} w$ in G', then $A \xrightarrow[L]{\varphi(\pi')} w$ in G.

Proof of Claim 1. Notice that $A \in N$. The proof is by induction on $|\pi'|$.

Basis. If $|\pi'| = 1$ then $\varphi(\pi') = \pi'$ and the result is clear.

Induction. Assume $|\pi'| = m$, $m > 1$. For $A \overset{\pi'}{\underset{R}{\Rightarrow}} w$ we may write

$$A \overset{i'}{\underset{R}{\Rightarrow}} aH_{ij_k}\gamma_k\gamma \overset{\rho'}{\underset{R}{\Rightarrow}} aH_{ij_k} w' \overset{j'}{\underset{R}{\Rightarrow}} abw',$$

where $i'\rho'j' = \pi'$ and $abw' = w$.

Since $|\rho'| < m$ and $\gamma_k\gamma \in N^*$ it is easily verified with the help of the induction hypothesis that

$$\gamma_k\gamma \xrightarrow[L]{\varphi(\rho')} w'$$

in G'. Moreover, $\varphi(i') = \varepsilon$ and $\varphi(j') = j_k i$, where $j_k.B \to b\gamma_k$ and $i.A \to aB\gamma$ are in P. Hence,

$$A \xrightarrow[L]{\varphi(\pi')} w$$

in G. □

CLAIM 2. If $A \overset{\pi}{\underset{L}{\Rightarrow}} w$ in G, then there exists $\pi' \in \Delta^*_{G'}$ such that $A \overset{\pi'}{\underset{R}{\Rightarrow}} w$ in G' and $\varphi(\pi') = \pi$.

Proof of Claim 2. The argument is similar to that of Claim 1. Notice that if $|\pi| > 1$ we can write

$$A \overset{i}{\underset{L}{\Rightarrow}} aB\gamma \overset{j}{\underset{L}{\Rightarrow}} ab\gamma_k\gamma \overset{\rho'}{\underset{L}{\Rightarrow}} abw' = w.$$

The details are left to the reader. □

In both claims we can take $A = S$ and we can conclude that $G'[\bar{r}/\ell]G$. □

If a grammar is in $\overline{GNF}$, then there exists a very simple proof to show the existence of a left-to-right covering grammar in GNF.

THEOREM 5.5. Any CFG G in $\overline{\text{GNF}}$ can be transformed to a CFG G' in GNF such that $G'[\ell/\bar{r}]G$.

Proof. Let $G = (N,\Sigma,P,S)$ be the CFG in $\overline{\text{GNF}}$. Define a grammar $G_R = (N,\Delta_G,P_R,S)$ by the set of productions

$$P_R = \{A \to \alpha i \mid i.A \to \alpha a \text{ is in } P,\ a \in \Sigma\}.$$

Define homomorphism $\varphi : \Delta_G^* \to \Sigma^*$ by letting $\varphi(i) = a$ if $i.A \to \alpha a$ is in P.

Notice that G_R is unambiguous. Find for G_R a weakly equivalent CFG $G_L = (N',\Delta_G,P_L,S')$ in GNF. Grammar G' and the associated cover homomorphism ψ are obtained from G_L by defining

$$P' = \{i'.A' \to a\alpha' \ \langle j\rangle \mid i'.A' \to j\alpha' \text{ is in } P_L \text{ and } \varphi(j) = a\}.$$

We may conclude that $G'[\ell/\bar{r}]G$ if we have verified that ψ is well-defined. That is, if $i'.A' \to i\alpha'$ and $j'.A' \to j\alpha'$ are in P_L, then $i \neq j$ implies $\varphi(i) \neq \varphi(j)$. But this property is trivially satisfied since otherwise G_L can generate sentences of the form $\pi_1 i\pi_2$ and $\pi_1 j\pi_2$. Hence, there exists $w \in L(G)$ such that $\varphi(\pi_1 i\pi_2) = \varphi(\pi_1 j\pi_2) = w$, and we have two different right parses for the same sentence. Since these right parses only differ in one production, this is impossible.

The usefulness of this theorem will become clear from the following observation. We know (Theorem 5.2 and 'symmetry') that any proper NRR grammar G can be transformed to a CFG G_0 in $\overline{\text{GNF}}$ such that $G_0[\bar{r}/\bar{r}]G$. From the above theorem it follows that we can transform G_0 to a grammar G' in GNF such that $G'[\ell/\bar{r}]G_0$ and from transitivity it follows that $G'[\ell/\bar{r}]G$.

COROLLARY 5.2. Any proper NRR grammar can be transformed to a CFG G' in GNF such that $G'[\ell/\bar{r}]G$.

A similar result was obtained in Ukkonen [162].

We conclude this section with some observations on production directed parses which are different from the left and right parses.

In section 5.2.2 it was shown that for any proper NLR grammar G there exist a CFG G' in GNF such that $G'[\ell/x]G$, $\ell \leq x \leq \ell p$. From transitivity and Theorem 5.4 of this section one can immediately conclude that any proper NLR grammar G can be given a CFG G' in GNF such that $G'[\bar{r}/x]G$, $\ell \leq x \leq \ell p$.

However, it is fairly simple to obtain more general results.

LEMMA 5.6. Let $G = (N,\Sigma,P,S)$ be a NLR grammar. Let x_G be a production directed parse relation. Then there exists a CFG G' in GNF such that $G'[\bar{r}/x]G$.

Proof. From Lemma 4.4 and Observation 4.2 it follows that there exists a grammar G_1 such that G_1 is NLR and $G_1[\bar{r}/x]G$. Grammar G_1 can be transformed to an ε-free NLR grammar G_2 (Corollary 4.1) such that $G_2[\bar{r}/\bar{r}]G_1$. Finally, for G_2 we can find a CFG G' in GNF such that $G'[\bar{r}/\bar{r}]G_2$ (Theorem 5.3). Hence, $G'[\bar{r}/x]G$. □

Another interesting result is obtained from the following argument. Consider a proper CFG G with a production directed parse relation x which satisfies $\ell c \leq x \leq \bar{r}$. Define a proper CFG G_1 in the following way.

For each production $i.A \to \alpha\beta$ of G with $|\alpha\beta| > 1$ and $\Gamma_G(i) = |\alpha| + 1$ define productions $A \to H_i\beta$ $\langle\varepsilon\rangle$ and $H_i \to \alpha$ $\langle i\rangle$ for grammar G_1. If $|\alpha\beta| = 1$, then $A \to \alpha\beta$ is also production of grammar G_1.

Clearly, $G_1[\bar{r}/x]G$. Hence, with the help of Theorem 5.3 and transitivity, it follows that there exists a CFG G' in GNF such that $G'[\bar{r}/x]G$.

COROLLARY 5.3.

(a) If G is a proper NLR grammar, then there exists a CFG G' in GNF such that $G'[\ell/x]G$, $\ell \leq x \leq \ell p$.

(b) If G is a NLR grammar, then there exists a CFG G' in GNF such that $G'[\bar{r}/x]G$, $\ell \leq x \leq \bar{r}$.

(c) If G is a proper CFG, then there exists a CFG G' in GNF such that $G'[\bar{r}/x]G$, $\ell c \leq x \leq \bar{r}$.

Note. Observe that if G is in GNF, then ℓc_G coincides with ℓ_G. Analogously, if G is in $\overline{\text{GNF}}$ then ℓp_G coincides with $\bar{r}_G$.

CHAPTER 6

THE COVER-TABLE FOR CONTEXT-FREE GRAMMARS

Once more we mention that the context-free grammars which we consider are cycle-free, they do not have useless symbols, and if the empty word is in the language then there is exactly one leftmost derivation for this word. Such a grammar is referred to as an amenable (AME) grammar. We will not pay attention to the special production $S_0 \rightarrow S\perp$ which may be introduced in the case of the elimination of single productions.

The cover-table, which is presented below, has five rows (AME, ε-FREE, NLR, ε-FREE NLR, GNF) and seven columns (AME, ε-FREE, NLR, ε-FREE NLR, GNF, NRR, ε-FREE NRR). Each row has four subrows, one for each type of cover which is considered, viz., ℓ/ℓ-, $\ell/\bar{r}$-, $\bar{r}/\ell$- and $\bar{r}/\bar{r}$-covers. For each of these covers a *yes/no*-answer is presented to the question whether certain types of grammars (indicated by the name of the column) can be covered by a grammar in some normal form (indicated by the name of the row).

A simple reference system to the entries of the table is used. Except for the AME-row all places are labeled with either letters (a.,...,p.) or numbers (1.,...,96.).

Example. Entry 25. is *no*, hence, not every ε-free grammar (satisfying the AME-conditions) can be left covered with a NLR grammar.

We have a short discussion on a negative cover result. In Ukkonen [164] it is shown, among others, that grammar G with productions

$$S \rightarrow 0SL \mid 0RL$$
$$R \rightarrow 1RL \mid 1$$
$$L \rightarrow \varepsilon$$

can not be left covered with an ε-free CFG. Now, consider CFG G_0 with productions

1. $S \rightarrow 0SL$
2. $S \rightarrow 1RL$
3. $R \rightarrow 1RL$
4. $R \rightarrow 2$
5. $L \rightarrow \varepsilon$

Clearly, if G does not have an ε-free CFG which left covers G, then G_0 does not have such a grammar. Grammar G_0 will be useful in the construction of the cover-table.

Next we list the productions of a CFG G_N which has the property that $G_N[\bar{r}/\ell]G_0$.

$S \rightarrow 0H_{00}S$	<55>	$H_{00} \rightarrow 0$	<11>
$S \rightarrow 0H_{01}R$	<55>	$H_{01} \rightarrow 1$	<12>
$S \rightarrow 1H_{11}R$	<55>	$H_{11} \rightarrow 1$	<23>
$S \rightarrow 1H_{12}$	<5 >	$H_{12} \rightarrow 2$	<24>
$R \rightarrow 1Q_{11}R$	<55>	$Q_{11} \rightarrow 1$	<33>
$R \rightarrow 1Q_{12}$	<5 >	$Q_{12} \rightarrow 2$	<34>
$R \rightarrow 2$	<4 >		

Grammar G_N is in GNF and since $G_N[\bar{r}/\ell]G_0$ we may immediately conclude that G_N does not have an ε-free CFG G' such that $G'[\ell/\bar{r}]G_N$.

Now we are sufficiently prepared to present the cover-table (Table VII) and the way it is obtained.

<u>Construction of the cover-table</u>

(6.1) All the ℓ/ℓ and $\bar{r}/\bar{r}$ entries of the AME-row are trivially *yes*. The $\ell/\bar{r}$ and $\bar{r}/\ell$ entries are *yes* because of Lemma 4.4.

(6.2) Trivially *yes* are also the entries 1., 4., 9., 12., 13., 16., 21., 24., 29., 32., 33., 36., 37. and 40. Because of Lemma 4.4 and Observation 4.2 the entries 30., 31., 34., 35., 38. and 39. are *yes*. Trivially *yes* are also the entries 57., 60., 61., 64., 85. and 88.

(6.3) Due to grammar G_0 we have that entry a. is *no* and from 'symmetry' it follows that entry d. is *no*. Therefore, also i., ℓ., m. and p. are *no*. Since G_0 is NLR it follows that entry 5. is *no* and again from 'symmetry' entry 20. is *no*. Thus, entries 68. and 92. are *no*.

(6.4) Next we consider grammar G_N. This grammar has the property that $G_N[\bar{r}/\ell]G_0$. Since G_0 has no ε-free grammar which left covers G_0 it follows that G_N does not have an ε-free grammar which left-to-right covers G_N. Moreover, G_N is in GNF, hence, the entries 14., 10., 6., 2. and b. are all *no*. Because of 'symmetry' it follows that the entries c., 3., 19. and 23. are *no*.

We have the following immediate consequences.

(i) Since entries b. and c. are *no* it follows that entries j., k., n. and o. are *no*.

(ii) Since entries 2. and 3. are *no* it follows that entries 50., 51., 74. and 75. are *no*.

(iii) Since entries 5. and 6. are *no* it follows that entries 53., 54., 77. and 78. are *no*.

(iv) Since entries 10. and 14. are *no* it follows that entries 58., 82., 62. and 86. are *no*.

G \ G'	COVER	AME	ε-FREE	NLR	ε-FREE NLR	GNF	NRR	ε-FREE NRR
AME	ℓ/ℓ	*yes*	*yes*	*yes*	*yes*	*yes*	*yes*	*yes*
	$\ell/\bar{r}$	*yes*	*yes*	*yes*	*yes*	*yes*	*yes*	*yes*
	$\bar{r}/\ell$	*yes*	*yes*	*yes*	*yes*	*yes*	*yes*	*yes*
	$\bar{r}/\bar{r}$	*yes*	*yes*	*yes*	*yes*	*yes*	*yes*	*yes*
ε-FREE	ℓ/ℓ	a. *no*	1. *yes*	5. *no*	9. *yes*	13. *yes*	17. *yes*	21. *yes*
	$\ell/\bar{r}$	b. *no*	2. *no*	6. *no*	10. *no*	14. *no*	18. *yes*	22. *yes*
	$\bar{r}/\ell$	c. *no*	3. *no*	7. *yes*	11. *yes*	15. *yes*	19. *no*	23. *no*
	$\bar{r}/\bar{r}$	d. *no*	4. *yes*	8. *yes*	12. *yes*	16. *yes*	20. *no*	24. *yes*
NLR	ℓ/ℓ	e. *no*	25. *no*	29. *yes*	33. *yes*	37. *yes*	41. *no*	45. *no*
	$\ell/\bar{r}$	f. *no*	26. *yes*	30. *yes*	34. *yes*	38. *yes*	42. *no*	46. *yes*
	$\bar{r}/\ell$	g. *no*	27. *no*	31. *yes*	35. *yes*	39. *yes*	43. *no*	47. *no*
	$\bar{r}/\bar{r}$	h. *no*	28. *yes*	32. *yes*	36. *yes*	40. *yes*	44. *no*	48. *yes*
ε-FREE NLR	ℓ/ℓ	i. *no*	49. *no*	53. *no*	57. *yes*	61. *yes*	65. *no*	69. *no*
	$\ell/\bar{r}$	j. *no*	50. *no*	54. *no*	58. *no*	62. *no*	66. *no*	70. *yes*
	$\bar{r}/\ell$	k. *no*	51. *no*	55. *yes*	59. *yes*	63. *yes*	67. *no*	71. *no*
	$\bar{r}/\bar{r}$	ℓ. *no*	52. *yes*	56. *yes*	60. *yes*	64. *yes*	68. *no*	72. *yes*
GNF	ℓ/ℓ	m. *no*	73. *no*	77. *no*	81. *yes*	85. *yes*	89. *no*	93. *no*
	$\ell/\bar{r}$	n. *no*	74. *no*	78. *no*	82. *no*	86. *no*	90. *no*	94. *yes*
	$\bar{r}/\ell$	o. *no*	75. *no*	79. *yes*	83. *yes*	87. *yes*	91. *no*	95. *no*
	$\bar{r}/\bar{r}$	p. *no*	76. *yes*	80. *yes*	84. *yes*	88. *yes*	92. *no*	96. *yes*

Table VII. Cover-table.

(v) Since entries 19. and 23. are *no* it follows that entries 67., 91., 71. and 95. are *no*.

(6.5) Due to the Corollaries 5.1 and 4.1 the entries 26., 28. and 52. are *yes*. From Theorem 5.2 it follows that entry 81. is *yes*. From Theorem 5.3 it follows that entries 76., 84. and 96. are *yes*. Since entry 96. is *yes* it follows that entries 72. and 48. are *yes*. From Corollary 5.2 it follows that entry 94. is *yes* and, consequently, entries 70., 46. and 22. are *yes*. Since the entries 81. and 85. are *yes* Theorem 5.4 tells us that entries 83. and 87. are *yes* and, consequently, entries 59., 11., 63. and 15. are *yes*.

With some simple observations, in which Theorem 5.4 can be used to obtain contradictions, it follows that the entries 73., 90., 93. and 89. are *no*.

Since the entries 73.,89., 93., and 90. are *no*, the entries 49., 69., 65. and 66. are *no*. Otherwise a contradiction with Theorem 5.2 can be obtained.

(6.6) Because of Corollary 4.1 we have that entry 8. is *yes* and from 'symmetry' it follows that entry 17. is *yes*. The assumption that entries h. and g. are *yes* leads, with the help of Corollary 4.1, to a contradiction with entries d. and c. which are *no*, respectively.

Similarly, with Corollary 4.1 and since entry 31. is *yes*, we must conclude that entries f. and e. are *no* in order to avoid contradictions with h. and g., respectively. Since both entry 19. and entry 20. are *no* we obtain with the same type of argument that entries 41., 42., 43. and 44. are *no*.

(6.7) Entry 56. is *yes* since the entries 8. and 52. are *yes*. The entries 25. and 27. are both *no* since otherwise a contradiction can be obtained (via entry 31. and 56. in the case of entry 25. and via entry 56. in the case of entry 27.) with entry 3. which is *no*.

For any NLR grammar G there exists a NLR grammar G' such that $G'[\bar{r}/\ell]G$. Grammar G' has an ε-free NLR grammar G" such that $G''[\bar{r}/\ell]G$. Hence, entry 55. is *yes* and therefore also entry 7. is *yes* and ('symmetry') entry 18. is *yes*. Since entries 55. and 56. are *yes* it follows (with entry 84. which is *yes*) that entries 79. and 80. are *yes*.

Both entries 45. and 47. are *no* because otherwise, with the help of 55. and 56., a contradiction with entry 71. is *no* is obtained. This concludes the construction of the cover-table.

We conclude this chapter with a few remarks on the cover-table in relation with section 3.2 ('Historical notes').

Our right cover result (entry 76.) deals with the comment of Griffiths and Petrick. That is, we have found a procedure for relating the structural descriptions of a standard form grammar (GNF grammar) to the context-free grammar from which it was constructed.

Both Kurki-Suonio and Foster solve (in their formalism) the problem of relating the structural descriptions in the case of elimination of left recursion. In the cover formalism (Soisalon-Soininen [156] and Nijholt [115]) there are corresponding right cover results (entry 28.)

Kuno's attempts are also illustrated in the table. He has no problem to relate a GNF grammar to the NLR grammar from which it is constructed (cf.entry 81.). However, his attempt to relate a NLR grammar to the context-free grammar from which it is obtained gives rise to a complicated procedure. It follows from our cover-table (cf. entry 25.) that a cover homomorphism is not strong enough to express this relation.

CHAPTER 7

NORMAL FORM COVERS FOR REGULAR GRAMMARS

In this chapter we present two techniques to transform left and right regular grammars into covering GNF grammars.

Given a left regular grammar G, the method described in the proof of Theorem 5.5 is adequate to obtain a grammar G' in GNF such that $G'[\ell/\bar{r}]G$. However, the first algorithm of this section shows that we can always find a right regular grammar G' such that $G'[\ell/\bar{r}]G$. The method in this algorithm is a slight adaptation of a method which is sometimes used to show that the classes of languages of left regular and right regular grammars coincide.

ALGORITHM 7.1.

Input. A left regular grammar $G = (N,\Sigma,P,S)$.

Output. A right regular grammar $G' = (N',\Sigma,P',S')$ such that $G'[\ell/\bar{r}]G$ under a very fine and faithful cover homomorphism.

Method. Initially, set $P' = \emptyset$. Each production in P' will be followed by its image under the cover homomorphism. Set N' will consist of the nonterminal symbols which occur in the productions. Start symbol S' is the only newly introduced nonterminal symbol.

(i) For any $A \in N$, $A \neq S$, if $i.A \to a$ is in P, then add $S' \to aA$ <i> to P'. Moreover, if $i.A \to Ba$ is in P, add $B \to aA$ <i> to P'.

(ii) a. If $i.S \to a$ is in P, add $S' \to a$ <i> to P'. Moreover, if S is left recursive, add $S' \to aS$ <i> to P'.

b. If $i.S \to Aa$ is in P, add $A \to a$ <i> to P'. Moreover, if S is left recursive, add $A \to aS$ <i> to P'. □

THEOREM 7.1. Any left regular grammar G can be transformed to a right regular grammar G' such that $G'[\ell/\bar{r}]G$ under a very fine and faithful cover homomorphism.

Proof. Use Algorithm 7.1. Obviously, G' is right regular and the homomorphism which is defined is very fine. Call this homomorphism ψ. Two claims are used.

CLAIM 1. Assume $B \neq S'$. If $B \overset{\pi'}{\underset{L}{\Rightarrow}} wA$ in G', then there exists a derivation $A \overset{\pi}{\underset{R}{\Rightarrow}} Bw$ in G, with $\psi(\pi') = \pi^R$.

Proof of Claim 1. The proof is by induction on $|w|$. Assume $|w| = 1$. Hence, $w \in \Sigma$ and we write $w = a$ and $\pi' = i'$. In this case there is a production $i'.B \to aA$ in P' and there exists a production $i.A \to Ba$ in P with $\psi(i') = i$.

Now assume $|w| > 1$. If we write $w = au$, with $a \in \Sigma$ and $u \in \Sigma^+$, and $\pi' = i'\rho'$, where $i'.B \rightarrow aC$ is in P', then we have a derivation

$$B \overset{i'}{\underset{L}{\Rightarrow}} aC \overset{\rho'}{\underset{L}{\Rightarrow}} auA$$

in G'.

Notice that, due to the construction of G', S' does not occur in a righthand side of a production. Therefore, $C \neq S'$ and since $C \overset{\rho'}{\underset{L}{\Rightarrow}} uA$ we may conclude from the induction hypothesis that $A \overset{\rho}{\underset{R}{\Rightarrow}} Cu$ in G, where $\psi(\rho') = \rho^R$. Moreover, there exists a production $i.C \rightarrow Ba$ in P with $\psi(i') = i$ and it follows that $A \overset{\pi}{\underset{R}{\Rightarrow}} Bw$ in G, with $\pi = \rho i$ and $\psi(\pi') = \pi^R$. This concludes the proof of Claim 1. □

It should be observed that if S is left recursive in G, then the existence of a derivation $S \overset{\pi}{\underset{R}{\Rightarrow}} Bw$ in G implies that the following derivations exist in G':

(a) $B \overset{\pi'}{\underset{L}{\Rightarrow}} wS$ for some sequence π' of productions such that $\psi(\pi') = \pi^R$ and π' can be written as $\pi' = \rho'i'$ for a production i' in P' which is of the form $A \rightarrow aS$,

(b) $B \overset{\delta'}{\underset{L}{\Rightarrow}} w$ for the sequence $\delta' = \rho'j'$ such that production j' is of the form $A \rightarrow a$ and $\psi(i') = \psi(j')$, hence $\psi(\pi') = \psi(\delta') = \pi^R$.

If S is not left recursive, then only situation (b) occurs. Formally,

CLAIM 2. Assume that S is not left recursive. For any $A \in N$, $A \neq S$, if $A \overset{\pi}{\underset{R}{\Rightarrow}} Bw$ in G, then there exists π' such that $B \overset{\pi'}{\underset{L}{\Rightarrow}} wA$ in G' and $\psi(\pi') = \pi^R$.

The proof of Claim 2 proceeds again by induction on $|w|$ and since it goes along the same lines as the proof of Claim 1 we omit it.

Now consider a derivation $S' \overset{\pi'}{\underset{L}{\Rightarrow}} w$ in G'. This derivation can be written as

$$S' \overset{i'}{\underset{L}{\Rightarrow}} aA \overset{\rho'}{\underset{L}{\Rightarrow}} auB \overset{j'}{\underset{L}{\Rightarrow}} aub,$$

where $w = aub$ and $\pi' = i'\rho'j'$. From the construction of G' it follows that there exist productions $j.S \rightarrow Bb$ and $i.A \rightarrow a$ in P with $\psi(i') = i$ and $\psi(j') = j$. From Claim 1 it follows that

$$B \overset{\rho}{\underset{R}{\Rightarrow}} Au, \text{ with } \psi(\rho') = \rho^R.$$

Hence, $S \overset{\pi}{\underset{R}{\Rightarrow}} w$ in G with $\pi = j\rho i$ and $\psi(\pi') = \pi^R$.

Now consider the second condition of the cover definition. Assume $S \overset{\pi}{\underset{R}{\Rightarrow}} w$ in G. We can write, with $a, b \in \Sigma$ and $u \in \Sigma^*$,

$$S \overset{j}{\underset{R}{\Rightarrow}} Ab \overset{\rho}{\underset{R}{\Rightarrow}} Bub \overset{i}{\underset{R}{\Rightarrow}} aub,$$

where $w = aub$ and $j\rho i = \pi$. Notice that if S is not left recursive then $A \neq S$. Hence, from Claim 2 it follows that $B \overset{\rho'}{\underset{L}{\Rightarrow}} uA$ in G', with $\psi(\rho') = \rho^R$. From the construction of G' it follows that there exist $i'.S' \to aB$ and $j'.A \to b$ in P', with $\psi(i') = i$ and $\psi(j') = j$. Hence, $S' \overset{\pi'}{\underset{L}{\Rightarrow}} w$, with $\pi' = i'\rho'j'$ and $\psi(\pi') = \pi^R$.

Since the construction is such that for any (rightmost) derivation $S \overset{\pi}{\underset{R}{\Rightarrow}} w$ in G there exists exactly one (leftmost) derivation $S' \overset{\pi'}{\underset{L}{\Rightarrow}} w$ in G' with $\psi(\pi') = \pi^R$, we can conclude that the cover is faithful. □

EXAMPLE 7.1.

Consider the well-known left regular grammar G_0 with productions

1. $S \to S0$
2. $S \to S1$
3. $S \to 0$
4. $S \to 1$

If we apply Algorithm 7.1, then step (i) is void and in the second step we obtain productions

(ii) a.	$S' \to 0$ <3>	(ii) b.	$S \to 0$ <1>
	$S' \to 1$ <4>		$S \to 1$ <2>
	$S' \to 0S$ <3>		$S \to 0S$ <1>
	$S' \to 1S$ <4>		$S \to 1S$ <2>

Since any right regular grammar is in GNF, Algorithm 5.6 can be used to obtain a GNF grammar which right covers the input grammar of Algorithm 7.1. If this is done for the grammar of Example 7.1, then grammar G', displayed in Table V (section 3.3), is obtained.

Notice that it would have been sufficient, in order to conclude that there exists a right regular grammar which left-to-right covers the left regular input grammar, to prove that Algorithm 7.1 is language preserving. Then we could have used the method of Theorem 5.5. For the unspecified transformation to GNF in this method one may use Algorithm 7.1.

Another method which preserves regularity is the Rosenkrantz method [142].

Before we can present a table which shows the possibilities of covering regular grammars with grammars in Greibach normal form we need one more algorithm.

In Chapter 6 we saw that not every GNF grammar G can be left-to-right covered with a GNF grammar G'. However, if GNF grammar G is right regular, then a GNF grammar G' such that $G'[\ell/\bar{r}]G$ exists.

ALGORITHM 7.2.

Input. A right regular grammar $G = (N,\Sigma,P,S)$.

Output. A grammar $G' = (N',\Sigma,P',S')$ in GNF such that $G'[\ell/\bar{r}]G$ under a faithful and very fine cover homomorphism.

Method. We construct a (nondeterministic) pushdown transducer $R = (Q,\Sigma,\Gamma,\Delta_G,\delta,q,S,\emptyset)$ which translates with empty pushdown stack, without ε-moves, and which satisfies

$$\tau_e(R) = \bar{r}_G.$$

Here, $Q = \{q,r\}$, Δ_G is the output set, $\Gamma = \{S\} \cup \{[ij] \mid i,j \in \Delta_G\}$ and S is the start symbol. Let $\Delta'_G = \{i \mid i.A \to a \text{ is in } P, a \in \Sigma\}$. Define the mapping δ as follows:

a. For each $a \in \Sigma$, $\delta(q,a,S)$ contains
   (i) $(p,[ij],j)$, if $p \in Q$, $j \in \Delta'_G$ and, for some $B \in N$, $i.\ S \to aB$ is in P. If $p = r$, then production j has lefthand side B.
   (ii) (r,ε,i), if $i.S \to a$ is in P.

b. For each $a \in \Sigma$, $\delta(q,a,[ij])$ contains
   (i) $(p,[mn][ij],n)$, if $p \in Q$, $n \in \Delta_G \backslash \Delta'_G$ and there exist $X,Z,U \in N$ and $Y \in \Sigma$ such that $i.X \to YZ$ and $m.Z \to aU$ are in P. If $p = r$, then production n has lefthand side U. If $n.X' \to bV$ is in P, then production j has lefthand side V.
   (ii) $(r,[ij],n)$, if there exist $X,Z,U \in N$ and $Y \in \Sigma$ such that $i.X \to YZ$ and $n.Z \to aU$ are in P and production j has lefthand side U.

c. For each $a \in \Sigma$, $\delta(r,a,[mn]) = (r,\varepsilon,m)$ if there exist $X \in N$ and $Y \in N \cup \{\varepsilon\}$ such that $n.X \to aY$ is in P.

This concludes the construction of PDT R. Now construct, using the Standard Construction (cf. section 1.3.1), a simple SDTS $T_1 = (N_1,\Sigma,\Delta_G,R_1,S')$ from pushdown transducer R.

All the rules of T_1 are of the form $A \to a\alpha, \pi\alpha$ with $a \in \Sigma$, $\pi \in \Delta_G$ and $\alpha \in N_1^*$. The desired GNF grammar $G' = (N',\Sigma,P',S)$ is obtained by removing the useless symbols from the input grammar of T_1.

Homomorphism ψ is defined by mapping each production $A \to a\alpha$ on π if $A \to a\alpha, \pi\alpha$ is a rule of T_1. □

Our first observation concerning this algorithm deals with the definition of ψ. We have to verify that ψ is well-defined, that is, there do not exist rules $A \to a\alpha$, $\pi_1\alpha$ and $A \to a\alpha$, $\pi_2\alpha$ in R with $\pi_1 \neq \pi_2$. This follows from the following lemma.

<u>LEMMA 7.1.</u> Pushdown transducer R is semantically unambiguous.

Proof. We have to verify that there do not exist $p \in Q$, $a \in \Sigma$ and $X \in \Gamma$ such that $\delta(p,a,X)$ contains elements which only differ in their output symbol. For the cases a., b.(i) and c. this is immediate. For step b.(ii) this property follows from the fact that the productions i and j, together with the input symbol a, uniquely determine production n. □

The following observation will clarify the behaviour of pushdown transducer R.

<u>OBSERVATION 7.1.</u> Assume R translates $w \in L(G)$ by empty pushdown list. If $|w|$ is even and $|w| > 2$, then translation of w can only take place in the following way:

A. one application of a step of the form a. (i), followed by
B. $(|w|/2) - 2$ applications of steps of the form b. (i) with $p = q$, followed by
C. one application of a step of the form b. (i) with $p = r$, followed by
D. $(|w|/2)$ applications of steps of the form c. .

Translating starts with one symbol on the stack. Each of the steps of b. (i) lets the stack grow with one symbol. After the application of a step b. (i) with $p = r$, there are $|w|/2$ symbols on the stack. Each of the $|w|/2$ steps of the form c. reduces the number of symbols on the stack with one.

Similar observations hold for $|w|$ is odd and some trivial cases ($|w| \leq 2$). Other ways of translating do not lead to acceptance. Either the stack is empty where there is still input to be read, or the input is read and the stack is not yet empty. End of Observation 7.1.

Now we are sufficiently prepared to present the following theorem.

<u>THEOREM 7.2.</u> Any right regular grammar G can be transformed to a CFG G' in GNF such that $G'[\ell/\bar{r}]G$ under a very fine and faithful cover homomorphism.

Proof. The proof is based on the following claim. This claim is used to prove that $\tau_e(R) = \bar{r}_G$, where R is the pushdown transducer of Algorithm 7.2.

<u>CLAIM.</u> Let $u \in \Sigma^*$, $|u| \geq 1$, $c \in \Sigma$ and $i.A \rightarrow aB$ and $j.C \rightarrow cX$ in P with $X \in N \cup \{\varepsilon\}$. Then,

$$(q,uc,[ij],\varepsilon) \overset{*}{\vdash} (r,\varepsilon,\varepsilon,\pi i)$$

in R if and only if

$$B \overset{\pi}{\underset{R}{\Rightarrow}} uC \overset{j}{\Rightarrow} ucX$$

is a derivation in G.

Proof of the claim. The proof is by induction on $|u|$.
Basis. Assume $|u| = 1$. Write $u = b$, $b \in \Sigma$. In this case the computation

$$(q,bc,[ij],\varepsilon) \overset{*}{\vdash} (r,\varepsilon,\varepsilon,\pi i)$$

is done with two moves and we must conclude the existence of

$$(r,[ij],\pi) \in \delta(q,b,[ij])$$

obtained from step b. (ii) of the algorithm, and of

$$(r,\varepsilon,i) \in \delta(r,c,[ij])$$

obtained from step c. of the algorithm. It follows that there exists a production $\pi.B \rightarrow bC$ in P and we have a derivation

$$B \overset{\pi}{\Rightarrow} bC \overset{i}{\Rightarrow} bcX$$

which had to be proved. Notice that $\pi^R = \pi$. In a similar way the other direction of the basis of the induction can be proved.

Induction. Assume $|u| > 1$. If

$$(q,uc,[ij],\varepsilon) \overset{*}{\vdash} (r,\varepsilon,\varepsilon,\pi i)$$

then, if we write $u = bv$ (with $b \in \Sigma$ and $v \in \Sigma^*$) and $\pi = n\gamma$ (with $n \in \Delta_G$ and $\gamma \in \Delta_G^*$), we can factor this computation into

$$(q,bvc,[ij],\varepsilon) \vdash (p,vc,[mn][ij],n) \overset{*}{\vdash} (r,\varepsilon,\varepsilon,n\gamma i),$$

where $p \in Q$.

First consider the case $p = r$. Then there exists

$$(r,[mn][ij],n) \in \delta(q,b,[ij])$$

obtained from step b (i) of the algorithm,

$$(r,\varepsilon,m) \in \delta(r,v,[mn])$$

and

$$(r,\varepsilon,i) \in \delta(r,c,[ij])$$

obtained from step c. of the algorithm, with $m = \gamma$, $m \in \Delta_G$ and $v \in \Sigma$. Hence, there exist productions $m.B \rightarrow bU$ and $n.U \rightarrow vC$ in P and we have a derivation

$$B \overset{m}{\Rightarrow} bU \overset{n}{\Rightarrow} bvC \overset{i}{\Rightarrow} bvcX$$

with $(mn)^R = n\gamma$ as had to be proved.

Now consider the case $p = q$. In this case we have

$$(q,[mn][ij],n) \in \delta(q,b,[ij])$$

which is obtained in step b. (i) of the algorithm. Hence, we have a production m of the form m.B → bU. Moreover, we have a computation

$$(q,vc,[mn][ij],\varepsilon) \overset{*}{\vdash} (r,\varepsilon,\varepsilon,\gamma i).$$

Clearly, we can write $v = v_1v_2$ and $\gamma = \gamma_1\gamma_2$ such that

$$(q,v_1,[mn],\varepsilon) \overset{*}{\vdash} (p,\varepsilon,\varepsilon,\gamma_1)$$

and

$$(p,v_2c,[ij],\varepsilon) \overset{*}{\vdash} (r,\varepsilon,\varepsilon,\gamma_2 i).$$

From the construction of δ it follows that $p = r$ and the last symbol of string γ_1 is m. Moreover, since $p = r$ we have also $v_2 = \varepsilon$ and $\gamma_2 = \varepsilon$. Therefore $v_1 = v$ and $\gamma_1 = \gamma$. Hence, we may write $\gamma = \gamma'm$ and

$$(q,v,[mn],\varepsilon) \overset{*}{\vdash} (r,\varepsilon,\varepsilon,\gamma'm)$$

and

$$(r,c,[ij],\varepsilon) \vdash (r,\varepsilon,\varepsilon,i).$$

We distinguish between two cases.

(a) $|v| > 1$. Write $v = v'd$, $d \in \Sigma$. Since, by assumption, production j is of the form j.C → cX we have by construction of δ (cf. the conditions mentioned in step b. (i)) that production n is of the form n.X' → dC. It follows from the induction hypothesis that

$$U \overset{\gamma',R}{\Rightarrow} v'X'$$

and since m.B → bU, n.X' → dC and j.C → cX are productions in P, we have a derivation

$$B \overset{m}{\Rightarrow} bU \overset{\gamma',R}{\Rightarrow} bv'X' \overset{n}{\Rightarrow} bv'dC \overset{j}{\Rightarrow} bv'dcX,$$

that is,

$$B \overset{\pi^R}{\Rightarrow} uC \overset{j}{\Rightarrow} ucX$$

where $bv'd = u$ and $\pi = n\gamma'm$, which had to be proved.

(b) $|v| = 1$. This would mean that

$$(q,v,[mn],\varepsilon) \vdash (r,\varepsilon,\varepsilon,\gamma'm),$$

with $\gamma' = \varepsilon$. However, with our definition of δ such a move is not possible. Therefore, this case does not occur. This concludes the 'only if'-part of the induction proof.

The 'if'-part of the proof is a straightforward reversal of the argument used in the 'only if'-proof. Therefore it is omitted. Moreover, we assume that it is clear that for any (rightmost) derivation

$$B \overset{\pi}{\underset{}{\Rightarrow}}^{R} uC \overset{j}{\Rightarrow} ucX$$

in the claim there is exactly one sequence of moves

$$(q,uc,[ij],\varepsilon) \vdash^{*} (r,\varepsilon,\varepsilon,\pi i).$$

This concludes the proof of the claim. □

With the help of this claim it is now fairly simple to verify that

$$S \overset{\pi}{\underset{L}{\Rightarrow}}^{R} w$$

if and only if

$$(q,w,S,\varepsilon) \vdash^{*} (r,\varepsilon,\varepsilon,\pi),$$

that is, $\tau_e(R) = \bar{r}_G$.

Now we want to show that $G'[\ell/\bar{r}]G$. However, this is an immediate consequence of the Standard Observation (cf. section 1.3.1). We know that simple SDTS T_1 performs the same translation as R, that is, $\tau(T_1) = \tau_e(R) = \bar{r}_G$. All the rules of T_1 are of the form $i.A \to a\alpha, b\alpha$ where $b \in \Delta_G$. Hence, if we define $\psi(i) = b$, then $(w,\pi') \in \ell_{G'}$ implies $(w,\psi(\pi')) \in \bar{r}_G$. It is also clear that $(w,\pi) \in \bar{r}_G = \tau(T_1)$ implies that there exists π' such that $(w,\pi') \in \ell_{G'}$ and $\psi(\pi') = \pi$. Therefore, $G'[\ell/\bar{r}]G$ and by definition of ψ the cover homomorphism is very fine.

For each derivation $S \overset{\pi}{\underset{L}{\Rightarrow}} w$ in G there is exactly one sequence of moves

$$(q,w,S,\varepsilon) \vdash^{*} (r,\varepsilon,\varepsilon,\pi^R)$$

(cf. the concluding remark in the proof of the claim.) Then it follows from the Standard Construction of a simple SDTS from a PDT that there is also exactly one derivation

$$(S,S) \overset{*}{\underset{L}{\Rightarrow}} (w,\pi^R).$$

Hence, if $(w,\pi^R) \in \bar{r}_G$, then there is exactly one element $(w,\pi') \in \ell_{G'}$ such that

$\psi(\pi') = \pi^R$. Therefore the cover is faithful. This concludes the proof of Theorem 7.2. □

In Table VIII we have collected the GNF cover results for regular grammars.

G' \ G	COVER	LEFT REGULAR	RIGHT REGULAR
GNF	ℓ/ℓ	1. *yes*	5. *yes*
	$\ell/\bar{r}$	2. *yes*	6. *yes*
	$\bar{r}/\ell$	3. *yes*	7. *yes*
	$\bar{r}/\bar{r}$	4. *yes*	8. *yes*

Table VIII. Cover-table for regular grammars.

The entries in this table are numbered from 1 to 8. The table shows that for any (left- or right-) regular grammar G a grammar G' in GNF can be found which covers G for each of the types of cover. The answers in this table are found in the following way.

Construction of the cover-table.

(7.1) The entries 5. and 8. follow trivially. Entry 2. is *yes* because of Theorem 7.1. Entry 6. is *yes* because of Theorem 7.2.

(7.2) Since entry 2. is *yes* we may conclude, with the help of Algorithm 5.6 (transitivity), that entry 4. is *yes*. Similarly, via entry 5., entry 7. is *yes*.

(7.3) Let G be a left regular grammar. Algorithm 7.1 yields a right regular grammar G' such that $G'[\ell/\bar{r}]G$. Hence, we have also that $G'[\bar{\ell}/r]G$, where we use $\bar{\ell}$ and r to denote the reverse of left parses and right parses, respectively. Since for regular grammars the leftmost and the rightmost derivations coincide, we obtain $G'[\bar{r}/\ell]G$. Therefore, entry 3. is *yes*.

(7.4) Let G be a left regular grammar. From the argument in (7.3) we know that there exists a right regular grammar G' such that $G'[\bar{r}/\ell]G$.
Since entry 6. is *yes* it follows that there exists a GNF grammar G" such that $G''[\ell/\bar{r}]G'$. From transitivity it follows that $G''[\ell/\ell]G$. Therefore entry 1. is *yes*.

It is worth noting that the GNF grammars of entries 2. and 3. are in fact right regular grammars. Moreover, except for entries 4. and 7., the cover homomorphisms are very fine. In particular the result that any left regular grammar can be transformed to a left covering GNF grammar under a very fine cover homomorphism (entry 1.) is interesting.

We illustrate Algorithm 7.2 with the following example.

EXAMPLE 7.2.
Consider the CFG G which is obtained in Example 7.1. If we apply Algorithm 7.2 to this grammar, then we obtain a grammar in GNF which left covers grammar G_0 under a very fine cover homomorphism. Notice that for right covers a similar result can not be obtained (cf. Chapter 3 and Gray and Harrison [49]). That is, grammar G_0 can not be right covered under a very fine cover homomorphism by a context-free grammar in Greibach normal form.

We start with grammar G with productions

1. $S' \to 0$ <3>	5. $S \to 0$ <1>
2. $S' \to 1$ <4>	6. $S \to 1$ <2>
3. $S' \to 0S$ <3>	7. $S \to 0S$ <1>
4. $S' \to 1S$ <4>	8. $S \to 1S$ <2>

Grammar G is such that $G[\bar{r}/\ell]G_0$. If we perform Algorithm 7.2 with input grammar G, then we obtain, after a suitable renaming of the nonterminal symbols, the GNF grammar with the following 98 (!) productions:

$S \to 0 \mid 1 \quad \langle 1,2\rangle$
$S \to 0A_0 \mid 0B_0 \mid 0A_1 \mid 0B_1 \quad \langle 5,5,6,6\rangle$
$S \to 1A_2 \mid 1B_2 \mid 1A_3 \mid 1B_3 \quad \langle 5,5,6,6\rangle$

$B_0 \to 0A_0 \mid 1A_0 \quad \langle 7,8\rangle$
$B_0 \to 0D_0A_0 \mid 0D_1A_0 \mid 1D_2A_0 \mid 1D_3A_0 \quad \langle 7,8,7,8\rangle$
$B_0 \to 0E_0A_0 \mid 0E_1A_0 \mid 1E_2A_0 \mid 1E_3A_0 \quad \langle 7,8,7,8\rangle$

$B_1 \to 0A_1 \mid 1A_1 \quad \langle 7,8\rangle$
$B_1 \to 0D_0A_1 \mid 0D_1A_1 \mid 1D_2A_1 \mid 1D_3A_1 \quad \langle 7,8,7,8\rangle$
$B_1 \to 0E_0A_1 \mid 0E_1A_1 \mid 1E_2A_1 \mid 1E_3A_1 \quad \langle 7,8,7,8\rangle$

$B_2 \to 0A_2 \mid 1A_2 \quad \langle 7,8\rangle$
$B_2 \to 0D_0A_2 \mid 0D_1A_2 \mid 1D_2A_2 \mid 1D_3A_2 \quad \langle 7,8,7,8\rangle$
$B_2 \to 0E_0A_2 \mid 0E_1A_2 \mid 1E_2A_2 \mid 1E_3A_2 \quad \langle 7,8,7,8\rangle$

$B_3 \rightarrow 0A_3 \mid 1A_3 \quad \langle 7,8\rangle$
$B_3 \rightarrow 0D_0A_3 \mid 0D_1A_3 \mid 1D_2A_3 \mid 1D_3A_3 \quad \langle 7,8,7,8\rangle$
$B_3 \rightarrow 0E_0A_3 \mid 0E_1A_3 \mid 1E_2A_3 \mid 1E_3A_3 \quad \langle 7,8,7,8\rangle$

$E_0 \rightarrow 0E_0D_0 \mid 0E_1D_0 \mid 1E_2D_0 \mid 1E_3D_0 \quad \langle 7,8,7,8\rangle$
$E_0 \rightarrow 0D_0D_0 \mid 0D_1D_0 \mid 1D_2D_0 \mid 1D_3D_0 \quad \langle 7,8,7,8\rangle$
$E_0 \rightarrow 0D_0 \mid 1D_0 \quad \langle 7,8\rangle$

$E_1 \rightarrow 0E_0D_1 \mid 0E_1D_1 \mid 1E_2D_1 \mid 1E_3D_1 \quad \langle 7,8,7,8\rangle$
$E_1 \rightarrow 0D_0D_1 \mid 0D_1D_1 \mid 1D_2D_1 \mid 1D_3D_1 \quad \langle 7,8,7,8\rangle$
$E_1 \rightarrow 0D_1 \mid 1D1 \quad \langle 7,8\rangle$

$E_2 \rightarrow 0E_0D_2 \mid 0E_1D_2 \mid 1E_2D_2 \mid 1E_3D_2 \quad \langle 7,8,7,8\rangle$
$E_2 \rightarrow 0D_0D_2 \mid 0D_1D_2 \mid 1D_2D_2 \mid 1D_3D_2 \quad \langle 7,8,7,8\rangle$
$E_2 \rightarrow 0D_2 \mid 1D_2 \quad \langle 7,8\rangle$

$E_3 \rightarrow 0E_0D_3 \mid 0E_1D_3 \mid 1E_2D_3 \mid 1E_3D_3 \quad \langle 7,8,7,8\rangle$
$E_3 \rightarrow 0D_0D_3 \mid 0D_1D_3 \mid 1D_2D_3 \mid 1D_3D_3 \quad \langle 7,8,7,8\rangle$
$E_3 \rightarrow 0D_3 \mid 1D_3 \quad \langle 7,8\rangle$

$A_0 \rightarrow 0 \quad \langle 3\rangle \qquad D_0 \rightarrow 0 \quad \langle 7\rangle$
$A_1 \rightarrow 1 \quad \langle 3\rangle \qquad D_1 \rightarrow 1 \quad \langle 7\rangle$
$A_2 \rightarrow 0 \quad \langle 4\rangle \qquad D_2 \rightarrow 0 \quad \langle 8\rangle$
$A_3 \rightarrow 1 \quad \langle 4\rangle \qquad D_3 \rightarrow 1 \quad \langle 8\rangle$

The reader may verify with a few examples that this GNF grammar indeed left covers grammar G_0. End of Example 7.2.

The transformation from a right regular grammar G to a GNF grammar G' such that $G'[\ell/\bar{r}]G$ is defined in terms of a PDT. We have not tried to give a grammatical characterization of this transformation. However, the idea in this transformation can be simply used in examples to obtain left covering or left-to-right covering grammars in GNF. This is illustrated in the following two examples.

<u>EXAMPLE 7.3.</u>

Consider again left regular grammar G_0. In Figure 7.1 we have displayed a typical parse tree for a sentence of G_0 and the way this tree is transformed to a parse tree of a grammar G in GNF such that $G[\ell/\ell]G_0$ and $G[\ell/\bar{r}]G_0$.

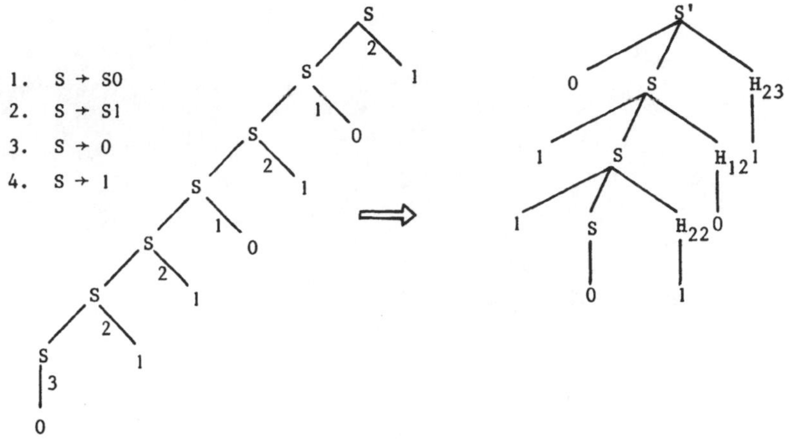

Figure 7.1. A left and left-to-right cover for G_0.

The indices of the symbols H_{23}, H_{12} and H_{22}, in this order, reflect the productions which are used in the parse tree with respect to G_0. The first index of H is used to describe the upper part of the tree of G_0 in a top-down manner (212). The second index describes the lower part of the tree of G_0 in a bottom-up manner (322).

Rather mechanically we can obtain all the productions of G. Each production of G is followed by its image under a left cover and a left-to-right cover, respectively.

$S' \to 0SH_{23} \mid 1SH_{24} \mid 0SH_{13} \mid 1SH_{14}$ <2,2,1,1> <3,4,3,4>
$S \to 0SH_{21} \mid 1SH_{22} \mid 0SH_{11} \mid 1SH_{12}$ <2,2,1,1> <1,2,1,2>

$S' \to 0H_{23} \mid 1H_{24} \mid 0H_{13} \mid 1H_{14}$ <2,2,1,1> <3,4,3,4>
$S \to 0H_{21} \mid 1H_{22} \mid 0H_{11} \mid 1H_{12}$ <2,2,1,1> <1,2,1,2>

$S' \to 0 \mid 1$ <3,4> <3,4>
$S \to 0 \mid 1$ <1,2> <1,2>

$H_{23} \to 1$	<3>	<2>		$H_{21} \to 1$	<1>	<2>
$H_{24} \to 1$	<4>	<2>		$H_{22} \to 1$	<2>	<2>
$H_{13} \to 0$	<3>	<1>		$H_{11} \to 0$	<1>	<1>
$H_{14} \to 0$	<4>	<1>		$H_{12} \to 0$	<2>	<1>

EXAMPLE 7.4.

Consider right regular grammar G with productions

1. $S \to 0S$ 3. $S \to 0$
2. $S \to 1S$ 4. $S \to 1$

In Figure 7.2 we have illustrated how a parse tree with respect to G can be converted to a parse tree with respect to a GNF grammar G' such that a left-to-right and a left cover can be defined. The complete definition of G' is left to the reader.

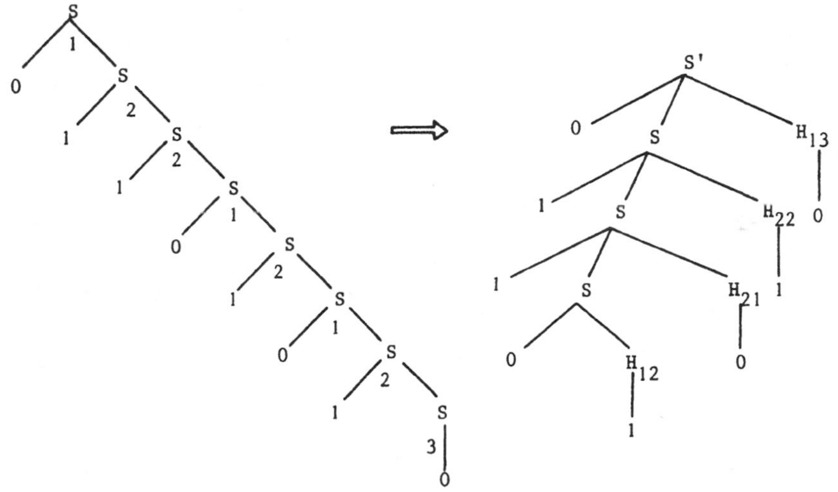

Figure 7.2. A left-to-right and left cover for G.

With this example we conclude Chapter 7.

CHAPTER 8

DETERMINISTICALLY PARSABLE GRAMMARS

8.1. INTRODUCTION

Various parsing methods for general context-free languages have been developed. However, for most of the practical applications the attention can be restricted to subclasses of the deterministic languages. The main parts of the syntactic structures of programming languages describe deterministic languages. Therefore it is not only legal to do so but also, since the time and space requirements for the parsing methods for the class of deterministic languages and its subclasses are modest in comparison with the methods for the general context-free languages, preferable to do so. Moreover, many of these methods can be easily implemented.

Suppose we have a language which is described by a context-free grammar. We want to build a parser for this grammar. This can be done by hand or with a *compiler writing system.*† If it is done by hand and a certain parsing method has been chosen, then one may expect that one has to manipulate the grammar, change it, apply transformations to it, etc. in order to make it suitable for this parsing method. The same may hold in the case of a compiler writing system. Such a system takes as input the syntactic rules of a grammar (together with semantic information) and produces as output a parser or, more generally, a compiler for this grammar. In a compiler writing system a choice has been made for a certain type of parsing method. If the system is provided with the syntactic rules then it will try to generate a parser of this specific type.

In their 'state-of-the-art' paper on 'Translator Writing Systems' Feldman and Gries [30] describe, among others, compiler writing systems where the syntactic analysis is based on 'precedence techniques'. Grammars which can be parsed with these techniques are called 'precedence grammars'. Feldman and Gries remark :

> *"Moreover, one must manipulate a grammar for an average programming language considerably before it is a precedence grammar ..... The final grammar could not be presented to a programmer as a reference to the language".*

Also in other situations where the chosen parsing method is based on other than precedence techniques one will need transformations to make the grammar suitable for the parsing method. Clearly, there is no need to worry about the final form of the grammar if the necessary transformations are done by the system itself.

† A lot of other names have been used, including translator writing system, parser generator and compiler-compiler.

These transformations can change the structure of the grammar. This can mean that the newly obtained grammar does not necessarily perform the same translation to semantic actions (which lead to code generation) as the original grammar. However, as the reader already did expect, if the transformations are done in such a way that a covering grammar is obtained, then we can 'fool' the user of a compiler writing system. This idea is illustrated in Figure 8.1.

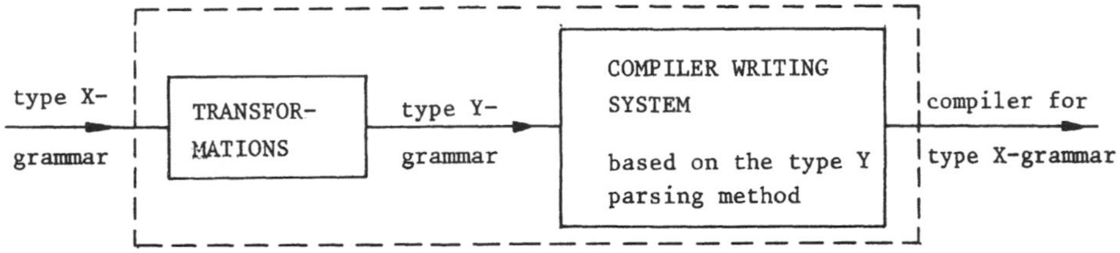

Figure 8.1. Compiler writing system for type X-grammars.

In the following chapters we will frequently refer to grammars which are LL(k) and LR(k). We will not confine ourselves to the formal introduction of these classes of grammars but we will give some introductory considerations on parsing. Moreover, these preliminaries make it possible to discuss a number of recent compiler writing systems and to mention those aspects which are of interest for our investigations in this monograph.

It is customary to distinguish between top-down and bottom-up parsing methods. The most important feature of (deterministic) top-down parsing is its simplicity.

TOP-DOWN

Consider a leftmost derivation

$$\omega_0 \overset{P_0}{\underset{L}{\Rightarrow}} \omega_1 \overset{P_1}{\underset{L}{\Rightarrow}} \ldots \omega_{n-1} \overset{P_{n-1}}{\underset{L}{\Longrightarrow}} \omega_n$$

where $\omega_0 = S$ and $\omega_n \in \Sigma^*$.

In top-down parsing the aim is to find the string $P_0 P_1 \ldots P_{n-1}$ of productions which have been used to derive ω_n from ω_0. If we know ω_{j-1} then the problem is how to find ω_j. Since we consider leftmost derivations we may write $\omega_{j-1} = wA\alpha$. If we know how A is rewritten at this point in order to obtain ω_n at the end, then the problem is solved. In deterministic (one-pass) top-down parsing this can be done, after we have seen $\omega_0, \omega_1, \ldots, \omega_{j-2}$ and $\omega_{j-1} = wA\alpha$, by looking at the symbols of ω_n which appear to the right of w. Notice that ω_n can be written as wv, where v is also a string of terminal symbols. If we allow a 'look-ahead' of at most k symbols then the class of grammars for which this method works is the class of LL(k) grammars.

Hence, if we have a leftmost derivation

$$S \overset{*}{\underset{L}{\Rightarrow}} wA\alpha$$

and productions $A \rightarrow \beta$ and $A \rightarrow \gamma$, then

$$FIRST_k(\beta\alpha) \cap FIRST_k(\gamma\alpha) \neq \emptyset$$

should imply $\beta = \gamma$.

LL-parsers and LL(k) grammars have been discussed in e.g. Lewis and Stearns [101], Rosenkrantz and Stearns [144], Culik [22], and Wood [173].

Because of the simplicity of the LL-parsing method much effort has been made to transform grammars into LL(k) or LL(1) grammars. For instance, in Wood [173], Foster [34], Stearns [158], Paull and Unger [130] and Lewis, Rosenkrantz and Stearns [100], algorithms are described to transform grammars into LL(1) form. In Paull and Unger [129] a transformation to simple deterministic grammars (a subclass of the LL(1) grammars) is described. Transformations into LL(k) grammars appear in Rosenkrantz and Lewis [143], Soisalon-Soininen and Ukkonen [157], Hunt and Rosenkrantz [69], Nijholt and Soisalon-Soininen [128] (cf. also Chapter 12) and Hammer [56].

In Beatty [10] various definitions of LL(k) grammars have been discussed and compared.

BOTTOM-UP

Many methods especially those which are used in compiler writing systems, are based on bottom-up techniques. Consider a rightmost derivation

$$\omega_n \overset{P_n}{\underset{R}{\Rightarrow}} \omega_{n-1} \underset{R}{\Rightarrow} \ldots\ldots \omega_2 \overset{P_2}{\underset{R}{\Rightarrow}} \omega_1 \overset{P_1}{\underset{R}{\Rightarrow}} \omega_0$$

where $\omega_n = S$ (the start symbol) and $\omega_0 \in \Sigma^*$.

In bottom-up parsing the goal is to find the string $P_1P_2\ldots P_n$ of productions which have been used (in the reversed order) to derive ω_0 from ω_n. If we write $\omega_j = \alpha Aw$ and $\omega_{j-1} = \alpha\beta w$, then the problem becomes to determine β and $|\alpha\beta|$ (the position of β) in ω_{j-1}, and by which symbol the substring β at position $|\alpha\beta|$ in ω_{j-1} should be replaced in order to obtain ω_j.
The pair $(A \rightarrow \beta, |\alpha\beta|)$ will be called the *handle* of ω_{j-1}. Bottom-up parsing starts with ω_0 and the process of determining the handle and replacing substring β by A

('reducing') should be continued, if possible, until the start symbol has been reached. In the deterministic one pass bottom-up parsing methods ω_j can be uniquely determined after having seen $\omega_0, \omega_1, \ldots, \omega_{j-2}$ and ω_{j-1}. The handle $(A \to \beta, |\alpha\beta|)$ of ω_{j-1} is determined from the uniqueness of the context of β. In these methods the context to the right of β which will be considered is restricted to a fixed number of k symbols $(k \geq 0)$.

In the most general case, if we have rightmost derivations.

$$S \overset{*}{\underset{R}{\Rightarrow}} \alpha A w \underset{R}{\Rightarrow} \alpha\beta w = \gamma w$$

and

$$S \overset{*}{\underset{R}{\Rightarrow}} \alpha' A' x \underset{R}{\Rightarrow} \alpha'\beta' x = \gamma w'$$

and the first k symbols of w and w' are the same, then the handles of γw and $\gamma w'$ should be the same. This conclusion implies that $\alpha = \alpha'$, $A = A'$, $\beta = \beta'$ and $x = w'$. Grammars which satisfy this condition are called LR(k) grammars. Consult section 8.2 for the formal definition. In Geller and Harrison [40] a detailed study of LR(k) grammars and languages is given. Numerous papers have appeared in which parsing methods for LR(k) grammars are described (e.g. in Knuth [76], DeRemer [25], Aho and Johnson [1] and Geller and Harrison [41]). Two subclasses, the SLR(1) grammars (*simple* LR(1)) and the LALR(1) grammars (*look-ahead* LR(1)) have become popular since they can be implemented efficiently and they can describe most of the usual programming language constructs. The context of β in ω_{j-1} can be used in a more restricted way. Other subclasses of the LR(k) grammars are then obtained. For example, the bounded (right) context grammars and the various classes of precedence grammars (cf. Aho and Ullman [3]).
The bottom-up parsing methods for these classes of grammars are also called *shift-reduce* methods. The reason is that in the implementation of these methods a stack is used and the operations of the parser are either *'shift* the next input symbol to the top of the stack' or *'reduce'* if a handle has been found and β, which is then on the top of the stack, will be replaced by A. For non-LR-grammars there will be action conflicts. That is, there will be situations where the parser can not decide whether a shift action or a reduce action should be done (a *shift/reduce conflict*) or the parser can not decide which reduce action has to be made *(a reduce/reduce conflict)*.

STRICT DETERMINISM

There is a third class of grammars, the class of strict deterministic grammars (Harrison and Havel [59 ,60,61]), which has turned out to be useful. This class is a subclass of the class of LR(0) grammars. Observations on the strict deterministic grammars and their parsing method, which has a hybrid character, that is, between top-down and bottom-up parsing, have lead to many useful ideas on parsing and translation (cf. Geller and Harrison [39,41], Lewis, Rosenkrantz and Stearns [99], Ukkonen [166] and Nijholt [116]). The definition of strict deterministic grammars (cf. Definition 8.5) is based on the productions of the grammar and not on the derivations. Therefore it is rather simple to decide whether a grammar is strict deterministic. In Chapter 9 the strict deterministic grammars will play an important role when we consider cover results for LR(k) grammars.

Before we will introduce the reader to the issues which will be treated in the following chapters we have a few remarks on developments in the theory of parsing and translation of context-free grammars.

Several authors have tried to generalize the ideas which are used in the parsing methods for LR(k) grammars, LL(k) grammars and some of their subclasses. For instance, deterministic context-sensitive parsing has been introduced for a subclass of the context-sensitive grammars (Walters [167]). Similarly, the class of indexed grammars has been subclassified into LL(k)- and LR(k)-type indexed grammars (Sebesta and Jones [152]).

Other authors have tried to define deterministic parsing methods for other than the well-known left and right parses. One may consult Colmerauer [20], Szymanski and Williams [159], Williams [169] and Kuo-Chung Tai [88]. In Demers [24], Brosgol [18] and Rosenkrantz and Lewis [143] parsing methods are defined which yield production directed parses. Semi-top-down parsing methods are discussed in Král and Demner [84] and in Kretinský [85].

Straightforward generalizations of the LL- and LR- grammar definitions are the LL-regular (Jarzabek and Krawczyk [73], Nijholt [114,126], Poplawsky [133]) and the LR-regular (Culik and Cohen [23]) grammar definitions.

Another approach in the theory of deterministic parsing has been the introduction of parsing methods for extended context-free grammars. In an extended context-free grammar each righthand side of a production consists of a regular expression (or, equivalently, a regular set or a finite automaton). In DeRemer [26], LaLonde [92,93], Madsen and Kristensen [105] and Thompson [161] extended LR-parsing is considered. In Lewi et al. [96,97] and in Heilbrunner [62] extended LL-grammars are discussed.

These ample discussions on parsing methods and grammar definitions are meant to give the reader some insight in the areas where the concept of grammar cover can be used. Many cover results, practically useful for parsing, have been obtained in Gray and Harrison [49]. As mentioned before, cover results can be used in compiler writing systems. Therefore we will consider some existing compiler writing systems.

Assume that the user of such a system provides the system with a set of productions (syntactic rules). The system will try to build a parser. This parser will be based on a specific parsing method. This may be, for example, a precedence method, an LALR-method or an LL-method.

If the syntactic rules, which are given as input, do not specify a grammar for which this type of parser can be built then the following may happen:

- the system reports its failure to build a parser to the user; it gives information why it failed and this information can be used by the user to change the syntactic rules (and the associated semantics) to make them appropriate for this system.
- the system can apply transformations to the input grammar in order to make it suitable for this method; clearly, it should be expected that this is done in such a way that the original semantics are preserved.
- although the syntactic rules do not specify a grammar which is suitable for the underlying parsing method of the compiler writing system, supplementary information, provided by the user as input to the system, will suffice to construct a correct parser.

Clearly, it is possible to combine the second and third alternative. Moreover, it is also possible that the system itself takes decisions which lead to a construction of a parser if the syntactic rules (whether or not with supplementary information) do not specify a grammar of the desired kind. In that case it remains for the user to verify that the parser has been built conform his intentions.

It should be mentioned that due to the latter possibilities it is possible to 'parse' ambiguous grammars. As was mentioned in Chapter 2 we use the name parser and parsing method even if the parser does not define a proper parse relation for a given grammar. Deterministic parsing of ambiguous grammars has been discussed by Aho, Johnson and Ullman [2]. Their ideas have not only been used in compiler writing systems but have also lead to more theoretical considerations (e.g., Ruzicka [145] Wharton [168] and Earley [29]).

We now want to mention a few examples of compiler writing systems. Feldman and Gries [30] gave an extensive survey of these systems until 1968. It is by no means our intention to give a new survey. In Räihä [135] and in Räihä and Saarinen [136] recent surveys can be found. Depending on the underlying top-down or bottom-up parsing method one can distinguish between the compiler writing systems.

<u>TOP-DOWN</u>

In Foster [34,35] a compiler writing system is described which is based on a top-down parsing method. The input grammar is made suitable for the top-down method by a special program SID (Syntax Improving Device) which performs some transformations on the grammar. One of these transformations is the elimination of left recursion. As we mentioned in section 5.1 this transformation yields a left-to-right and a right cover, thus preserving the original semantics.

Other examples of compiler writing systems which are based on LL(1) parsing methods can be found in Lewi et al.[96,97] (based on extended LL(1) grammars), Bochmann and Ward [16] and Milton, Kirchhoff and Rowland [112]. This latter system can use supplementary information, in this case obtained from the so-called 'inherited attributes', to build the parser. A consequence is that parsers can be constructed for non-LL(1) grammars. Cf. also Madsen and Jones [104].

BOTTOM-UP

In Lecarme and Bochmann [95] transformations are mentioned in their compiler writing system which make the input grammar suitable for the underlying precedence parsing method.

In Mickunas and Schneider [111] a parser generating system is described where the first phase of the system converts the input grammar into a simplified normal form for internal use. The transformation to this normal form preserves the original semantics. In fact, the authors give a definition of what we call a right cover. It is announced that an approach for their system is being developed which will involve transforming LR(k) grammars into grammars that can be parsed without considering look-ahead. These transformations to SLR(1) and LALR(1) grammars have been described in Mickunas and Schneider [110], Mickunas, Lancaster and Schneider [109] and Mickunas [108]. These transformations yield right covers.

Building compiler writing systems based on an LALR(1) parsing method has become a popular occupation. The Yacc (Yet another compiler-compiler) system of Johnson [74] is, due to its availability on the UNIX time sharing system, probably the most wide-spread system which is based on the LALR(1) method. The syntactic rules which are given as input to the system are converted to an LALR(1) parsing algorithm. If the input grammar is not LALR(1), then there will be parsing actions conflicts. Supplementary information provided by the user can help to resolve these conflicts and to produce a correct parser. Otherwise the system uses some built-in rules to resolve these conflicts. Hence, non-LALR(1) grammars can be converted to parsers and these parsers do not necessarily define proper parse relations.

The first LALR(1) based system is described in LaLonde, Lee and Horning [94]. Joliat [75] describes another LALR(1) based compiler writing system. In the compiler writing system HLP (Helsinki Language Processor), described in Räihä et al.[137], it is also required that the input grammar is LALR(1). The system produces diagnostic information to help the user to change his grammar to an LALR(1) grammar if the LALR (1) condition is not satisfied. Similar ideas as have been used in the Yacc system can be found in the system described by Kron, Hoffmann and Winkler [86]. In Lewi et al.[98] another system based on the LALR(1) method is described. Druseikis [28] has designed an SLR(1) parser generator.

Because of the popularity of the LALR(1) parsing method much effort has been made to investigate 'error-recovery' techniques for LR- and LALR-grammars (cf. Sippu and Soisalon-Soininen [153,154] and Graham, Haley and Joy [47]) and to obtain methods for efficient implementations for their parsing methods (cf. Thompson [161], DeRemer and Pennello [27] and Fisher and Weber [31]).

This section is concluded with a few remarks on the contents of the forthcoming sections.

In Harrison [57] and in Aho and Ullman [3] the question was raised whether each LR(k) grammar can be (right) covered with an LR(1) grammar. Starting form their work on the development of a compiler-compiler this question was answered affirmatively by Mickunas and Schneider [110], Mickunas, Lancaster and Schneider [109] and Mickunas [108]. In Nijholt [116] a more simple proof was given and some more general results were obtained. The following chapter is based on the latter paper. However, our treatment here will be more general.

In Chapter 9 we will introduce the concept of a valid DPDT (deterministic pushdown transducer). This transducer will be the model for the parsing methods which we will consider. Grammars will be called parsable with respect to a certain parse relation. We shall have the convention that the parsing methods assign one parse to each sentence. We can deterministically parse ambiguous grammars since the parse relation may be chosen in such a manner that for each sentence w in the language there is exactly one element (w,π) in the parse relation. For example, in Aho, Johnson and Ullman [2] LL(k) and LR(k) parsing methods are used to parse ambiguous grammars. The parse relations which are used are subclasses of the left and right parse relations. If a grammar G is parsable with respect to a certain parse relation f_G, then it will be shown that we can obtain a strict deterministic grammar or LR(1) grammar G' and a cover homomorphism ψ which is defined between $\ell_{G'}$ or $\bar{r}_{G'}$ and f_G.

In Chapter 10 we continue our discussion on cover results for normal forms of context-free grammars. Instead of arbitrary context-free grammars we will now consider the classes of LR-, LL-, and strict deterministic grammars.

8.2. PRELIMINARIES

We shall reproduce below a few definitions of grammars and automata which will frequently be referred to in the forthcoming sections. From now on we will only consider automata and transducers which are deterministic.

<u>DEFINITION 8.1.</u> A *deterministic pushdown automaton* (DPDA for short) is a pushdown

automaton $P = (Q,\Sigma,\Gamma,\delta,q_0,Z_0,F)$ which has the property that δ is a partial function from $Q \times (\Sigma \cup \{\varepsilon\}) \times \Gamma$ to $Q \times \Gamma^*$ and, for any $q \in Q$ and $Z \in \Gamma$, if $\delta(q,\varepsilon,Z)$ is defined then, for all $a \in \Sigma$, $\delta(q,a,Z)$ is undefined.

A CFL is said to be *deterministic* if it is accepted by some DPDA.

DEFINITION 8.2. A *deterministic pushdown transducer* (DPDT for short) is a pushdown transducer $(Q,\Sigma,\Gamma,\Sigma',\delta,q_0,Z_0,F)$ which has the property that δ is a partial function from $Q \times (\Sigma \cup \{\varepsilon\}) \times \Gamma$ to $Q \times \Gamma^* \times \Sigma'^*$ and, for any $q \in Q$ and $Z \in \Gamma$, if $\delta(q,\varepsilon,Z)$ is defined then, for all $a \in \Sigma$, $\delta(q,a,Z)$ is undefined.

DEFINITION 8.3. A *deterministic finite transducer* (DFT for short) is a six-tuple $M = (Q,\Sigma,\Sigma',\delta,q_0,F)$, where

(i) Q is a finite set of state symbols, Σ and Σ' are alphabets of input symbols and output symbols, respectively; $q_0 \in Q$ is the initial state and $F \subseteq Q$ is the set of final states.

(ii) δ is a partial function from $Q \times (\Sigma \cup \{\varepsilon\})$ to $Q \times \Sigma'^*$ such that, for any $q \in Q$, $\delta(q,\varepsilon)$ is defined implies $\delta(q,a)$ is undefined for all $a \in \Sigma$.

Definitions similar to those for a PDT (Definition 1.15) can be given for a configuration and a binary relation $\vdash$ on the configurations of a DFT. Likewise we define a translation

$$\tau(M) = \{(w,w') \mid (q_0,w,\varepsilon) \overset{*}{\vdash} (q,\varepsilon,w') \text{ for some } q \in F\}.$$

For any set $L \subseteq \Sigma^*$ we define

$$M(L) = \{y \mid x \in L \text{ and } (x,y) \in \tau(M)\}.$$

We need three definitions of subclasses of the context-free grammars. Again, we assume that each grammar which is considered is reduced. Our definition of LR(k) grammars is the same as the one used in Geller and Harrison [40].

DEFINITION 8.4. Let $k \geq 0$ and $G = (N,\Sigma,P,S)$ be a CFG such that $S \overset{+}{\underset{R}{\Rightarrow}} S$ is not possible in G. Grammar G is LR(k) if for each $w,w',x \in \Sigma^*$; $\gamma,\alpha,\alpha',\beta,\beta' \in V^*$; $A,A' \in N$, if

(i) $S \overset{*}{\underset{R}{\Rightarrow}} \alpha A w \underset{R}{\Rightarrow} \alpha\beta w = \gamma w$,

(ii) $S \overset{*}{\underset{R}{\Rightarrow}} \alpha' A' x \underset{R}{\Rightarrow} \alpha'\beta' x = \gamma w'$,

(iii) $k : w = k : w'$,

then $(A \to \beta, |\alpha\beta|) = (A' \to \beta', |\alpha'\beta'|)$.

For any $k \geq 1$, the class of LR(k) languages coincides with the class of deterministic languages. A language L is said to be *prefix-free* if u and uv in L implies $v = \varepsilon$. The class of prefix-free deterministic languages is a proper subclass of the class of LR(0) languages. Let $G = (N,\Sigma,P,S)$ be an LR(k) grammar. If S' is a symbol not already in N and $\perp$ is a symbol not already in Σ, then

$$G' = (N \cup \{S'\}, \Sigma \cup \{\perp\}, P \cup \{S' \to S\perp\}, S')$$

is LR(k) and L(G') is a prefix-free deterministic language (cf. Geller and Harrison [40]). The strict deterministic grammars (Harrison and Havel [59] generate exactly the prefix-free deterministic languages.

DEFINITION 8.5. A CFG $G = (N,\Sigma,P,S)$ is *strict deterministic* if there exists a partition π of V such that

(i) $\Sigma \in \pi$,

(ii) For any A, A' $\in$ N and $\alpha,\beta,\beta' \in V^*$, if $A \to \alpha\beta$, $A' \to \alpha\beta'$ and $A \equiv A'$ (mod π), then either

(a) both $\beta, \beta' \neq \varepsilon$ and $1 : \beta \equiv 1 : \beta'$ (mod π)

or

(b) $\beta = \beta' = \varepsilon$ and $A = A'$.

The class of strict deterministic grammars is a proper subclass of the class of LR(0) grammars. No strict deterministic grammar is left recursive. Moreover, if A, B $\in$ N and $\alpha \in V^*$, then $A \overset{+}{\Rightarrow} B\alpha$ implies $A \not\equiv B$. Any partition of V which satisfies (i) and (ii) is called a *strict* partition.

In general a strict deterministic grammar can have more than one strict partition. The set of strict partitions of a strict deterministic grammar is a semi-lattice under the meet operation. Therefore there exists a *minimal* strict partition. An algorithm which is presented in Harrison and Havel [59] computes this minimal strict partition. We recall this algorithm since it can be used to check our example grammars on strict determinism.

Let $G = (N,\Sigma,P,S)$ be a CFG. Let α, $\beta \in V^*$ and let A, B $\in$ V such that $A \neq B$ and we have $\alpha = \gamma A\alpha_1$ and $\beta = \gamma B\beta_1$ for some γ, α_1, $\beta_1 \in V^*$. Then the pair (A,B) is said to be the *distinguishing pair* of α and β.

ALGORITHM 8.1.

Input. A CFG $G = (N,\Sigma,P,S)$. The productions of P are denoted in the following way

$$P = \{A_i \to \alpha_i \mid i = 1,\ldots,|P|\}$$

Output. If G is strict deterministic, then the minimal strict partition is computed.
Method. [A] will denote the (unique) block of the partition which contains A.

Step 1. Initially define $\pi = \{\{A\} \mid A \in N\} \cup \{\Sigma\}$. Set $i = 0$.

Step 2. Set $i = j = i + 1$. If $i > |P|$ go to step 8.

Step 3. Set $j = j + 1$. If $j > |P|$ go to step 2.

Step 4. If $A_i \not\equiv A_j$ go to step 3. If α_i and α_j have no distinguish pair go to step 7.

Step 5. Let (B,C) be the (unique) distinguishing pair of α_i, α_j. If $B \equiv C$ go to step 3. If $B \in \Sigma$ or $C \in \Sigma$ go to step 7.

Step 6. Replace [B] and [C] in π by one new block $[B] \cup [C]$. Set $i = 0$ and go to step 2.

Step 7. Halt. G is not a strict deterministic grammar.

Step 8. Halt. G is strict deterministic under π.

End of the algorithm. □

There are three subclasses of the class of strict deterministic grammars which will be referred to in the forthcoming sections.

DEFINITION 8.6.

a. (Korenjak and Hopcroft [80]) A CFG $G = (N,\Sigma,P,S)$ is said to be a *simple deterministic grammar* if it is in GNF and, for each $A \in N$, if $A \to a\alpha$ and $A \to a\beta$ are in P, then $\alpha = \beta$.
b. (Pittl [131]) A CFG $G = (N,\Sigma,P,S)$ is said to be a *uniform grammar* if it is in GNF and there exists a strict partition π of V which satisfies: For all A, $A' \in N$, $a \in \Sigma$ and $\alpha, \alpha' \in N^*$, if $A \to a\alpha$ and $A' \to a\alpha'$ are in P, then $A \equiv A' \pmod{\pi}$ implies $|\alpha| = |\alpha'|$.
c. (Harrison and Havel [61]) A CFG $G = (N,\Sigma,P,S)$ is said to be a *real-time* strict deterministic grammar if it is ε-free and it has a minimal strict partition π such that, for all $A,A',B,B' \in N$ and $\alpha, \beta \in V^*$, if $A \to \alpha B$ and $A' \to \alpha B'\beta$ are in P, then $A \equiv A' \pmod{\pi}$ implies $\beta = \varepsilon$.

Any simple deterministic grammar $G = (N,\Sigma,P,S)$ is strict deterministic with respect to the partition $\pi = \{\Sigma,N\}$ and with respect to the minimal partition $\pi_0 = \{\Sigma\} \cup \{\{A\} \mid A \in N\}$. Any simple deterministic grammar is a uniform grammar, since π_0 is a uniform strict partition. Clearly, any uniform grammar is a real-time strict deterministic grammar. The following relation between these classes of grammars can be shown:

SIMPLE DET. $\subsetneq$ UNIFORM $\subsetneq$ REAL-TIME $\subsetneq$ STRICT.DET.

The third class of grammars which we will consider is the class of LL(k) grammars.

DEFINITION 8.7. Let $k \geq 0$ and $G = (N,\Sigma,P,S)$ a CFG. Grammar G is LL(k) if for each $w \in \Sigma^*$, $A \in N$ and $\alpha,\beta,\gamma \in V^*$, if $A \rightarrow \beta$ and $A \rightarrow \gamma$ are in P and

$$S \overset{*}{\underset{L}{\Rightarrow}} wA\alpha$$

then $FIRST_k(\beta\alpha) \cap FIRST_k(\gamma\alpha) \neq \emptyset$ implies $\beta = \gamma$.

Each LL(k) grammar is an LR(k) grammar. The class of LL(k) languages is properly included in the class of deterministic languages. For each $k \geq 1$ there exists an LL(k) language which is not LL(k-1). Clearly, the classes of simple deterministic grammars and LL(1) grammars in GNF coincide (except for a possible production $S \rightarrow \varepsilon$).

Whenever we speak of an LL- or an LR-grammar, then we mean a grammar for which there exists a non-negative integer k such that it is LL(k) or LR(k), respectively. It should be noted that instead of Definition 8.7 we could have given the following equivalent definition:

Let $k \geq 0$ and $G = (N,\Sigma,P,S)$ be a CFG. Grammar G is LL(k) if for each $w,x,y \in \Sigma^*$, $A \in N$ and $\alpha,\beta,\gamma \in V^*$, if $A \rightarrow \beta$ and $A \rightarrow \gamma$ are in P and

(i) $S \overset{*}{\underset{L}{\Rightarrow}} wA\alpha \underset{L}{\Rightarrow} w\beta\alpha \overset{*}{\underset{L}{\Rightarrow}} wx$

(ii) $S \overset{*}{\underset{L}{\Rightarrow}} wA\alpha \underset{L}{\Rightarrow} w\gamma\alpha \overset{*}{\underset{L}{\Rightarrow}} wy$

(iii) $k : x = k : y$

then $\beta = \gamma$.

This definition can easily be changed to a definition of strong LL(k) grammars.

DEFINITION 8.8. Let $k \geq 0$ and $G = (N,\Sigma,P,S)$ a CFG. Grammar G is *strong* LL(k) if for each $w_1,w_2,x,y \in \Sigma^*$, $A \in N$ and $\alpha_1,\alpha_2,\beta,\gamma \in V^*$, if $A \rightarrow \beta$ and $A \rightarrow \gamma$ are in P and

(i) $S \overset{*}{\underset{L}{\Rightarrow}} w_1A\alpha_1 \underset{L}{\Rightarrow} w_1\beta\alpha_1 \overset{*}{\underset{L}{\Rightarrow}} w_1x$

(ii) $S \overset{*}{\underset{L}{\Rightarrow}} w_2A\alpha_2 \underset{L}{\Rightarrow} w_2\gamma\alpha_2 \overset{*}{\underset{L}{\Rightarrow}} w_2y$

(iii) $k : x = k : y$

then $\beta = \gamma$.

It can be shown (cf. Rosenkrantz and Stearns [144]) that any LL(k) grammar can be converted into a structurally equivalent strong LL(k) grammar (cf. Definition

1.7. c). For k = 1 the notions of LL(k) and strong LL(k) coincide. Each simple deterministic grammar is LL(1) and instead of simple deterministic grammars they are also called simple LL(1) grammars. Cf. section 10.2 for a further discussion on LL(k) and strong LL(k) grammars.

CHAPTER 9

COVERS AND DETERMINISTICALLY PARSABLE GRAMMARS

9.1. DETERMINISTICALLY PARSABLE GRAMMARS

The well-known parsing methods for deterministic languages can be implemented by a DPDT. In Aho and Ullman [3] this has been made clear for a k-predictive parsing algorithm (for LL(k) grammars) and for a shift-reduce parsing algorithm (e.g. for LR(k) grammars). In Harrison and Havel [59,60] the same has been done for strict deterministic parsing. For other methods, although not always explicitly shown, it is mostly intuitively clear that the method can be implemented by a DPDT.

For LL(k) and LR(k) grammars this means that the proper parse relations ℓ_G and $\bar{r}_G$, respectively, are obtained as the translation of a DPDT. Clearly, each of these translations can also be obtained from a simple SDTS which has the LL(k) or LR(k) grammar as underlying grammar. Lewis and Stearns [101] have investigated this type of (simple) syntax directed translations. We list the two main theorems. The terminology is of Aho and Ullman [3]. The symbol $\perp$ is used as an endmaker.

<u>THEOREM 9.1.</u> Let $T = (N,\Sigma,\Delta,R,S)$ be a semantically unambiguous simple SDTS with an underlying LL(k) grammar. Then $\{(x\perp,y) \mid (x,y) \in \tau(T)\}$ can be defined by a DPDT.

Proof. See Aho and Ullman [3 ,p.731]. □

It follows that any production directed parse relation f_G of an LL(k) grammar G can be defined by a DPDT.

This is not the case for LR(k) grammars. We have to restrict the notion of a simple SDTS such that its translation can be defined by a DPDT. A simple SDTS $T = (N,\Sigma,\Delta,R,S)$ where each rule is of the form $A \to \alpha,\beta$ with β in $N^*\Delta^*$, is called a *simple postfix* SDTS.

<u>THEOREM 9.2.</u> Let $T = (N,\Sigma,\Delta,R,S)$ be a semantically unambiguous simple postfix SDTS with an underlying LR(k) grammar. Then $\{(x\perp,y) \mid (x,y) \in \tau(T)\}$ can be defined by a DPDT.

Proof. See Aho and Ullman [3 ,p.733]. □

It follows from this theorem that the right parse relation $\bar{r}_G$ of an LR(k) grammar G can be defined by a DPDT.

There exist classes of grammars which properly include the class of LL(k) grammars and which are properly included in the class of LR(k) grammars. For these classes less severe restrictions on the simple SDTS than are necessary for LR(k) grammars need to be introduced. Cf. Soisalon-Soininen [155] and Rosenkrantz and Lewis [143] for such classes of grammars.

These observations motivate us to consider deterministic pushdown transducers as a model for parsers. If f_G is a parse relation for CFG G, then we call DPDT P a parser for G and f_G if $\tau(P) = f_G$. A more formal definition will be given shortly.

We require that at most one parse will be given to each sentence of L(G). This condition restricts the class of deterministic pushdown transducers. This can be seen with the help of the following example.

<u>EXAMPLE 9.1.</u>

Consider grammar G with productions

1. $S \rightarrow S$
2. $S \rightarrow a$

A production directed parse relation is the set

$$\bar{r}_G = \{(a,21^k) \mid k \geq 0\}$$

A DPDT for G and $\bar{r}_G$ is defined by

$$P = (\{q_0,q_e\},\{a\},\{S\},\{1,2\},\delta,q_0,S,\{q_e\})$$

such that

$$\delta(q_0,a,S) = (q_e,S,2)$$

and

$$\delta(q_e,\varepsilon,S) = (q_e,S,1).$$

Here we have $\tau(P) = \{(a,21^k) \mid k \geq 0\} = \bar{r}_G$. We do not want to consider this DPDT as a deterministic parser. End of Example 9.1.

A DPDT will be called a *parser* for G and f_G if and only if it is valid for G and f_G.

<u>DEFINITION 9.1.</u> A DPDT P is *valid* for CFG G and parse relation f_G if

(i) $\tau(P) = \{(x\bot,y) \mid (x,y) \in f_G\}$

(ii) no moves can be made in the final states of P.

LEMMA 9.1. Let P be a valid DPDT for CFG G and parse relation f_G. If $(w,\pi_1) \in f_G$ and $(w,\pi_2) \in f_G$, then $\pi_1 = \pi_2$.

Proof. Assume that pushdown transducer P is a valid DPDT for CFG G and parse relation f_G. Suppose (w,π_1) and (w,π_2) are in f_G. Since P is deterministic all the moves which are made to reach a final state with w are the same for a translation from $w\perp$ to π_1 and a translation from w to π_2. Since there are no possible moves in this final state it follows that $\pi_1 = \pi_2$. □

Let us call a parse relation f_G *unambiguous* if (w,π_1) and (w,π_2) in f_G implies $\pi_1 = \pi_2$.

LEMMA 9.2. If f_G is an unambiguous parse relation of CFG G, then any DPDT P with $\tau(P) = \{(w\perp,\pi) \mid (w,\pi) \in f_G\}$ can be converted to a valid DPDT for G and f_G.

Proof. Suppose that

$$(q_0,w\perp,Z_0,\varepsilon) \overset{*}{\vdash} (q_e,\varepsilon,\gamma,u)$$

in $P = (Q,\Sigma,\Gamma,\delta,q_0,Z_0,F)$, where $q_e \in F$ and q_e is the first final state which is reached after the symbols of $w\perp$ have been read. Hence, $(w\perp,u) \in \tau(P)$. It is possible that ε-moves are made from q_e to an other final state q_e'. However, during these moves no output can be given. Otherwise f_G would not be unambiguous. It follows that we can delete $\delta(q_e,\varepsilon,1\!:\!\gamma)$ from the definition of δ. This can be done for each final state. The modified DPDT is a valid DPDT for G and f_G. □

Any LR(k) grammar G is unambiguous. Therefore the parse relation $\bar{r}_G$ is unambiguous. Since, by Theorem 9.2, for any LR(k) grammar G and parse relation $\bar{r}_G$ there exists a DPDT P which satisfies $\tau(P) = \{(w\perp,x) \mid (w,x) \in \bar{r}_G\}$ it follows from Lemma 9.2 that G and $\bar{r}_G$ have a valid DPDT.

Notice that any CFG G which generates a deterministic language has a DPDT which is valid for G and parse relation $\{(w,\varepsilon) \mid w \in L(G)\}$. If DPDT P is valid for G and parse relation f_G, then, necessarily, L(G) is deterministic.

Now classes of grammars can be defined with respect to parse relations.

DEFINITION 9.2. A CFG G is an f_G-*parsable grammar* if there exists a DPDT which is valid for G and f_G.

With this definition we can introduce, among others, *left parsable* grammars ($f_G = \ell_G$), *right parsable* grammars ($f_G = \bar{r}_G$), *left corner parsable* grammars ($f_G = \ell c_G$) and *left part parsable* grammars ($f_G = \ell p_G$).

In Aho and Ullman [3] the left and right parsable grammars were introduced with the help of a simple SDTS.

Notice that if G is an f_G-parsable grammar, then it is not necessarily the case that G is unambiguous since we have not required that f_G is a proper parse relation. Therefore we can deterministically parse ambiguous grammars in the sense described in Aho, Johnson and Ullman [2]. It follows from the discussion before Definition 9.2 that each f_G-parsable grammar generates a deterministic language.

The left parsable and the right parsable grammars are also discussed in Aho and Ullman [3]. There we can find the following inclusion diagram

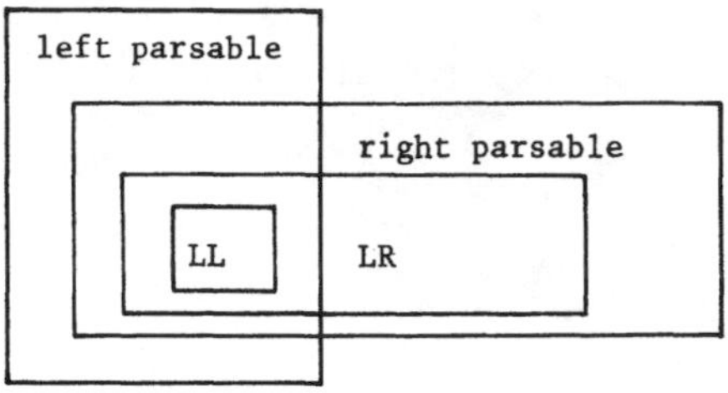

Figure 9.1. Diagram for the left and right parsable grammars.

Clearly, any LL(k) grammar is left parsable and any LR(k) grammar is right parsable. The classes of LR-grammars and left parsable grammars are incomparable. Examples showing this and showing the proper inclusions in the diagram can be found in [3].

To show that, e.g. an example grammar G is not left parsable one can use the argument of [3,p.272]. That is, try to construct a (valid) DPDT for G and ℓ_G. If this turns out to be impossible, then G is not left parsable.

We show some results which are not in the diagram. Mostly these results are of the form: Grammar G is f_G-parsable but not h_G-parsable, thus establishing incomparability of classes of grammars. Except for the first example we will confine ourselves to the presentation of some example grammars and mention their properties. This is justified by the simplicity of the examples. The properties of each grammar can be checked by using the type of argument mentioned above.

Consider the grammar G with productions

1. $S \to 1S1$
2. $S \to 1S2$
3. $S \to 1$

Grammar G is not left parsable. Suppose there is a valid DPDT P for G and ℓ_G. In translating P can only start with emitting output after the last symbol of a sentence $u \in L(G)$ has been read. (Formally this can be seen as follows. Consider two sentences w1 and w2 in L(G). Translation of w1 with P leads to a sequence of moves such that

$$(q_0,w1\perp,Z_0,\varepsilon) \overset{*}{\vdash} (r,1\perp,\gamma,\pi_w) \overset{*}{\vdash} (q_e,\varepsilon,\gamma',\pi')$$

where q_0 is the initial state, r is an intermediate state and q_e is a final state. Suppose that $\pi_w \neq \varepsilon$. Necessarily, $1 : \pi_w = 1$. Now consider the translation of w2 with P. Here we have

$$(q_0,w2\perp,Z_0,\varepsilon) \overset{*}{\vdash} (r,2\perp,\gamma,\pi_w).$$

Since $1 : \pi_w = 1$ we can not have that a final state is reached form the configuration $(r,2\perp,\gamma,\pi_w)$. Since P is deterministic there is no other way for $w2\perp$ to reach a final state via $(r,2\perp,\gamma,\pi_w)$. It follows that $\pi_w = \varepsilon$. End of the formal argument.)

To recognize a sentence of the form 1^n11^k2v with $k + 1 + |v| = n$ we have to verify that $|2v| \leq n$. To make this possible we should have shifted the symbols 1 on the stack. Verification can now be done by popping one symbol from the stack for this first symbol and for each following symbol until the endmarker is read. (It is left to the reader to formalize this argument.) It follows that when we have read the endmarker we do not have available the information on the stack which is necessary to give the correct output (It is left to the reader to formalize this argument.) Therefore grammar G is not left parsable.

In a similar way it can be shown that G is not right parsable. Since the left corner parses coincide with the left parses and the left part parses with the right parses it follows that G is not left corner parsable and not left part parsable. However, G is parsable with respect to the proper parse relation

$$f_G = \{(1^m u, u31^n) \mid u \in \{\varepsilon\} \cup 2\{1,2\}^*,\ m > 0,\ n \geq 0$$
$$|u| \leq m - 1$$
$$|u| + m \text{ is odd}$$
$$|u| + n = (m + |u| - 1)/2\}.$$

Informally, read 1's and shift them onto the stack until the first 2 (if any) is encountered. Continue reading, emit for each symbol 2 (including the first 2) the symbol 2 and for each symbol 1 the symbol 1 and pop for each symbol which is read (including the first 2) one symbol from the stack. If the endmarker is read, emit the symbol 3 and pop one symbol from the stack. It remains to check whether the stack contains an even number of 1's. For each pair of 1's the symbol 1 should be emitted.

EXAMPLE 9.2.

(a) G_0: $S \rightarrow AEa \mid DBd$

$A \rightarrow a$

$D \rightarrow a$

$E \rightarrow bEc \mid bc$

$B \rightarrow bBc \mid bc$

Grammar G_0 is unambiguous. $L(G_0)$ is a deterministic language. There does not exist a proper parse relation f_G such that G_0 is f_G-parsable.

(b) G_1: $S \rightarrow 1A \mid 1B \mid 0$

$A \rightarrow S0$

$B \rightarrow S1$

Grammar G_1 is strict deterministic. G_1 is right parsable but not left parsable, left corner parsable or left part parsable.

(c) G_2: $S \rightarrow 0S0 \mid 0S1$

$S \rightarrow BAb \mid CAc$

$C \rightarrow a$

$B \rightarrow a$

$A \rightarrow BA \mid a$

Grammar G_2 is left part parsable (for a proper parse relation ℓp_G) but not left parsable, left corner parsable or right parsable.

(d) G_3: $S \rightarrow AH \mid BCb \mid DCc$

$A \rightarrow S$

$H \rightarrow 0$

$C \rightarrow BC \mid a$

$D \rightarrow a$

Grammar G_3 is left corner parsable (for a proper parse relation ℓc_G) but not left parsable, left part parsable or right parsable.

(e) G_4: $S \rightarrow A0 \mid A1 \mid BDb \mid CDc$

$A \rightarrow S$

$B \rightarrow a$

$C \rightarrow a$

$D \rightarrow E \mid a$

$E \rightarrow BD$

Grammar G_4 is left parsable, but not left corner parsable, left part parsable or right parsable.

Notice that for all these examples the parse relations ℓc_G and ℓp_G are proper. The properties of the grammars are collected in Table IX.

	G_0	G_1	G_2	G_3	G_4
left parsable	no	no	no	no	yes
left corner parsable	no	no	no	yes	no
left part parsable	no	no	yes	no	no
right parsable	no	yes	no	no	no

Table IX. Parsability and proper parse relations.

9.2. ON THE COVERING OF DETERMINISTICALLY PARSABLE GRAMMARS.

In this section we show that the part of the grammar which is parsed by the DPDT is covered with a strict deterministic or LR(1) grammar. The part of the grammar which is parsed is defined by the parse relation. The proof of this cover result is in fact well-known. Any DPDA which satisfies a few simple conditions can be converted to a strict deterministic grammar. The generalization of this conversion to a DPDT is the 'Standard Construction' of section 1.3.1 when applied to a DPDT. In this way we obtain a simple SDTS T with an underlying grammar G which has the property that each leftmost derivation (left parse) of a sentence $w \in L(G)$ can be mapped on the translation of w by T. This observation (the 'Standard Observation' of section 1.3.1) is well-known; it can be concluded from the results in Aho and Ullman [3] and it is explicitly mentioned in Brosgol [17]. This observation was related to covers in Nijholt [116] by considering parsing as a restricted way of translating. We need a few technical preliminaries before we can give the full argument.

Many of the transformations which will be used in the forthcoming sections are well-known or have been treated in the preceding sections. This means that we already know that they preserve language. Now consider two grammars G' and G, and parse relations $f_{G'}$ and h_G. We will mostly be in a situation where $L(G') = L(G)$, $g = \langle \varphi, \psi \rangle$ is a (total) parse homomorphism and φ is the identity homomorphism.

<u>LEMMA 9.3.</u> Let G' and G be grammars with parse relations $f_{G'}$ and h_G, respectively. Let $g = \langle \varphi, \psi \rangle$ be a parse homomorphism, $g : f_{G'} \to h_G$, such that φ is the identity homomorphism. If $L(G') = L(G)$ and G is unambiguous then g is a cover homomorphism.

Proof. Trivial. □

Hence, if we know that G is unambiguous, L(G') = L(G) and we restrict ourselves to parse homomorphisms $g = \langle\varphi,\psi\rangle$ where φ is the identity homomorphism, then we may conclude that G' covers G if $(w,\pi') \in f_{G'}$ implies $(w,\psi(\pi')) \in h_G$. Now we return to our discussion on valid DPDT's. As we mentioned in section 3.3 we will no longer consider homomorphism φ.

We will convert an arbitrary valid DPDT to a valid DPDT which is more amenable for a conversion to a strict deterministic grammar.

<u>LEMMA 9.4.</u> Let P be a valid DPDT for CFG G and parse relation f_G. Then we can construct a valid DPDT P' for G and f_G which accepts with empty pushdown list in one final state.

Proof. Let $P = (Q,\Sigma,\Gamma,\Delta,\delta,q_0,Z_0,F)$ be valid for CFG G and parse relation f_G. Define DPDT

$$P' = (Q \cup Q_1 \cup \{q_e\},\Sigma,\Gamma \cup \{Z_{00}\},\Delta,\delta',q_0,Z_{00},\{q_e\})$$

where $Q_1 = \{q' \mid q \in F\}$ and where q_e and the states q' in Q_1 are newly introduced states. Z_{00} is a new pushdown symbol not already in Γ and δ' is equal to δ except for the following cases:

(i) Define $\delta'(q_0,\varepsilon,Z_{00}) = (q_0,Z_0Z_{00},\varepsilon)$

(ii) For all $q \in F$, for all corresponding $q' \in Q_1$ and for all $X \in \Gamma$, define

$$\begin{aligned}
\delta'(q,\varepsilon,Z_{00}) &= (q_e,\varepsilon,\varepsilon) \\
\delta'(q,\varepsilon,X) &= (q',\varepsilon,\varepsilon), \qquad X \neq Z_{00} \\
\delta'(q',\varepsilon,X) &= (q',\varepsilon,\varepsilon), \qquad X \neq Z_{00} \\
\delta'(q',\varepsilon,Z_{00}) &= (q_e,\varepsilon,\varepsilon).
\end{aligned}$$

It can easily be verified that P' satisfies the desired conditions. □

<u>LEMMA 9.5.</u> Let P be a valid DPDT for CFG G and parse relation f_G. Suppose that L(G) is prefix-free. Then we can construct a DPDT P' which accepts with empty pushdown list in one final state such that $\tau(P') = f_G$.

Proof. Let $P = (Q,\Sigma,\Gamma,\Delta,\delta,q_0,Z_0,\{q_e\})$ be valid for CFG G and parse relation f_G. Due to Lemma 9.4 we may assume that P accepts with empty pushdown list in one final state. P defines the set $\tau(P) = \{(w\bot,\pi) \mid (w,\pi) \in f_G\}$. If $(w\bot,\pi) \in \tau(P)$, then

$$(q_0,w\bot,Z_0,\varepsilon) \overset{*}{\vdash} (q,\bot,\gamma,u) \vdash (q',\varepsilon,\gamma',u') \overset{*}{\vdash} (q_e,\varepsilon,\varepsilon,\pi).$$

Since $\delta(q,\perp,1:\gamma)$ is defined, $\delta(q,\varepsilon,1:\gamma)$ is undefined. Otherwise P would be non-deterministic. If $\delta(q,a,1:\gamma)$ is defined for $a \neq \perp$, then since L(G) is prefix-free, application of this step can never lead to a final state. Therefore, for each $a \in \Sigma$, $a \neq \perp$ we can delete $\delta(q,a,1:\gamma)$ from the definition of δ. If we replace in the definition of δ

$$\delta(q,\perp,Z) = (q',\alpha,\beta)$$

by

$$\delta(q,\varepsilon,Z) = (q',\alpha,\beta),$$

for any q, q' in Q, Z in Γ, α in Γ^* and β in Δ^*, then $\tau(P) = f_G$. □

For convenience we repeat the 'Standard Construction' of section 1.3.1. If it is applied to a DPDT which accepts with empty pushdown list in one final state, then a simple SDTS is obtained which has an underlying strict deterministic grammar. Only the productions of the underlying grammar are given. Each production is followed by the output which is given in the rule of the DPDT from which this production has been obtained.

<u>ALGORITHM 9.1.</u>

Input. A DPDT $P = (Q,\Sigma,\Gamma,\Delta,\delta,q_0,Z_0,\{q_e\})$ which accepts with empty pushdown list in one final state.

Output. A strict deterministic grammar $G' = (N',\Sigma,P',S')$.

Method. (1) Define $N' = \{[pAq] \mid p,q \in Q, A \in \Gamma\}$ and $S' = [q_0Z_0q_e]$.

(2) P is defined as follows. Let $\delta(p,a,A) = (r,X_1\ldots X_k,y)$, with $a \in \Sigma \cup \{\varepsilon\}$. If $k > 0$, then P' contains the productions

$$[pAq_k] \rightarrow a[rX_1q_1]\ldots[q_{k-1}X_kq_k] \quad \langle y\rangle$$

for all sequences of states $q_1,\ldots,q_k$ in Q. If $k = 0$, then P' will contain $[pAR] \rightarrow a \quad \langle y\rangle$. □

It follows from Harrison and Havel [59] that G' is a strict deterministic grammar. In the sequel we assume that in a grammar obtained with this construction all useless symbols and productions are removed. This removal can be done such that strict determinism is preserved (Harrison and Havel [59]). Grammar G' simulates with leftmost derivations the moves of the DPDT. Therefore we have the following theorem.

<u>THEOREM 9.3.</u> Let G be an f_G-parsable grammar. Assume that L(G) is prefix-free. Then there exists a strict deterministic grammar G' such that $G'[\ell/f]G$.

Proof. If G is f_G-parsable then there exists a valid DPDT P for G and f_G. We may assume that P accepts with empty pushdown list in one final state. Moreover, since L(G) is prefix-free we may assume that $\tau(P) = f_G$.
With the help of Algorithm 9.1 P can be converted into a strict deterministic grammar G' with label set $\Delta_{G'}$. Define a homomorphism $\psi : \Delta_{G'}^* \to \Delta_G^*$ such that each production which is obtained from a step

$$\delta(p,a,A) = (r, X_1X_2 \ldots X_k, y),$$

where $a \in \Sigma \cup \{\varepsilon\}$, $k \geq 0$, is mapped on the string $y \in \Delta_G^*$.

Now, if $(w,\pi') \in \ell_{G'}$ then $(w,\psi(\pi')) \in \tau(P)$. Hence $(w,\psi(\pi')) \in f_G$. Moreover, due to the construction, for each $(w,\pi) \in f_G$ there exists a π' such that $(w,\pi') \in \ell_{G'}$ and $\psi(\pi') = \pi$. Notice that this is the 'Standard Observation' of section 1.3.1. We conclude that $G'[\ell/f]G$. □

It follows that each right parsable grammar (e.g. an LR(k) grammar) with a prefix-free language is left-to-right covered with a strict deterministic grammar. Any left parsable grammar (e.g. an LL(k) grammar) with a prefix-free language is left covered with a strict deterministic grammar. We will deal with the prefix-free condition shortly.

First we notice that this result is not quite satisfactory from the point of view of our model of parsing. A strict deterministic or LR-parsing method yields right parses. Moreover, there exist strict deterministic grammars which are not left parsable. Therefore we try to change Theorem 9.3 so that the right parse relation of the strict deterministic grammar can be considered.

<u>THEOREM 9.4.</u> Let G be an f_G-parsable grammar. Assume that L(G) is prefix-free. Then there exists a strict deterministic grammar G" such that $G''[\bar{r}/f]G$.

Proof. Our starting point is the valid DPDT P in the proof of Theorem 9.3 from which a strict deterministic grammar G' is constructed. Hence, $G'[\ell/f]G$. We will construct a strict deterministic grammar G" such that G' will play the role of the intermediate grammar of Observation 4.1.

Let $P = (Q,\Sigma,\Gamma,\Delta,\delta,q_0,Z_0,\{q_e\})$ be the DPDT. We assume that the elements of δ are uniquely labeled by numbers from the set $H = \{1,2,\ldots,h\}$, where h is the total number of three-tuples for which δ is defined. From P we construct a new DPDT P', also valid for G and f_G. Define

$$P' = (Q,\Sigma,\Gamma \cup \{H_i \mid i \in H\}, \Delta,\delta',q_0,Z_0,\{q_e\})$$

with $\{H_i \mid i \in H\} \cap \Gamma = \emptyset$ and δ' is defined as follows.

(i) If in P, for $k > 0$ and $a \in \Sigma \cup \{\varepsilon\}$

$$i.\delta(p,a,A) = (r,X_1\ldots X_k,y) \qquad (1)$$

then define in P'

$$i'.\delta'(p,a,A) = (r,H_iX_1\ldots X_k,\varepsilon) \qquad (2)$$

and

$$i''.\delta'(r,\varepsilon,H_i) = (r,\varepsilon,y). \qquad (3)$$

(ii) If in P, for $a \in \Sigma \cup \{\varepsilon\}$

$$j.\delta(p,a,A) = (r,\varepsilon,z) \qquad (4)$$

then define in P'

$$j'.\delta'(p,a,A) = (r,\varepsilon,z). \qquad (5)$$

Notice that for any input string the final state of P is reached with an application of a step of the form $\delta(p,a,A) = (q_e,\varepsilon,z)$ with $a \in \Sigma \cup \{\varepsilon\}$. Such a step remains unaltered and P' accepts with empty pushdown list in one final state and $\tau(P') = \tau(P)$. If P' is converted to a CFG then a strict deterministic grammar G" is obtained. Clearly, $G''[\ell/f]G$. We show that also $G''[\bar{r}/f]G$.

Define a partition π_t of $\Delta_{G'}$ as follows. Two productions of G' are in the same block of π_t if and only if they are obtained from the same step $\delta(p,a,A) = (r,X_1\ldots X_k,y)$ of P ($a \in \Sigma \cup \{\varepsilon\}, k \geq 0$). Clearly all the productions in a block B of π_t are mapped on the same string $y \in \Delta_G^*$ by the cover homomorphism ψ. Therefore π_t is a transitivity partition. Define $\delta_t : \Delta_{G'}^* \to \pi_t^*$ by $\delta_t(i) = B$, for $i \in B$. We have the transitivity relation

$$\tilde{\ell}_{G'} = \{(w,\pi) \mid (w,\pi') \in \ell_{G'} \text{ and } \delta_t(\pi') = \pi\}.$$

It remains to verify that there exists a homomorphism $\psi_t : \Delta_{G''}^* \to \pi_t^*$ such that, if $(w,\pi) \in \bar{r}_{G''}$, then $(w,\psi_t(\pi)) \in \tilde{\ell}_{G'}$. Notice that $\tilde{\ell}_{G'}$ can play the role of parse relation h_G in Lemma 9.3. Therefore we do not have to verify the surjectivity of ψ_t (the second condition of Observation 4.1).

The verification can be done by induction on the length of the derivations using an argument almost similar to that of the proof of Theorem 5.4. We confine ourselves to the definition of ψ_t. We refer to the situations (i) and (ii) displayed above.

(i) Productions of the form

$$[pAq_k] \rightarrow a[rX_1q_1]....[q_{k-1}X_kq_k] \quad \langle y\rangle$$

are obtained from (1) (for CFG G') and productions of the form

$$[pAq_k] \rightarrow a[rH_ir][rX_1q_1]...[q_{k-1}X_kq_k] \quad \langle\varepsilon\rangle$$

$$[rH_ir] \rightarrow \varepsilon \quad \langle y\rangle$$

are obtained from (2) and (3) (for CFG G"). Define

$$\psi_t([pAq_k] \rightarrow a[rH_ir][rX_1q_1]...[q_{k-1}X_kq_k]) = \varepsilon,$$

for any sequence of states $q_1,\ldots,q_k$, and

$$\psi_t([rH_ir] \rightarrow \varepsilon) = \{[pAq_k] \rightarrow a[rX_1q_1]...[q_{k-1}X_kq_k] \mid q_1,\ldots,q_k \in Q\}.$$

(ii) A production

$$[pAr] \rightarrow a \quad \langle z\rangle$$

is obtained from (4) for CFG G', and a production

$$[pAr] \rightarrow a \quad \langle z\rangle$$

is obtained from (5) for CFG G". Define

$$\psi_t([pAr] \rightarrow a) = \{[pAr] \rightarrow a\}.$$

With this definition of $\psi_t : \Delta^*_{G"} \rightarrow \pi^*_t$ we conclude from Observation 4.1 that $G"[\bar{r}/f]G$. □

Up to this point we have been concerned with context-free grammars with prefix-free languages. In the following theorem we show the existence of an LR(1) grammar G' which covers an f_G-parsable grammar G.

<u>THEOREM 9.5.</u> Let G be an f_G-parsable grammar. Then there exists an LR(1) grammar G' such that $G'[\ell/f]G$ and $G'[\bar{r}/f]G$.

Proof. Let $G = (N,\Sigma,P,S)$ be an f_G-parsable grammar. Define grammar $G_0 = (N \cup \{S_0\}, \Sigma \cup \{\bot\}, P \cup \{S_0 \rightarrow S\bot\}, S_0)$ where S_0 is a newly introduced nonterminal and $\bot$ is the endmarker. Production $S_0 \rightarrow S\bot$ will be given label 0. $L(G_0)$ is prefix-free. The set $h_{G_0} = \{(w\bot,\pi 0) \mid (w,\pi) \in f_G\}$ is a parse relation for G_0. Since G is f_G-parsable there exists a valid DPDT $P' = (Q,\Sigma \cup \{\bot\},\Gamma,\Delta,\delta,q_0,Z_0,\{q_e\})$ such that $\tau(P') = \{(w\bot,\pi) \mid (w,\pi) \in f_G\}$.

Notice that P' has steps of the form $\delta(q,X,Z) = (q_e,\varepsilon,\rho)$, where $q \in Q$, $X \in \Sigma \cup \{\varepsilon\} \cup \{\bot\}$, $Z \in \Gamma$, q_e is a final state and $\rho \in \Delta^*$. Each of these steps may be replaced by $\delta(q,X,Z) = (q_e,\varepsilon,\rho 0)$. In this way we obtain a DPDT $P_0 = (Q,\Sigma \cup \{\bot\},\Gamma,\Delta \cup \{0\},\delta',q_0,Z_0,\{q_e\})$, where δ' represents the modified δ. Clearly, $\tau(P_0) = h_{G_0}$. P_0 can be converted to a strict deterministic grammar G_1 such that $G_1[\bar{r}/h]G_0$ and $G_1[\ell/h]G_0$. We modify grammar G_1 in such a way that an LR(1) grammar G' is obtained which satisfies $G'[\bar{r}/f]G$ and $G'[\ell/f]G$.

Grammar $G_1 = (N_1,\Sigma \cup \{\bot\},P_1,S_1)$ has productions with $\bot$ in the righthand side. These productions are of the form $A \to \bot B_1B_2\ldots B_n$, $n \geq 0$ and $A,B_1,B_2,\ldots,B_n \in N_1$. Necessarily, $B_1B_2\ldots B_n \overset{*}{\Rightarrow} \varepsilon$. Let $P_\bot$ be the subset of P_1 which contains only productions of this form. Define

$$R = \{A \to B_1B_2\ldots B_n \mid A \to \bot B_1B_2\ldots B_n \in P_\bot\},$$

where each production in R has the same label as the corresponding production in $P_\bot$. Notice that, due to the fact that P_0 is deterministic, if $A \to \bot B_1B_2\ldots B_n$ is in P_1, then there does not exist $A \to B_1B_2\ldots B_n$ in P_1. Let R' be the complement of $P_\bot$ in P_1. Define $G' = (N',\Sigma',P',S')$, where $N' = N_1$, $\Sigma' = \Sigma$, $P' = R \cup R'$ and $S' = S_1$. Clearly, $L(G') = L(G)$.

Let $\psi : \Delta^*_{G_1} \to \Delta^*_{G_0}$ be the cover homomorphism for which we have $G_1[\bar{r}/h]G_0$ and $G_1[\ell/h]G_0$. Define $\psi' : \Delta^*_{G'} \to \Delta^*_G$ as follows:
For each $p \in P'$,

$$\psi'(p) = \pi_1\pi_2 \text{ if } \psi(p) = \pi_1 0 \pi_2, \text{ for some } \pi_1, \pi_2 \in \Delta^*_G, \text{ and}$$

$$\psi'(p) = \psi(p), \text{ otherwise.}$$

Now it should be clear that $G'[\bar{r}/f]G$ and $G'[\ell/f]G$. We prove that G' is an LR(1) grammar. Suppose that G' is not LR(1). Then there exist $\gamma,\alpha,\alpha',\beta,\beta' \in (N' \cup \Sigma')^*$; $w,w',x \in \Sigma'^*$; $A,A' \in N'$ such that

(1) $S' \overset{*}{\underset{R}{\Rightarrow}} \alpha Aw \underset{R}{\Rightarrow} \alpha\beta w = \gamma w$,

(2) $S' \overset{*}{\underset{R}{\Rightarrow}} \alpha'A'x \underset{R}{\Rightarrow} \alpha'\beta'x = \gamma w'$, and

(3) $1 : w = 1 : w'$ and $(A \to \beta,|\alpha\beta|) \neq (A' \to \beta',|\alpha'\beta'|)$.

We prove that this assumption leads to a contradiction with G_1 being strict deterministic (and hence LR(0)). Notice that the only difference between G' and G_1 is the sets R and $P_\bot$. For the derivations (1) and (2) we have corresponding derivations (1') and (2') in G_1. That is, if in (1) or (2) a production of R is used, then the corresponding production of $P_\bot$ is used in (1') or (2'). Otherwise the same productions are used. We distinguish between two cases.

Case 1. Assume $1 : w = \varepsilon$. Then $w = w' = \varepsilon$ and G' is ambiguous. The corresponding derivations for (1) and (2) can be written as

$$(1')\ S' \overset{*}{\underset{R}{\Rightarrow}} \gamma'$$

and

$$(2')\ S' \overset{*}{\underset{R}{\Rightarrow}} \gamma''$$

where

$\gamma' = \gamma_1 \bot \gamma_2$, with $\gamma_1\gamma_2 = \gamma$, if a production of R is used in (1),

$\gamma' = \gamma$, if no production of R is used in (1),

$\gamma'' = \gamma_3 \bot \gamma_4$, with $\gamma_3\gamma_4 = \gamma$, if a production of R is used in (2),

$\gamma'' = \gamma$, if no production of R is used in (2).

It is sufficient to consider the following three cases.

a. The case $\gamma' = \gamma'' = \gamma$ is impossible since G_1 is unambiguous.

b. Let $\gamma' = \gamma_1 \bot \gamma_2$ and $\gamma'' = \gamma = \gamma_1\gamma_2$. Notice that $\gamma_2 \overset{*}{\Rightarrow} \varepsilon$. If $v \in L(\gamma_1)$ then both v and $v\bot$ in $L(G_1)$. This is impossible.

c. Let $\gamma' = \gamma_1 \bot \gamma_2$ and $\gamma'' = \gamma_3 \bot \gamma_4$. Assume that γ_1 is a proper prefix of γ_3. The symmetric case, γ_3 is a proper prefix of γ_1, is omitted. We can write $\gamma' = \gamma_1 \bot \rho \gamma_4$ and $\gamma'' = \gamma_1 \rho \bot \gamma_4$. For any $w \in L(\gamma_1)$ we have $w\bot \in L(\gamma')$ and $w\bot \in L(\gamma'')$. Therefore, since G_1 is unambiguous, either $\gamma' \overset{*}{\underset{R}{\Rightarrow}} \gamma''$ or $\gamma'' \overset{*}{\underset{R}{\Rightarrow}} \gamma'$. We consider the first case. The second case needs a similar argument. If $\gamma_1 \bot \rho \gamma_4 \overset{*}{\underset{R}{\Rightarrow}} \gamma_1 \rho \bot \gamma_4$, then $\gamma_1 \overset{*}{\underset{R}{\Rightarrow}} \gamma_1 \rho$. Since $\rho \overset{*}{\Rightarrow} \varepsilon$, we have a derivation $\gamma_1 \overset{*}{\underset{R}{\Rightarrow}} \gamma_1 \rho \overset{*}{\underset{R}{\Rightarrow}} \gamma_1$, which means that G_1 is ambiguous. Contradiction.

There remains the situation $\gamma' = \gamma'' = \gamma_1 \bot \gamma_2$. In this case it should be verified that the pairs in G_1 which correspond with the pairs $(A \to \beta, |\alpha\beta|)$ and $(A' \to \beta', |\alpha'\beta'|)$ of G' are also different. This can easily be done and therefore we obtain a contradiction with G_1 being LR(0).

Case 2. Assume $1 : w \in \Sigma$. The derivations in G_1 corresponding to (1) and (2) are

$$(1')\ S' \overset{*}{\underset{R}{\Rightarrow}} \alpha A w \bot \underset{R}{\Rightarrow} \alpha\beta w \bot = \gamma w \bot,$$

and

$$(2a')\ S' \overset{*}{\underset{R}{\Rightarrow}} \alpha' A' x \bot \underset{R}{\Rightarrow} \alpha'\beta' x \bot = \gamma w' \bot,$$

or

$$(2b')\ S' \overset{*}{\underset{R}{\Rightarrow}} \alpha'A' \underset{R}{\Rightarrow} \alpha'\bot = \gamma w'\bot.$$

Since G_1 is LR(0) it follows that we can not have $(A \to \beta, |\alpha\beta|) \neq (A' \to \beta', |\alpha'\beta'|)$ for these derivations.

We may conclude from Case 1 and Case 2 that the assumption that G' is not LR(1) leads to a contradiction with G_1 being LR(0). □

A consequence of this theorem is that any LR(k) grammar is right covered and left-to-right covered by an LR(1) grammar.

We conclude this section with a few observations on the relation between parsability and covers.

THEOREM 9.6. Let h_G be a parse relation for CFG G. If G is not an h_G-parsable grammar, then there does not exist an $f_{G'}$-parsable grammar G' such that G'[f/h]G.

Proof. If G' is $f_{G'}$-parsable then there exists a DPDT P such that $\tau(P) = \{(w\bot,\pi) \mid (w,\pi) \in f_{G'}\}$. Assume that G'[f/h]G under a cover homomorphism $\psi : \Delta_{G'}^{*} \to \Delta_{G}^{*}$. A DPDT P' is obtained from P by changing any rule $\delta(q,X,Z) = (r,X_1\ldots X_k,y)$ from P to $\delta(q,X,Z) = (r,X_1\ldots X_k,\psi(y))$. DPDT P' is valid for G and h_G. However, this is in contradiction with G is not h_G-parsable. Therefore G'[f/h]G is not possible. □

This theorem is simple but useful. Consider e.g. the CFG G with productions

$$S \to aAc \mid aAd$$
$$A \to aAb \mid b$$

Grammar G can be simply transformed to LL(1) grammar G' with productions

$$S \to aAH$$
$$A \to aAb \mid b$$
$$H \to c \mid d$$

However, since G is not a left parsable grammar, it follows from Theorem 9.6 that there does not exist an LL(1) grammar which left covers G.

Suppose that we are in a situation as described in Theorem 9.6. Hence G'[f/h]G is not possible. Can we obtain the result that G' covers G for these two parse relations if we use, instead of a homomorphism, a DFT to map the parses of $f_{G'}$ on the parses of h_G? The answer is negative because of the following argument. If G' is

$f_{G'}$-parsable then there exists a valid DPDT P for G' and $f_{G'}$. If M is the DFT which maps the parses of $f_{G'}$ on the parses of h_G, then we can combine DPDT P and DFT M to a DPDT P' which is valid for G and h_G. Since grammar G is not h_G-parsable, we have obtained a contradiction.

The construction of P' is defined below. Without loss of generality we may assume that DFT M has no ε-moves. We assume that it is clear from the construction that P' has the desired properties.

ALGORITHM 9.2.

Input. A DPDT $P = (Q,\Sigma,\Gamma,\Delta_G,\delta,q_0,Z_0,F)$ and a DFT $M = (Q_M,\Delta_G,\Delta_{G'},\delta_M,p_0,Q_M)$.

Output. A DPDT P' such that $\tau(P') = \{(w\bot,M(\pi)) \mid (w\bot,\pi) \in \tau(P)\}$.

Method. Define

$$P' = (Q \times Q_M,\Sigma,\Gamma,\Delta_{G'},\delta', (q_0,p_0),Z_0,F \times Q_M),$$

where δ' is defined as follows.

For each step $\delta(q,a,Z) = (r,\alpha,\omega)$ in P, with $a \in \Sigma \cup \{\varepsilon\}$, define

(i) $\delta'((q,p),a,Z) = ((r,t),\alpha,\omega')$, if $|\omega| \geq 1$ and $(p,\omega,\varepsilon) \overset{*}{\vdash} (t,\varepsilon,\omega')$ in M

(ii) $\delta'((q,p), a,Z) = ((r,p),\alpha ,\varepsilon)$ if $|\omega| = 0$. This concludes the construction of P'.□

It follows that replacing the homomorphism in the cover definition by a DFT-mapping does not help in finding a left covering grammar for the example grammar G displayed above.

CHAPTER 10

NORMAL FORM COVERS FOR DETERMINISTICALLY PARSABLE GRAMMARS

In the three sections of this chapter we will frequently refer to the algorithms which were introduced in the Chapters 4 and 5. The cover properties of the transformations defined by these algorithms were proved in these chapters.

To obtain similar cover properties for LL(k), strict deterministic and LR(k) grammars one has to prove that these algorithms preserve LL-ness, strict determinism and LR-ness, respectively. This is done in the forthcoming sections. Cover-tables will be constructed for these three classes of grammars.

10.1. NORMAL FORM COVERS FOR LL(k) GRAMMARS

As we did in Chapter 6 for context-free grammars, here we will construct a cover-table for LL(k) grammars. We start with some general results and then we will actually construct the table. This section is concluded with a short evaluation of the results from a more practical point of view.

Our first lemma is in fact Lemma 4.4, but now formulated for LL(k) grammars.

LEMMA 10.1. For any LL(k) grammar G and production directed parse relation h_G there exists an LL(k) grammar G' such that both $G'[\ell/h]G$ and $G'[\bar{r}/h]G$, $(k \geq 0)$.

Proof. It is sufficient to show that CFG G' of Lemma 4.4 is LL(k) if grammar G is. CFG G' is obtained from G by inserting new nonterminal symbols in the righthand sides of the productions. For each production the inserted nonterminal symbol is unique. The argument that this does not change the LL(k) property is elementary and is therefore omitted. □

We do not know whether ε-productions in an LL(k) grammar can be eliminated in such a way that a right covering LL-grammar is obtained. It is well-known that any LL(k) language can be given an LL(k+1) grammar without ε-productions. This change from k to k + 1 is necessary, since there exist LL(k) languages which can not be generated by ε-free LL(k) grammars. We will consider a subclass of the LL(k) grammars.

DEFINITION 10.1. Let $G = (N,\Sigma,P,S)$ be a CFG which has ε-productions. Grammar G is said to have *strict ε-productions* if, for any $A \in N, \varepsilon \in L(A)$ implies $L(A) = \{\varepsilon\}$.

We recall the definition of a representation of a righthand side of a production (Definition 4.3). If $A \to \alpha$ is a production, $L(\alpha) \neq \{\varepsilon\}$, then a representation of α is a factorization $\alpha = \alpha_0X_1\alpha_1X_2 \dots \alpha_{n-1}X_n\alpha_n$, $n > 0$, which satisfies

(i) $X_i \in N \cup \Sigma$ and $L(X_i) \neq \{\varepsilon\}$, $1 \leq i \leq n$.

(ii) $\alpha_i \in N^*$ and $\varepsilon \in L(\alpha_i)$, $0 \leq i \leq n$.

<u>LEMMA 10.2.</u> Let $G = (N,\Sigma,P,S)$ be a CFG with strict ε-productions. Each righthand side α, with $L(\alpha) \neq \{\varepsilon\}$, of a production $A \rightarrow \alpha$ in P has exactly one representation.

Proof. Straightforward and therefore omitted. □

<u>THEOREM 10.1.</u> Any LL(k) grammar with strict ε-productions can be right covered with an ε-free LL(k) grammar ($k \geq 0$).

Proof. Since each LL(k) grammar is non-left-recursive, we can use Algorithm 4.1 to eliminate the ε-productions of an LL(k) grammar G. Grammar G' which is obtained by this algorithm is ε-free and $G'[\bar{r}/\bar{r}]G$. We show that if G has strict ε-productions, then G' is LL(k).

Assume for the sake of contradiction that G' is not LL(k). Then there exists a derivation

$$S' \overset{*}{\underset{L}{\Rightarrow}} wC\omega'$$

and productions $C \rightarrow \alpha'$ and $C \rightarrow \beta'$ in G' such that $\alpha' \neq \beta'$ and

$$\text{FIRST}_k(\alpha'\omega') \cap \text{FIRST}_k(\beta'\omega') \neq \emptyset.$$

Hence, $|\text{rhs}(C)| \geq 2$. Suppose C is of the form $[\gamma\underline{X}\alpha]$ with $\alpha \neq \varepsilon$. It follows from step (2) of the algorithm that there exist productions of the form $B \rightarrow \beta_1$ and $B \rightarrow \beta_2$ in P with $\beta_1 \neq \beta_2$ and $\varepsilon \in L(\beta_1) \cap L(\beta_2)$. This implies that G is ambiguous which is impossible for an LL(k) grammar. Therefore C can not be of the form $[\gamma\underline{X}\alpha]$ with $\alpha \neq \varepsilon$. Similarly, C can not be of the form $[\gamma\underline{X}]$ with $\gamma \neq \varepsilon$ and $X \in \Sigma$.

There remains the case that $C = [\gamma\underline{A}]$ with $A \in N$ and $\gamma \in N^*$. Therefore, we can write

$$S' \overset{*}{\underset{L}{\Rightarrow}} w[\gamma\underline{A}]\omega'$$

A straightforward induction on the lengths of the derivations learns that

$$S' \overset{*}{\underset{L}{\Rightarrow}} w[\gamma\underline{A}]\omega'$$

implies

$$S \overset{*}{\underset{L}{\Rightarrow}} wA\omega$$

where ω is obtained from ω' by deleting the square brackets '[' and ']'.

We consider possible righthand sides for the nonterminal $[\gamma\underline{A}]$. If $A \to \alpha$ and $A \to \beta$ are in P, with $\alpha \neq \beta$, $L(\alpha) \neq \{\varepsilon\}$ and $L(\beta) \neq \{\varepsilon\}$, then we have productions $[\gamma\underline{A}] \to \alpha'$ and $[\gamma\underline{A}] \to \beta'$ in P', where α' is the unique representation of α and β' is the unique representation of β. Any nonterminal symbol $[\gamma\underline{X}\delta]$ of N' has the property that if $[\gamma\underline{X}\delta] \stackrel{*}{\Rightarrow} w$ for some $w \in \Sigma^+$, then $\gamma X\delta \stackrel{*}{\Rightarrow} w$ in G, and w is derived from X (cf. the remarks which follow Algorithm 4.1). It immediately follows that if in G' the condition

$$\mathrm{FIRST}_k(\alpha'\omega') \cap \mathrm{FIRST}_k(\beta'\omega') = \emptyset$$

is not satisfied then we obtain a corresponding situation in G with $\alpha \neq \beta$ and

$$\mathrm{FIRST}_k(\alpha\omega) \cap \mathrm{FIRST}_k(\beta\omega) \neq \emptyset,$$

which is not possible since G is LL(k). It follows that G' is LL(k). □

When applied to an arbitrary LL(k) grammar, Algorithm 4.1 does not necessarily produce an LL-grammar.

The next transformation which we want to consider is the left part transformation (Algorithm 5.3). Since any LL(k) grammar is unambiguous, we do not have to bother about single productions (cf. the remark following Algorithm 5.3).

It should be noted that the usual transformation from an ε-free LL(k) grammar to an LL(k) grammar in GNF gives rise to a more simple proof. However, apart from including this proof for completeness sake, we will also use it in the proof of Lemma 10.4

<u>THEOREM 10.2.</u> For any ε-free LL(k) grammar G there exists an LL(k) grammar G' in GNF such that $G'[\ell/x]G$, $\ell \leq x \leq \ell p$ and $k \geq 0$.

Proof. From Theorem 5.2 we may conclude that Algorithm 5.3, when applied to an ε-free NLR grammar G, yields a CFG G' in GNF such that $G'[\ell/x]G$. Since any ε-free LL(k) grammar is ε-free NLR, it remains to verify that G' is LL(k) when G is LL(k).

Assume for the sake of contradiction that G' is not LL(k). Then there exists a derivation

$$[S] \stackrel{*}{\underset{L}{\Rightarrow}} w[Ai\alpha]\omega$$

and productions

$$[Ai\alpha] \to \beta$$

and

$$[Ai\alpha] \rightarrow \gamma$$

with $\beta \neq \gamma$, such that

$$FIRST_k(\beta\omega) \cap FIRST_k(\gamma\omega) \neq \emptyset.$$

Let $A \rightarrow \alpha X_0\varphi$ be the ith production of P. Since $\beta \neq \gamma$, there exist chains

$$\pi_1 = X_0X_1 \ldots X_{n-1}X_n$$

and

$$\pi_2 = Y_0Y_1 \ldots Y_{m-1}Y_m$$

with $X_0 = Y_0$, in $CH(X_0)$ and left production chains

$$\rho_1 = i_0i_1 \ldots i_{n-1} \text{ in } LP(\pi_1)$$

and

$$\rho_2 = j_0j_1 \ldots j_{m-1} \text{ in } LP(\pi_2)$$

such that $\rho_1 \neq \rho_2$ and

$$[Ai\alpha] \rightarrow X_n\xi([X_{n-1}i_{n-1}X_n] \ldots [X_0i_0X_1][Ai\alpha X_0]) = [Ai\alpha] \rightarrow \beta$$

and

$$[Ai\alpha] \rightarrow Y_m\xi([Y_{m-1}j_{m-1}Y_m] \ldots [Y_0j_0Y_1][Ai\alpha Y_0]) = [Ai\alpha] \rightarrow \gamma.$$

Write $\omega = [C_0k_0\delta_0][C_1k_1\delta_1] \ldots [C_\ell k_\ell \delta_\ell]$.
We omit the proof of the following claim.

<u>CLAIM 1.</u> If

$$[S] \overset{*}{\underset{L}{\Rightarrow}} w[Ai\alpha][C_0k_0\delta_0][C_1k_1\delta_1] \ldots [C_\ell k_\ell \delta_\ell]$$

where

$$i.\ A \to \alpha X_0\varphi$$

$$k_0.\ C_0 \to \delta_0\varphi_0$$

$$k_1.\ C_1 \to \delta_1\varphi_1$$

$$\cdot$$

$$\cdot$$

$$\cdot$$

$$\cdot$$

$$\cdot$$

$$k_\ell.\ C_\ell \to \delta_\ell\varphi_\ell$$

are productions in P, then

$$S \overset{*}{\underset{L}{\Rightarrow}} uA\varphi_0\varphi_1\ldots\varphi_\ell \overset{i}{\underset{L}{\Rightarrow}} u\alpha X_0\varphi\varphi_0\varphi_1\ldots\varphi_\ell \overset{*}{\underset{L}{\Rightarrow}} uvX_0\varphi\varphi_0\ldots\varphi_\ell$$

where $uv = w$.

The following claim, which is also independent of the fact that G is LL(k), follows from the two more general claims which are used in the proof of Theorem 5.2. Compare also the remark which follows Lemma 5.3.

CLAIM 2. If $i.A \to \alpha\varphi$ in P, $\varphi \neq \varepsilon$, then

$[Ai\alpha] \overset{*}{\Rightarrow} w$ if and only if $\varphi \overset{*}{\Rightarrow} w$.

Since

$$FIRST_k(X_n\xi([X_{n-1}i_{n-1}X_n]\ldots.[X_0i_0X_1][Ai\alpha X_0])\omega)$$
$$\cap$$
$$FIRST_k(Y_m\xi([Y_{m-1}j_{m-1}Y_m]\ldots.[Y_0j_0Y_1][Ai\alpha Y_0])\omega)$$
$$\neq \emptyset,$$

there exist

$$x_1 \in L(X_n\xi([X_{n-1}i_{n-1}X_n]\ldots[X_0i_0X_1][Ai\alpha X_0])),$$

$$y_1 \in L(\omega),$$

$$x_2 \in L(Y_m\xi([Y_{m-1}j_{m-1}Y_m]\ldots[Y_0j_0Y_1][Ai\alpha Y_0])),\ \text{and}$$

$$y_2 \in L(\omega),$$

such that $k : x_1y_1 = k : x_2y_2$.

From the two claims it follows that there exist $x_1 \in L(X_0\varphi)$, $x_2 \in L(Y_0\varphi)$, $y_1 \in L(\varphi_0\varphi_1\ldots\varphi_\ell)$ and $y_2 \in L(\varphi_0\varphi_1\ldots\varphi_\ell)$ such that $k : x_1y_1 = k : x_2y_2$. However, since $\rho_1 \neq \rho_2$ it follows that we have obtained a contradiction with G being LL(k). We conclude that G' is LL(k). □

Next we consider the possibility to obtain a right covering LL(k) grammar in GNF from an ε-free LL(k) grammar. We use Algorithm 5.4 to obtain an almost-GNF grammar which is LL(k) and Algorithm 5.5 to transform an almost-GNF LL(k) grammar to a GNF LL(k+1) grammar. However, first we have to show that any ε-free LL(k) grammar can be made to satisfy the input conditions of Algorithm 5.4.

Notice that if a grammar is LL(k) and we replace a production of the form $A \to \alpha a \beta$, $\alpha \neq \varepsilon$, by the productions $A \to \alpha H_a \beta$ and $H_a \to a$, then the newly obtained grammar is also LL(k). We now have to verify that the elimination of single productions does not change the LL(k) property of a grammar.

<u>LEMMA 10.3.</u> For any ε-free LL(k) grammar G there exists an ε-free LL(k) grammar G' without single productions such that $G'[\ell/\ell]G$ and $G'[\bar{r}/\bar{r}]G$ $(k \geq 0)$.

Proof. We can use the method for eliminating single productions which is described in the proof of Lemma 4.6. However, since any LL(k) grammar is unambiguous, we can simplify this method. Only step (i) of this method needs to be considered.

Let $G = (N,\Sigma,P,S)$ be an ε-free LL(k) grammar. Define

$$P_1 = \{A \to \alpha \, \langle i \rangle \mid i.A \to \alpha \text{ is in } P - P_0\}$$

where P_0 is the subset of P which contains all the single productions.

For any $A \in N$, if $A \overset{\delta}{\Rightarrow} B \overset{i}{\Rightarrow} \gamma$ is a derivation in G such that $\delta \neq \varepsilon$ and either $|\gamma| \geq 2$ or $\gamma \in \Sigma$, then add $A \to \gamma \, \langle \pi \rangle$ to the set P_1. To obtain a left cover, define $\pi = \delta i$. To obtain a right cover, define $\pi = i\delta^R$. The desired grammar G' is now obtained by reducing the grammar (N,Σ,P_1,S). Clearly, G' is LL(k) when grammar G is LL(k). □

It follows that we can use Algorithm 5.4 to obtain an almost-GNF grammar G' such that G' is LL(k).

<u>LEMMA 10.4.</u> Any ε-free LL(k) grammar G can be transformed to an almost-GNF grammar G' such that $G'[\bar{r}/\bar{r}]G$ and G' is LL(k) $(k \geq 0)$.

Proof. If Algorithm 5.4 is applied to an LL(k) grammar G which satisfies the input conditions, then an almost-GNF grammar G' which right covers G is produced. We show that G' is LL(k). The following trick is used.

If Algorithm 5.3 is applied to an LL(k) grammar G with $P \subseteq N \times (\Sigma N^* \cup NN^+)$, then we obtain a grammar G_1 which is LL(k) and which has productions which are of the following forms:

(i) $[S] \to X_n\xi([X_{n-1}i_{n-1}X_n]\ldots[X_1i_1X_2][Si_0X_1])$

and

(ii) $[A i\alpha] \to X_n\xi([X_{n-1}i_{n-1}X_n]\ldots[X_0i_0X_1][Ai\alpha X_0])$.

Grammar G' which is obtained by using Algorithm 5.4 can be constructed from G_1 in the following way.

(a) If in (i) $\xi([X_{n-1}i_{n-1}X_n]\ldots[Si_0X_1]) = \varepsilon$ (hence, i_0. $S \to X_n$ in P), then $[S] \to X_n$ in P'. If in (i) $\xi([X_{n-1}i_{n-1}X_n]\ldots[Si_0X_1]) \neq \varepsilon$, then

$$[S] \to H_{i_{n-1}}\xi([X_{n-1}i_{n-1}X_n]\ldots[Si_0X_1])$$

and

$$H_{i_{n-1}} \to X_n$$

are in P'.

(b) If in (ii) $\xi([X_{n-1}i_{n-1}X_n]\ldots[X_0i_0X_1][Ai\alpha X_0]) = \varepsilon$, then $[Ai\alpha] \to X_n$ is in P'. If in (ii) $\xi([X_{n-1}i_{n-1}X_n]\ldots[X_0i_0X_1][Ai\alpha X_0]) \neq \varepsilon$, then

$$[Ai\alpha] \to H_{i_{n-1}}\xi([X_{n-1}i_{n-1}X_n]\ldots[X_0i_0X_1][Ai\alpha X_0])$$

and

$$H_{i_{n-1}} \to X_n$$

are in P'.

It follows that either we have the same productions for G_1 and G' (viz. $[S] \to X_n$ or $[Ai\alpha] \to X_n$) or we have a simple change of a production of the form $C \to c\gamma$ for LL(k) grammar G_1 to productions $C \to H\gamma$ and $H \to c$. It is easily verified that a situation $C \to H_1\gamma$, $C \to H_2\gamma$, $H_1 \to c$ and $H_2 \to c$ can never be introduced because of our choice of nonterminal symbols $H_{i_{n-1}}$. This simple transformation on the productions of an LL(k) grammar does not change the LL(k) property. This concludes the proof of Lemma 10.4. □

Any almost-GNF LL-grammar can be transformed to a GNF LL-grammar which right covers the original grammar. Algorithm 5.5 is used to show this.

LEMMA 10.5. Any almost-GNF LL(k) grammar G can be transformed to a GNF LL(k+1) grammar G' such that $G'[\bar{r}/\bar{r}]G$ ($k \geq 0$).

Proof. When Algorithm 5.5 is applied to an almost-GNF LL(k) grammar G, then a GNF grammar G' is obtained which satisfies $G'[\bar{r}/\bar{r}]G$. We show that G' is LL(k+1).

Consider Figure 10.1 where, once more, the general idea of the transformation is displayed. In this figure the part of the transformation which changes the parse

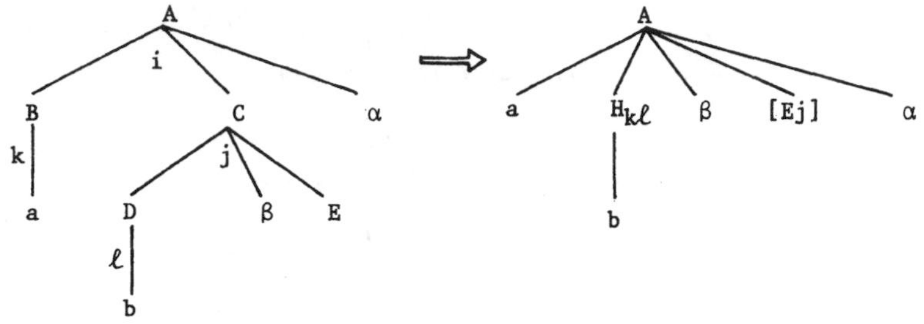

Figure 10.1. Step 1 of Algorithm 5.5.

trees is displayed. In step 2 of the algorithm it is possible that the production

$$A \to aH_{k\ell}\beta[Ej]\alpha$$

of this figure is changed to a production

$$[Ap] \to aH_{k\ell}\beta[Ej]\alpha$$

for some $p \in \Delta_G$. Now consider a derivation

$$S \overset{*}{\underset{L}{\Rightarrow}} wC'\omega'$$

in G' and two productions $C' \to \beta'$ and $C' \to \gamma'$ in P' with $\beta' \neq \gamma'$.

For the nonterminal symbols of N' we can distinguish the following forms:

(i) [Ap] with $A \in N$ and $p \in \Delta_G$

(ii) A with $A \in N$

(iii) $H_{k\ell}$ with k, ℓ in Δ_G

Any nonterminal symbol of the form $H_{k\ell}$ can only be lefthand side of one production. It follows that A' is of the form [Ap] or A. Let N" be the subset of N' which contains the nonterminal symbols of the form A and [Ap]. Define a homomorphism $f : N''^* \to N^*$ by defining f(A) = A and f([Ap]) = A.

<u>CLAIM.</u> Let $C \in N''$. If $S \overset{*}{\underset{L}{\Rightarrow}} wC'\omega'$ in G', then $S \overset{*}{\underset{L}{\Rightarrow}} wC\omega$ in G, where $C\omega = f(C'\omega')$.

Proof of the Claim. The proof can be done by a straightforward induction on the lengths of the derivations. Instead of doing the proof for startsymbol S, the proof should be done for an arbitrary nonterminal symbol $A' \in N''$. □

Notice that in this claim ω' is always in N''^*. It follows from Claim 1 of the proof of Lemma 5.5 that, for any $A' \in N''$, if $A' \overset{*}{\Rightarrow} w$ in G', then $f(A') \overset{*}{\Rightarrow} w$ in G.

Now suppose that G' is not LL(k+1). Then we can have a situation described above with

$$\text{FIRST}_{k+1}(\beta'\omega') \cap \text{FIRST}_{k+1}(\gamma'\omega') \neq \emptyset.$$

Now it should be verified that for all possible occurences of β' and γ' this situation gives rise to a contradiction with G being LL(k). We confine ourselves to the verification of the situation where

$$C' \to \beta' = C \to aH_{k\ell}\beta_1[Ei]\alpha_1$$

and

$$C' \to \gamma' = C \to aH_{mn}\beta_2[Fj]\alpha_2.$$

It follows that in G we have a derivation $S \overset{*}{\underset{L}{\Rightarrow}} wC\omega$ and productions $C \to D_1Q_1\alpha_1$, $C \to D_2Q_2\alpha_2$, $D_1 \to a$, $D_2 \to a$, $Q_1 \to D_3\beta_1E$, $Q_2 \to D_4\beta_2F$, $D_3 \to b$ and $D_4 \to c$.

This situation is illustrated in Figure 10.2.

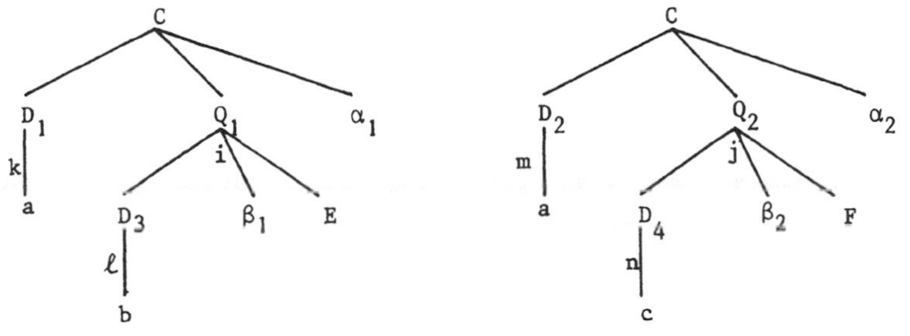

Figure 10.2. Productions of grammar G.

Due to our assumption we have strings

$$x_1 \in L(ab\beta_1[Ei]\alpha_1)$$

$$y_1 \in L(\omega')$$

$$x_2 \in L(ac\beta_2[Fj]\alpha_2)$$

$$y_2 \in L(\omega')$$

such that $k + 1 : x_1y_1 = k + 1 : x_2y_2$.

It follows that in G we can not distinguish the productions $C \to D_1Q_1\alpha_1$ and $C \to D_2Q_2\alpha_2$. Therefore, $C \to D_1Q_1\alpha_1 = C \to D_2Q_2\alpha_2$. This implies that in G we have a derivation

$$S \overset{*}{\underset{L}{\Rightarrow}} waQ\omega_0$$

with $Q = Q_1 = Q_2$ and $\omega_0 = \alpha_1\omega = \alpha_2\omega$. Moreover, we have productions $Q \to D_3\beta_1E$ and $Q \to D_4\beta_2F$. Since $k + 1 : x_1y_1 = k + 1 : x_2y_2$ we have that

$$\mathrm{FIRST}_k(D_3\beta_1E\omega_0) \cap \mathrm{FIRST}_k(D_4\beta_2F\omega_0) \neq \emptyset.$$

Since G is LL(k) we must conclude that $D_3\beta_1E = D_4\beta_2F$. But this implies that $\beta' = \gamma'$, contradicting $\beta' \neq \gamma'$.

The verification of the other possibilities for β' and γ' can be done along similar lines. It follows that G' is LL(k+1). □

From Lemma 10.4 and Lemma 10.5 we obtain the following corollary.

<u>COROLLARY 10.1.</u> Any ε-free LL(k) grammar G can be transformed to an LL(k+1) grammar G' in GNF such that $G'[\bar{r}/\bar{r}]G$ $(k \geq 0)$.

<u>THEOREM 10.3.</u> Any LL(k) grammar G with strict ε-productions can be transformed to an LL(k+1) grammar G' in GNF such that $G'[\bar{r}/\bar{r}]G$ $(k \geq 0)$.

Proof. Combine Theorem 10.1 and Corollary 10.1. □

Notice that for any LL(k) grammar G with strict ε-productions we can find an LL(k) grammar G' such that $G'[\bar{r}/x]G$, with $\ell \leq x \leq \bar{r}$ (Lemma 10.1). Grammar G' has also strict ε-productions and we can use Theorem 10.3 to obtain the following corollary.

<u>COROLLARY 10.2.</u> Any LL(k) grammar G with strict ε-productions can be transformed to an LL(k+1) grammar G' in GNF such that $G'[\bar{r}/x]G$, with $\ell \leq x \leq \bar{r}$ and $k \geq 0$.

Note. There remain two problems which have not been investigated. Firstly, can we eliminate ε-productions from an arbitrary LL(k) grammar in such a way that a right covering LL(k+1) grammar is obtained? Secondly, can the transformation from almost-GNF LL(k) to GNF LL(k+1) be done in such a way that the right covering grammar is LL(k) instead of LL(k+1)?

We now show negative cover results for LL(k) grammars. In Chapter 6 we presented a grammar G_0 with productions

$$S \to 0SL \mid 1RL$$
$$R \to 1RL \mid 2$$
$$L \to \varepsilon$$

Grammar G_0 has the property that there does not exist an ε-free CFG G' by which it is left covered. Since grammar G_0 is LL(1) we have the following corollary.

COROLLARY 10.3. Not every LL(k) grammar ($k \geq 1$) can be left covered with an ε-free grammar.

Consider the grammar G_N with productions

$S \to 0H_{00}S$	$H_{00} \to 0$
$S \to 0H_{01}R$	$H_{01} \to 1$
$S \to 1H_{11}R$	$H_{11} \to 1$
$S \to 1H_{12}$	$H_{12} \to 2$
$R \to 1Q_{11}R$	$Q_{11} \to 1$
$R \to 1Q_{12}$	$Q_{12} \to 2$
$R \to 2$	

This grammar was introduced in Chapter 6. Grammar G_N satisfies $G_N[\bar{r}/\ell]G_0$. Notice that G_N is LL(2) and, moreover, G_N is in GNF. From the transitivity of the cover relation we obtain the following corollary.

COROLLARY 10.4. Not every LL(k) grammar ($k \geq 2$) in GNF can be left-to-right covered with an ε-free CFG.

Now we are sufficiently prepared to construct the cover-table for LL(k) grammars.

G' \ G	COVER	ARB LL	STRICT ε-LL	ε-FREE LL	GNF LL
ARB LL	ℓ/ℓ	1. *yes*	5. *yes*	9. *yes*	13. *yes*
	$\ell/\bar{r}$	2. *yes*	6. *yes*	10. *yes*	14. *yes*
	$\bar{r}/\ell$	3. *yes*	7. *yes*	11. *yes*	15. *yes*
	$\bar{r}/\bar{r}$	4. *yes*	8. *yes*	12. *yes*	16. *yes*
ε-FREE LL	ℓ/ℓ	17. *no*	21. *no*	25. *yes*	29. *yes*
	$\ell/\bar{r}$	18. *no*	22. *no*	26. *no*	30. *no*
	$\bar{r}/\ell$	19. *?*	23. *yes*	27. *yes*	31. *yes*
	$\bar{r}/\bar{r}$	20. *?*	24. *yes*	28. *yes*	32. *yes*
GNF LL	ℓ/ℓ	33. *no*	37. *no*	41. *yes*	45. *yes*
	$\ell/\bar{r}$	34. *no*	38. *no*	42. *no*	46. *no*
	$\bar{r}/\ell$	35. *?*	39. *yes*	43. *yes*	47. *yes*
	$\bar{r}/\bar{r}$	36. *?*	40. *yes*	44. *yes*	48. *yes*

Table X. Cover-table for LL-grammars.

In Table X we have collected the cover results. The entries in this table are numbered from 1. to 48. The column with name STRICT ε-LL indicates the LL(k) grammars with strict ε-productions. In the table it is not displayed that in some cases the necessary look-ahead may change from k to k + 1. The answers in this table can be found in the following way.

Construction of the cover-table

(10.1.1) Trivially *yes* are the entries 1., 4., 5., 8., 9., 12., 13., 16., 25., 28., 29., 32., 45. and 48. Because of Lemma 10.1 we may conclude that the entries 2., 3., 6., 7., 10., 11., 14. and 15. are *yes*.

(10.1.2) From Corollary 10.2 it follows that the entries 40., 39., 24., 23., 44., 43., 27., 47. and 31. are *yes*.

(10.1.3) Due to Theorem 10.2 we have that entry 41. is *yes*.

(10.1.4) From Corollary 10.3 it follows that entry 17. is *no*. Since grammar G_0 has strict ε-productions we have also that entry 21. is *no*. Therefore, entries 33. and 37. are *no*. From Corollary 10.4 we may conclude that entry 30. is *no*. Therefore, the entries 26., 22., 18., 46., 42., 38. and 34. are *no*.

(10.1.5) The entries 19., 20., 35. and 36. are open. Cf. the note which follows Corollary 10.2.

This concludes the construction of the cover-table. It should be observed that all the no-entries in this table are *no* because of a more general negative cover result. That is, we do no obtain positive results if we relax the condition that the covering grammar should be an LL-grammar.

Let us consider transformations which deal with LL(k) grammars from a more practical point of view. If we have a CFG which should be made suitable for a top-down parsing method (for example as the first phase in a compiler writing system), then there exist transformations which can be applied and which sometimes, depending on the starting grammar, yield an LL(k) grammar. Some of these transformations can be found in Stearns [158] and in Appendix A of Lewis, Rosenkrantz and Stearns [100]. As remarked in Stearns:

"Although these transformations are not guaranteed to make grammars LL(1) they seem to work out when applied to real programming languages".

The two most well-known transformations which can be used to obtain an LL(k) grammar are the elimination of left recursion and left factorisation. The elimination of left recursion (cf. Table VII) can yield a right covering and a left-to-right covering grammar. Now consider left factorisation. If a grammar is not left factored (Definition 1.10), then there exist productions of the form $i.A \to \alpha\beta$ and $j.A \to \alpha\gamma$ with $\alpha \neq \varepsilon$ and $\beta \neq \gamma$. A straightforward process of left factorisation consists of replacing these productions by the productions $A \to \alpha H$ $<\varepsilon>$ and $H \to \beta \mid \gamma$ $<i,j>$, where H is a newly introduced nonterminal symbol. This can be repeated for all such pairs $A \to \alpha\beta \mid \alpha\gamma$ until the grammar is left factored. In this way a right covering grammar is obtained. However, in our model of parsing we prefer a left-to-right covering grammar. If the newly obtained grammar is LL(k), then the LL-parsing method can yield a left parse and this parse can be mapped on the right parse of the original grammar. In Chapter 12 a process of left factoring will be introduced which yields a left-to-right cover.

Now, if we consider the results of this section then we see that for each ε-free LL-grammar G we can obtain a GNF LL-grammar G' such that $G'[\bar{r}/\bar{r}]G$.

One might think that this result, like other right cover results, is not useful for practical applications. Grammar G' is constructed to be parsed top-down and in our model of parsing top-down parsing is assumed to yield left parses. Therefore one might expect results of the form $G'[\ell/\bar{r}]G$. However, it follows from Theorem 9.1 that any production directed parse relation of an LL-grammar G' can be defined by a DPDT. Therefore right parses can be obtained from parsing (in a top-down manner) LL-grammars. The intuitive idea is as follows (cf. Aho and Ullman [3] for the whole story).

If A is a nonterminal symbol at the top of the stack then it should be replaced by a righthand side α of a production $i.A \to \alpha$ and i should be emitted as the next symbol in the left parse. This righthand side is uniquely determined by the look-ahead which is allowed. Now we can obtain a right parse if A is replaced by αi (the top of the stack is assumed to be on the left) and i is emitted in a DPDT-step of the form $\delta(q,\varepsilon,i) = (r,\varepsilon,i)$.

It should be observed that if we 'translate' this way of parsing to the grammatical model in the case of GNF LL-grammars, then it would have been sufficient to have a grammar G' which has productions of the form $A \to a\alpha H$ $\langle\varepsilon\rangle$ and $H \to \varepsilon$ $\langle\pi\rangle$ instead of $A \to a\alpha$ $\langle\pi\rangle$, to make this type of parsing possible. That is we could have transformed the original grammar G to a less restricted normal form than GNF and still have the same practical result.

Now we turn to the last topic of this section, the relation between LL(k) and strong LL(k) grammars. As mentioned in section 8.2 it has been shown in Rosenkrantz and Stearns [144] that each LL(k) grammar can be converted into a structurally equivalent strong LL(k) grammar.

The property $G_1 \cong G_2$ (G_1 is structurally equivalent with G_2) does not necessarily imply that G_1 covers G_2. Consider the following counter-example:

$$
\begin{array}{llll}
G_1: & S_1 \to aB & G_2: & S_2 \to aB \mid aC \mid aD \\
 & B \to aB & & B \to aB \mid aC \mid aD \\
 & B \to b \mid c & & C \to b \\
 & & & D \to c
\end{array}
$$

In this case we have that both G_1 and G_2 are LL-grammars and $G_1 \cong G_2$. However, we do not have $G_1[\ell/\ell]G_2$ or $G_1[\bar{r}/\bar{r}]G_2$.

The conversion from an LL(k) grammar to a strong LL(k) grammar as described in Rosenkrantz and Stearns is such that a left and a right cover is obtained.

<u>THEOREM 10.4.</u> Any LL(k) grammar G can be transformed to a strong LL(k) grammar G' such that $G'[\ell/\ell]G$ and $G'[\bar{r}/\bar{r}]G$ $(k \geq 0)$.

Proof. We use the following notation. Let L be a set of strings. Use the notation

$$k : L = \{x \mid k : w = x \text{ for some } w \in L\}$$

and

$$2^{k:L}$$

for the set of all subsets of k : L.

Let $G = (N,\Sigma,P,S)$ be an LL(k) grammar. Define

$$\Sigma'' = \Sigma \times 2^{k:\Sigma^*},$$

$$N'' = N \times 2^{k:\Sigma^*},$$

$$S'' = (S,\{\varepsilon\}),$$

$$P'' = P \times 2^{k:\Sigma^*}$$

The pair (p,R) represents the production

$$(A,R) \to (X_n,R_n)....(X_1,R_1)$$

where $A \to X_n....X_1$ is the production p and R_{i+1} satisfies the condition

$$R_{i+1} = k : (L(X_i...X_1)R)$$

for all $n > i \geq 1$. Define $R_1 = R$ and if $p = A \to \varepsilon$ then $(A,R) \to \varepsilon$. Reduce grammar $G'' = (N'',\Sigma'',P'',S'')$ and replace each occurrence of a terminal (a,R) by terminal symbol a. In this way we obtain grammar $G' = (N',\Sigma,P',S')$.

Given a leftmost (rightmost) derivation in G' a corresponding leftmost (rightmost) derivation in G is obtained by replacing each nonterminal (A,R) by A. Instead of applying production p to an instance of A one can apply (p,R) to the corresponding (A,R) in order to obtain a leftmost (rightmost) derivation of G" from a leftmost (rightmost) derivation of G. A corresponding derivation in G' is immediate.

The cover homomorphism $\psi : \Delta_{G'}^* \to \Delta_G^*$ is defined by $\psi((p,R)) = p$, for each (modified) production (p,R) of P'. Hence, $G'[\ell/\ell]G$ and $G'[\bar{r}/\bar{r}]G$. In [144] it is shown that G' is strong LL(k). This concludes the proof. □

10.2. NORMAL FORM COVERS FOR STRICT DETERMINISTIC GRAMMARS

This section is concerned with the construction of a cover-table for strict deterministic grammars.

Just like the LL(k) grammars, the strict deterministic grammars are non-left-recursive. Therefore, the construction of the table does not differ very much from the construction of the LL cover-table in section 10.1.

For strict deterministic grammars we have the following version of Lemma 4.4.

LEMMA 10.6. For any strict deterministic grammar G there exists a strict deterministic grammar G' such that $G'[\ell/\bar{r}]G$.

Proof. This is a direct consequence of Theorem 9.3. However, it is more simple to construct grammar G' in the following way. Suppose that grammar G is strict deterministic with partition π. Define G' by introducing productions $A \to \alpha H_i$ $<\varepsilon>$ and $H_i \to \varepsilon$ $<i>$ for each production $i.A \to \alpha$ in P. Symbol H_i is a newly introduced nonterminal symbol. Clearly, $G'[\ell/\bar{r}]G$.

Notice that for any pair of productions $A \to \alpha$ and $A' \to \alpha\beta$ of G with $A \equiv A'$ (mod π), we have $\beta = \varepsilon$ and $A = A'$. Therefore, the new nonterminal symbols do not interfere with the original nonterminal symbols. Thus, we can define a strict partition π' for G' by $\pi' = \pi \cup \{\{H_i\} \mid 1 \leq i \leq |P|\}$. □

Notice that we can slightly generalize this result. If strict deterministic grammar G is h_G-parsable, then it follows from Theorem 9.3 that there exists a strict deterministic grammar G' such that $G'[\ell/h]G$. Moreover, from Theorem 9.4 it follows that there exists a strict deterministic grammar G' such that $G'[\bar{r}/h]G$.

Since not every strict deterministic grammar G is left parsable, we can not have the general result $G'[\bar{r}/\ell]G$, where G' is strict deterministic.

We want to show that ε-productions in a strict deterministic grammar can be eliminated in such a way that a right covering strict deterministic grammar is obtained. Before doing so we need a few preliminaries on strict deterministic grammars.

It is clear that the set of productions of a strict deterministic grammar is prefix-free. That is, if $A \to \alpha$ and $A \to \alpha\beta$ are in P, then $\beta = \varepsilon$. Clearly, this property holds for all nonterminals in a block of the strict partition. That is, if $A \to \alpha$ and $A' \to \alpha\beta$, then $A \equiv A'$ (mod π) implies $\beta = \varepsilon$.

LEMMA 10.7. Let $G = (N,\Sigma,P,S)$ be a CFG with strict partition π. For any $A, A' \in N$, if $A \equiv A'$ (mod π), then $L(A) \cup L(A')$ is prefix-free and, if moreover $A \neq A'$, $L(A) \cap L(A') = \emptyset$.

Proof. Do the proof of Theorem 2.2 from Harrison and Havel [59] for A and A' instead of for S. This gives the result $L(A) \cup L(A')$ is prefix-free. The property

$L(A) \cap L(A') = \emptyset$ can be proved by a simple induction on the lengths of the derivations starting from A and A'. □

LEMMA 10.8. A strict deterministic grammar can only have strict ε-productions.

Proof. It follows from Lemma 10.7 that for any nonterminal A the set L(A) is prefix-free. Thus, if $\varepsilon \in L(A)$, then $L(A) = \{\varepsilon\}$. □

It follows directly from Lemma 10.2 that each righthand side α, $L(\alpha) \neq \{\varepsilon\}$, of a production $A \to \alpha$ of a strict determinisitic grammar, has exactly one representation.

LEMMA 10.9. Let $G = (N,\Sigma,P,S)$ be a CFG with strict partition π. Let $A \to \alpha$ and $A' \to \beta$ be productions in P with $L(\alpha) \neq \varepsilon$, $L(\beta) \neq \varepsilon$ and $A \equiv A' \pmod{\pi}$. If $\alpha_0X_1\ldots X_{i-1}\alpha_{i-1}X_i\ldots X_n\alpha_n$ and $\alpha_0X_1\ldots X_{i-1}\beta_{i-1}Y_i\ldots Y_m\beta_m$ are representations of α and β, respectively, then $\alpha_{i-1} = \beta_{i-1}$.

Proof. We have that $i \geq 1$, $i \leq n$ and $i \leq m$. Consider the case $i < n$ and $i < m$. If $\alpha_{i-1} \neq \beta_{i-1}$, then there are two possibilities.

(i) α_{i-1} is a prefix of β_{i-1} (or the symmetric case, which we omit). Hence, $\beta_{i-1} = \alpha_{i-1}\rho$ and we have $1 : \rho \equiv X_i \pmod{\pi}$. However, $\varepsilon \in L(1:\rho)$ and $L(X_i) \neq \{\varepsilon\}$. Therefore, $L(1:\rho) \cup L(X_i)$ is not prefix-free which contradicts Lemma 10.7.

(ii) α_{i-1} can be written as $\rho Q_1\delta_1$ and β_{i-1} as $\rho Q_2\delta_2$, with $Q_1 \neq Q_2$. Since $\varepsilon \in L(Q_1)$, $\varepsilon \in L(Q_2)$ and $Q_1 \equiv Q_2 \pmod{\pi}$ we have again a contradiction with Lemma 10.7.

We conclude that in this case $\alpha_{i-1} = \beta_{i-1}$.

Now consider the case $i = n$ and $i < m$ (or the symmetric case, which we omit). Then we have $\alpha = \alpha_0X_1\ldots\alpha_{n-1}X_n\alpha_n$ and $\beta = \alpha_0X_1\ldots\alpha_{n-1}X_n\beta_nY_{n+1}\ldots Y_m\beta_m$. Since $L(\alpha) \cup L(\beta)$ should be a prefix-free set, we can conclude that $Y_{n+1}\ldots Y_m\beta_m = \varepsilon$. Assume $\alpha_n \neq \beta_n$. If α_n is a prefix of β_n (or the symmetric case), then we obtain an immediate contradiction with the definition of a strict deterministic grammar. With a similar argument as used above we can conclude that a situation $\alpha_n = \rho Q_1\delta_1$ and $\beta_n = \rho Q_2\delta_2$ with $Q_1 \neq Q_2$ can not occur. It follows that $\alpha_n = \beta_n$. This concludes the proof of Lemma 10.9. □

We can now show that ε-productions can be eliminated in such a way that strict determinism is preserved.

THEOREM 10.5. Any strict deterministic grammar can be right covered with an ε-free strict deterministic grammar.

Proof. Since any strict deterministic grammar is non-left-recursive, we can use

Algorithm 4.1 to eliminate the ε-productions from a strict deterministic grammar G. Grammar G' which is obtained by this algorithm is ε-free and $G'[\bar{r}/\bar{r}]G$. Unfortunately, we do not necessarily have that G' is strict deterministic. We will modify the input grammar G such that G' will be strict deterministic.

Let $G = (N,\Sigma,P,S)$ be a CFG with strict partition π. Let $j.A \to \alpha$ be a production in P with $L(\alpha) \neq \{\varepsilon\}$. If $\alpha_0X_1\alpha_1X_2\ldots X_n\alpha_n$ is a representation of α, then replace this rule by

$$A \to H_{\alpha 0}X_1H_{\alpha 1}X_2\ldots X_nH_{\alpha n} \quad \langle j \rangle$$

where each

$$H_{\alpha i}\ , \quad 0 \leq i \leq n$$

is a newly introduced nonterminal symbol, and introduce the productions

$$H_{\alpha i} \to \varepsilon \quad \langle \pi_i \rangle, \quad 0 \leq i \leq n$$

if

$$\alpha_i \overset{\pi_i^R}{\underset{R}{\Longrightarrow}} \varepsilon.$$

If $\alpha_i = \varepsilon$, then define $\pi_i = \varepsilon$. This can be done for each production $A \to \alpha$ in P. Clearly, the newly obtained grammar $G' = (N',\Sigma,P',S)$ right covers the original grammar.

Notice, that if for some α and β the productions $H_\alpha \to \varepsilon \ \langle \pi_1 \rangle$ and $H_\beta \to \varepsilon \ \langle \pi_2 \rangle$ are introduced and $\alpha = \beta$, then $\pi_1 = \pi_2$.

Let H be the set of all newly introduced nonterminal symbols. The new grammar is strict deterministic under a partition π' which is defined by the following conditions:

(i) $\Sigma \in \pi'$

(ii) For any A, A' in N such that $A \equiv A' \pmod{\pi}$ we have $A \equiv A' \pmod{\pi'}$.

(iii) For each newly introduced nonterminal symbol $H_{\alpha i}$ we have that $\{H_{\alpha i}\}$ is a block of the partition π'.

We verify that π' is a strict partition. Consider two productions

$$A \to \alpha\beta$$

and

$$A' \to \alpha\beta'$$

in P', with $A \equiv A'$ (mod π'). If both A and A' are newly introduced nonterminal symbols, then $\beta = \beta' = \varepsilon$, $\alpha = \varepsilon$ and $A = A'$, as is required. Now consider the case that both A and A' are in N. We distinguish two subcases.

(i) Write $\alpha = H_{\alpha 0}X_1H_{\alpha i}$, $\beta = X_{i+1}\ldots X_nH_{\alpha n}$ and $\beta' = Y_{i+1}\ldots Y_mH_{\beta m}$. By considering the corresponding productions in P, it immediately follows that either β and β' are not empty and $X_{i+1} \equiv Y_{i+1}$ (mod π') or $\beta = \beta' = \varepsilon$ and $A = A'$.

(ii) Write $\alpha = H_{\alpha 0}X_1H_{\alpha 1}\ldots X_i$, $\beta = H_{\alpha i}X_{i+1}\ldots X_nH_{\alpha n}$ and $\beta' = H_{\beta i}Y_{i+1}\ldots Y_mH_{\beta m}$. Due to the construction of G' it follows that $\beta, \beta' \neq \varepsilon$. It follows from Lemma 10.9 that $H_{\alpha i} = H_{\beta i}$ and, therefore, $H_{\alpha i} \equiv H_{\beta i}$ (mod π'). This concludes the proof that π' is strict.

We now show that G' can be transformed to a strict deterministic grammar G" which has no ε-productions and which right covers G'. From transitivity it then follows that $G''[\bar{r}/\bar{r}]G$.

Apply Algorithm 4.1 to grammar G'. The newly obtained grammar $G'' = (N'',\Sigma,P'',S')$ right covers G' and has no ε-productions. We show that G" is strict deterministic under a partition π'' which is defined as follows:

(i) $\Sigma \in \pi''$

(ii) $[\gamma\underline{X}\alpha] \equiv [\gamma'\underline{Y}\beta]$ (mod π'') if and only if

- $\gamma = \gamma'$
- $X \equiv Y$ (mod π)
- both α and β are in H or $\alpha = \beta = \varepsilon$
- if $X = Y$, then $\alpha = \beta$

We show that this partition is strict. We distinguish the following five cases.

(1) Consider nonterminal symbols $[\gamma\underline{A}]$ and $[\gamma\underline{B}]$ with $A \equiv B$ (mod π) and A, B in N. Hence, $[\gamma\underline{A}] \equiv [\gamma\underline{B}]$ (mod π''). Suppose we have productions

$$[\gamma\underline{A}] \to \alpha\beta$$

and

$$[\gamma\underline{B}] \to \alpha\beta'$$

in P". These productions have been introduced in step (1) of Algorithm 4.1. If $\alpha \neq \varepsilon$, then we can write

$$\alpha = [\gamma H_0\underline{X}_1H_1][\underline{X}_2H_2]\ldots.[\underline{X}_iH_i]$$

$$\beta = [\underline{X}_{i+1}H_{i+1}]\ldots.[\underline{X}_nH_n]$$

$$\beta' = [\underline{X}'_{i+1}H'_{i+1}]\ldots.[\underline{X}'_mH'_m]$$

Assume $\beta = \beta' = \varepsilon$. Then there exist productions

$$A \rightarrow H_0X_1H_1X_2H_2 \ldots X_iH_i$$

$$B \rightarrow H_0X_1H_1X_2H_2 \ldots X_iH_i$$

in P' and necessarily A = B. Hence, $[\gamma\underline{A}] = [\gamma\underline{B}]$, as is required.

Assume $\beta \neq \varepsilon$ and $\beta' \neq \varepsilon$. In this case we have that $X_{i+1} \equiv X'_{i+1}$ (mod π') in G'. Moreover, if $X_{i+1} = X'_{i+1}$, then $H_{i+1} = H'_{i+1}$, since otherwise G' can not be strict deterministic. Therefore, $[\underline{X}_{i+1}H_{i+1}] \equiv [\underline{X}'_{i+1}H'_{i+1}]$ (mod π''), as is required.

It is left to the reader to verify that the case $\beta = \varepsilon$ and $\beta' \neq \varepsilon$ (or the symmetric case) can not occur.

Consider the case $\alpha = \varepsilon$. Since G" does not have ε-productions, it follows that $\beta, \beta' \neq \varepsilon$. We can write $1 : \beta = [\gamma H_0\underline{X}_1H_1]$ and $1 : \beta' = [\gamma H'_0\underline{X}'_1H'_1]$. Since G' is strict deterministic it follows that $H'_0 = H_0$ (H_0 and H'_0 are equivalent and they are left-hand sides of ε-productions) and $X_1 \equiv X'_1$ (mod π). Moreover, if $X_1 = X'_1$, then $H_1 = H'_1$. Therefore, $[\gamma H_0\underline{X}_1H_1] \equiv [\gamma H'_0\underline{X}'_1H'_1]$ (mod π''), as is required.

(2) Consider nonterminal symbols $[\underline{X}H_1]$ and $[\underline{Y}H_2]$ with X, Y $\in \Sigma$. If $[\underline{X}H_1] \equiv [\underline{Y}H_2]$ (mod π'') and we have (unique) productions $[\underline{X}H_1] \rightarrow X$ and $[\underline{Y}H_2] \rightarrow Y$, then $X \equiv Y$ (mod π''), as is required. Moreover, it follows from the definition of π'' that if X = Y, then $H_1 = H_2$ and $[\underline{X}H_1] = [\underline{Y}H_2]$, as is required.

(3) Consider nonterminal symbols $[\gamma\underline{X}H_1]$ and $[\gamma\underline{Y}H_2]$ with $X \equiv Y$ (mod π) and $\gamma \neq \varepsilon$ or $X \in N$. If $[\gamma\underline{X}H_1] \equiv [\gamma\underline{Y}H_2]$ (mod π'') and we have (unique) productions

$$[\gamma\underline{X}H_1] \rightarrow [\gamma\underline{X}]$$

$$[\gamma\underline{Y}H_2] \rightarrow [\gamma\underline{Y}]$$

then $[\gamma\underline{X}] \equiv [\gamma\underline{Y}]$ (mod π'') as is required. Moreover. If $[\gamma\underline{X}] = [\gamma\underline{Y}]$ then it follows from the definition of π'' that $H_1 = H_2$. Thus, $[\gamma\underline{X}H_1] = [\gamma\underline{Y}H_2]$, as is required.

(4) Consider nonterminal symbols $[\gamma H_1\underline{X}]$ and $[\gamma H_1\underline{Y}]$ with X, Y $\in \Sigma$ and $\gamma \in H^*$. Then $[\gamma H_1\underline{X}] \equiv [\gamma H_1\underline{Y}]$ (mod π'') and we have unique productions

$$[\gamma H_1\underline{X}] \rightarrow [\gamma\underline{X}]$$

$$[\gamma H_1\underline{Y}] \rightarrow [\gamma\underline{Y}]$$

Clearly, $[\gamma\underline{X}] \equiv [\gamma\underline{Y}]$ (mod π'') and if $[\gamma\underline{X}] = [\gamma\underline{Y}]$, then $[\gamma H_1\underline{X}] = [\gamma H_1\underline{Y}]$, as is required.

(5) Consider nonterminal symbols $[H_1\underline{X}]$ and $[H_1\underline{Y}]$ with X, Y $\in \Sigma$. Then $[H_1\underline{X}] \equiv [H_1\underline{Y}]$

(mod π'') and we have unique productions

$$[H_1\underline{X}] \to X$$

$$[H_1\underline{Y}] \to Y$$

Clearly, $X \equiv Y \pmod{\pi''}$ and if $X = Y$, then $[H_1\underline{X}] = [H_1\underline{Y}]$, as is required.

The cases (1) to (5) cover all possible pairs of equivalent nonterminal symbols. Therefore we can conclude that G" is strict deterministic under partition π''. □

The next transformation which will be considered is the left part transformation (Algorithm 5.3). Due to the fact that strict deterministic grammars are unambiguous and due to the remark which follows Algorithm 5.3, we do not have to bother about single productions.

In Nijholt [123] we used Algorithm 5.2 to show that any ε-free strict deterministic grammar can be transformed to a weakly equivalent strict deterministic grammar in GNF. In Geller, Harrison and Havel [42] another algorithm was presented to show the same result. They use this result to show that any deterministic language can be generated by an LR(1) grammar in GNF. Their algorithm modestly utilizes properties of strict deterministic grammars.

The result that any deterministic language is generated by an LR(1) grammar in GNF was first shown by Lomet [102].

Here we show that the left part transformation (which does not make use of specific properties of strict deterministic grammars) when it is applied to a strict deterministic grammar G, will produce a GNF grammar G' which is strict deterministic and which has the property that $G'[\ell/x]G$, $\ell \le x \le \ell p$.

<u>THEOREM 10.6.</u> For any ε-free strict deterministic grammar G there exists a strict deterministic grammar G' in GNF such that $G'[\ell/x]G$, $\ell \le x \le \ell p$.

Proof. Apply Algorithm 5.3 to the ε-free strict deterministic grammar $G = (N,\Sigma,P,S)$ with strict partition π. The newly obtained grammar $G' = (N',\Sigma,P',[S])$ is in GNF and $G'[\ell/x]G$. We show that G' is strict deterministic under the following partition π':

(i) $\Sigma \in \pi'$, $\{[S]\} \in \pi'$.

(ii) For any $[Ai\alpha]$, $[Bj\beta]$ in N', with $A, B \in N$ and $\alpha, \beta \in V^+$, $[Ai\alpha] \equiv [Bj\beta] \pmod{\pi'}$ if and only if $\alpha = \beta$ and $A \equiv B \pmod{\pi}$.

In the following observations we will show some properties of the productions of G'. These properties are needed to show that π' is strict.

OBSERVATION 10.1. Consider two productions in P' which are of the form

$$[Ai\gamma] \rightarrow a\rho$$

and

$$[Bj\gamma] \rightarrow a\delta$$

where A, B $\in$ N, $\gamma \in V'^{+}$, $a \in \Sigma$, $\rho, \delta \in N'^{*}$ and $A \equiv B \pmod{\pi}$. Because of the construction of P' it follows that there exist productions i. $A \rightarrow \gamma X_0\varphi$ and j. $B \rightarrow \gamma Y_0\psi$ in P with $X_0, Y_0 \in V$ and $\varphi, \psi \in V^*$. Moreover, there exist chains $X_0X_1\ldots X_{n-1}X_n$ and $Y_0Y_1\ldots Y_{m-1}Y_m$ in $CH(X_0)$ and $CH(Y_0)$, respectively, where $X_n = Y_m = a$ and associated left production chains $i_0i_1\ldots i_{n-1}$ and $j_0j_1\ldots j_{m-1}$, such that

$$\rho = \xi([X_{n-1}i_{n-1}a]\ldots[X_0i_0X_1][Ai\gamma X_0])$$

and

$$\delta = \xi([Y_{m-1}j_{m-1}a]\ldots[Y_0j_0Y_1][Bj\gamma Y_0]).$$

Since grammar G is strict deterministic we have $X_0 \equiv Y_0 \pmod{\pi}$ and it follows also that $m = n$ and $X_k \equiv Y_k \pmod{\pi}$, $1 \leq k \leq n$. □

Notice that a similar observation holds for productions of the form $[S] \rightarrow a\rho$ and $[S] \rightarrow a\delta$. Since our observations can easily be converted to similar observations for the cases that the productions in question have lefthand sides [S], we will not treat this nonterminal separately. Notice that [S] can not occur in the righthand sides of the productions of G'.

We will need the following claim.

CLAIM 1. If $\xi([Ci\gamma]) = \xi([Dj\gamma])$, where $C \equiv D \pmod{\pi}$, then $C = D$ and $i = j$.

Proof of Claim 1. For some $\varphi, \psi \in V^*$ there exist productions i. $C \rightarrow \gamma\varphi$ and j. $D \rightarrow \gamma\psi$ in P. Since $C \equiv D \pmod{\pi}$ we may distinguish between two cases:

(a) either both φ and ψ are empty, hence $C = D$ and $i = j$, or

(b) both φ and ψ are not empty and by definition of ξ it follows that $\xi([Ci\gamma]) = [Ci\gamma]$ and $\xi([Dj\gamma]) = [Dj\gamma]$, hence $C = D$ and $i = j$. □

OBSERVATION 10.2. Let $C \rightarrow \alpha\beta$ and $C' \rightarrow \alpha\beta'$ be in P', with $C \equiv C' \pmod{\pi'}$. From Observation 10.1 and the definition of π' it follows that we may write

$$C \rightarrow \alpha\beta = [Ai\gamma] \rightarrow a\xi([X_{n-1}i_{n-1}a]\ldots[X_0i_0X_1][Ai\gamma X_0])$$

and

$$C' \to \alpha\beta' = [Bj\gamma] \to a\xi([Y_{n-1}j_{n-1}a]\ldots[Y_0j_0Y_1][B_j\gamma Y_0]).$$

Consider a situation in which we have

$$\xi([X_{n-1}i_{n-1}X_n]\ldots[\zeta X_k]) = \xi([Y_{n-1}j_{n-1}Y_n]\ldots[\zeta' Y_k])$$

where $X_n = Y_n = a$, k satisfies $0 \le k \le n$ and either

(i) $\zeta = Ai\gamma$, $\zeta' = Bj\gamma$ and $k = 0$, or
(ii) $\zeta = X_{k-1}i_{k-1}$, $\zeta' = Y_{k-1}j_{k-1}$ and $k \ge 1$.

In this situation we have the following result.

<u>CLAIM 2.</u> $[X_{n-1}i_{n-1}X_n]\ldots[\zeta X_k] = [Y_{n-1}j_{n-1}Y_n]\ldots[\zeta' Y_k]$.

Proof of Claim 2. If $n = 0$, then the situation amounts to showing that $\xi([\zeta a]) = \xi([\zeta' a])$ implies $\zeta = \zeta'$ and this follows immediately from Claim 1. Assume $n > 0$. First we show, by induction on m where $k \le m < n$, that $X_m = Y_m$ and $i_m = j_m$. As basis we take $m = n - 1$. Since $X_n = Y_n$ one can easily verify, using Claim 1, that $X_{n-1} = Y_{n-1}$ and $i_{n-1} = j_{n-1}$. Assume inductively that $X_p = Y_p$ and $i_p = j_p$ for all p such that $k \le m < p < n$. We show that $X_m = Y_m$ and $i_m = j_m$. In this case the situation can be reduced to

$$\xi([X_m i_m X_{m+1}]\ldots[\zeta X_k]) = \xi([Y_m j_m Y_{m+1}]\ldots[\zeta' Y_k]).$$

Use of Claim 1 and its proof yields again $X_m = Y_m$ and $i_m = j_m$. This concludes the induction. It follows that $X_k = Y_k$ and again with Claim 1 we conclude $\zeta = \zeta'$. This concludes the proof of Claim 2. □

We continue with Observation 10.2. Now we consider a situation in which we have $\beta, \beta' \neq \varepsilon$. Then there exist p and q, $0 \le p, q \le n$ such that

$$1 : \beta = \xi([\zeta X_p]) = [\zeta X_p],$$

where either $\zeta = X_{p-1}i_{p-1}$ or $\zeta = Ai\gamma$ and $p = 0$, and

$$1 : \beta' = \xi([\zeta' Y_q]) = [\zeta' Y_q],$$

where either $\zeta' = Y_{q-1}j_{q-1}$ or $\zeta' = Bj\gamma$ and $q = 0$.

In this situation we have the following result.

CLAIM 3. $1 : \beta \equiv 1 : \beta'$ (mod π') and $p = q$.

Proof of Claim 3. Assume $p > q$ (the case $p < q$ is symmetric and therefore omitted). In this case we have

$$\alpha = a\xi([X_{n-1}i_{n-1}X_n]\ldots[X_pi_pX_{p+1}]) = a\xi([Y_{n-1}j_{n-1}Y_n]\ldots[Y_qj_qY_{q+1}]).$$

It follows (see also Claim 2.) that

$$\xi([Y_{p-1}j_{p-1}Y_p]\ldots[Y_{q-1}j_{q-1}Y_q]) = \varepsilon$$

so that necessarily, $\xi([Y_{p-1}j_{p-1}Y_p]) = \varepsilon$. This means that we have productions in P of the form $i_{p-1} \to X_p\varphi$ for some $\varphi \in V^+$ and $j_{p-1}.\ Y_{p-1} \to Y_p$. Notice that $X_p = Y_p$ and $X_{p-1} \equiv Y_{p-1}$ (mod π). But then we have a contradiction with condition (ii) of Definition 8.5. Therefore $p = q$. Since $p = q$ we have that $1 : \beta = [\zeta X_p]$, $1 : \beta' = [\zeta' Y_p]$ with $X_p = Y_p$ and either

(i) $\zeta = X_{p-1}i_{p-1}$ and $\zeta' = Y_{p-1}j_{p-1}$ with $X_{p-1} \equiv Y_{p-1}$ (mod π) and by definition of π' it follows that $[\zeta X_p] \equiv [\zeta' Y_p]$ (mod π'), or

(ii) $\zeta = Ai\gamma$ and $\zeta' = Bj\gamma$ with $A \equiv B$ (mod π) and also in this case, by definition of π', it follows that $[\zeta X_p] \equiv [\zeta' Y_p]$ (mod π').

Thus $1 : \beta \equiv 1 : \beta'$. This concludes the proof of Claim 3. □

With the proof of this claim we conclude Observation 10.2. □

Now it is straightforward to show that π' is strict. By definition of π' we have $\Sigma \in \pi'$. It remains to verify that π' satisfies condition (ii) of Definition 8.5. First we consider case (a) of this condition. Consider two productions $C \to \alpha\beta$ and $C' \to \alpha\beta'$ in P' where $C \equiv C'$ (mod π') and $\beta, \beta' \neq \varepsilon$. If $\alpha = \varepsilon$, then $1 : \beta$, $1 : \beta' \in \Sigma$ hence $1 : \beta \equiv 1 : \beta'$ (mod π'). Case (b) of condition (ii) follows immediately from Claim 2. Since G is strict deterministic, other cases are not possible. □

Before examining other cover properties of strict deterministic grammars we shortly discuss the strict partition π'. The set of strict partitions of a strict deterministic grammar forms a semi-lattice under the meet operation. Therefore there exists a minimal strict partition. In section 8.2 we presented the algorithm which computes this minimal strict partition. If the algorithm is applied to CFG G', which is obtained by the left part transformation, then π' is obtained. That is, independent of the definition of π we have that π' is the minimal strict partition of G'.

It can be verified that if the input grammar G is a real-time strict deterministic grammar (Definition 8.6.c), then the left part transformation produces a grammar which is not only real-time strict deterministic but also uniform (Definition 8.6.b).

As we mentioned in section 5.2.2, if the left part transformation is applied twice, then the newly obtained grammar is at the same time in standard 2-form.

We want to consider the possibility of obtaining a right covering almost-GNF strict deterministic grammar from an ε-free strict deterministic grammar. Algorithm 5.4 will be slightly adapted in order to make it suitable for strict deterministic grammars. However, first we have to show that any ε-free strict deterministic grammar can be made to satisfy the input conditions of Algorithm 5.4. Notice that if a grammar is strict deterministic and we replace each production of the form $A \rightarrow \alpha a \beta$, $\alpha \neq \varepsilon$, by the productions $A \rightarrow \alpha H_a \beta$ and $H_a \rightarrow a$, then the newly obtained grammar is also strict deterministic. That is, if π is the original strict partition, then the new partition is $\pi \cup \{\{H_a \mid a \in \Sigma\}\}$.

Unfortunately, the single productions of a strict deterministic grammar can not be eliminated in a straightforward way. The reason is that, whenever we have two nonterminal symbols A and A' with $A \equiv A'$, then $\pi_1 \in CH(A)$ and $\pi_2 \in CH(A')$ implies $|\pi_1| = |\pi_2|$. However, if we have a derivation

$$A \overset{\pi_1}{\underset{L}{\Rightarrow}} a$$

and

$$A' \overset{\pi_2}{\underset{L}{\Rightarrow}} b\varphi$$

with $|\pi_1| > 1$, then eliminating the single productions in the 'usual' way yields a production $A \rightarrow a$, while, if $\varphi \neq \varepsilon$, the derivation which uses π_2 does not necessarily change under the elimination of single productions. Hence, such an elimination does not preserve strict determinism. Therefore we will include this elimination in the algorithm which transforms an ε-free strict deterministic grammar into a strict deterministic grammar in almost-GNF. It should be noted that if a grammar is real-time strict deterministic, then we can eliminate the single productions in the same way as was described for the LL(k) grammars (cf. Lemma 10.3).

One more remark should be made. We need to adapt the definition of almost-GNF in order to be able to deal with strict deterministic grammars. This is done in the following definition.

<u>DEFINITION 10.2.</u> (*Almost-GNF, second version*) A CFG $G = (N,\Sigma,P,S)$ is said to be an *almost*-GNF grammar if for any production $A \rightarrow \alpha$ in P either

(i) $\alpha \in \Sigma$, or
(ii) $\alpha \in N^+$ and $rhs(1{:}\alpha) \subseteq \Sigma$.

Notice that in Definition 5.5 we had the condition

(ii) $\alpha \in NN^+$ and $rhs(1:\alpha) \subseteq \Sigma$.

Therefore, the new definition is slightly more general.

LEMMA 10.10. Each ε-free strict deterministic grammar G can be transformed to an almost-GNF grammar G' such that $G'[\bar{r}/\bar{r}]G$ and G' is strict deterministic.

Proof. We have to adapt Algorithm 5.4 in order to deal with the single productions and the strict determinism. As we did for LL(k) grammars, we will first consider Algorithm 5.3. If this algorithm is applied to a strict deterministic grammar G with $P \subseteq N \times (\Sigma N^* \cup N^+)$, then we obtain a grammar G_1 which is strict deterministic and which has productions with the following forms:

(i) $[S] \to X_n\xi([X_{n-1}i_{n-1}X_n]\ldots.[X_1i_1X_2][Si_0X_1])$

and

(ii) $[Ai\alpha] \to X_n\xi([X_{n-1}i_{n-1}X_n]\ldots.[X_0i_0X_1][Ai\alpha X_0])$

We will proceed in the following way. Firstly, we construct a strict deterministic grammar G' which is in almost GNF. In this construction we do not have to bother about single productions. At the same time a homomorphism will be defined under which $G'[\bar{r}/\bar{r}]G$ if G has no single productions. Secondly, we will slightly change grammar G' and the definition of the homomorphism in order to deal with the case that G has single productions.

Consider the strict partition π of grammar G. Let $\pi = \{\Sigma\} \cup \{V_1,V_2,\ldots,V_m\}$. Let $V_k \in \pi - \{\Sigma\}$. For each $a \in \Sigma$, define

$$Q_k^a = \{i \mid i.\ A \to a\alpha \text{ in P, } A \in V_k \text{ and } \alpha \in N^*\}.$$

Clearly, for each $i,j \in Q_k^a$ such that $i.\ A \to a\alpha$ and $j.\ B \to a\beta$ are in P, we have that either $\alpha = \beta = \varepsilon$ and $i = j$, or both α and β are not equal to ε.

Grammar G_1, which is obtained by Algorithm 5.3, is strict deterministic under a partition π_1 which is defined by

(1) $\Sigma \in \pi_1$, $\{[S]\} \in \pi_1$

(2) $[Ai\alpha] \equiv [Bj\beta] \pmod{\pi_1}$ if and only if $A \equiv B \pmod{\pi}$ and $\alpha = \beta$.

Grammar $G' = (N',\Sigma,P',[S])$ is obtained from grammar $G_1 = (N_1,\Sigma,P_1,[S])$ in the following way. Initially, set $P' = \emptyset$. The symbols Q_k^a which denote the sets defined above will be used as nonterminal symbols. They will be added to N_1 in order to obtain N'.

Now we define the productions of G'. Each production is followed by its image under a mapping of which it will be shown that it is a cover homomorphism.

(a) If in (i) $\xi([X_{n-1}i_{n-1}X_n]\ldots.[Si_0X_1]) = \varepsilon$ (hence, with our assumption that G has no single productions, $i_0.\ S \rightarrow X_n$ is in P), then

$$[S] \rightarrow Q_k^{X_n} \quad \langle\varepsilon\rangle$$

where $S \in V_k$, and

$$Q_k^{X_n} \rightarrow X_n \quad \langle i_0\rangle$$

are added to P'.

(b) If in (i) $\xi([X_{n-1}i_{n-1}X_n]\ldots[Si_0X_1]) \neq \varepsilon$, then

$$[S] \rightarrow Q_k^{X_n}\ \xi([X_{n-1}i_{n-1}X_n]\ldots[Si_0X_1]) \quad \langle\varepsilon\rangle,$$

where $X_{n-1} \in V_k$, and

$$Q_k^{X_n} \rightarrow X_n \quad \langle p\rangle$$

are added to P'. Here, $p = i_{n-1}$ if $i_{n-1}.\ X_{n-1} \rightarrow X_n$ is in P and $p = \varepsilon$ otherwise.

(c) If in (ii) $\xi([X_{n-1}i_{n-1}X_n]\ldots[X_0i_0X_1][Ai\alpha X_0]) = \varepsilon$ (hence, with our assumption that G has no single productions, i. $A \rightarrow \alpha X_0$ and $i_0.\ X_0 \rightarrow X_1$ are in P and $n = 1$), then

$$[Ai\alpha] \rightarrow Q_k^{X_n} \quad \langle i\rangle$$

where $X_0 \in V_k$, and

$$Q_k^{X_n} \rightarrow X_n \quad \langle i_0\rangle$$

are added to P'.

(d) If in (ii) $\xi([X_{n-1}i_{n-1}X_n]\ldots[X_0i_0X_1][Ai\alpha X_0]) \neq \varepsilon$, then

$$[Ai\alpha] \rightarrow Q_k^{X_n}\ \xi([X_{n-1}i_{n-1}X_n]\ldots[X_0i_0X_1][Ai\alpha X_0]) \quad \langle p\rangle,$$

where $X_{n-1} \in V_k$, and

$$Q_k^{X_n} \to X_n \quad \langle q\rangle$$

are added to P'. Here, $p = i$, if $i.\ A \to \alpha X_0$ is in P and $p = \varepsilon$ otherwise, and $q = i_{n-1}$ if $i_{n-1}.\ X_{n-1} \to X_n \in P$ and $q = \varepsilon$, otherwise.

CLAIM 1. Grammar G' is strict deterministic.

Proof of Claim 1. Grammar G' is strict deterministic under a partition π' which is defined as follows

(1') $\pi_1 \subseteq \pi'$

(2') For each k, $1 \le k \le m$, the set $\{Q_k^a \mid a \in \Sigma \text{ and } Q_k^a \neq \emptyset\}$ is a block of the partition.

We prove that π' is strict. Since we know that G_1 is strict deterministic under partition π_1 it is sufficient to notice that the new nonterminal symbols do not interfere with this partition. Moreover, if $Q_k^a \equiv Q_k^b \pmod{\pi'}$, then if $Q_k^a \to a$ and $Q_k^b \to b$ are in P', then $a = b$ implies that $Q_k^a = Q_k^b$ as is desired. We conclude that G' is strict deterministic. □

CLAIM 2. If G has no single productions, then $G'[\bar{r}/\bar{r}]G$.

Proof of Claim 2. We should compare grammar G' with the grammar which is obtained in the proof of Lemma 5.4. The grammar of Lemma 5.4 right covers grammar G. It should be clear from the definition of the sets Q_k^a that the mapping defined by $Q_k^a \to X_n$ $\langle q\rangle$ coincides with the mapping defined by the productions $H_{i_{n-1}} \to X_n$ $\langle q\rangle$ with $i_{n-1} \in Q_k^a$. Therefore, $G'[\bar{r}/\bar{r}]G$. □

Now suppose that G has single productions. Grammar G_1 which is obtained by Algorithm 5.3 is strict deterministic. We show how to modify the steps (a), (b), (c) and (d) in order to obtain a right covering strict deterministic grammar G'.

First consider case (a). If G has single productions and $\xi([X_{n-1}i_{n-1}X_n]\ldots.[Si_0X_1]) = \varepsilon$, then

$$[S] \to Q_k^{X_n} \quad \langle\varepsilon\rangle$$

where $X_{n-1} \in V_k$, and

$$Q_k^{X_n} \to X_n \quad \langle i_{n-1}\ldots i_0\rangle$$

are added to P'. Notice that since G is strict deterministic, a situation $Q_k^{X_n} \to X_n \langle\rho_1\rangle$ and $Q_k^{X_n} \to X_n \langle\rho_2\rangle$ with $\rho_1 \neq \rho_2$ can not occur.

A similar modification is done in case (c). If $\xi([X_{n-1}i_{n-1}X_n]\ldots[X_0i_0X_1][Ai\alpha X_0]) = \varepsilon$, then

$$[Ai\alpha] \to Q_k^{X_n} \quad \langle i\rangle$$

where $X_{n-1} \in V_k$, and

$$Q_k^{X_n} \to X_n \quad \langle i_{n-1}\ldots i_0\rangle$$

are added to P'.

The situations described under (b) and (d) are more complicated. Consider the situation described under (d). Situation (b) can be treated similarly and therefore it is omitted. We assume that the detailed proof of Theorem 10.6 has provided the reader with sufficient insight in the properties of the strings of the form $\xi([X_{n-1}i_{n-1}X_n]\ldots.[X_0i_0X_1][Ai\alpha X_0])$. Therefore we omit detailed proof of the properties which will be used. First we show how to treat some special single productions. If

$$\xi([X_{n-1}i_{n-1}X_n]\ldots[X_0i_0X_1][Ai\alpha X_0]) \neq \varepsilon,$$

then we have

$$\xi([X_{n-1}i_{n-1}X_n]) \neq \varepsilon$$

or there exists an integer ℓ, $0 \le \ell \le n-1$ such that

$$\xi([X_{n-1}i_{n-1}X_n]\ldots[X_\ell i_\ell X_{\ell+1}]) = \varepsilon$$

and

$$\xi([Zj\zeta]) \neq \varepsilon$$

where

$$Z = A,\ j = i \text{ and } \zeta = \alpha X_0 \text{ if } \ell = 0$$

and

$$Z = X_{\ell-1},\ j = i_{\ell-1} \text{ and } \zeta = X_\ell \text{, otherwise.}$$

Since G is strict deterministic, for any other production

$$[A'i'\alpha] \rightarrow Q_k^{X_n}\ \xi([X'_{n-1}i'_{n-1}X_n]\ldots[X'_0i'_0X'_1][A'i'\alpha X'_0])$$

with $A \equiv A'$ (mod π), we have the same situation. That is, if $\xi([X_{n-1}i_{n-1}X_n]) \neq \varepsilon$, then $\xi([X'_{n-1}i'_{n-1}X_n]) \neq \varepsilon$ and otherwise we have

$$\xi([X'_{n-1}i'_{n-1}X_n]\ldots[X'_\ell i_\ell X'_{\ell+1}]) = \varepsilon$$

and

$$\xi([Z'j'\zeta']) \neq \varepsilon$$

where

$$Z' = A',\ j' = i' \text{ and } \zeta' = \alpha X'_0 \text{ if } \ell = 0$$

and

$$Z' = X'_{\ell-1},\ j' = i'_{\ell-1} \text{ and } \zeta' = X'_\ell\ , \text{ otherwise.}$$

Moreover, in the latter case, $i'_{n-1}\ldots\ldots i'_\ell = i_{n-1}\ldots i_\ell$. It follows that we can handle these single productions if we define

$$Q_k^{X_n} \rightarrow X_n \quad \langle\rho\rangle$$

where $\rho = \varepsilon$ if $\xi([X_{n-1}i_{n-1}X_n]) \neq \varepsilon$ and $\rho = i_{n-1}\ldots\ldots i_\ell$ otherwise, where ℓ is as above.

Next we consider situations (d) (and similarly (b)) where we have a nonterminal

$$[X_{\ell-1}i_{\ell-1}X_\ell], \quad n \le \ell \le 2$$

(hence, $\xi([X_{\ell-1}i_{\ell-1}X_\ell]) \neq \varepsilon$) and there exists an integer ℓ', $0 \le \ell' \le \ell - 2$, such that

$$\xi([X_{\ell-2}i_{\ell-2}X_{\ell-1}]\ldots\ldots[X_{\ell'}i_{\ell'}X_{\ell'-1}]) = \varepsilon$$

and

$$\ell' = 0 \text{ or } \xi([X_{\ell'-1}i_{\ell'-1}X_{\ell'-2}]) \neq \varepsilon.$$

Now we have the following two steps. Define $\hat{P}$ to be the set of productions which are obtained in step (a) or (c) together with the productions of the form $Q_k^a \rightarrow a\ \langle\rho\rangle$.

Step 1 (Righthand sides).

For each production

$$[Ai\alpha] \rightarrow Q_k^{X_n} \xi([X_{n-1}i_{n-1}X_n]\ldots.[X_0 i_0 X_1][Ai\alpha X_0])$$

which is defined in step (d) (or, similarly, (b)) add to $\hat{P}$ the production which is obtained if each of the described occurences of $[X_{\ell-1}i_{\ell-1}X_\ell]$ in the righthand side is replaced by a nonterminal $[X_{\ell-1}i_{\ell-1}X_\ell\rho]$, with $\rho = i_{\ell-2}\ldots i_{\ell'}$.

Step 2 (Lefthand sides).

Set $P' = \hat{P}$. For each nonterminal $[X_{\ell-1}i_{\ell-1}X_\ell\rho]$ and for each δ which is righthand side of a production $[X_{\ell-1}i_{\ell-1}X] \rightarrow \delta \quad <\rho'>$ in $\hat{P}$ add $[X_{\ell-1}i_{\ell-1}X_\ell\rho] \rightarrow \delta \quad <\rho'\rho>$ to P'.

We assume that it is clear that grammar G' with the set of productions P' right covers grammar G. It remains to verify that G' is strict deterministic.

Define a partition π' in the following way:

(1") $\Sigma \in \pi'$, $\{[S]\} \in \pi'$

(2") For each k, $1 \leq k \leq m$, the set $\{Q_k^a \mid a \in \Sigma \text{ and } Q_k^a \neq \emptyset\}$ is a block of π'.

(3") $[Ai\alpha\rho] \equiv [Bj\beta\omega] \pmod{\pi'}$, with $\rho, \omega \in \Delta_G^*$, if and only if $A \equiv B \pmod{\pi}$, $\alpha = \beta$ and if $A = B$, then $\rho = \omega$.

Now it is straightforward (since we know that π_1 is strict and since the nonterminals of the form Q_k^a can be treated as in Claim 1) to show that partition π' is strict. This concludes the proof of Lemma 10.10. □

It is not difficult to verify that if grammar G is real-time strict deterministic, then grammar G' is also real-time strict deterministic. Notice that partition π' is a minimal partition since nonterminals are defined to be equivalent if and only if it is necessary.

We can transform grammar G' with the same method. Then a right covering grammar G" is obtained with productions of the form $A \rightarrow \alpha$, with $\alpha \in \Sigma$ or $\alpha \in N \cup N^2 \cup N^3$ and $rhs(1:\alpha) \subseteq \Sigma$ (almost-standard 2-form). This almost-standard 2-form will be used when transforming an almost-GNF strict deterministic grammar to a GNF strict deterministic grammar.

<u>LEMMA 10.11.</u> Any almost-GNF strict deterministic grammar G can be transformed to a GNF strict deterministic grammar G' such that $G'[\bar{r}/\bar{r}]G$.

Proof. We may assume that G is in almost-standard 2-form. We need a preliminary transformation on G before we can use Algorithm 5.5.

Let $G = (N,\Sigma,P,S)$ be strict deterministic under a partition $\pi = \{\Sigma,V_1,V_2,\ldots,V_n\}$. For each k, $1 \le k \le n$ and for each $\beta \in N \cup N^2$ define

$$Q_k^\beta = \{A \to \beta\alpha \mid A \to \beta\alpha \text{ in } P,\ A \in V_k,\ \alpha \in N \cup N^2\}.$$

Let $Q = \{Q_k^\beta \mid 1 \le k \le n,\ \beta \in N \cup N^2 \text{ and } Q_k^\beta \ne \emptyset\}$. Each element Q_k^β in Q will be given a unique number, denoted by $L(Q_k^\beta)$.

We now transform grammar $G = (N,\Sigma,P,S)$ into a strict deterministic grammar $G_1 = (N_1,\Sigma,P_1,S)$ such that G_1 is in almost-GNF and $G_1[\bar{r}/\bar{r}]G$. The transformation is such that the nonterminals of G_1 will contain information on the productions of G. Initially, set $P_1 = \{A \to X \text{ <i>} \mid i.A \to X \text{ in } P,\ X \in V\}$ and set $N_1 = N$. There are the following three steps.

(1) For each rule i. $A \to BC$ in P such that $A \to BC$ in Q_k^B and $j = L(Q_k^B)$, add the rule

$$A \to B[jC] \quad \text{<i>}$$

to P_1. Add the newly introduced symbol $[jC]$ to N_1.

(2) For each rule i. $A \to BCD$ in P such that $A \to BCD$ in $Q_k^B \cap Q_k^{BC}$, $j = L(Q_k^B)$ and $\ell = L(Q_k^{BC})$, add the rule

$$A \to B[jC][\ell D] \quad \text{<i>}$$

to P_1. The newly introduced nonterminal symbols $[jC]$ and $[\ell D]$ are added to N_1.

(3) For each nonterminal symbol $[jC]$ (hence, $C \in N$) and for each δ such that $C \to \delta$ <i> is in P_1, add the rule

$$[jC] \to \delta \quad \text{<i>}$$

to P_1.

We show that grammar G_1 has the desired properties. The useless symbols may be removed from G_1.

<u>CLAIM 1.</u> Grammar G_1 is in almost-standard 2-form and $G_1[\bar{r}/\bar{r}]G$.

Proof of Claim 1. The argument is straightforward and therefore omitted. □

<u>CLAIM 2.</u> Grammar G_1 is strict deterministic.

Proof of Claim 2. Define a partition π_1 of $V_1 = N_1 \cup \Sigma$ in the following way:

(i) $\Sigma \in \pi_1$

(ii) For each A, B $\in$ N, A $\equiv$ B (mod π_1) if and only if A $\equiv$ B (mod π).

(iii) For each [iC], [jD] $\in N_1 - N$, [iC] $\equiv$ [jD] (mod π_1) if and only if i = j and C $\equiv$ D (mod π).

The verification that π_1 is a strict partition is straightforward and therefore omitted. □

The third claim shows why we are interested in grammar G_1.

<u>CLAIM 3.</u> Let [jC] $\in N_1 - N$. There exists a function f, $f : N_1 - N \to \Delta_G \cup \{\varepsilon\}$ such that

$$f([jC]) = i,$$

if $j = L(Q_k^\beta)$ and i. $A \to \beta C$ is in Q_k^β and

$$f([jC]) = \varepsilon,$$

otherwise.

Proof of Claim 3. Consider a nonterminal [jC] in $N_1 - N$. If $j = L(Q_k^\beta)$, then there exists a production in Q_k^β from which [jC] is obtained. We want to determine this production. Consider the case $\beta \in N$. Assume that there are productions $A \to \beta C$ and $B \to \beta CD$ in Q_k^β. However, A $\equiv$ B (mod π), therefore this is not possible. Suppose that there exist different productions $A \to \beta C$ and $B \to \beta C$ in Q_k^β. Also in this case, since A $\equiv$ B (mod π), this can not happen.

It follows that we can uniquely determine whether [jC] is obtained from a production of the form $A \to \beta C$ or from a production of the form $A \to \beta CD$. In the former case the production is completely determined and we define f([jC]) = i if it is the ith production of P. In the latter case we define f([jC]) = ε. If $\beta \in N^2$, then, with a similar argument, there exists exactly one production of the form i. $A \to \beta C$ in Q_k^β and we define f([jC]) = i. □

We extend $f : N_1 - N \to \Delta_G \cup \{\varepsilon\}$ to $f : N_1 \to \Delta_G \cup \{\varepsilon\}$ by defining f(A) = ε for each A $\in$ N. We continue the proof with the steps of Algorithm 5.5. Grammar $G_1 = (N_1,\Sigma,P_1,S)$ will be transformed to a GNF grammar $G' = (N',\Sigma,P',S)$ such that $G'[\bar{r}/\bar{r}]G$.

Initially, set $P' = \{A \to a <\psi(i)f(A)> \mid i.\ A \to a \in P_1\}$ and $N' = N_1$. Let ψ be the cover homomorphism under which $G_1[\bar{r}/\bar{r}]G$.

Step 1. For each production i. $A \to BC\alpha$ in P_1 (with B, C $\in N_1$ and $\alpha \in N_1 \cup \{\varepsilon\}$) the following is done.

(i) If $C \to D\beta E$ is in P_1 (with $D, E \in N_1$ and $\beta \in N_1 \cup \{\varepsilon\}$), then, for any pair of productions k. $B \to a$ and ℓ. $D \to b$ in P_1 add

$$A \to aH_{k\ell}\beta E\alpha \quad <\rho_1>$$

with $\rho_1 = \psi(i)f(A)$ if $\alpha = \varepsilon$ and $\rho_1 = f(A)$ otherwise, and

$$H_{k\ell} \to b \quad <\rho_2>$$

with $\rho_2 = \psi(k\ell)$, to P'. Add $H_{k\ell}$ to N'.

(ii) For each pair of productions j. $C \to b$ and k. $B \to a$ in P_1 add

$$A \to aH_{kj}\alpha \quad <\rho_1>$$

with $\rho_1 = \psi(i)f(A)$ if $\alpha = \varepsilon$ and $\rho_1 = f(A)$ otherwise, and

$$H_{kj} \to b \quad <\rho_2>$$

with $\rho_2 = \psi(kj)$, to P'. Add H_{kj} to N'. (Notice that in the grammar which is obtained in Lemma 10.10 this situation does not occur.)

(iii) For each production k. $B \to a$ in P_1 and pair of productions j. $C \to D$ and ℓ. $D \to b$ add

$$A \to aH_{kj}\alpha \quad <\rho_1>$$

with $\rho_1 = \psi(i)f(A)$ if $\alpha = \varepsilon$ and $\rho_1 = f(A)$ otherwise, and

$$H_{kj} \to b \quad <\rho_2>$$

with $\rho_2 = \psi(k\ell j)$ to P'. Add H_{kj} to N'.

Step 2. For each pair of productions i. $A \to B$ and j. $B \to a$ in P_1 add the production

$$A \to a \quad <\rho>$$

with $\rho = \psi(ji)f(A)$, to P'.

It is not difficult to verify that the cover homomorphism is well-defined. That is, since G_1 is strict deterministic and because of our choice of nonterminal symbols, a situation $A \to \alpha <\rho_1>$ and $A \to \alpha <\rho_2>$ with $\rho_1 \neq \rho_2$ can not occur. In order to conclude that $G'[\bar{r}/\bar{r}]G$ the proof which follows Algorithm 5.5 should be slightly modified.

The algorithm preserves strict determinism. Let π_1 be a strict partition for grammar G_1. Define a partition π' for grammar G' in the following way.

(i) $\pi_1 \subseteq \pi'$

(ii) The set H of newly introduced nonterminal symbols (of the form $H_{k\ell}$) is partitioned as follows. For each pair of productions $A \to BC\alpha$ and $A' \to BC'\alpha'$ in P_1 and for each production k. $B \to a$ in P_1 such that $A \equiv A'$ (mod π_1), define

$$H_{k\ell} \equiv H_{km} \pmod{\pi'}$$

if and only if one of the following situations does occur:

(a) Productions of the form $C \to D\beta E$, $C' \to D\beta' E'$, ℓ. $D \to b$ and m. $D' \to c$ are in P_1.

(b) Productions of the form ℓ. $C \to b$ and m. $C' \to d$ are in P_1.

(c) Productions of the form j. $C \to D$, $D \to b$, m. $C' \to D'$ and $D' \to c$ are in P_1.

Clearly, relation $\equiv$ which is defined in this way is an equivalence relation. Symmetry, reflexivity and transitivity can easily be verified. Therefore we have a partition π' of $V' = N' \cup \Sigma$. The verification that π' is strict is straightforward and therefore omitted. This concludes the proof that $G'[\bar{r}/\bar{r}]G$ and G' is strict deterministic. □

It can be verified that if G is real-time strict deterministic, then both G_1 and G' are real-time strict deterministic. From Lemma 10.10 and Lemma 10.11 we obtain the following corollary.

<u>COROLLARY 10.5.</u> Any ε-free strict deterministic grammar G can be transformed to a strict deterministic grammar G' in GNF such that $G'[\bar{r}/\bar{r}]G$.

<u>THEOREM 10.7.</u> Any strict deterministic grammar G can be transformed to a strict deterministic grammar G' in GNF such that $G'[\bar{r}/\bar{r}]G$.

Proof. Combine Theorem 10.5 and Corollary 10.5. □

Finally we consider negative results for the covering of strict deterministic grammars. Consider the following CFG G with productions

$$S \to aCB \mid aCD \qquad B \to c$$
$$C \to aCb \mid b \qquad D \to d$$

Grammar G is strict deterministic under a partition $\pi = \{\{a,b,c,d\}, \{S\}, \{C\}, \{B,D\}\}$. Grammar G is in GNF, and with the argument presented in Chapter 9 it can be shown that G is not a left parsable grammar.
It follows that there does not exist a right parsable grammar G' such that $G'[\bar{r}/\ell]G$. Hence, there does not exist a strict deterministic or LR-grammar G' which right-to-left covers G.

COROLLARY 10.6. Not every strict deterministic grammar in GNF can be right-to-left covered with a right parsable grammar.

Now consider grammar G_0 (also presented in Chapter 6 and section 10.1) with productions

$$S \to 0SL \mid 1RL$$
$$R \to 1RL \mid 2$$
$$L \to \varepsilon$$

Grammar G_0 is strict deterministic under a partition $\pi = \{\{0,1,2\},\{S\},\{R\},\{L\}\}$. We know (cf. Chapter 6) that G_0 does not have an ε-free left covering CFG.

COROLLARY 10.7. Not every strict deterministic grammar can be left covered with an ε-free grammar.

Consider grammar G_N (also presented in Chapter 6 and in the preceding section) with productions

$S \to 0H_{00}S$	$H_{00} \to 0$
$S \to 0H_{01}R$	$H_{01} \to 1$
$S \to 1H_{11}R$	$H_{11} \to 1$
$S \to 1H_{12}$	$H_{12} \to 2$
$R \to 1Q_{11}R$	$Q_{11} \to 1$
$R \to 1Q_{12}$	$Q_{12} \to 2$
$R \to 2$	

Grammar G_N is strict deterministic under partition
$\pi = \{\{0,1,2\},\{S\},\{H_{00},H_{01}\},\{H_{11},H_{12}\},\{Q_{11},Q_{12}\},\{R\}\}$. Since $G_N[\bar{r}/\ell]G_0$, we may conclude that there does not exist a left-to-right covering ε-free grammar for G_N.

COROLLARY 10.8. Not every strict deterministic grammar in GNF can be left-to-right covered with an ε-free context-free grammar.

We can now construct the cover-table for strict deterministic grammars. In Table XI the cover results are collected. The entries of the table are numbered from 1. to 36. The answers in this table can be found in the following way.

<u>Construction of the cover-table.</u>

(10.2.1) Trivially *yes* are the entries 1., 4., 5., 8., 9., 12., 17., 20., 21., 24., 33. and 36.

G' \ G	COVER	ARB SD	ε-FREE SD	GNF SD
ARB SD	ℓ/ℓ	1. *yes*	5. *yes*	9. *yes*
	$\ell/\bar{r}$	2. *yes*	6. *yes*	10. *yes*
	$\bar{r}/\ell$	3. *no*	7. *no*	11. *no*
	$\bar{r}/\bar{r}$	4. *yes*	8. *yes*	12. *yes*
ε-FREE SD	ℓ/ℓ	13. *no*	17. *yes*	21. *yes*
	$\ell/\bar{r}$	14. *no*	18. *no*	22. *no*
	$\bar{r}/\ell$	15. *no*	19. *no*	23. *no*
	$\bar{r}/\bar{r}$	16. *yes*	20. *yes*	24. *yes*
GNF SD	ℓ/ℓ	25. *no*	29. *yes*	33. *yes*
	$\ell/\bar{r}$	26. *no*	30. *no*	34. *no*
	$\bar{r}/\ell$	27. *no*	31. *no*	35. *no*
	$\bar{r}/\bar{r}$	28. *yes*	32. *yes*	36. *yes*

Table XI. Cover-table for strict deterministic grammars.

(10.2.2) Because of Lemma 10.6 we may conclude that the entries 2., 6. and 10. are *yes*.

(10.2.3) From Theorem 10.5 it follows that entry 16. is *yes*. Because of Theorem 10.6 we may conclude that entry 29. is *yes*.

(10.2.4) From Theorem 10.7 it follows that the entries 28. and 32. are *yes*.

(10.2.5) The entries 3., 7., 11., 15., 19., 23., 27., 31. and 35. are *no* because of Corollary 10.6.

(10.2.6) From Corollary 10.7 it follows that the entries 13. and 25. are *no*. From Corollary 10.8 it follows that the entries 14., 18., 22., 26., 30. and 34. are *no*.

This concludes the construction of the cover-table. The results in this table can be compared with those in Table VI.

10.3. NORMAL FORM COVERS FOR LR(k) GRAMMARS

This section is devoted to the construction of the LR cover-table. At some points we will be less detailed than in the preceeding sections. We make systematic use of the results of Chapter 9. Therefore our treatment and the sequence of results will be different from that of the previous two sections. Our only concern is to fill the LR cover-table and we do not bother about direct transformations on LR-grammars. Moura [113] has found similar results as are presented in this section by directly transforming LR-grammars.

<u>THEOREM 10.8.</u> Any LR(k) grammar can be right covered with an LR(1) grammar in GNF.

Proof. Let $G = (N,\Sigma,P,S)$ be an LR(k) grammar. Define

$$G_0 = (N \cup \{S_0\},\ \Sigma \cup \{\perp\},\ P \cup \{S_0 \rightarrow S\perp\},\ S_0).$$

Provide production $S_0 \rightarrow S\perp$ with label 0. For G_0 we can find a strict deterministic grammar G_1 such that $G_1[\bar{r}/\bar{r}]G_0$ (Theorem 9.4). Grammar G_1 can be transformed to a strict deterministic grammar G_2 in GNF (Theorem 10.7) such that $G_2[\bar{r}/\bar{r}]G_1$. Hence, $G_2[\bar{r}/\bar{r}]G_0$.

Let ψ be the corresponding cover homomorphism. Since G_2 is in GNF, each production whose righthand side contains $\perp$ is of the form $A \rightarrow \perp \langle\pi_1\rangle$. Each production which has A in its righthand side is of the form $C \rightarrow a\alpha A \langle\pi_2\rangle$, for some $C \in N_2$, $a \in \Sigma$ and $\alpha \in N_2^*$.

If we replace each of the productions of the form $A \rightarrow \perp \langle\pi_1\rangle$ by a production $A \rightarrow \varepsilon \langle\pi_1\rangle$, then (modified) grammar G_2 is LR(1) (cf. the proof of Theorem 9.5) and $G_2[\bar{r}/\bar{r}]G$ under a cover homomorphism ψ' which is defined by

$$\psi'(p) = \pi, \quad \text{if } \psi(p) = \pi 0$$
$$\psi'(p) = \psi(p), \text{ otherwise.}$$

If, moreover, for each production $C \rightarrow a\alpha A \langle\pi_2\rangle$ discussed above, with $A \rightarrow \varepsilon \langle\pi_1\rangle$

obtained from $A \rightarrow \bot <\pi_1>$, we let also $C \rightarrow a\alpha <\pi_1\pi_2>$ be a production rule and we delete the rule $A \rightarrow \varepsilon <\pi_1>$, then the resulting grammar is LR(1), in GNF and it right covers grammar G.

Notice that we do not delete the production $C \rightarrow a\alpha A$ from the set of productions since it is not necessarily the case that $|rhs(A)| = 1$. Since $L(G_2)$ is prefix-free we can not have that in G_2 there already existed a production $C \rightarrow a\alpha$.

This change in the productions does not change the LR(1) property of the grammar. If it is possible, before the transformation, to determine by one symbol of look-ahead the productions $A \rightarrow \varepsilon$ and $C \rightarrow a\alpha A$, then it is also possible, after the transformation, to determine production $C \rightarrow a\alpha$ by one symbol of look-ahead. □

The next theorem deals with the left cover result for ε-free and NLR LR(k) grammars.

THEOREM 10.9. Any ε-free NLR LR(k) grammar G can be transformed to an LR(k) grammar G' in GNF such that $G'[\ell/\ell]G$.

Proof. We assume that it is sufficiently clear that a simple substitution in the left corner of a production preserves the LR(k) property of a grammar.

That is, if $C \rightarrow A\beta$ and $A \rightarrow \alpha_j$ are productions in an LR(k) grammar G, then replacing these productions by

$$C \rightarrow \alpha_j\beta, \quad j = 1,\ldots,|rhs(A)|$$

will yield a grammar which is also LR(k). One possible way to show this is to construct the sets of LR(k)-items (Aho and Ullman [3]) and observe that they can not contain inconsistent items.

Once we have observed this we can use the usual algorithm to transform an ε-free and NLR LR(k) grammar to a GNF grammar. Since any LR(k) grammar is unambiguous, it is not necessary to use the more complicated algorithm of section 5.1. A left cover is obtained if we define $C \rightarrow \alpha_j\beta <ik_j>$ for each substitution of productions

$$i.\ C \rightarrow A\beta \text{ and } k_j.\ A \rightarrow \alpha_j,\ j = 1,\ldots,|rhs(A)|.$$

This concludes the proof of Theorem 10.9. □

Before passing to our negative cover results for LR(k) grammars we observe that the LR(1) grammar which is obtained in Theorem 9.5 is NLR. Thus we have the following corollary.

COROLLARY 10.9. Any LR(k) grammar G can be transformed to a NLR LR(1) grammar G' such that $G'[\ell/\bar{r}]G$ and $G'[\bar{r}/\bar{r}]G$.

Finally, we turn our attention to some negative results for LR(k) grammars. Grammar G_0 with productions

$$S \rightarrow 0SL \mid 1RL$$
$$R \rightarrow 1RL \mid 2$$
$$L \rightarrow \varepsilon$$

has the property that there does not exist an ε-free CFG G' such that $G'[\ell/\ell]G$. Grammar G_0 is strict deterministic (cf. section 10.2) and therefore LR(0).

<u>COROLLARY 10.10.</u> Not every LR(0) grammar can be left covered with an ε-free grammar.

Grammar G_N with productions

$$\begin{array}{ll} S \rightarrow 0H_{00}S & H_{00} \rightarrow 0 \\ S \rightarrow 0H_{01}R & H_{01} \rightarrow 1 \\ S \rightarrow 1H_{11}R & H_{11} \rightarrow 1 \\ S \rightarrow 1H_{12} & H_{12} \rightarrow 2 \\ R \rightarrow 1Q_{11}R & Q_{11} \rightarrow 1 \\ R \rightarrow 1Q_{12} & Q_{12} \rightarrow 2 \\ R \rightarrow 2 & \end{array}$$

has the property that there does not exist an ε-free CFG G' such that $G'[\ell/\bar{r}]G_N$. Grammar G_N is strict deterministic (cf. section 10.2) and therefore LR(0).

<u>COROLLARY 10.11.</u> Not every LR(0) grammar in GNF can be left-to-right covered with an ε-free grammar.

Grammar G with productions

$$S \rightarrow aCB \mid aCD$$
$$C \rightarrow aCb \mid b$$
$$B \rightarrow c$$
$$D \rightarrow d$$

is not left parsable (cf.section 10.2). Since grammar G is strict deterministic and therefore LR(0), the following corollary is immediate.

<u>COROLLARY 10.12.</u> Not every LR(0) grammar in GNF can be right-to-left covered with a right parsable grammar.

Now we come to a less straightforward obtainable negative result. We want to show that not every LR-grammar can be left covered with a non-left-recursive (LR-) grammar.

Consider grammar G_0. Since there does not exist an ε-free CFG G' such that $G'[\ell/\ell]G_0$, we know that there does not exist an ε-free grammar G' such that $G'[\bar{r}/\bar{r}]G_0^R$. Here, G_0^R is the 'symmetric' version of grammar G_0, conform Observation 4.3. Grammar G_N^R satisfies $G_N^R[\ell/\bar{r}]G_0^R$. It follows that there does not exist an ε-free CFG G' such that $G'[\bar{r}/\ell]G_N^R$.

Now suppose that there exists a NLR grammar G' such that $G'[\ell/\ell]G_N^R$. However, due to entry 7 of Cover-Table VII we must conclude that then there exists an ε-free grammar G" such that $G''[\bar{r}/\ell]G'$, thus $G''[\bar{r}/\ell]G_N^R$, and we have a contradiction. However, grammar G_N^R is not an LR-grammar. If we want to use this argument, then we need to construct an LR-grammar which can play the role of G_N^R in this argument. This is done below.

We start with a CFG G with productions

1. $S \rightarrow 0AL$
2. $A \rightarrow 1SL$
3. $S \rightarrow 3RL$
4. $A \rightarrow 2RL$
5. $R \rightarrow 4BL$
6. $B \rightarrow 5RL$
7. $R \rightarrow 6$
8. $B \rightarrow 7$
9. $L \rightarrow \varepsilon$

Grammar G can not be left covered with an ε-free CFG. This should be clear by comparing grammar G with grammar G_0. From G we can construct a grammar G_M such that $G_M[\bar{r}/\ell]G$. Grammar G_M has the following productions

$S \rightarrow 0H_{01}S$	<99>	$H_{01} \rightarrow 1$	<12>
$S \rightarrow 0H_{02}R$	<99>	$H_{02} \rightarrow 2$	<14>
$S \rightarrow 3A$	<9>	$B \rightarrow 4$	<35>
$S \rightarrow 3BC$	<99>	$C \rightarrow 7$	<8>
$S \rightarrow 3D$	<9>	$D \rightarrow 6$	<37>
$A \rightarrow 4ER$	<99>	$E \rightarrow 5$	<356>
$R \rightarrow 4H_{45}R$	<99>	$H_{45} \rightarrow 5$	<56>
$R \rightarrow 4F$	<9>	$F \rightarrow 7$	<58>
$R \rightarrow 6$	<7>		

It is not difficult to verify that $G_M[\bar{r}/\ell]G$ and, moreover, G_M^R is an LR(k) grammar. Thus, we may conclude that there does not exist a NLR grammar G' such that $G'[\ell/\ell]G_M^R$.

<u>COROLLARY 10.13.</u> Not every LR-grammar (in $\overline{GNF}$) can be left covered with a NLR grammar.

In Table XII we have collected the cover results for LR-grammars. The entries in this table are numbered from 1. to 100. The answers can be found in the following way.

<u>Construction of the cover-table.</u>

(10.3.1) Trivially *yes* are the entries 1., 4., 5., 8., 9., 12., 13., 16., 17., 20., 25., 28., 32., 36., 37., 40., 49., 52., 53., 56., 57., 60., 73., 76., 77., 80., 97. and 100.

(10.3.2) From Corollary 10.9 it follows that for any LR-grammar G we can find a NLR grammar G' which is LR(1) such that $G'[\ell/\bar{r}]G$ and $G'[\bar{r}/\bar{r}]G$. Hence, we have *yes* for the entries 2., 6., 10., 14., 18., 42., 46., 50., 54., 58., 44. and 48.

(10.3.3) From Corollary 10.10 it follows that the entries 21., 29., 61., 69., 81. and 89. are *no*.
Due to Corollary 10.11 we may conclude that the entries 38., 34., 30., 26., 22., 78., 74., 70., 66., 62., 98., 94., 90., 86. and 82. are *no*.
From Corollary 10.12 we may conclude that we have *no* for the entries 3., 7., 11., 15., 19., 23., 27., 31., 35., 39., 43., 47., 51., 55., 59., 63., 67., 71., 75., 79., 83., 87., 91., 95. and 99.

(10.3.4) From Theorem 10.8 it follows that the entries 84., 64., 24., 88., 68., 92., 72., 32. and 96. are *yes*.
From Theorem 10.9 it follows that entry 93. is *yes*. We may conclude from Corollary 10.13 that the entries 45., 65., 85. and 41. are *no*.

G' \ G	COVER	ARB LR	ε-FREE LR	NLR LR	ε-FREE NLR LR	GNF LR
ARB LR	ℓ/ℓ	1. *yes*	5. *yes*	9. *yes*	13. *yes*	17. *yes*
	$\ell/\bar{r}$	2. *yes*	6. *yes*	10. *yes*	14. *yes*	18. *yes*
	$\bar{r}/\ell$	3. *no*	7. *no*	11. *no*	15. *no*	19. *no*
	$\bar{r}/\bar{r}$	4. *yes*	8. *yes*	12. *yes*	16. *yes*	20. *yes*
ε-FREE LR	ℓ/ℓ	21. *no*	25. *yes*	29. *no*	33. *yes*	37. *yes*
	$\ell/\bar{r}$	22. *no*	26. *no*	30. *no*	34. *no*	38. *no*
	$\bar{r}/\ell$	23. *no*	27. *no*	31. *no*	35. *no*	39. *no*
	$\bar{r}/\bar{r}$	24. *yes*	28. *yes*	32. *yes*	36. *yes*	40. *yes*
NLR LR	ℓ/ℓ	41. *no*	45. *no*	49. *yes*	53. *yes*	57. *yes*
	$\ell/\bar{r}$	42. *yes*	46. *yes*	50. *yes*	54. *yes*	58. *yes*
	$\bar{r}/\ell$	43. *no*	47. *no*	51. *no*	55. *no*	59. *no*
	$\bar{r}/\bar{r}$	44. *yes*	48. *yes*	52. *yes*	56. *yes*	60. *yes*
ε-FREE NLR LR	ℓ/ℓ	61. *no*	65. *no*	69. *no*	73. *yes*	77. *yes*
	$\ell/\bar{r}$	62. *no*	66. *no*	70. *no*	74. *no*	78. *no*
	$\bar{r}/\ell$	63. *no*	67. *no*	71. *no*	75. *no*	79. *no*
	$\bar{r}/\bar{r}$	64. *yes*	68. *yes*	72. *yes*	76. *yes*	80. *yes*
GNF LR	ℓ/ℓ	81. *no*	85. *no*	89. *no*	93. *yes*	97. *yes*
	$\ell/\bar{r}$	82. *no*	86. *no*	90. *no*	94. *no*	98. *no*
	$\bar{r}/\ell$	83. *no*	87. *no*	91. *no*	95. *no*	99. *no*
	$\bar{r}/\bar{r}$	84. *yes*	88. *yes*	92. *yes*	96. *yes*	100. *yes*

Table XII. Cover-table for LR-grammars.

Except for the negative results which are caused by the property that not every LR-grammar is left parsable, the main difference between this table and Table VI is the possibility of a right cover of an arbitrary LR-grammar with a GNF grammar. Notice that not every ε-free LR-grammar can be left covered with a NLR (LR-) grammar.

CHAPTER 11

COVER PROPERTIES OF SIMPLE CHAIN GRAMMARS

In the preceeding chapters we have been concerned with transformations of context-free grammars. One of the key-concepts has been the 'chain'. We have used 'left part' transformations (Algorithms 5.2 and 5.3) and we have introduced 'left-part' parses.

In this chapter we show the origins of these concepts. Historically seen, the results in this chapter precede most results of the preceeding chapters. Most results in this chapter were first published in Nijholt [118,119,122].

We consider a subclass of the LR(0) grammars. This class of grammars, called the simple chain grammars has a very simple and natural bottom-up parsing method. The definition of a simple chain grammar was originally motivated by the parsing method for production prefix grammars, as introduced by Geller, Graham and Harrison [38]. However, they start by constructing a parsing graph for a context-free grammar and give conditions which ensure that the parsing algorithm works correctly. In our approach we start with a grammatical definition and, as can be shown, a slightly adapted version of their parsing method can be used.

This chapter is concerned with the properties of simple chain grammars, their languages, their grammatical trees and their parsing and covering properties. For the time being we consider only simple chain grammars for which no look-ahead is allowed. An extension with look-ahead is straightforward and in Chapter 12 a few notes will be spent on this extension. The class of simple chain grammars is such that it properly contains the class of simple deterministic grammars (Korenjak and Hopcroft [80]). However, each simple chain grammar can be transformed to a weakly equivalent simple deterministic grammar. Thus, the simple chain grammars generate exactly the simple deterministic languages.

Material which is closely related to the parsing method which can be used for simple chain grammars appears in the work of Kràl [82] and Kràl and Demner [83]. They consider top-down properties of DeRemers LR(0) parsing method. A comparison of this work will not be given here.

The organization of this chapter is as follows. In section 11.1 we introduce the simple chain grammars. We develop some of their properties and give examples of simple chain grammars which are not, for any k, LL(k), LC(k) or left parsable. Section 11.2 is devoted to relationships with some other classes of grammars and in section 11.3 simple chain languages are discussed. We present transformations to Greibach normal form and to simple deterministic grammars. Section 11.4 is concerned with the grammatical trees of simple chain grammars. In analogy with Harrison and

Havel [60] a left part property for simple chain grammars is obtained. With the help of this left part property we can (in section 11.5) introduce left part parses and discuss the parsing and covering properties of simple chain grammars.

It should be noted that until Chapter 8 we have been using simple SDTS's (or equivalently, pushdown transducers) without further restrictions. In Chapter 8, 9 and 10 we used deterministic pushdown transducers (DPDT) to obtain cover results. In this chapter we use a simple DPDT to obtain cover results for simple chain grammars.

11.1. SIMPLE CHAIN GRAMMARS

In this section we introduce the class of simple chain grammars and discuss some of their properties.

DEFINITION 11.1. An ε-free CFG $G = (N,\Sigma,P,S)$ is said to be a *simple chain grammar* if P is prefix-free and for any $A \in N$, $\alpha,\varphi,\psi \in V^*$ and $X,Y \in V$ with $X \neq Y$, if $A \to \alpha X\varphi$ and $A \to \alpha Y\psi$ are in P, then $\text{FIRST}(X) \cap \text{FIRST}(Y) = \emptyset$.

Our first task is to prove that each ε-free LL(1) grammar is a simple chain grammar. After that we will be concerned with a definition of simple chain grammars which is equivalent to Definition 11.1 but in which some useful properties of simple chain grammars are explicitly mentioned.

LEMMA 11.1. Every ε-free LL(1) grammar is a simple chain grammar.

Proof. Let $G = (N,\Sigma,P,S)$ be an ε-free LL(1) grammar and assume that G is not a simple chain grammar. If P is not prefix-free then there is $A \in N$ and $\alpha,\beta \in V^*$ such that $A \to \alpha$, $A \to \alpha\beta$ and $\beta \neq \varepsilon$. This obviously contradicts the LL(1) definition. Now suppose there exist $A \in N, \alpha,\varphi,\psi \in V^*$, $X,Y \in V$ and rules $A \to \alpha X\varphi$, $A \to \alpha Y\psi$ with $X \neq Y$ and $\text{FIRST}(X) \cap \text{FIRST}(Y) \neq \emptyset$. Since $\alpha X\varphi \neq \alpha Y\psi$ and $\text{FIRST}(\alpha X\varphi) \cap \text{FIRST}(\alpha Y\psi) \neq \emptyset$ this contradicts the LL(1) definition. □

In Definition 5.1 chains were introduced. We recall this definition. Let $G = (N,\Sigma,P,S)$ be an ε-free CFG. If $X_0 \in N$, then $CH(X_0)$, the set of chains of X_0, is defined by $CH(X_0) = \{X_0X_1\ldots X_n \in N^+\Sigma \mid X_0 \underset{L}{\Rightarrow} X_1\psi_1 \underset{L}{\Rightarrow} \ldots \underset{L}{\Rightarrow} X_n\psi_n,\ \psi_i \in V^*,\ 1 \leq i \leq n\}$ and, for each $X_0 \in \Sigma$, $CH(X_0) = \{X_0\}$. For each $\pi \in CH(X_0)$, let $\ell(\pi)$ denote the last element of π. Thus, if $\pi = X_0X_1\ldots X_n$, then $\ell(\pi) = X_n$ and $\ell(\pi) \in \Sigma$.

DEFINITION 11.2. Let $X \in V$. X is said to be *chain-independent* if for each pair π_1, π_2 in CH(X), if $\pi_1 \neq \pi_2$, then $\ell(\pi_1) \neq \ell(\pi_2)$. If each element of V is chain-independent, then V is said to be *chain-independent*.

Clearly, each terminal symbol is chain-independent. Some other properties are listed in the following lemma.

LEMMA 11.2.

a. Let $X \in V$. If V is chain-independent, then $CH(X)$ is a finite set.

b. If V is chain-independent, then G is NLR.

Proof. Part a. is trivial. Part b. follows from Theorem 5.1. □

DEFINITION 11.3. Let $X,Y \in V$, $X \neq Y$. The symbols X and Y are said to be *mutually* chain-independent, and we write $X \not\equiv Y$, if for each pair $\pi_1 \in CH(X)$ and $\pi_2 \in CH(Y)$, $\ell(\pi_1) \neq \ell(\pi_2)$.

Recall that if $k = 1$ then we omit the index k of the notation $FIRST_k$.

LEMMA 11.3. Let $X,Y \in V$, $X \neq Y$. Then $X \not\equiv Y$ if and only if $FIRST(X) \cap FIRST(Y) = \emptyset$.

Proof. Trivial. □

Notice that for each pair a,b in Σ with $a \neq b$ we have $a \not\equiv b$. The following corollary will be obvious. Recall that a set P of productions is said to be prefix-free if for each pair $A \to \alpha$ and $A \to \alpha\beta$ in P, $\beta = \varepsilon$.

COROLLARY 11.1. CFG $G = (N,\Sigma,P,S)$ is a simple chain grammar if and only if P is prefix-free and for any $\alpha,\varphi,\psi \in V^*$, $A \in N$ and $X,Y \in V$ with $X \neq Y$, if $A \to \alpha X\varphi$ and $A \to \alpha Y\psi$ are in P, then $X \not\equiv Y$.

LEMMA 11.4. If $FIRST(X) \cap FIRST(Y) = \emptyset$ for each pair $A \to \alpha X\varphi$, $A \to \alpha Y\psi$ with $\alpha,\varphi,\psi \in V^*$, $X,Y \in V$ and $X \neq Y$, then V is chain-independent.

Proof. Assume that V is not chain-independent. Hence there exist $A \in N$ and $\pi_1,\pi_2 \in CH(A)$ such that $\pi_1 \neq \pi_2$ and $\ell(\pi_1) = \ell(\pi_2)$. Let $\pi_1 = X_0X_1\ldots X_n$ and $\pi_2 = Y_0Y_1\ldots Y_m$, where $X_0 = Y_0 = A$ and $X_n = Y_m$. Then there exists a maximal $i \geq 0$ such $X_0X_1\ldots X_i = Y_0Y_1\ldots Y_i$, there exists a derivation $A \stackrel{*}{\Rightarrow}_L X_i\psi_i$ for some $\psi_i \in V^*$ and there exist productions $X_i \to X_{i+1}\psi_{i+1}$, $X_i \to Y_{i+1}\psi'_{i+1}$, for some $\psi_{i+1}, \psi'_{i+1} \in V^*$ such that $X_{i+1} \neq Y_{i+1}$. By hypothesis $FIRST(X_{i+1}) \cap FIRST(Y_{i+1}) = \emptyset$. But this contradicts the assumption that $\ell(\pi_1) = \ell(\pi_2)$. □

From Corollary 11.1 and Lemma 11.4 the following corollary is now immediate.

COROLLARY 11.2. An ε-free CFG $G = (N,\Sigma,P,S)$ is a simple chain grammar if and only if the following three conditions are satisfied.

(i) V is chain-independent.

(ii) If there exist $\alpha \in V^+$, $\varphi,\psi \in V^*$, $A \in N$ and $X,Y \in V$ with $X \neq Y$ such that $A \to \alpha X\varphi$ and $A \to \alpha Y\psi$ are in P, then $X \not\Rightarrow Y$.

(iii) P is prefix-free.

Hence, the three conditions in this corollary can be used as a definition of a simple chain grammar. These three conditions will be useful in proofs of properties of simple chain grammars.

To illustrate the definition of a simple chain grammar we consider a few examples.

EXAMPLE 11.1.

Consider grammar G with productions

$$S \to AF \qquad C \to dF \mid dD$$
$$A \to Ba \qquad G \to Cb$$
$$B \to Cd \qquad D \to b$$
$$F \to Ga \mid a$$

For example, $CH(C) = \{Cd\}$, $CH(a) = \{a\}$ and $CH(F) = \{Fa,FGCd\}$. One can easily verify that G satisfies the conditions of a simple chain grammar.

In the following two examples we list simple chain grammars which are not LL(k) or LC(k) (for any $k > 0$) and left parsable, respectively. For the definitions of these classes of grammars the reader should consult Chapter 8 and 9. The proofs are straightforward from these definitions.

EXAMPLE 11.2.

CFG G with productions

$$S \to aEc \mid aEd$$
$$E \to aE \mid ab$$

is a simple chain grammar. However, there is no k such that G is LL(k) or LC(k).

EXAMPLE 11.3.

CFG G with productions

$$S \to aEc \mid aEd$$
$$E \to aEb \mid ab$$

is a simple chain grammar. However, G is not left parsable, that is, there does not exist a DPDT which acts as a left parser for G.

The grammar of Example 11.2 is not ε-free LL(1). Therefore the class of ε-free LL(1) grammars is properly included in the class of simple chain grammars.

<u>DEFINITION 11.4.</u> Let $G = (N,\Sigma,P,S)$ be a CFG. String $\alpha \in V^*$ is said to be *prefix-free* if, for any $w_1,w_2 \in \Sigma^*$, $\alpha \overset{*}{\Rightarrow} w_1$ and $\alpha \overset{*}{\Rightarrow} w_1w_2$ implies $w_2 = \varepsilon$. Grammar G is said to be *prefix-free* if all the nonterminal symbols are prefix-free.

Notice that if a grammar G is prefix-free, then L(G) is prefix-free. That is, if $w_1 \in L(G)$ and $w_1w_2 \in L(G)$, then $w_2 = \varepsilon$.

<u>THEOREM 11.1.</u> Every simple chain grammar is prefix-free.

Proof. We have to prove that every nonterminal of a simple chain grammar is prefix-free. Let $G = (N,\Sigma,P,S)$ be a simple chain grammar. By induction on the length of the derivations we prove that any $\mu \in V^+$ is prefix-free.

Basis. Consider two derivations of length 1 which can be used to obtain w_1 and w_1w_2 in Σ^*; the case in which one derivation is of length 1 and the other is of length 0 cannot occur. If $\mu \underset{R}{\Rightarrow} w_1$ and $\mu \underset{R}{\Rightarrow} w_1w_2$ then there exists a nonterminal $C \in N$ and strings $w',w'',z_1,z_2 \in \Sigma^*$ such that

$$\mu = w'Cw'' \underset{R}{\Rightarrow} w'z_1w'' = w_1,$$

and

$$\mu = w'Cw'' \underset{R}{\Rightarrow} w'z_2w'' = w_1w_2$$

If $w_2 \neq \varepsilon$ then z_1 is a prefix of z_2 and P is not prefix-free, whence $w_2 = \varepsilon$.

Induction. Assume for all $\mu \in V^+$ and derivations $\mu \underset{R}{\overset{*}{\Rightarrow}} w_1$ and $\mu \underset{R}{\overset{*}{\Rightarrow}} w_1w_2$ with lengths less than n, we have $w_2 = \varepsilon$. Now consider derivations $\mu \underset{R}{\overset{*}{\Rightarrow}} w_1$ and $\mu \underset{R}{\overset{*}{\Rightarrow}} w_1w_2$ with lengths less than or equal to n. Then there exist $C \in N$, $\rho,\rho_1,\varphi_1,\varphi_2 \in V^*$, $v_1,v_2,w' \in \Sigma^*$ and $X,Y \in V$ such that $C \to \rho_1X\varphi_1$ and $C \to \rho_1Y\varphi_2$ are in P, with $X \neq Y$ and

$$\mu \underset{R}{\overset{*}{\Rightarrow}} \rho Cw' \underset{R}{\Rightarrow} \rho\rho_1X\varphi_1w' \underset{R}{\overset{*}{\Rightarrow}} \rho\rho_1Xv_1w' \underset{R}{\overset{*}{\Rightarrow}} w_1,$$

and

$$\mu \underset{R}{\overset{*}{\Rightarrow}} \rho Cw' \underset{R}{\Rightarrow} \rho\rho_1Y\varphi_2w' \underset{R}{\overset{*}{\Rightarrow}} \rho\rho_1Yv_2w' \underset{R}{\overset{*}{\Rightarrow}} w_1w_2,$$

where $\rho Cw'$ is the last right sentential form which these two derivations have in common. Since $FIRST(X) \cap FIRST(Y) = \emptyset$ we must have $\rho\rho_1 \neq \varepsilon$. Moreover, to obtain both w_1 and w_1w_2 there exist $w \neq \varepsilon$ and $\bar{w} \neq \varepsilon$ such that $\rho\rho_1 \overset{*}{\underset{R}{\Rightarrow}} w\bar{w}$ and $\rho\rho_1 \overset{*}{\underset{R}{\Rightarrow}} w$, where both w and $w\bar{w}$ are prefixes of w_1, and both derivations are of length less than n. Since this contradicts the induction hypothesis we must conclude $w_2 = \varepsilon$. This concludes the proof that every $\mu \in V^+$ and hence every $A \in N$ is prefix-free. □

<u>THEOREM 11.2.</u> Every simple chain grammar is unambiguous.

Proof. We have to prove that each $w \in L(G)$, where $G = (N,\Sigma,P,S)$ is a simple chain grammar, has exactly one (rightmost) derivation from S. Suppose $S \overset{*}{\underset{R}{\Rightarrow}} w$ by at least two rightmost derivations. Then there exists $A \in N$, $\rho,\varphi_1,\varphi_2 \in V^*$ and $X,Y \in V$, where $X \neq Y$, such that there are derivations

$$A \Rightarrow \rho X\varphi_1 \overset{*}{\underset{R}{\Rightarrow}} w'$$

and

$$A \Rightarrow \rho Y\varphi_2 \overset{*}{\underset{R}{\Rightarrow}} w'$$

where $w' \neq \varepsilon$ is a substring of w. Since $X \neq Y$ we must conclude that ρ is not prefix-free which is in contradiction with Theorem 11.1. Therefore there are no two such derivations. □

A characteristic feature of simple chain grammars is mentioned in the following theorem. The notation $\overset{n}{\underset{L}{\Rightarrow}}$ is used to indicate that the derivation is of length n.

<u>THEOREM 11.3.</u> Let $G = (N,\Sigma,P,S)$ be a simple chain grammar. Suppose there exist $n \geq 1$, $X,Y \in V$ and $\alpha,\varphi,\psi \in V^*$ such that $S \overset{n}{\underset{L}{\Rightarrow}} \alpha X\varphi$ and $S \overset{n}{\underset{L}{\Rightarrow}} \alpha Y\psi$. If $X \neq Y$, then $X \not\equiv Y$.

Proof. The proof is by induction on the length of the derivations. To facilitate the induction proof we take an arbitrary string $\mu \in V^+$ instead of the start symbol S.

Basis. Let $\mu \overset{1}{\underset{L}{\Rightarrow}} \alpha X\varphi$ and $\mu \overset{1}{\underset{L}{\Rightarrow}} \alpha Y\psi$. Suppose $\mu = \gamma C\rho$, $C \in N$, $\gamma \in \Sigma^*$ and $\rho \in V^*$. Then there are productions $C \to \gamma_1 X\rho_1$ and $C \to \gamma_1 Y\rho_2$ in P such that $\gamma\gamma_1 = \alpha$, $\rho_1\rho = \varphi$ and $\rho_2\rho = \psi$. Since $X \neq Y$ we obtain $X \not\equiv Y$.

Induction. Let $\mu \overset{n}{\underset{L}{\Rightarrow}} \alpha X\varphi$ and $\mu \overset{n}{\underset{L}{\Rightarrow}} \alpha Y\psi$ where $X \neq Y$ and assume the property holds for all $\mu \in V^*$ and leftmost derivations with length less than n. There exist $\alpha_1 \in \Sigma^*$, δ, φ_1, $\psi_1,\rho \in V^*$, $X_1,Y_1 \in V$ and $C \in N$ such that $C \to \delta X_1\varphi_1$ and $C \to \delta Y_1\psi_1$, where $X_1 \neq Y_1$, and

$$\mu \overset{k}{\underset{L}{\Rightarrow}} \alpha_1 C\rho \underset{L}{\Rightarrow} \alpha_1 \delta X_1 \varphi_1 \rho \overset{m}{\underset{L}{\Rightarrow}} \alpha X\varphi$$

and

$$\mu \overset{k}{\underset{L}{\Rightarrow}} \alpha_1 C\rho \underset{L}{\Rightarrow} \alpha_1 \delta Y_1 \psi_1 \rho \overset{m}{\underset{L}{\Rightarrow}} \alpha Y\psi$$

with $n = k + m + 1$. If $m = 0$ then $X_1 = X$, $Y_1 = Y$ and since $X_1 \not\equiv Y_1$ we have also $X \not\equiv Y$. Otherwise, since $\alpha_1\delta$ is prefix-free, there are two possibilities:

(i) $\alpha_1\delta \overset{m}{\underset{L}{\Rightarrow}} \alpha X\varphi_1'$, where $\varphi_1' X_1 \varphi_1 \rho = \varphi$,

and

$\alpha_1\delta \overset{m}{\underset{L}{\Rightarrow}} \alpha Y\psi_1'$, where $\psi_1' Y_1 \psi_1 \rho = \psi$.

Since $m < n$ we have $X \not\equiv Y$.

(ii) $\alpha_1\delta \overset{*}{\Rightarrow} \alpha'$, where α' is a prefix of α, that is $\alpha = \alpha'\alpha''$,

and

$X_1 \overset{*}{\underset{L}{\Rightarrow}} \alpha'' X\varphi_1'$, where φ_1' is a prefix of φ,

and

$Y_1 \overset{*}{\underset{L}{\Rightarrow}} \alpha'' Y\psi_1'$, where ψ_1' is a prefix of ψ.

Since $X_1 \not\equiv Y_1$ we have $\alpha'' = \varepsilon$ and $X \not\equiv Y$. □

It follows that $S \overset{n}{\underset{L}{\Rightarrow}} wX\varphi$ and $S \overset{n}{\underset{L}{\Rightarrow}} wY\psi$ with $X \neq Y$ implies $X \not\equiv Y$.

In the remainder of this section we present some results on the rightmost derivations of a simple chain grammar. First we have the following results. In this lemma π denotes the concatenation of the productions in the rightmost derivation.

<u>LEMMA 11.5.</u> Let $G = (N,\Sigma,P,S)$ be a simple chain grammar. Assume $A \in N$, $X \in V$, $\varphi \in V^*$ and $v_1, v_2 \in \Sigma^*$ such that

$$S \overset{*}{\underset{R}{\Rightarrow}} \varphi A v_1 \overset{\pi}{\underset{R}{\Rightarrow}} \varphi X v_2$$

where $A \neq X$. Then there is $v' \in \Sigma^*$ such that $v'v_1 = v_2$ and

$$A \overset{\pi}{\underset{R}{\Rightarrow}} Xv'.$$

Proof. Notice that we can not have $\varphi \overset{*}{\underset{R}{\Rightarrow}} \varphi Xu$ for some $u \in \Sigma^*$ since φ is prefix-free.

Neither can we have $\varphi \underset{R}{\overset{*}{\Rightarrow}} \varphi'$, where φ' is a proper prefix of φ since there are no ε-productions. Therefore we must conclude that $A \underset{R}{\overset{\pi}{\Rightarrow}} Xv'$ for $v' \in \Sigma^*$ and $v'v_1 = v_2$. □

<u>THEOREM 11.4.</u> Let $G = (N,\Sigma,P,S)$ be a simple chain grammar. Let $\alpha \in V^*$, $X,Y \in V$ and $w_1,w_2 \in \Sigma^*$ such that $S \underset{R}{\overset{*}{\Rightarrow}} \alpha X w_1$ and $S \underset{R}{\overset{*}{\Rightarrow}} \alpha Y w_2$, where $X \neq Y$. Then, either $X \not\equiv Y$ or there is a string $u \in \Sigma^*$ such that

$$S \underset{R}{\overset{*}{\Rightarrow}} \alpha X u \underset{R}{\overset{*}{\Rightarrow}} \alpha Y w_2$$

(or the symmetric case:

$$S \underset{R}{\overset{*}{\Rightarrow}} \alpha Y u \underset{R}{\overset{*}{\Rightarrow}} \alpha X w_1)$$

Proof. The proof is by induction on the length of the derivations. Let $\mu \in V^+$. As basis we consider derivations of length one or less.

Basis. First consider derivations

$$\mu \underset{R}{\Rightarrow} \alpha X w_1$$

and

$$\mu \underset{R}{\Rightarrow} \alpha Y w_2$$

where $X \neq Y$. Then there exist $\rho \in V^*$, $C \in N$, $w \in \Sigma$ and $C \to \rho_1 X v_1$, $C \to \rho_1 Y v_2$ in P, such that $\rho\rho_1 = \alpha$, $v_1 w = w_1$ and $v_2 w = w_2$. Since G is a simple chain grammar, $X \not\equiv Y$.

Now suppose that $\mu = \alpha X w_1$ and $\mu \underset{R}{\Rightarrow} \alpha Y w_2$. Then $\alpha X w_1 \underset{R}{\Rightarrow} \alpha Y w_2$. It follows that we have a derivation

$$\mu \underset{R}{\overset{*}{\Rightarrow}} \alpha X w_1 \underset{R}{\overset{*}{\Rightarrow}} \alpha Y w_2$$

which is of the desired form. The basis of the induction is now satisfied.

Induction. Now suppose we have derivations

$$\mu \underset{R}{\overset{*}{\Rightarrow}} \alpha X w_1$$

and

$$\mu \underset{R}{\overset{*}{\Rightarrow}} \alpha Y w_2$$

with $X \neq Y$ and the lengths of the derivations are less than or equal to n. Assume the property holds for all derivations with lengths less than n. There exist $\rho,\rho_1,\varphi_1,\varphi_2 \in V^*$, $C \in N$, $X_1,Y_1 \in V$ such that $C \to \rho_1X_1\varphi_1$ and $C \to \rho_1Y_1\varphi_2$ are in P, with $X_1 \neq Y_1$ and there exist derivations

$$\mu \overset{*}{\underset{R}{\Rightarrow}} \rho Cw \underset{R}{\Rightarrow} \rho\rho_1X_1\varphi_1 w \overset{*}{\underset{R}{\Rightarrow}} \alpha Xw_1$$

and

$$\mu \overset{*}{\underset{R}{\Rightarrow}} \rho Cw \underset{R}{\Rightarrow} \rho\rho_1Y_1\varphi_2 w \overset{*}{\underset{R}{\Rightarrow}} \alpha Yw_2.$$

Since $X_1 \neq Y_1$ and $\rho\rho_1$ is prefix-free there are two possibilities:

(i) $$\rho\rho_1 \overset{*}{\underset{R}{\Rightarrow}} \alpha Xv_1$$

and

$$\rho\rho_1 \overset{*}{\underset{R}{\Rightarrow}} \alpha Yv_2$$

where v_1 is a prefix of w_1 and v_2 is a prefix of w_2. But then, since the lengths of these derivations are less than n, we have by the induction hypothesis either $X \neq Y$ or there is $v \in \Sigma^*$ such that

$$\rho\rho_1 \overset{*}{\underset{R}{\Rightarrow}} \alpha Xv \overset{*}{\underset{R}{\Rightarrow}} \alpha Yv_2$$

where v_2 is a prefix of w_2. If

$$\rho\rho_1 \overset{*}{\underset{R}{\Rightarrow}} \alpha Yv_2$$

then there is a derivation

$$\mu \overset{*}{\underset{R}{\Rightarrow}} \rho\rho_1Y_1\varphi_2 w \overset{*}{\underset{R}{\Rightarrow}} \rho\rho_1 w' \overset{*}{\underset{R}{\Rightarrow}} \alpha Yv_2w' = \alpha Yw_2.$$

Moreover, since

$$\rho\rho_1 \overset{*}{\underset{R}{\Rightarrow}} \alpha Xv \overset{*}{\underset{R}{\Rightarrow}} \alpha Yv_2$$

we can write

$$\mu \overset{*}{\underset{R}{\Rightarrow}} \rho\rho_1Y_1\varphi_2 w \overset{*}{\underset{R}{\Rightarrow}} \rho\rho_1 w' \overset{*}{\underset{R}{\Rightarrow}} \alpha Xvw' \overset{*}{\underset{R}{\Rightarrow}} \alpha Yv_2w' = \alpha Yw_2.$$

Therefore there is $u = vw' \in \Sigma^*$ such that

$$\mu \overset{*}{\underset{R}{\Rightarrow}} \alpha Xu \overset{*}{\underset{R}{\Rightarrow}} \alpha Yw_2.$$

(ii) $$X_1 \overset{*}{\underset{R}{\Rightarrow}} \rho' X w'_1$$

and

$$Y_1 \overset{*}{\underset{R}{\Rightarrow}} \rho' Y w'_2$$

where ρ' is a suffix of α and w'_1 and w'_2 are prefixes of w_1 and w_2, respectively. But then, since $X_1 \not\equiv Y_1$ we have $\rho' = \varepsilon$ and $X \not\equiv Y$.

The proof of the theorem is now complete if we take $\mu = S$. □

Note. It follows from this theorem that, if $S \overset{*}{\underset{R}{\Rightarrow}} \alpha X w_1$ and $S \overset{*}{\underset{R}{\Rightarrow}} \alpha Y w_2$, where $X \neq Y$ and we do not have $X \not\equiv Y$, then there exists $v \in \Sigma^*$ such that

$$S \overset{*}{\underset{R}{\Rightarrow}} \alpha X v \overset{\pi}{\underset{R}{\Rightarrow}} \alpha Y w_2$$

where $X \overset{\pi}{\underset{R}{\Rightarrow}} Yw'$ and w' is such that $w'v = w_2$ (or the symmetric case).

The following corollary is immediate from Theorem 11.4. We use the following notation. For $X,Y \in V$ we write $X \perp Y$ if there does not exist $\psi \in V^*$ such that either $X \overset{*}{\Rightarrow} Y\psi$ or $Y \overset{*}{\Rightarrow} X\psi$. Notice that if $X \neq Y$, then $X \not\equiv Y$ implies $X \perp Y$. If $X \perp Y$, then $X \neq Y$.

<u>COROLLARY 11.3.</u> Let $G = (N,\Sigma,P,S)$ be a simple chain grammar. Suppose there exist $\alpha \in V^*$, $X,Y \in V$ and $w_1,w_2 \in \Sigma^*$ such that $S \overset{*}{\underset{R}{\Rightarrow}} \alpha X w_1$ and $S \overset{*}{\underset{R}{\Rightarrow}} \alpha Y w_2$. If $X \perp Y$, then $X \not\equiv Y$.

Note. Notice that we do not have $S \overset{*}{\underset{R}{\Rightarrow}} \alpha X w_1$ and $S \overset{*}{\underset{R}{\Rightarrow}} \alpha Y w_2$ implies $X \not\equiv Y$. A counter-example is grammar G with productions $S \to aXb$, $X \to Yc$ and $Y \to a$. Grammar G is a simple chain grammar, $S \overset{*}{\underset{R}{\Rightarrow}} aXb$ and $S \overset{*}{\underset{R}{\Rightarrow}} aYcb$ but we do not have $X \not\equiv Y$.

Another example is the grammar with productions $S \to aXD \mid aXe$, $X \to Y$, $Y \to b$ and $D \to d$, which is also a simple chain grammar. Here we have derivations $S \overset{2}{\underset{R}{\Rightarrow}} aXd$ and $S \overset{2}{\underset{R}{\Rightarrow}} aYe$, but we do not have $X \not\equiv Y$.

11.2. RELATIONSHIPS BETWEEN SIMPLE CHAIN GRAMMARS AND OTHER CLASSES OF GRAMMARS

We already saw that each ε-free LL(1) grammar is a simple chain grammar. Moreover, there exist simple chain grammars which are not LL(k) or LC(k), for any $k \geq 0$. In Chapter 12 we will return to the relation between simple chain grammars and LC-grammars. Here we will compare the class of simple chain grammars with the classes of grammars that are simple precedence, strict deterministic or LR(0). For the definition of simple precedence the reader is referred to [3]. The definition of strict deterministic grammars can be found in section 8.2.

The CFG with productions $S \to Ab \mid Bc$, $A \to a$ and $B \to ad$ is not a simple chain grammar. By constructing the 'Wirth-Weber precedence matrix' one can easily verify that there are no precedence conflicts. Since the grammar is also *uniquely invertible* (i.e., if $A \to \alpha$ and $B \to \alpha$ are in P, then $A = B$) it follows that the grammar is simple precedence. On the other hand, the CFG with only productions $S \to aA \mid bB$, $A \to dc$, $B \to dC$ and $C \to c$ is a simple chain grammar and not a simple precedence grammar.

COROLLARY 11.4. The classes of simple chain grammars and of (ε-free) simple precedence grammars are incomparable.

The CFG with only productions $S \to cb \mid Ab$ and $A \to a$ is a simple chain grammar but not a strict deterministic grammar. The CFG with only productions $S \to Ab \mid Bc$, $A \to ad$ and $B \to ae$ is a strict deterministic grammar but not a simple chain grammar.

COROLLARY 11.5. The classes of simple chain grammars and of (ε-free) strict deterministic grammars are incomparable.

There is a nontrivial hierarchy of strict deterministic grammars and their languages according to their degree (cf. Harrison and Havel [59]). The simplest class in this hierarchy is the class of strict deterministic grammars of degree 1. The following definition is a reformulation of Theorem 3.1 of [61].

DEFINITION 11.5. A CFG $G = (N,\Sigma,P,S)$ is said to be *strict deterministic of degree one* if P is prefix-free and if $A \to \alpha X \varphi$ and $A \to \alpha Y \psi$ are in P (hence, α,φ and ψ in V^* and X and Y in V), with $X \neq Y$, then X and Y are in Σ.

LEMMA 11.6. Any ε-free strict deterministic grammar of degree 1 is a simple chain grammar.

Proof. Trivial. □

In order to prove that every simple chain grammar is LR(0) we have to show that if

$$S \overset{*}{\underset{R}{\Rightarrow}} \alpha A w \underset{R}{\Rightarrow} \alpha\beta w = \gamma w$$

and

$$S \overset{*}{\underset{R}{\Rightarrow}} \alpha' A' x \underset{R}{\Rightarrow} \alpha'\beta' x = \gamma w'$$

then $A \to \beta = A' \to \beta'$ and $|\alpha\beta| = |\alpha'\beta'|$.

Notice that $S \overset{+}{\Rightarrow} S$ is not possible in a simple chain grammar.

One possible way to do this is to assume that there exists a simple chain grammar which is not LR(0) and to do a tedious case analysis based on the following four situations:

(i) $|\alpha'| \leq |\alpha|$

(ii) $|\alpha| < |\alpha'| < |\alpha\beta|$

(iii) $|\alpha'| > |\alpha\beta|$, and

(iv) $|\alpha'| = |\alpha\beta|$

Each of these cases can actually occur for a non-LR(0) grammar and it can be shown that for each of these cases the assumption that G is not LR(0) leads to a contradiction with G being a simple chain grammar.

The following proof, however, which was suggested by a referee of [122], uses the construction of the state sets of the usual LR(0) parsing algorithm. It is shown that if a CFG G is a simple chain grammar, then these state sets do not contain inconsistent items. Therefore we may conclude that G is LR(0).

We recall a few definitions. However, to avoid too much repetition of terminology we assume that the reader is familiar with the construction of the LR(0) parsing algorithm ([3,58]).

DEFINITION 11.7. Suppose that $S \overset{*}{\underset{R}{\Rightarrow}} \alpha Aw \underset{R}{\Rightarrow} \alpha\beta w$ in a CFG G. String γ is a *viable prefix* of G if γ is a prefix of $\alpha\beta$. We say that $[A \to \beta_1.\beta_2]$ is an LR(0) *item* for G if $A \to \beta_1\beta_2$ is a production in P. LR(0) item $[A \to \beta_1.\beta_2]$ is *valid* for $\alpha\beta_1$ (a viable prefix of G) if there is a derivation $S \overset{*}{\underset{R}{\Rightarrow}} \alpha Aw \underset{R}{\Rightarrow} \alpha\beta_1\beta_2 w$.

For any viable prefix γ of G define $V(\gamma)$ to be the set of LR(0) items valid for γ. Define

$$S = \{\sigma \mid \sigma = V(\gamma) \text{ for some viable prefix } \gamma \text{ of } G\},$$

the collection of LR(0) *state sets* for G.

In the construction of S each $\sigma \in S$ is obtained as the union of a *basis set* and a set which is achieved by taking the *'closure'* of this basis set. We denote the basis set of a set $\sigma \in S$ by basis(σ).

THEOREM 11.5. Every simple chain grammar is an LR(0) grammar.

Proof. Let S be the collection of state sets for simple chain grammar $G = (N,\Sigma,P,S)$. First we have the following claim.

<u>CLAIM.</u> Let $\sigma \in S$. If $[A \to \alpha_1.\alpha_2]$ and $[B \to \beta_1.\beta_2]$ are any two distinct items in basis (σ), then $A = B$ and $\alpha_1 = \beta_1$.

Proof of the Claim. By definition of S there exists $\gamma \in V^*$ such that $\sigma = V(\gamma)$. It is convenient to prove the claim by induction on $|\gamma|$.

Basis. $|\gamma| = 0$. By convention (see Algorithm 5.8 [3]) basis$(V(\varepsilon))$ = $= \{[S \to .\alpha] \mid S \to \alpha \text{ is in } P\}$ for which the claim is easily verified. Notice that for every state set σ other than $V(\varepsilon)$ an item $[A \to \alpha_1.\alpha_2]$ can only be in basis(σ) if $\alpha_1 \neq \varepsilon$.

Induction. Consider a string γX where $\gamma \in V^*$ and $X \in V$. Assume that the claim is true for $\sigma = V(\gamma)$; we will show that it is likewise true for $\sigma' = V(\gamma X)$. Let $[A \to \alpha_1 X.\alpha_2]$ and $[B \to \beta_1 X.\beta_2]$ be any two items in basis(σ'). Then both $[A \to \alpha_1.X\alpha_2]$ and $[B \to \beta_1.X\beta_2]$ are in σ. There are now several cases:

(I) $\alpha_1 \neq \varepsilon \neq \beta_1$: By the induction hypothesis $A = B$ and $\alpha_1 = \beta_1$, as desired since both items belong to basis(σ).

(II) $\alpha_1 \neq \varepsilon$ and $\beta_1 = \varepsilon$: In this case $[B \to .X\beta_2]$ is obtained from some item $[C \to \gamma_1.Y\gamma_2] \in$ basis(σ), so that $Y \overset{+}{\underset{L}{\Rightarrow}} X\varphi$ for some $\varphi \in V^*$ and because of the induction hypothesis, $C = A$ and $\gamma_1 = \alpha_1$. Hence we have productions $A \to \alpha_1 Y\gamma_2$ and $A \to \alpha_1 X\alpha_2$. If $X = Y$ then X is left recursive, which is not possible in a simple chain grammar. If $X \neq Y$ then, since FIRST(X) $\cap$ FIRST(Y) $\neq \emptyset$, we obtain a contradiction with the definition of a simple chain grammar.

(III) $\alpha_1 = \varepsilon$ and $\beta_1 \neq \varepsilon$: This case is symmetric to (II).

(IV) $\alpha_1 = \varepsilon = \beta_1$: Then either $A = B = S$, hence the claim is satisfied, or $[A \to .X\alpha_2]$ and $[B \to .X\beta_2]$ are obtained from items $[C \to \gamma_1.U\gamma_2]$ and $[C \to \gamma_1.U'\gamma'_2]$, respectively, in basis$(\sigma)$. If $U = U'$ then either U is not chain-independent, which is impossible, or $A = B$, as desired. If $U \neq U'$ then, since FIRST(U) $\cap$ FIRST(U') $\neq \emptyset$, G is not a simple chain grammar.

This concludes the proof of the claim. □

Now suppose that G is not LR(0). Then there is some LR(0) state set σ of G which contains two ore more inconsistent items. There are two cases (see Definition 2.4 in Geller and Harrison [41])

(i) A *shift/reduce conflict*: There are two items $[A \to \alpha_1.a\alpha_2]$ and $[B \to \beta.]$ in σ, where $\alpha_1,\alpha_2,\beta \in V^*$ and $a \in \Sigma$. Since $\beta = \varepsilon$ we have that $[B \to \beta]$ is in basis(σ). There are two cases:

(a) $\alpha_1 \neq \varepsilon$: It follows that $\alpha_1 = \beta$, $A = B$ and P is not prefix-free which is impossible.

(b) $\alpha_1 = \varepsilon$: In this case there exists a production $B \to \beta X\varphi$ in P, where $X\varphi \in NV^*$ and $X \overset{+}{\underset{L}{\Rightarrow}} A\psi$ for some $\psi \in V^*$, and also in this case we have that P is not prefix-free, which is impossible.

(ii) A *reduce/reduce conflict*: There are two items $[A \to \alpha.]$ and $[B \to \beta.]$ in σ. Since G is ε-free $\alpha \neq \varepsilon \neq \beta$ and both items belong to basis(σ). It follows from the claim that $A = B$ and $\alpha = \beta$, so that, in fact, no conflict exists in σ.

It follows that every simple chain grammar is an LR(0) grammar. □

Observe that, since we are only concerned with ε-free grammars, the combination of Lemma 11.1 and Theorem 11.5 does not lead to the incorrect result that any LL(1) grammar (not necessarily ε-free) is an LR(0) grammar. Clearly, every simple deterministic grammar is a simple chain grammar. The class of simple chain grammars is properly included in the LR(0) grammars since the CFG with only productions $S \to aB$, $S \to eB$, $B \to cD$, $B \to cF$, $D \to b$ and $F \to b$ is LR(0) but it is not a simple chain grammar.

In Reichardt [139] and in Schlichtiger [147,148] (cf. also Chapter 12) simple chain grammars are compared with some other classes of grammars.

11.3. SIMPLE CHAIN LANGUAGES

In this section we show that the class of simple chain languages coincides with the class of simple deterministic languages. First we show that every simple chain grammar can be transformed to an equivalent simple chain grammar in Greibach normal form. A transformation which is similar to ours can be found in [42] where it is shown that each strict deterministic grammar can be transformed to a strict deterministic grammar in GNF.

<u>OBSERVATION 11.1.</u> Let $G = (N,\Sigma,P,S)$ be a simple chain grammar. Let $A \in N$ and $a \in$ FIRST(A). The chain from A to a in CH(A) is uniquely determined and therefore also its length. Denote this length by $n_A(a)$. Hence, if $A \overset{n}{\underset{L}{\Rightarrow}} a\alpha$ for some $\alpha \in V^*$, then $n \geq n_A(a)$.

<u>THEOREM 11.6.</u> Each simple chain grammar can be transformed to a weakly equivalent simple chain grammar in GNF.

Proof. Let $G = (N,\Sigma,P,S)$ be a simple chain grammar. Let $P' = \{A \to a\alpha \mid A \in N, \alpha \in V^*$ and $a \in \Sigma$ such that $A \overset{n'}{\underset{L}{\Rightarrow}} a\alpha$ with $n' = n_A(a)\}$ and let $G' = (N,\Sigma,P',S)$. In this way G' is well-defined, G' has no ε-productions and moreover, G' is in quasi-GNF. CFG G' can be reduced in the usual way.

CLAIM 1. G' is a simple chain grammar.

Proof of Claim 1. Consider Definition 11.1. Assume P' is not prefix-free, so that there exist productions $A \to \alpha$ and $A \to \alpha\beta$ in P' with $\beta \neq \varepsilon$. Then, by definition of P' there exist derivations $A \overset{*}{\underset{L}{\Rightarrow}} \alpha$ and $A \overset{*}{\underset{L}{\Rightarrow}} \alpha\beta$ in G with $\beta \neq \varepsilon$. Since G is a simple chain grammar it follows from Theorem 11.1 that this is not possible. Thus P' is prefix-free.

Now assume there exist $A \in N$, $\alpha,\varphi,\psi \in V^*$ and $X,Y \in V$ with $X \neq Y$ such that $A \to \alpha X\varphi$ and $A \to \alpha Y\psi$ are in P'. Let $\alpha \neq \varepsilon$ and assume $1 : \alpha = a$. Then both derivations in G can be written as

$$A \overset{n'}{\underset{L}{\Rightarrow}} \alpha X\varphi$$

and

$$A \overset{n'}{\underset{L}{\Rightarrow}} \alpha Y\psi$$

where $n' = n_A(a)$.
Then, by Theorem 11.3, $X \not\equiv Y$. If $\alpha = \varepsilon$, then X and Y are in Σ, $X \neq Y$ and therefore also in this case $X \not\equiv Y$. This completes the proof of Claim 1. □

It is not difficult to see that transforming G' in quasi-GNF to a CFG in GNF by replacing terminals inside the righthand sides of the productions in the usual way does not disturb the simple chain properties of G'. Therefore we may assume that G' is in GNF.

CLAIM 2. L(G') = L(G).

Proof of Claim 2. It is clear that for any $w \in \Sigma^*$, $S \overset{*}{\underset{L}{\Rightarrow}} w$ in G' implies $S \overset{*}{\underset{L}{\Rightarrow}} w$ in G. For the converse, consider $A \overset{n}{\underset{L}{\Rightarrow}} w$ in G. If $n = 1$, then trivially, also $A \underset{L}{\Rightarrow} w$ in G'.

Suppose that $A \overset{*}{\underset{L}{\Rightarrow}} w$ in G implies $A \overset{*}{\underset{L}{\Rightarrow}} w$ in G' be true for all derivations of length less than n in G. Factor the derivation $A \overset{n}{\underset{L}{\Rightarrow}} w$ in G to get $A \overset{n'}{\underset{L}{\Rightarrow}} a\alpha$, where $n' = n_A(a)$ and it is assumed that $1 : w = a$. By construction, $A \to a\alpha$ is in P'. Let $\alpha = A_1A_2\ldots A_m \in N^*$. Notice that according to the remark following Claim 1 we may assume $\alpha \in N^*$. Each A_i derives a subword of w, that is, $A_i \overset{*}{\underset{L}{\Rightarrow}} w_i$ in G for $1 \leq i \leq m$ and $w = aw_1w_2\ldots w_m$. Since these derivations are of length less than n, $A_i \overset{*}{\underset{L}{\Rightarrow}} w_i$ in G'. The combination of $A \to aA_1A_2\ldots A_m$ is in P' and $A_i \overset{*}{\underset{L}{\Rightarrow}} w_i$ in G' gives $A \overset{*}{\underset{L}{\Rightarrow}} w$ in G'. Therefore, $S \overset{*}{\underset{L}{\Rightarrow}} w$ in G implies $S \overset{*}{\underset{L}{\Rightarrow}} w$ in G'. It follows that L(G') = L(G). □

With these two claims the proof of Theorem 11.6 is complete. □

Grammar G' which is now in GNF is not necessarily a simple deterministic grammar.

The second transformation of this section will produce a simple deterministic grammar from a simple chain grammar in GNF. In section 11.5 we will give an immediate transformation from a simple chain grammar to a simple deterministic grammar. There we will also discuss the cover properties of these transformations.

The transformation which we are now to present is in fact a simple process of left factoring. That is, we are going to replace productions $A \to \alpha\beta$ and $A \to \alpha\gamma$ with $\alpha \neq \varepsilon$ and $\beta \neq \gamma$ by productions $A \to \alpha H$, $H \to \beta$ and $H \to \gamma$. However, since we want to preserve the Greibach normal form we need to adapt the process of left factoring.

NOTATION 11.1. Let $G = (N,\Sigma,P,S)$ be a CFG. For any $A \in N$ and $\alpha \in V^*$,

$$Q_A^\alpha = \{A \to \alpha\varphi \in P \mid \varphi \in V^*\}.$$

Let $A \to \alpha_1$ and $A \to \alpha_2$ be two productions. The longest string $\alpha \in V^*$ such that α is both a prefix of α_1 and α_2 is called the *common prefix* of $A \to \alpha_1$ and $A \to \alpha_2$. Similarly, we can define the common prefix of a set of productions.

ALGORITHM 11.1.

Input. A simple chain grammar $G = (N,\Sigma,P,S)$ in GNF.

Output. A weakly equivalent simple deterministic grammar $G' = (N',\Sigma,P',S)$.

Method. Initially, set $N' = N$ and $P' = \emptyset$. Define $R = \{(A,a) \mid A \to a\alpha \in P$ for some $\alpha \in V^*\}$. The elements of R are numbered in an arbitrary way. Starting with the first element we shal consider for each element $(A,a) \in R$ the set Q_A^a. The set Q_A^a is not fixed but will change in the course of the computation. Initially,

$$Q_A^a = \{A \to a\varphi \in P \mid \varphi \in N^*\}.$$

Step 1.

(i) Let $|Q_A^a| = 1$. Then add the only production of Q_A^a to P'. If all the elements of R have been considered go to Step 2. Otherwise, start again with the next element of R.

(ii) Let $|Q_A^a| > 1$. Consider $\alpha \in \{a\}N'^*$ such that α satisfies:

a. α is a common prefix of at least two productions in Q_A^a, and

b. there are no productions $A \to a\varphi$ and $A \to a\psi$ with $\varphi \neq \psi$ in Q_A^a with common prefix α' such that α is a proper prefix of α'.

If $|Q_A^\alpha| = n$, then denote the elements of Q_A^α by $\{A \to \alpha X_i\varphi_i \mid 1 \leq i \leq n\}$. Replace in Q_A^a the subset Q_A^α by the only production $A \to \alpha[A\alpha,X_1\varphi_1,\ldots,X_n\varphi_n]$, where $[A\alpha,X_1\varphi_1,\ldots,X_n\varphi_n]$ is a newly introduced nonterminal which is added to N'. Repeat Step 1.

Step 2.
For each newly introduced nonterminal of the form $Q = [B\beta, Y_1\psi_1, \ldots, Y_m\psi_m]$ add to P', for each i, $1 \leq i \leq m$, the set of productions $\{Q \rightarrow \gamma\psi_i \mid Y_i \rightarrow \gamma \in P'\}$.

Step 3.
Remove the useless symbols. □

Note. In general, string α in Step 1 (ii) is not uniquely determined. If there is more than one such α then it does not matter which one is taken first. Notice, that since G is in GNF the strings $Y_i\psi_i$, $1 \leq i \leq m$, are in N'^*. A newly introduced nonterminal symbol $[B\beta, Y_1\psi_1, \ldots, Y_m\psi_m]$ is associated by $B\beta$ with the productions in Q_B^β from which it is obtained.

<u>EXAMPLE 11.4.</u>
Consider the simple chain grammar in GNF with the following list of productions.

$S \rightarrow cA$	$A \rightarrow aBD$	$A \rightarrow aAB$	$D \rightarrow e$
$A \rightarrow aBCBD$	$A \rightarrow aBA$	$A \rightarrow f$	$B \rightarrow b$
$A \rightarrow aBCBA$	$A \rightarrow aACA$	$D \rightarrow d$	$C \rightarrow c$

The subsequent results of Step 1 on Q_A^a can be given in the following order:

1. For $\alpha = aBCB$. $A \rightarrow aBCBD$ and $A \rightarrow aBCBA$ are replaced by $A \rightarrow aBCBQ_0$, where $Q_0 = [AaBCB, D, A]$.
2. For $\alpha = aB$. $A \rightarrow aBCBQ_0$, $A \rightarrow aBD$ and $A \rightarrow aBA$ are replaced by $A \rightarrow aBQ_1$, where $Q_1 = [AaB, CBQ_0, D, A]$.
3. For $\alpha = aA$. $A \rightarrow aACA$ and $A \rightarrow aAB$ are replaced by $A \rightarrow aAQ_2$, where $Q_2 = [AaA, CA, B]$.
4. For $\alpha = a$ (the common prefix of Q_A^a). $A \rightarrow aAQ_2$ and $A \rightarrow aBQ_1$ are replaced by $A \rightarrow aQ_3$, where $Q_3 = [Aa, AQ_2, BQ_1]$.

The result of Step 2 for Q_0, Q_1, Q_2 and Q_3 are:

$Q_0 \rightarrow d$	$Q_1 \rightarrow cBQ_0$	$Q_1 \rightarrow f$	$Q_3 \rightarrow fQ_2$
$Q_0 \rightarrow e$	$Q_1 \rightarrow d$	$Q_2 \rightarrow cA$	$Q_3 \rightarrow bQ_1$
$Q_0 \rightarrow aQ_3$	$Q_1 \rightarrow e$	$Q_2 \rightarrow b$	
$Q_0 \rightarrow f$	$Q_1 \rightarrow aQ_3$	$Q_3 \rightarrow aQ_3Q_2$	

<u>THEOREM 11.7.</u> Each simple chain grammar can be transformed to a weakly equivalent simple deterministic grammar.

Proof. By Theorem 11.6 we may assume that $G = (N,\Sigma,P,S)$ is a simple chain grammar in GNF. Let $G' = (N',\Sigma,P',S)$ be the CFG which is obtained by Algorithm 11.1. The proof that G' is a simple deterministic grammar which is weakly equivalent to G is divided into three claims.

<u>CLAIM 1.</u> Let $Q = [A\alpha,X_1\varphi_1,\ldots,X_n\varphi_n]$ be a newly introduced nonterminal symbol. Each X_i, $1 \leq i \leq n$, is in N and if $i \neq j$, where $1 \leq i, j \leq n$, then $X_i \neq X_j$ and $X_i \not\equiv X_j$.

Proof of Claim 1. Observe that the prefix α in step 1 (ii) is always in ΣN^* (that is, it does not contain newly introduced nonterminals). Moreover, since all the productions in Q^a_A are considered at the same time we can not have productions $A \rightarrow \alpha Q'\varphi$ for some newly introduced Q' and $\varphi \in N'^*$ and $A \rightarrow \alpha B\psi$ for some $B \in N$ and $\psi \in N'^*$. Thus, each $X_i\varphi_i$ which is mentioned in Q has $X_i \in N$. Moreover, $X_i \neq X_j$ since otherwise the α which was chosen was not the longest applicable prefix as is demanded in part b of Step 1 (ii). Since X_i, $X_j \in N$ there exist productions $A \rightarrow \alpha X_i\varphi$ and $A \rightarrow \alpha X_j\psi$ in P, for some φ and ψ in V^*. For $i \neq j$ we have $X_i \neq X_j$ and since P is the set of productions for simple chain grammar G, we have $X_i \not\equiv X_j$. □

<u>CLAIM 2.</u> G' is a simple deterministic grammar.

Proof of Claim 2. We have to show that for each $A \in N'$ and $a \in \Sigma$ there is at most one production $A \rightarrow a\alpha$ in P', for some $\alpha \in V'^*$.

A set Q^a_A, where $A \in N$ and $a \in \Sigma$, is reduced to only one production whose right-hand side has as prefix the common prefix of Q^a_A. Therefore, after step 1 has been performed, for each $A \in N$ and $a \in \Sigma$ there is at most one production $A \rightarrow a\alpha$ in P' for some $\alpha \in N'^*$.

In step 2 productions are introduced for the new nonterminals of the form $Q = [A\alpha,X_1\varphi_1,\ldots,X_n\varphi_n]$. Since, by Claim 1, $X_i \not\equiv X_j$ for $i \neq j$, we can not have $X_i \rightarrow a\gamma$ and $X_j \rightarrow a\gamma'$ for some $a \in \Sigma$ and $\gamma,\gamma' \in V'^*$. Therefore, for any newly introduced Q and for any $a \in \Sigma$ there is also at most one production in Q^a_Q. This concludes the proof that G' is simple deterministic. □

<u>CLAIM 3.</u> $L(G') = L(G)$.

Proof of Claim 3. In Figure 11.1 the transformation is illustrated. Only local transformations as presented in this figure are performed. Therefore the transformation is language preserving. □

From Claim 2 and Claim 3 it follows that Theorem 11.7 is proved. □

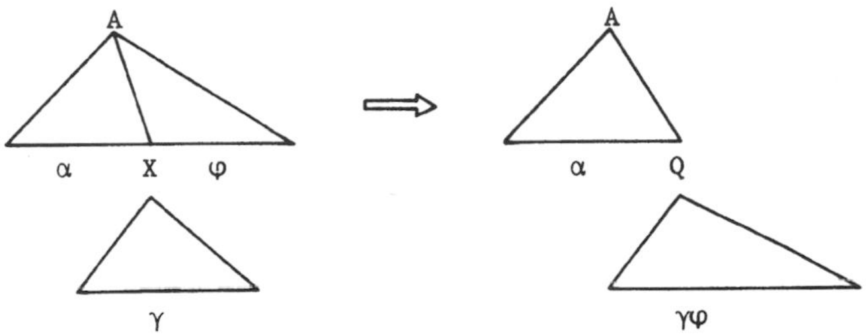

Figure 11.1. Transformation to simple deterministic grammars.

Since each simple deterministic grammar is a simple chain grammar and since it is decidable whether two simple deterministic grammars are weakly equivalent we have the following corollary.

COROLLARY 11.6.

a. The class of simple chain languages coincides with the class of simple deterministic languages.

b. It is decidable whether two simple chain grammars are weakly equivalent.

11.4. A LEFT PART THEOREM FOR SIMPLE CHAIN GRAMMARS

In this section we consider a global property of the grammatical trees of context-free grammars. This property can be considered as a restricted version of the left part property for the trees of strict deterministic grammars (Harrison and Havel [60]). It will be shown that this left part property is satisfied by the set of grammatical trees of a left part grammar, a type of context-free grammar which is a slight generalization of a simple chain grammar.

If a context-free grammar is unambiguous, then each terminal string generated by this grammar has a unique parse tree. Informally, our left part property requires that every prefix of such a terminal string has a unique 'partial'tree. This notion of 'partial' tree will be specified.

To present the left part property and to describe grammatical trees we use the notations and definitions from Harrison and Havel [60]. For convenience we repeat, as far as necessary, some of these notions here. For more details the reader is referred to [60].

Among others, an intuitive assumption on 'translations' of prefixes of sentences which is discussed in Kràl [82] motivated us to introduce this left part property.

The organization of this section is as follows. We continue with some definitions and notational conventions on trees and grammatical trees. Then we present the left part property and we introduce the left part grammars. We show that a context-free grammar is a left part grammar if and only if its set of grammatical trees satisfies the left part property.

PRELIMINARIES ON TREES

To introduce the concepts of the theory of trees which we need here we will frequently refer to the tree *T* given in Figure 11.2. This introduction goes along similar lines as in [60].

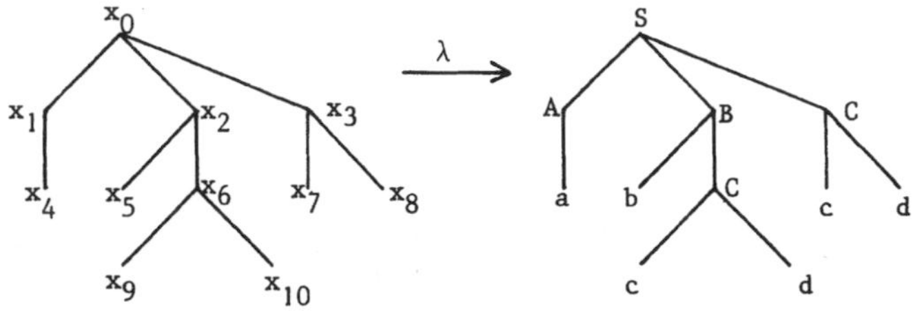

Figure 11.2. Tree *T* and its labeling.

Tree *T* has *nodes* $(x_0,x_1,\ldots,x_{10})$ and it has a *root* (x_0). The relation of *immediate descendancy* is denoted by $\ulcorner$ (for example x_5 is an immediate descendant of x_2, $x_2 \ulcorner x_5$). The *transitive closure* of $\ulcorner$ is denoted by $\ulcorner^+$ and the *reflexive* and *transitive closure* by $\ulcorner^*$. If $x \ulcorner^* y$ then there is a *path* from x to y, which is the sequence of all nodes, including x and y, between x and y. For example, x_0,x_2,x_6,x_{10} is the path in *T* from x_0 to x_{10}. A *leaf* is a node x in *T* for which there is no y in *T* such that $x \ulcorner y$; in Figure 11.2 the leaves are $x_4,x_5,x_9,x_{10},x_7,x_8$, given here in the *left-right order*, which is in general, for a tree *T* with m leaves, denoted by $y_1,y_2,\ldots,y_m$. We introduce the binary relation $\llcorner$ as follows; $x \llcorner y$ if and only if:

(i) x and y are not on the same path and

(ii) for some leaves y_i,y_{i+1} in the left-right order we have $x \ulcorner^* y_i$ and $y \ulcorner^* y_{i+1}$.

Thus, for instance, $x_4 \llcorner x_2$ and, by introducing transitive and transitive-reflexive closures of $\llcorner$ in an obvious way, $x_4 \llcorner^* x_8$.

Two trees *T*, *T'* are *structurally isomorphic*, $T \cong T'$, if and only if there is a bijection g: $T \rightarrow T'$ such that $x \ulcorner_y$ if and only if $g(x) \ulcorner g(y)$ and $x \llcorner y$ if and only if $g(x) \llcorner g(y)$, that is, except for a possible relabeling the trees are identical.

GRAMMATICAL TREES

Let T be a tree. Then every node x of T has a *label* $\lambda(x)$. For instance, in Figure 11.2 x_3 has label C. We will be concerned with grammatical trees, therefore $\lambda(x) \in V$, where $V = N \cup \Sigma$ for a given CFG $G = (N,\Sigma,P,S)$. The *root label* of tree T is denoted by $rt(T)$ (in Figure 11.2 $rt(T) = S$) and the *frontier* of tree T is the concatenation of the labels of the leaves (in the left-right order) of T, notation: $fr(T)$. In Figure 11.2 $fr(T) = abcdcd$. We write $T = T'$ when $T \cong T'$ and T and T' will be treated as identical. The productions in P are elementary subtrees (see Figure 11.3 for a production $A \to X_1X_2...X_n$).

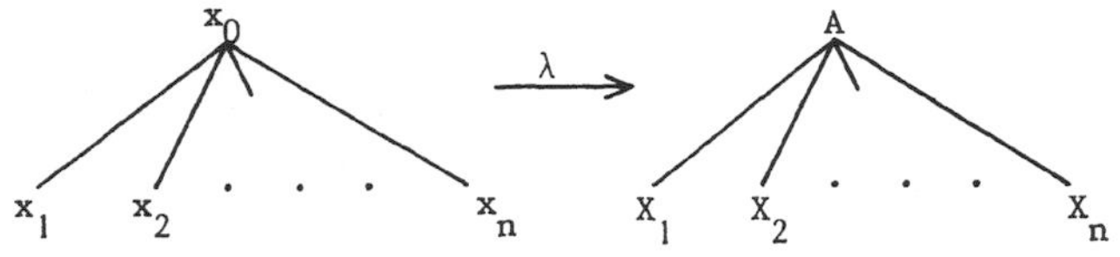

Figure 11.3. An elementary subtree.

Formally, T is said to be a *grammatical* tree for a CFG $G = (N,\Sigma,P,S)$ iff

(i) for every elementary subtree T' of T there exists a production in P corresponding to T', and

(ii) $fr(T) \in \Sigma^*$.

The set of grammatical trees for a CFG G is denoted by J_G. Define $J_G(A) = \{T \in J_G \mid rt(T) = A\}$ and trees in $J_G(S)$ are the *parse trees* of G (cf.Definition 1.5).

Having introduced the necessary preliminaries we now can turn our attention to the left part property.

Let $G = (N,\Sigma,P,S)$ be a CFG. Informally, the left part property says that for each $A \in N$ and for each prefix u of $w = uv \in L(A)$, u uniquely determines the "left part" (up to the first symbol of v) of the grammatical tree which corresponds to the derivation of w from A. Clearly such a property can only be satisfied (take for instance $v = \varepsilon$ and $A = S$) by grammatical trees for which the CFG is unambiguous. The following definition of left part is from Harrison and Havel [60].

<u>DEFINITION 11.8.</u> Let T be a grammatical tree of some grammar G. For any $n \geq 0$ define ${}^{(n)}T$, the *left n-part* of T(or the *left part* when n is understood) as follows. Let $(x_1,\ldots,x_m)$ be the sequence of all leaves in T (from the left to the right). Then ${}^{(n)}T = \{x \in T \mid x \llcorner^* \ulcorner^* x_n\}$ if $n \leq m$ and ${}^{(n)}T = T$ if $n > m$. ${}^{(n)}T$ is considered to be a tree under the same relations $\ulcorner$, $\llcorner$ and the same labeling λ as T.

For instance, in Figure 11.2 ${}^{(3)}T$ is the subtree with the nodes x_0, x_1, x_2, x_4, x_5, x_6 and x_9. In the following definition we introduce our simple left part property for a set of grammatical trees.

<u>DEFINITION 11.9.</u> Let $J \subseteq J_G$, for some CFG G. J is said to satisfy the *left part property* if for any $n > 0$ and $T, T' \in J$, if $rt(T) = rt(T')$ and ${}^{(n)}fr(T) = {}^{(n)}fr(T')$ then ${}^{(n)}T = {}^{(n)}T'$.

This definition is illustrated in Figure 11.4 where two trees T and T' in a set $J \subseteq J_G$ are given with their labeling. In this figure we have ${}^{(2)}T = {}^{(2)}T'$. However, since ${}^{(3)}T \neq {}^{(3)}T'$ and ${}^{(3)}fr(T) = {}^{(3)}fr(T')$ we may conclude that J does not satisfy the left part property. Clearly, not for every CFG G we have that J_G satisfies the left part property. We introduce the left part grammars, a modest generalization of simple chain grammars, defined in such a way that CFG G is a left part grammar if and only if J_G satisfies the left part property.

Let $G = (N, \Sigma, P, S)$ be a CFG. Set P is said to be *prefix(1)* if for each pair $A \to \beta$, $A \to \beta\gamma$ in P, with $\gamma \neq \varepsilon$ and for $\alpha \in V^*$ and $w \in \Sigma^*$, if $S \overset{*}{\underset{L}{\Rightarrow}} wA\alpha$, then $FIRST(\gamma) \cap FIRST(\alpha) = \emptyset$. To avoid an empty α we add, if necessary, the production $S' \to S\perp$ to P, where S' is a new start symbol and $\perp$ is an endmarker, $\perp \notin V$.

<u>DEFINITION 11.10.</u> An ε-free CFG $G = (N, \Sigma, P, S)$ is said to be a *left part grammar* if P is prefix(1) and $FIRST(X) \cap FIRST(Y) = \emptyset$ for each pair $A \to \alpha X\varphi$, $A \to \alpha Y\psi$ in P, with $X \neq Y$.

The following corollary is now self-evident (cf. Corollary 11.2).

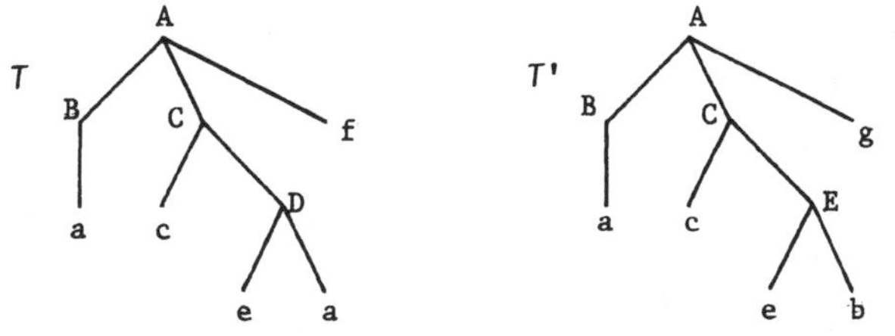

Figure 11.4. Two trees, ${}^{(3)}T \neq {}^{(3)}T'$.

<u>COROLLARY 11.7.</u> A CFG $G = (N, \Sigma, P, S)$ is a left part grammar if and only if

(i) P is prefix(1)

(ii) V is chain-independent

(iii) $X \not\sim Y$ for each pair $A \to \alpha X\varphi$, $A \to \alpha Y\psi$ in P with $X \neq Y$ and $\alpha \neq \varepsilon$.

EXAMPLE 11.5.

Grammar G with only productions $S \to Ac$ and $A \to a \mid ab$ is a left part grammar. G is not a simple chain grammar.

The class of simple deterministic languages is properly included in the class of left part languages. Consider CFG G with productions

$$S \to aSa \mid aA$$
$$A \to bd \mid b \mid c$$

Obviously, G is a left part grammar. However the language generated by G is not a simple deterministic language, since L(G) can not be generated by an ε-free LL(1) grammar (see Aho and Ullman [3]). Since each simple deterministic grammar is an ε-free LL(1) grammar, the proper inclusion follows.

From Definition 11.9 and Definition 11.10 we now can achieve the main result of this section.

THEOREM 11.8. Let $G = (N,\Sigma,P,S)$ be a CFG. The set J_G of the grammatical trees of G satisfies the left part property if and only if G is a left part grammar.

Proof. (The 'if'-direction). Let G be a left part grammar. To prove: J_G satisfies the left part property. Assume J_G does not satisfy the left part property. Hence there exist $n > 0$ and trees T_1 and T_2 in J_G with $rt(T_1) = rt(T_2)$, ${}^{(n)}fr(T_1) = {}^{(n)}fr(T_2)$ and ${}^{(n)}T_1 \neq {}^{(n)}T_2$. Suppose $n = 1$, then ${}^{(1)}T_1 \neq {}^{(1)}T_2$ and ${}^{(1)}fr(T_1) = {}^{(1)}fr(T_2)$ hence, since $rt(T_1) = rt(T_2)$ we must conclude that V is not chain-independent. Contradiction.

Now consider the case $n > 1$. For T_1 and T_2 we can choose n such that ${}^{(n-1)}T_1 = {}^{(n-1)}T_2$ and ${}^{(n)}T_1 \neq {}^{(n)}T_2$. Let T_1 be labeled by λ_1 and T_2 by T_2. The restriction of λ_1 to ${}^{(n-1)}T_1$ which is equal to the restriction of λ_2 to ${}^{(n-1)}T_2$ is denoted by λ. We use the same convention for the relations $\ulcorner_1$, $\llcorner_1$ on T_1 and $\ulcorner_2$, $\llcorner_2$ on T_2. Let the leaves of ${}^{(n)}T_1$ have a left-right order $x_1,x_2,\ldots,x_n$. Since ${}^{(n)}fr(T_1) = {}^{(n)}fr(T_2)$ we have the same order and labels for the leaves of ${}^{(n)}T_2$. Since ${}^{(n-1)}T_1 = {}^{(n-1)}T_2$, the path in T_1 from the root of T_1 to x_{n-1} is the same (including the labeling) as the path in T_2 from the root of T_2 to x_{n-1}. Let this path be $p = (y_0,y_1,\ldots,y_m)$, where y_0 is the root, $y_m = x_{n-1}$ and $y_0 \ulcorner y_1 \ulcorner \ldots \ulcorner y_m$. Since ${}^{(n)}T_1 \neq {}^{(n)}T_2$ there exist nodes y_i and y_j on p $(0 \leq i,\ j < m)$ such that

a. $y_i \ulcorner_1^* x_n$ in T_1 and not $y_{i+1} \ulcorner_1^* x_n$ in T_1

b. $y_j \ulcorner_2^* x_n$ in T_2 and not $y_{j+1} \ulcorner_2^* x_n$ in T_2.

First we show that i = j. Suppose i > j (the case i < j is symmetric). See also Figure 11.5. Since T_1 and T_2 are grammatical trees and since we have no ε-productions there exist $\lambda(y_i) \to \beta\lambda(y_{i+1})$ and $\lambda(y_i) \to \beta\lambda(y_{i+1})\varphi$ in P, for some $\varphi \in V^+$ and $\beta \in V^*$. Notice that $\varphi \neq \varepsilon$ since $\lambda_1(x_n) \in \mathrm{FIRST}(\varphi)$.

Tree T_1 corresponds with a derivation
$\mathrm{rt}(T_1) \overset{*}{\underset{L}{\Rightarrow}} w\lambda(y_i)\alpha_1 \underset{L}{\Rightarrow} w\beta\lambda(y_{i+1})\varphi\alpha_1 \overset{*}{\underset{L}{\Rightarrow}} {}^{(n-1)}\mathrm{fr}(T_1)\varphi\alpha_1 \overset{*}{\underset{L}{\Rightarrow}} \mathrm{fr}(T_1)$, for some $w \in \Sigma^*$ and $\alpha_1 \in V^*$.

Tree T_2 corresponds with a derivation
$\mathrm{rt}(T_2) \overset{*}{\underset{L}{\Rightarrow}} w\lambda(y_i)\ \alpha_2 \underset{L}{\Rightarrow} w\beta\lambda(y_{i+1})\alpha_2 \overset{*}{\underset{L}{\Rightarrow}} {}^{(n-1)}\mathrm{fr}(T_2)\alpha_2 \overset{*}{\underset{L}{\Rightarrow}} \mathrm{fr}(T_2)$, for some $w \in \Sigma^*$ and $\alpha_2 \in V^*$.

Since $\lambda_1(x_n) = \lambda_2(x_n)$ we have that $\mathrm{FIRST}(\alpha_2) \cap \mathrm{FIRST}(\varphi) \neq \emptyset$. Since the CFG is reduced and since $\mathrm{rt}(T_1) = \mathrm{rt}(T_2)$ it immediately follows that if P contains

$$\lambda(y_i) \to \beta\lambda(y_{i+1}) \text{ and } \lambda(y_i) \to \beta\lambda(y_{i+1})\varphi$$

then P is not prefix(1). Therefore we must conclude that i = j.

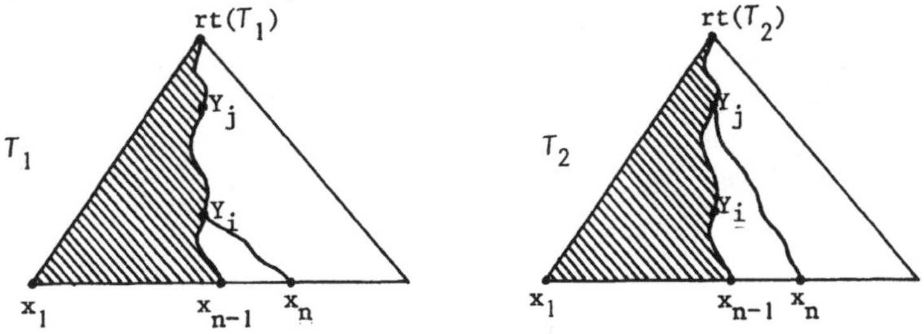

Figure 11.5. Trees T_1 and T_2.

We proceed with i. There are corresponding nodes, z_1 in T_1 and z_2 in T_2, which will again be treated as identical, hence we omit the indexes, such that $y_i \ulcorner_1 z$, $y_i \ulcorner_2 z$, $y_{i+1} \llcorner_1 z$, $y_{i+1} \llcorner_2 z$ and $z \ulcorner_1^* x_n$ and $z \ulcorner_2^* x_n$. Left part ${}^{(n)}T_1$ is obtained by adding in an obvious way the path from y_i to x_n to ${}^{(n-1)}T_1$. Left part ${}^{(n)}T_2$ is obtained in an analogous way. Hence there are paths $y_i \ulcorner_1 z \ulcorner_1 \ldots \ulcorner_1 x_n$ and $y_i \ulcorner_2 z \ulcorner_2 \ldots \ulcorner_2 x_n$. Since ${}^{(n-1)}T_1 = {}^{(n-1)}T_2$ and ${}^{(n)}T_1 \neq {}^{(n)}T_2$ these labeled paths are different. Since T_1 and T_2 are grammatical trees there exist productions $\lambda(y_i) \to \beta\lambda(y_{i+1})\lambda_1(z)\psi_1$ and $\lambda(y_i) \to \beta\lambda(y_{i+1})\lambda_2(z)\psi_2$, for some β, ψ_1 and ψ_2 in V^*. If $\lambda_1(z) = \lambda_2(z_2)$ then V is not chain-independent. If $\lambda_1(z) \neq \lambda_2(z)$ then the necessary condition that $\lambda_1(z) \neq \lambda_2(z)$ is not satisfied. We must conclude that also the case n > 1 leads to a contradiction. This concludes the 'if'-part of the proof.

(The 'only if'-direction). Let G be a CFG such that J_G satisfies the left part property. Assume that G is not a left part grammar, then, according to Corollary 11.7 there are three possibilities:

(i) V is not chain-independent. Then there is $A \in N$ and $\pi_1, \pi_2 \in CH(A)$, $\pi_1 \neq \pi_2$ such that $\ell(\pi_1) = \ell(\pi_2)$. Then we can construct trees T_1 and T_2 in J_G with $rt(T_1) = rt(T_2) = A$ and where the first leaf of each of the trees has label $\ell(\pi_1)$. Let the path (and the labeling) from the root of T_1 to the first leaf of T_1 be according to π_1 and the path (and the labeling) from the root of T_2 to the first leaf of T_2 be according to π_2, then ${}^{(1)}fr(T_1) = {}^{(1)}fr(T_2)$ and ${}^{(1)}T_1 \neq {}^{(1)}T_2$. Contradiction.

(ii) Suppose there exist productions $A \to \alpha X \varphi$ and $A \to \alpha Y \psi$ in P, $X \neq Y$, $\alpha \neq \varepsilon$ and X and Y are not mutually chain-independent. Let $w \in L(\alpha)$, where $|w| = n - 1$. Let $\pi_1 \in CH(X)$, $\pi_2 \in CH(Y)$ and $\ell(\pi_1) = \ell(\pi_2)$. Obviously there exist trees T_1 and T_2 in J_G with $rt(T_1) = rt(T_2) = A$, ${}^{(n-1)}fr(T_1) = {}^{(n-1)}fr(T_2) = w$ and ${}^{(n-1)}T_1 = {}^{(n-1)}T_2$. By adding paths corresponding to the chains π_1 and π_2 to ${}^{(n-1)}T_1$ and to ${}^{(n-1)}T_2$ respectively we obtain a situation such that ${}^{(n)}fr(T_1) = {}^{(n)}fr(T_2)$ and ${}^{(n)}T_1 \neq {}^{(n)}T_2$. Contradiction.

(iii) Suppose P is not prefix(1). Then there exist productions $A \to \beta$ and $A \to \beta\gamma$, $\gamma \neq \varepsilon$ and there is $a \in \Sigma$, $w \in \Sigma^*$ and $\alpha \in V^*$ such that $S \overset{*}{\underset{L}{\Rightarrow}} wA\alpha$ and $a \in FIRST(\gamma) \cap FIRST(\alpha)$. Also in this case we can construct trees T_1 and T_2 in J_G, $rt(T_1) = rt(T_2) = S$. Let $w_1 \in L(\beta)$ and let $|ww_1|$ be $n - 1$. Then we construct T_1 and T_2 such that ${}^{(n)}fr(T_1) = {}^{(n)}fr(T_2) = ww_1a$ and where ${}^{(n)}T_1 \neq {}^{(n)}T_2$, since ${}^{(n)}T_1$ is obtained from ${}^{(n-1)}T_1$ by adding the (rightmost) path from the node corresponding to ${}^{(1)}\alpha$ to the nth leaf of T_1, and ${}^{(n)}T_2$ is obtained by adding to ${}^{(n-1)}T_1$ (= ${}^{(n-1)}T_2$) the path from the node corresponding to A to the nth leaf of T_2. Since ${}^{(n)}T_1 \neq {}^{(n)}T_2$ we have again a contradiction with the left part property. This concludes the 'only if' part of the proof and therefore the proof of Theorem 11.8 is now complete. □

We may conclude that the grammatical trees of a simple chain grammar satisfy the left part property.

In Harrison and Havel [60] the left part property for strict deterministic grammars is used to prove relationships between strict deterministic grammars and other classes of grammars. Moreover, the property is used to develop an iteration theorem for deterministic languages. In Beatty [10,11] a left part property of LL(k) grammars is considered and iteration theorems for LL(k) languages are obtained.

11.5. LEFT PART PARSING AND COVERING OF SIMPLE CHAIN GRAMMARS

In section 11.3 we have seen that each simple chain grammar can be transformed to a weakly equivalent simple deterministic grammar. Unfortunately, this transformation can not be done in such a way that always a left cover or a left-to-right cover can be defined. This will be shown in the present section.

With the help of the simple left part property we will then show that a positive cover result can be obtained if we use the left part parse. The method which will be used to show this does not differ from the methods use in Chapter 7 and Chapter 9. That is, we construct a (left part) parser for a simple chain grammar and then convert it into a (simple deterministic) grammar.

The first algorithm of this section, however, shows how right parsing can be done for simple chain grammars. From the proof of Theorem 11.5 it will already be clear that a simplified version of the LR(0) parsing method can be used. Moreover, it is possible to modify the construction of the parsing-graphs for production prefix grammars (Geller, Graham and Harrison [38]) so that they are suitable for a parsing method for simple chain grammars. We will confine ourselves to the presentation of a DPDT which acts as a right parser for the simple chain grammar from which it is constructed.

<u>ALGORITHM 11.2.</u>

Input. A simple chain grammar $G = (N,\Sigma,P,S)$.

Output. A DPDT $R = (Q,\Sigma,\Gamma,\Delta,\delta,q_0,Z,F)$ which is a right parser for G.

Method. Define $Q = \{q\}$, $q_0 = q$, $F = \{q\}$, $\Delta = \Delta_G$, $\Gamma = \{[A\alpha] \mid A \to \alpha\beta \text{ in } P, A \in N$ and $\alpha,\beta \in V^*\}$, $Z = [S]$ and the function δ is defined in the following way:

(i) For each $i.A \to \alpha$ in P, define $\delta(q,\varepsilon,[A\alpha]) = (q,\varepsilon,i)$.

(ii) For any $[A\alpha] \in \Gamma$, with $A \to \alpha\beta$ in P and $\beta \neq \varepsilon$, and any chain $X_0X_1\ldots X_n \in CH(1:\beta)$, define:

(a) $\delta(q,X_n,[A\alpha]) = (q,[A\alpha X_0],\varepsilon)$ if $X_0 = X_n \in \Sigma$ and otherwise

(b) $\delta(q,X_n,[A\alpha]) = (q,[X_{n-1}X_n]\ldots.[X_0X_1][A\alpha X_0],\varepsilon)$.

This concludes Algorithm 11.2. □

Define a simple SDTS T on simple chain grammar $G = (N,\Sigma,P,S)$ such that if $i.A \to \alpha$ is in P, then $A \to \alpha$, $h_\Sigma(\alpha i)$ is a rule of T. We have to show that Algorithm 11.2 yields a right parser for G, that is, it should be proved that $\tau(R) = \tau(T) = \bar{r}_G$. This proof can be based on the following two claims. Since the proofs of the claims and the proof of $\tau(R) = \tau(T)$ hardly differ from the proofs which are used for a more interesting result stated in Corollary 11.7, we confine ourselves to the presentation of the two claims.

<u>CLAIM 1.</u> Let $A \to \alpha X_0 \varphi$ be in P and let $X_0 X_1 \dots X_{n-1} Y \in N^* V$ be a prefix of a chain in $CH(X_0)$. Then

$$(Y, h_\Sigma(Y)) \overset{*}{\underset{R}{\Rightarrow}} (y, \pi)$$

for some $m \geq 0$, $y \in \Sigma^+$ and $\pi \in \Delta^*$, implies

$$(q, y, [A\alpha], \varepsilon) \overset{*}{\vdash} (q, \varepsilon, [X_{n-1} Y] \dots [X_0 X_1][A\alpha X_0], \pi).$$

<u>CLAIM 2.</u> If $(q, w, [A\alpha X], \varepsilon) \overset{*}{\vdash} (q, \varepsilon, \varepsilon, \pi)$, then

$$(A, A) \overset{*}{\underset{R}{\Rightarrow}} (\alpha X w, h_\Sigma(\alpha X \pi)).$$

In the preceding chapters pushdown transducers (PDT) and deterministic pushdown transducers (DPDT) have been used. The class of simple deterministic languages is exactly the class of languages which can be accepted with a simple deterministic pushdown automaton. Here we immediately define the notion of a simple deterministic pushdown transducer (simple DPDT).

<u>DEFINITION 11.11.</u> A *simple* DPDT is a five-tuple $R = (\Sigma, \Delta, \Gamma, \delta, S)$, where Σ is the input alphabet, Δ is the output alphabet, Γ is the alphabet of pushdown list symbols, δ is a mapping from $\Sigma \times \Gamma$ to $\Gamma^* \times \Delta^*$ and $S \in \Gamma$ is the initial pushdown list symbol.

A *configuration* of a simple DPDT is a triple (w, α, y) in $\Sigma^* \times \Gamma^* \times \Delta^*$, where w will stand for the unused portion of the input string, α represents the contents of the pushdown list and y is the output string emitted sofar. The *binary relation* $\vdash$ on configurations is defined by

$$(aw, Z\alpha, y) \vdash (w, \gamma\alpha, yz)$$

if and only if $\delta(a, Z) = (\gamma, z)$, for some $a \in \Sigma$, $Z \in \Gamma$, $\gamma \in \Gamma^*$ and $z \in \Delta^*$. An *initial configuration* of R is of the form (w, S, ε) for some $w \in \Sigma^*$.

The *transitive* and *transitive-reflexive* closures of $\vdash$ are denoted by $\overset{+}{\vdash}$ and $\overset{*}{\vdash}$, respectively. The *translation* defined by a simple DPDT R is the set $\tau(R) = \{(w,x) \mid (w, S, \varepsilon) \overset{*}{\vdash} (\varepsilon, \varepsilon, x)\}$. If $(w,x) \in \tau(R)$, then x is said to be a translation of w. We will always have that $\Delta = \Delta_G$ for some grammar G.

Observe that if a simple DPDT is converted into a simple SDTS, then the underlying input grammar is simple deterministic. Note also that a simple DPDT can act as a left parser for a simple deterministic grammar; define $\delta(a, A) = (\alpha, i)$ for each production $i.A \to a\alpha$. It will be clear that we do not have to bother about an endmarker.

<u>DEFINITION 11.12.</u> A simple DPDT R is *valid* for CFG G and parse relation f_G if $\tau(R) = f_G$.

Instead of f_G-parsable grammars (cf.Definition 9.2) we can now introduce *simple* f_G-parsable grammars for a parse relation f_G. We will not repeat definitions and theorems of Chapter 9, but observations similar to those in that chapter will be used.

Each simple deterministic grammar is both left parsable and right parsable. Now consider the simple chain grammar G with productions:

$$S \to aEc \mid aEd$$
$$E \to aEb \mid ab$$

Grammar G is not left parsable. This will be clear from the arguments presented in Chapter 9. It follows that there does not exist a left parsable grammar G' such that $G'[\ell/\ell]G$ or $G'[\bar{r}/\ell]G$ (cf.Theorem 9.6). Since any simple deterministic grammar is left parsable, we may conclude that a transformation from a simple chain grammar G to a simple deterministic grammar G' will not always satisfy $G'[\ell/\ell]G$ or $G'[\bar{r}/\ell]G$. Now consider simple chain grammar G with productions:

1. $S \to aB$	3. $B \to b$
2. $B \to aB$	4. $B \to c$

Notice that G is not only a simple chain grammar but also a simple deterministic grammar. However, G is not simple right parsable. That is, there does not exist a simple DPDT which is valid for G and $\bar{r}_G$. This follows from the following claim.

<u>CLAIM.</u> There does not exist a valid simple DPDT for G and $\bar{r}_G$.

Proof. If a simple DPDT is valid, then no ε-moves can be made. For G we have parse relation $\bar{r}_G = \{(a^n b, 32^{n-1}1) \mid n \geq 1\} \cup \{(a^n c, 42^{n-1}1) \mid n \geq 1\}$. For any DPDT which performs the translation $\bar{r}_G$ the first symbol on the output tape should be 3 or 4, depending on whether a string $a^n b$ or $a^n c$ is parsed.

In both cases the DPDT can not emit this first symbol until symbol b or c has been read. After a^n has been read there is only one symbol left on the input tape while an unbounded amount of output symbols must be generated. Therefore ε-moves are needed. □

We may conclude that there does not exist a simple deterministic grammar G' such that $G'[\ell/\bar{r}]G$.

It is possible to construct a left part parser for each simple chain grammar.

The intuitive idea behind the method is as follows. In Figure 11.6 it is displayed how a parse tree T is obtained from partial subtrees (left parts) by considering the next terminal symbol, reading from left to right.

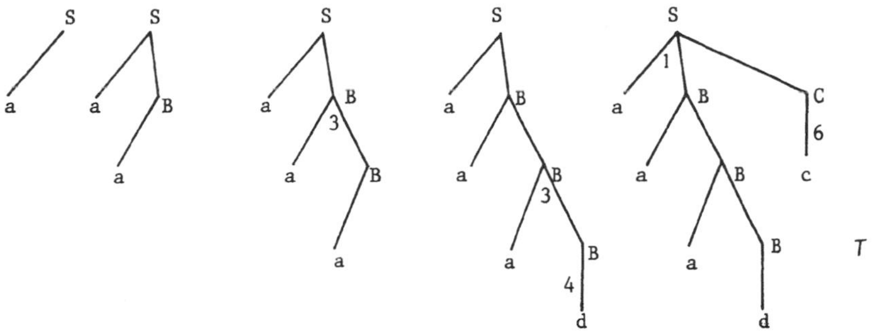

Figure 11.6. Tree T and its left parts.

The left part parse of tree T is 33416. In ${}^{(1)}T$ and in ${}^{(2)}T$ there are only 'partial' productions. In ${}^{(3)}T$ it can be seen that production 3 is completely displayed. In ${}^{(4)}T$ the following production 3 and production 4 are complete. Finally, in ${}^{(5)}T$ the productions 1 and 6 follow.

The left parts of a simple chain grammar are unique. That is, each string u which is prefix of a sentence w has exactly one left part. It follows that for simple chain grammars parsing can be done in the following way: Suppose the nth terminal symbol has been read. Now read the next terminal symbol. The productions which are complete in ${}^{(n+1)}T$ and which are partial in ${}^{(n)}T$ can now be given as output. Due to the uniqueness of the left parts these productions are unique.

In the following algorithm, which is a modification of Algorithm 11.2, this idea is formalized and a left part parser is constructed. The algorithm, which takes as input a simple chain grammar $G = (N,\Sigma,P,S)$, will use two special alphabets Γ and Γ' and a homomorphism $\xi: \Gamma'^* \to \Gamma^*$.

Define

$$\Gamma' = \{[S]\} \cup \{[Ak\alpha] \mid i.A \to \alpha\beta \text{ in P for some } \alpha \neq \varepsilon,\ k = i \text{ if } \beta = \varepsilon \text{ and } k = \varepsilon, \text{ otherwise}\}$$

and

$$\Gamma = \{[S]\} \cup \{[A\alpha] \mid A \to \alpha\beta \text{ is in P for some } \alpha,\beta \neq \varepsilon\}.$$

Define homomorphism $\xi: \Gamma'^* \to \Gamma^*$ by defining $\xi([S]) = [S]$ and, for any $[Ak\alpha]$ in Γ',

$$\xi([Ak\alpha]) = \varepsilon \text{ if } [Ak\alpha] \text{ in } \Gamma' - \Gamma$$

and

$$\xi([Ak\alpha]) = [A\alpha], \text{ otherwise.}$$

Notice that for a simple chain grammar P is prefix-free. Therefore, if $[Ak\alpha] \in \Gamma'$ with $k \neq \varepsilon$, then $[A\alpha]$ is not in Γ', and conversely.

ALGORITHM 11.3.

Input. A simple chain grammar $G = (N,\Sigma,P,S)$.

Output. A simple DPDT $R = (\Sigma,\Delta,\Gamma,\delta,[S])$ which is a left part parser for G.

Method. Set Γ is defined as above, $[S] \in \Gamma$, $\Delta = \Delta_G$ and δ is specified below.

(i) For each $X_0X_1\ldots X_n \in CH(X_0)$, with $X_0 = S$, define

$$\delta(X_n,[S]) = (\xi([X_{n-1}k_nX_n]\ldots[X_1k_2X_2][X_0k_1X_1]),k_1\ldots k_n).$$

(ii) For each $A \to \alpha X_0\varphi$ in P, $\alpha \neq \varepsilon$ and $X_0X_1\ldots X_n \in CH(X_0)$, define

$$\delta(X_n,[A\alpha]) = (\xi([X_{n-1}k_nX_n]\ldots[X_0k_1X_1][Ak_0\alpha X_0]),k_0k_1\ldots k_n).$$

This concludes Algorithm 11.3. □

Obviously, R has no ε-rules. It is an immediate consequence of the definition of a simple chain grammar that, for each X_n, $|\delta(x_n,[S])| = 1$ and for each X_n and $[A\alpha]$, $|\delta(X_n,[A\alpha])| = 1$. Therefore δ is well-defined and R is indeed deterministic. That R transduces with empty pushdown list follows from the lemma which will be proved below.

Let Q be the simple SDTS which is defined on simple chain grammar G and which satisfies $\tau(Q) = \ell p_G$. We have to show $\tau(R) = \tau(Q)$. The proof of the following lemma resembles the proof of Theorem 5.2.

LEMMA 11.7. Let G, R and Q be as above. Then

$$(S,S) \overset{*}{\Rightarrow} (w,\pi)$$

in Q if and only if

$$(w,[S],\varepsilon) \overset{*}{\vdash} (\varepsilon,\varepsilon,\pi)$$

in R.

Proof. For the 'only if part' of the proof the following claim is used.

<u>CLAIM 1.</u> Let $A \to \alpha X_0 \varphi$ be in P and let $X_0 X_1 \ldots X_{n-1} Y \in N^* V$ be a prefix of a chain in $CH(X_0)$. Then

$$(Y, h_\Sigma(Y)) \overset{m}{\Rightarrow} (y, \pi)$$

for some $m \geq 0$, $y \in \Sigma^+$ and $\pi \in \Delta^*$, implies

$$(y, [A\alpha], \varepsilon) \overset{*}{\vdash} (\varepsilon, \xi([X_{n-1} k' X_n] \ldots [Ak\alpha X_0]), k \ldots k'\pi)$$

where $X_n = Y$.

Proof of Claim 1. The proof is by induction on m. If $m = 0$, then $y = Y \in \Sigma$ and $\pi = \varepsilon$. In this case we have a production $A \to \alpha X_0 \varphi$ and a chain $X_0 X_1 \ldots X_{n-1} y \in CH(X_0)$. Thus, by construction,

$$\delta(y, [A\alpha]) = (\xi([X_{n-1} k' y] \ldots [Ak\alpha X_0]), k \ldots k').$$

Therefore,

$$(y, [A\alpha], \varepsilon) \vdash (\varepsilon, \xi([X_{n-1} k' X_n] \ldots [Ak\alpha X_0]), k \ldots k'\pi)$$

with $X_n = Y = y$.

Now assume $m > 0$ and assume the claim holds for all $m' < m$ (induction hypothesis). If $j.\ Y \to Y_1 Y_2 \ldots Y_q$ is the first production which is used, then we can write

$$(Y, Y) \Rightarrow (Y_1 Y_2 \ldots Y_q, h_\Sigma(Y_1 Y_2 \ldots Y_{q-1} j Y_q)) \overset{*}{\Rightarrow} (y_1 y_2 \ldots y_q, \pi_1 \pi_2 \ldots \pi_{q-1} j \pi_q)$$

where $y_1 y_2 \ldots y_q = y$, $\pi_1 \pi_2 \ldots \pi_{q-1} j \pi_q = \pi$ and

$$(Y_i, h_\Sigma(Y_i)) \overset{m_i}{\Rightarrow} (y_i, \pi_i)$$

for $y_i \in \Sigma^*$, $m_i < m$ and $1 \leq i \leq q$. From the induction hypothesis it follows that we may conclude

$$(y_1, [A\alpha], \varepsilon) \overset{*}{\vdash} (\varepsilon, \xi([Yk_1 Y_1][X_{n-1} k' X_n] \ldots [Ak\alpha X_0]), k \ldots k' k_1 \pi_1)$$

and

$$(y_i, [YY_1 \ldots Y_{i-1}], \varepsilon) \overset{*}{\vdash} (\varepsilon, \xi([Yk_i Y_1 \ldots Y_{i-1} Y_i]), k_i \pi_i)$$

for $1 < i \leq q$. Notice that $k_i = \varepsilon$, $1 \leq i < q$ and $k_q = j$. We may conclude that

$$(y_1 y_2 \ldots y_q, [A\alpha], \varepsilon) \overset{*}{\vdash} (\varepsilon, \xi([X_{n-1} k' X_n] \ldots [Ak\alpha X_0]), k \ldots k' \pi_1 \ldots \pi_{q-1} j \pi_q)$$

which had to be proved. □

Now let $A \rightarrow \alpha X\varphi$ in P and suppose $(X,X) \overset{*}{\Rightarrow} (x,\pi)$. It follows from Claim 1 that

$$(x,[A\alpha],\varepsilon) \overset{*}{\vdash} (\varepsilon,\xi([Ak\alpha X]),k\pi).$$

Notice that Claim 1 holds for $\alpha = \varepsilon$ and $A = S$. Let 1. $S \rightarrow Z_1Z_2\ldots Z_n$ be the first production which is used in a derivation of $w = z_1z_2\ldots z_n \in \Sigma^*$, where

$$(Z_i,h_\Sigma(Z_i)) \overset{*}{\Rightarrow} (z_i,\pi_i)$$

for $1 \leq i \leq n$. It follows that

$$(S,S) \Rightarrow (Z_1Z_2\ldots Z_n,h_\Sigma(Z_1Z_2\ldots Z_{n-1}1Z_n)) \overset{*}{\Rightarrow} (w,\pi_1\ldots\pi_{n-1}1\pi_n)$$

implies

$$(w,[S],\varepsilon) \overset{*}{\vdash} (\varepsilon,\varepsilon,\pi_1\ldots\pi_{n-1}1\pi_n),$$

which had to be proved for the 'only if part'. Now we show the 'if part' of the proof.

<u>CLAIM 2.</u> If $(w,[A\alpha X],\varepsilon) \overset{m}{\vdash} (\varepsilon,\varepsilon,\pi)$, then

$$(A,A) \overset{*}{\Rightarrow} (\alpha Xw,h_\Sigma(\alpha X\pi)).$$

Proof of Claim 2. The proof is by induction on m. Write $w = ax$, $a \in \Sigma$ and $x \in \Sigma^*$. If $m = 1$, then $w = a$. In that case we have

$$\delta(a,[A\alpha X]) = (\xi([X_{n-1}k_nX_n]\ldots[X_0k_1X_1][Ak_0\alpha XX_0]),k_0k_1\ldots k_n)$$

with $X_0X_1\ldots X_n \in CH(X_0)$, $X_n = a$, $\xi([X_{n-1}k_nX_n]\ldots[X_0k_1X_1][Ak_0\alpha XX_0]) = \varepsilon$ and $\pi' = k_1..k_n$ is the left part parse associated with $X_0 \overset{*}{\Rightarrow} X_n$. Thus,

$$[\alpha,[A\alpha X],\varepsilon) \vdash (\varepsilon,\varepsilon,k_0\pi')$$

implies

$$(A,A) \Rightarrow (\alpha XX_0,h_\Sigma(\alpha Xk_0X_0)) \overset{*}{\Rightarrow} (\alpha Xa,h_\Sigma(\alpha Xk_0\pi'))$$

Now let $m > 1$. Let the first step be done with the transition

$$\delta(a,[A\alpha X]) = (\xi([X_{n-1}k_nX_n]\ldots[X_0k_1X_1][Ak_0\alpha XX_0]),k_0k_1\ldots k_n)$$

with $X_n = a$. Then we have

$$(ax,[A\alpha X],\varepsilon) \vdash (x,\xi([X_{n-1}kX_n]\ldots[X_0k_1X_1][Ak_0\alpha XX_0]),k_0k_1\ldots k_n) \overset{*}{\vdash} (\varepsilon,\varepsilon,\pi).$$

Obviously, there exist $x_i \in \Sigma^*$, $0 \le i \le n$, such that $x = x_nx_{n-1}\ldots x_2x_1x_0$ and $\pi_i \in \Delta^*$, $0 \le i \le n$, such that $\pi = k_0k_1\ldots k_n\pi_n\pi_{n-1}\ldots\pi_2\pi_1\pi_0$, with $\pi_i = x_i = \varepsilon$ if $k_i \neq \varepsilon$, and such that, for those k_i equal to ε,

$$(x_i,[X_{i-1}X_i],\varepsilon) \overset{m_i}{\vdash} (\varepsilon,\varepsilon,\pi_i)$$

and

$$(x_0,[A\alpha XX_0],\varepsilon) \overset{m_0}{\vdash} (\varepsilon,\varepsilon,\pi_0).$$

Since m_0, $m_i < m$, we obtain

$$(X_{i-1},h_\Sigma(X_{i-1})) \overset{*}{\Rightarrow} (X_ix_i,k_ih_\Sigma(X_i)\pi_i)$$

for $1 \le i \le n$, and

$$(A,A) \overset{*}{\Rightarrow} (\alpha XX_0x_0,h_\Sigma(\alpha XX_0)\pi_0).$$

It follows that

$$(A,A) \overset{*}{\Rightarrow} (\alpha Xax,h_\Sigma(\alpha X)\pi).$$

This concludes the proof of Claim 2. □

Now let $(w,[S],\varepsilon) \overset{m}{\vdash} (\varepsilon,\varepsilon,\pi)$. The first step, with $w = ax$ can be written as

$$(ax,[S],\varepsilon) \vdash (x,\xi([X_{n-1}k_nX_n]\ldots[X_0k_1X_1][Sk_0X_0]),k_0k_1\ldots k_n)$$

where $X_n = a$ and the other notations are as usual. From Claim 2, with an analogous partition of x and π as in its proof, we obtain

$$(S,S) \overset{*}{\Rightarrow} (X_0x_0,k_0h_\Sigma(X_0)\pi_0)$$

and for $1 \le i \le n$,

$$(X_{i-1},X_{i-1}) \overset{*}{\Rightarrow} (X_ix_i,k_ih_\Sigma(X_i)\pi_i).$$

Hence,

$$(S,S) \overset{*}{\Rightarrow} (X_nx_n\ldots x_1x_0,k_0k_1\ldots k_n\pi_n\ldots\pi_1\pi_0) = (w,\pi)$$

which had to be proved.

This conclues the proof of Lemma 11.7. □

The following corollary is immediate

<u>COROLLARY 11.7.</u> Each simple chain grammar G has a simple DPDT R such that $\tau(R) = \ell p_G$.

Corollary 11.7 has the following consequence.

<u>COROLLARY 11.8.</u> For each simple chain grammar G there exists a simple deterministic grammar G' such that $G'[\ell/\ell p]G$.

Recall that not for every CFG G the parse relation ℓp_G is proper (cf.Chapter 2).

It should be observed that when Algorithm 5.3 is applied to a simple chain grammar G, then a CFG G' in GNF is obtained such that $G'[\ell/x]G$, $\ell \leq x \leq \ell p$. However, grammar G' is not necessarily a simple chain grammar and therefore not a simple deterministic grammar. The construction of the simple DPDT should be compared with the transformation presented in Algorithm 5.2. This algorithm, when applied to a simple chain grammar, yields a simple deterministic grammar.

CHAPTER 12

TRANSFORMATIONS AND PARSING STRATEGIES: A CONCRETE APPROACH

12.1. INTRODUCTION

In this chapter we study classes of grammars which can be transformed to grammars with 'better' parsing properties. This notion of 'better' will not be made explicit. However, in many cases it will just mean that for the new grammars we can make use of a simpler parsing technique than is possible for the original grammar. Obviously, this does not necessarily imply that parsing will be done faster or that less space is required.

In general we have the following point of view. Consider a well-amenable class of grammars Γ_0. We are interested in the question which grammars can be transformed to grammars belonging to Γ_0. Moreover, the necessary transformations have to be language preserving and, preferably, it should be possible to define a cover homomorphism between the grammars. Hence, we are looking for a class of grammars Γ_1 for which we can find covering grammars in Γ_0.

As a first approach, one can try to find a new parsing method. This will lead to a definition of a class of grammars for which this method can be used. Clearly, in finding a new method we can use ideas and techniques of existing methods. Maybe this new class of grammars can be transformed to the existing class Γ_0 of well-amenable grammars. If we can find such a transformation τ, then we have

$$\tau(\Gamma_1) \subseteq \Gamma_0$$

Transformation τ is an already existing or a newly introduced transformation. In both cases we can try to find the largest class Γ of grammars such that

$$\tau(\Gamma) \subseteq \Gamma_0$$

If we can find this class Γ, then we have the situation that grammar G is in Γ if and only if G can be transformed by τ to a grammar in Γ_0. A next step in this process could possibly be finding a parsing method for Γ and, maybe, by taking instead of Γ_0 the class Γ or Γ_1 as starting point, start a new cycle.

In a second approach it is not the parsing method but the transformation which is the source for the definition of a new class of grammars. Suppose we have a subclass Γ_0 of the class of context-free grammars. There exist many well-known transformations of context-free grammars. If τ is such a transformation, then we can try to characterize the class $\tau^{-1}(\Gamma_0)$ or, for some subclass $\Gamma_0' \subseteq \Gamma_0$, the class $\tau^{-1}(\Gamma_0')$. Consider for example Hotz [66] where three transformations τ_1, τ_2 and τ_3 to Greibach normal form grammars are studied and where it is observed that these transformations may transform non-LR(k) grammars into LR(k) grammars.

From a theoretical point of view one will always be interested in a precise characterization, that is, in the form of a grammatical definition, of Γ_1 and $\tau^{-1}(\Gamma_0)$ and in parsing methods for these classes of grammars. Examples will be given in this chapter.

Clearly, if we have a grammatical definition and a transformation, then, in the case of a cover, we may say that we have enlarged the 'domain' of a given parsing method to the class which satisfies this definition. In a more practical environment one is not always interested in such a precise characterization. For example, the first phase of a compiler writing system can contain one or more transformations which try to make the input grammar suitable for the parser generating part of the system. This can be done without knowledge of a grammatical definition of the class of grammars to which the input grammar belongs. The system recognizes whether these transformations succeed, in which case automatically a correct parser will be constructed , or whether these transformations fail. In the latter case it depends on the design philosophy of the system what will happen (cf. Chapter 8).

Not only enlarging the domain of a given parsing method but also other considerations can lead to transformations of grammars. For example, it can be done to improve the error-correcting capabilities or one can consider transformations, often performed on the parser instead of on the grammar, which improve the time and space requirements of the parsing algorithms. Another example can be found in the description of the Yacc system (Johnson [74]), where the user is advised to use, 'wherever possible', left recursion in the syntax of a programming language. Instead of this advice it would have been possible to include an elimination of right recursion in the system.

In this final chapter of this monograph we will illustrate the above given remarks with some grammatical definitions and transformations. The results mentioned here are a sampling of recent results which have been obtained by various authors. Because of this recentness we are not yet able to give a thorough investigation of this area. However, the reader will recognize that the approaches which we give here are useful.

The class of grammars which will play the role of Γ_0 in the forthcoming two sections will be the class of LL(k) grammars. A first step to a discussion on LL(k) grammar transformations has been given in section 10.1 immediately after the construction of the cover-table for LL(k) grammars. As mentioned in that section, LL(k) grammars can be transformed to covering strong LL(k) grammars.

In section 12.2 we have an informal discussion on parsing strategies which lead to classes of grammars 'between' the LL(k) and LR(k) grammars. The formal approach will be given in section 12.3. Most of the results in these sections first appeared in Rosenkrantz and Lewis [143], Soisalon-Soininen and Ukkonen [157] and Nijholt and Soisalon-Soininen [128]. In section 12.4 we informally introduce an analogous research area where, instead of LL(k) grammars strict deterministic grammars play a central role.

12.2. FROM LL(k) TO LR(k) GRAMMARS: PARSING STRATEGIES

Especially from the point of view of parsing the LL(k) grammars constitute a very attractive class of context-free grammars. For each LL(k) grammar a top-down parsing algorithm can be devised which is essentially an one-state deterministic pushdown transducer, Efficient implementations of LL-parsing algorithms are known (either by a table or by recursive descent), there exist compiler writing systems which are based on LL-parsing methods and error-recovery algorithms for LL-grammars have been developed. Consult Wood [175] for a general overview and an associated bibliography.

There are many reasons why it is interesting to focus on the gap between LL(k) and LR(k) grammars and languages. We mention four of them.

(i) Parsing methods for LL(k) grammars are easy to understand and efficiently implementable. Therefore it is desirable to find subclasses of the LR(k) grammars which can be transformed to the LL(k) grammars.

(ii) It is interesting to study the different parsing properties of LL(k) and LR(k) grammars. Every LL(k) grammar is left parsable (cf.Chapter 9) while not every LR(k) grammar is left parsable.

(iii) The definitions and parsing strategies which can be found for classes of grammars between the LL(k) and LR(k) grammars can, hopefully, be generalized in order to find and investigate parsing methods for more general classes of grammars (cf. section 12.4).

(iv) It is decidable whether two LL(k) grammars generate the same language. The answer is unknown for LR(k) (and LR(0)) grammars. Therefore, in order to obtain an answer for LR-grammars, it seems to be useful to define more general classes of grammars than the LL(k) grammars for which the decidability question can be answered affirmatively.

Many authors have contributed to the research which deals with the 'gap' between LL(k) and LR(k) grammars. At this point we want to mention Rosenkrantz and Lewis [143],

Brosgol [17], Hammer [56], Rechenberg [138], Cho [19], Demers [24] and Soisalon-Soininen and Ukkonen [157].

In order to intuitively characterize the different classes of grammars to be defined we give an intuitive idea of their parsing strategies. In Figure 12.1 we have displayed a parse tree of a context-free grammar $G = (N,\Sigma,P,S)$. In this tree we have described the following situation. There exist terminal strings w, x, y and z, a nonterminal A and symbols $X_1,\ldots,X_p$ in V, such that $A \rightarrow X_1\ldots X_p$ is a production and there exist derivations

$$S \stackrel{*}{\Rightarrow} wAz,$$

$$X_1 \stackrel{*}{\Rightarrow} x,$$

and

$$X_2\ldots X_p \stackrel{*}{\Rightarrow} y.$$

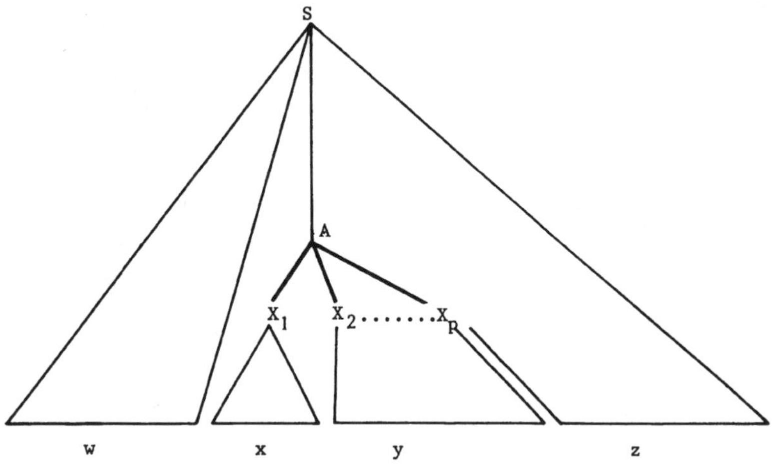

Figure 12.1. Parsing strategies.

In the following table we have collected six parsing strategies which are illustrated with the help of Figure 12.1. The following abbreviations are used:

LL : reading from the left using left parses

PLC: predictive left corner grammars

LP : left part grammars†

† In Nijholt and Soisalon-Soininen [128] the left part grammars were called chain-k (or Ch(k)-) grammars.

LC : left corner grammars

PLR: predictive LR-grammars

LR : reading from the left using right parses

GRAMMAR	READ	RECOGNITION of A	READ	RECOGNITION of $A \rightarrow X_1 \ldots . X_p$
LL	w	k : xyz	w	k : xyz
PLC	w	k : xyz	wx	k : yz
LP	w	k : xyz	wxy	k : z
LC	wx	k : yz	wx	k : yz
PLR	wx	k : yz	wxy	k : z
LR	wxy	k : z	wxy	k : z

Table XIII. Parsing strategies.

With the help of Figure 12.1 the table should be read as follows. Consider the terminal string wxyz. The production $A \rightarrow X_1X_2 \ldots X_p$ depicted in this parse tree of wxyz can be recognized with certainty after scanning

(i) w and k : xyz if the grammar is LL(k)

(ii) wx and k : yz if the grammar is PLC(k) or LC(k)

(iii) wxy and k : z if the grammar is LP(k), PLR(k) or LR(k).

However, if the grammar is PLC(k) or LP(k), then the lefthand side A of the production $A \rightarrow X_1X_2 \ldots X_p$ is already recognized after scanning w and k : xyz. If the grammar is PLR(k), then A is recognized after scanning wx and k : yz.

In Table XIII we have distinguished between the recognition of the lefthand side of a production and the recognition of the whole production rule. In Demers [24] this distinction is not made. He considers a generalization of the LC(k) parsing method. In his approach it is possible to specify arbitrarily for each production rule the position in the righthand side at which that rule is to be recognized.

Clearly, this idea can also be used if we want to distinguish between recognition of the lefthand side of a production and recognition of the whole production. In Table XIII we have only considered a left corner which consists of one symbol. In general we can define strategies and classes of grammars as depicted in Figure 12.2.

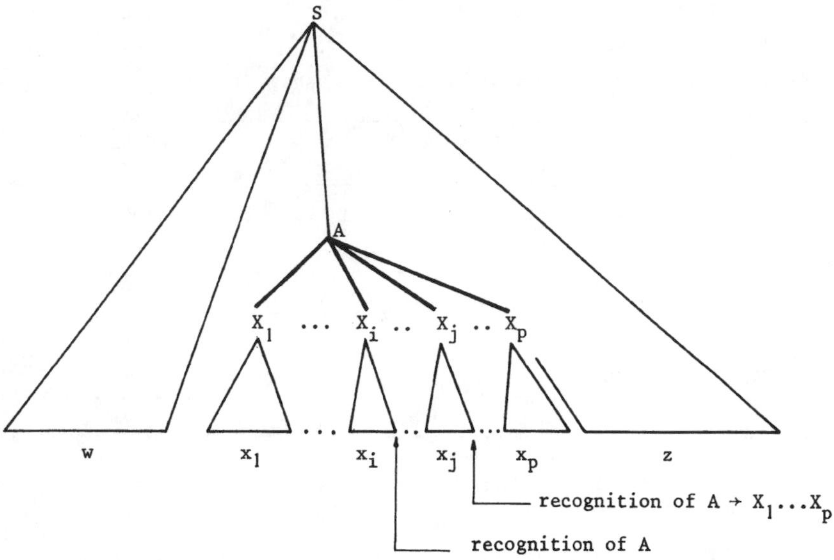

Figure 12.2. Generalized parsing strategies.

In Figure 12.2 we have that for each i, $0 \leq i \leq p$, we can specify where A has to be recognized (by considering $FIRST_k(X_{i+1}...X_p z)$) and for each j, $i \leq j \leq p$, we can specify where the production $A \rightarrow X_1...X_p$ has to be recognized.

It should be noted that when grammar G is in Chomsky normal form, that is, with production which are of the form, $A \rightarrow BC$ or $A \rightarrow a$, then the generalization of Figure 12.1 to Figure 12.2 does not play a role. Moreover, it will be clear that if a grammar is in Chomsky normal form then the strategies for LP-parsing and PLC-parsing coincide. This observation was first made, in a less general setting, by Reichardt [139].

Unfortunately, the representation of classes of grammars in Table XIII does not really expose the differences between LP(k) grammars on the one side and PLR(k) and LR(k) grammars on the other side. In the next section we will return to this drawback of our table-representation of classes of grammars.

12.3. TRANSFORMATIONS TO LL(k) GRAMMARS

We introduce classes of grammars which are properly included in the class of LR(k) grammars and which properly include the class of LL(k) grammars. First we recall the definition of an LL(k) grammar.

A grammar $G = (N,\Sigma,P,S)$ is said to be an LL(k) grammar if, for a terminal string w, a nonterminal A and strings γ, δ_1 and δ_2 in $(N \cup \Sigma)^*$ such that $A \to \delta_1$ and $A \to \delta_2$ are distinct productions of G, the condition

$$S \overset{*}{\underset{L}{\Rightarrow}} wA\gamma$$

implies that

$$\mathrm{FIRST}_k(\delta_1\gamma) \cap \mathrm{FIRST}_k(\delta_2\gamma) = \emptyset.$$

It is instructive to consider the following characterization of LL(k) grammars.

<u>LEMMA 12.1.</u> Let $k \geq 0$. Grammar $G = (N,\Sigma,P,S)$ is an LL(k) grammar if and only if for $n \geq 0$ and for any $w \in \Sigma^*$, $A, A' \in N$, $\gamma, \gamma', \delta_1, \delta_2 \in V^*$ such that $\delta_1 \neq \delta_2$, the conditions

$$S \overset{n}{\underset{L}{\Rightarrow}} wA\gamma \underset{L}{\Rightarrow} w\delta_1\gamma$$

and

$$S \overset{n}{\underset{L}{\Rightarrow}} wA'\gamma' \underset{L}{\Rightarrow} w\delta_2\gamma'$$

always imply that $\mathrm{FIRST}_k(\delta_1\gamma) \cap \mathrm{FIRST}_k(\delta_2\gamma) = \emptyset$.

Proof . The 'if'-part is trivially satisfied. For the 'only if'-part we use the following claim.

<u>CLAIM.</u> Let $v,w \in \Sigma^*$, $A \in N$, $\alpha,\beta,\gamma \in V^*$ and $n \geq 0$. If $S \overset{*}{\underset{L}{\Rightarrow}} wA\alpha$, $A \overset{n}{\underset{L}{\Rightarrow}} v\beta$ and $A \overset{n}{\underset{L}{\Rightarrow}} v\gamma$, then $\mathrm{FIRST}_k(\beta\alpha) \cap \mathrm{FIRST}_k(\gamma\alpha) \neq \emptyset$ implies that $\beta = \gamma$.

Proof of the Claim. Induction on n. If $n = 0$, then $A = v\beta = v\gamma$, whence $\beta = \gamma$. Let $n > 0$ and assume that the claim holds for derivations of length $n - 1$. We can write

$$A \Rightarrow uB\delta \overset{n-1}{\underset{L}{\Rightarrow}} uz\beta = v\beta$$

$$A \Rightarrow u'B'\delta' \overset{n-1}{\underset{L}{\Rightarrow}} u'z'\gamma = v\gamma$$

for some $u, u', z, z' \in \Sigma^*$, $B, B' \in N$ and $\delta, \delta' \in V^*$. Since $\mathrm{FIRST}_k(\beta\alpha) \cap \mathrm{FIRST}_k(\gamma\alpha) \neq \emptyset$

we have also $FIRST_k(uB\delta\alpha) \cap FIRST_k(u'B'\delta'\alpha) \neq \emptyset$. Since G is LL(k) it follows that $uB\delta = u'B'\delta'$. We obtain

$$S \overset{*}{\underset{L}{\Rightarrow}} wuB\delta\alpha$$

$$B \overset{n-1}{\underset{L}{\Rightarrow}} z\beta_1$$

$$B \overset{n-1}{\underset{L}{\Rightarrow}} z\gamma_1$$

for some $\beta_1, \gamma_1 \in V^*$ such that $\beta = \beta_1\delta$, $\gamma = \gamma_1\delta$ and $FIRST_k(\beta_1\delta\alpha) \cap FIRST_k(\gamma_1\delta\alpha) \neq \emptyset$. From the induction hypothesis it follows that $\beta_1 = \gamma_1$. Therefore the claim is proved.□

This Claim and its proof is also in Pittl [132]. Now assume that G is LL(k) and we have derivations

$$S \overset{n}{\underset{L}{\Rightarrow}} wA\gamma \underset{L}{\Rightarrow} w\delta_1\gamma$$

and

$$S \overset{n}{\underset{L}{\Rightarrow}} wA'\gamma' \underset{L}{\Rightarrow} w\delta_2\gamma'$$

with $\delta_1 \neq \delta_2$. That is, we have derivations $S \overset{*}{\underset{L}{\Rightarrow}} S$, $S \overset{n}{\underset{L}{\Rightarrow}} wA\gamma$ and $S \overset{n}{\underset{L}{\Rightarrow}} wA'\gamma'$. Assume for the sake of contradiction that $FIRST_k(\delta_1\gamma) \cap FIRST_k(\delta_2\gamma') \neq \emptyset$. It follows from the Claim that $A\gamma = A'\gamma'$. That is, $A = A'$ and $\gamma = \gamma'$. However, if $A = A'$ and $\gamma = \gamma'$ then it follows from the LL(k) definition that $FIRST_k(\delta_1\gamma) \cap FIRST_k(\delta_2\gamma') = \emptyset$. Contradiction. □

In Lemma 12.1 it is more clearly displayed that in Figure 12.1, once we have seen w and k : xyz, the next production in the left parse is uniquely determined since for any pair of productions $A \to \delta_1$ and $A \to \delta_2$ in this situation we have that $A = A'$ and $\delta_1 = \delta_2$. In what follows we will also refer to the class of strong LL(k) grammars (cf. Definition 8.8). The following lemma gives a useful characterization of strong LL(k) grammars. The function $FOLLOW_k$ which is used is defined as follows.

<u>DEFINITION 12.1.</u> Let $G = (N,\Sigma,P,S)$ be a CFG and let $k \geq 0$. For any $A \in N$, define

$$FOLLOW_k(A) = \{k : w \mid S \overset{*}{\Rightarrow} \alpha A w \text{ for some } \alpha \in V^* \text{ and } w \in \Sigma^*\}.$$

<u>LEMMA 12.2.</u> Let $k \geq 0$. A CFG $G = (N,\Sigma,P,S)$ is a strong LL(k) grammar if and only if for distinct productions $A \to \alpha$ and $A \to \beta$ the condition

$$FIRST_k(\alpha\ FOLLOW_k(A)) \cap FIRST_k(\beta\ FOLLOW_k(A)) = \emptyset$$

holds.

Proof. Trivial. □

Our first definition of a new class of grammars concerns the so-called PLC(k) grammars (predictive left corner grammars).

DEFINITION 12.2. Let $k \geq 0$. A CFG $G = (N,\Sigma,P,S)$ is said to be a PLC(k) *grammar* if, for a terminal string w, a nonterminal A and strings α, γ, γ', δ_1 and δ_2 in $(N \cup \Sigma)^*$ such that $A \to \alpha\delta_1$ and $A \to \alpha\delta_2$ are distinct productions of G and α is the longest common prefix of $\alpha\delta_1$ and $\alpha\delta_2$ with length less than or equal to one, the conditions

$$S \overset{*}{\underset{L}{\Rightarrow}} wA\gamma \underset{L}{\Rightarrow} w\alpha\delta_1\gamma$$

and

$$S \overset{*}{\underset{L}{\Rightarrow}} wA\gamma' \underset{L}{\Rightarrow} w\alpha\delta_2\gamma'$$

always imply that

$$FIRST_k(\delta_1\gamma) \cap FIRST_k(\delta_2\gamma') = \emptyset.$$

This definition is included for completeness sake. Clearly, we can also introduce strong PLC(k) grammars. Then we have for distinct productions $A \to \alpha\delta_1$ and $A \to \alpha\delta_2$ with α is the longest common prefix of $\alpha\delta_1$ and $\alpha\delta_2$ with length less than or equal to one, the condition

$$FIRST_k(\delta_1\ FOLLOW_k(A)) \cap FIRST_k(\delta_2\ FOLLOW_k(A)) = \emptyset.$$

We immediately turn our attention to the class of LP(k) grammars. This class includes the PLC(k) grammars.

DEFINITION 12.3. A CFG $G = (N,\Sigma,P,S)$ is said to be an LP(k) *grammar* if, for a terminal string w, a nonterminal A and strings α, γ, γ', δ_1 and δ_2 in $(N \cup \Sigma)^*$ such that $A \to \alpha\delta_1$ and $A \to \alpha\delta_2$ are distinct productions of G and α is the longest common prefix of $\alpha\delta_1$ and $\alpha\delta_2$, the conditions

$$S \overset{*}{\underset{L}{\Rightarrow}} wA\gamma \underset{L}{\Rightarrow} w\alpha\delta_1\gamma$$

and

$$S \overset{*}{\underset{L}{\Rightarrow}} wA\gamma' \underset{L}{\Rightarrow} w\alpha\delta_2\gamma'$$

always imply that

$$\mathrm{FIRST}_k(\delta_1\gamma) \cap \mathrm{FIRST}_k(\delta_2\gamma') = \emptyset.$$

Observe the obvious difference with the characterization of LL(k) grammars in Lemma 12.1. In that case the implication

$$\mathrm{FIRST}_k(\alpha\delta_1\gamma) \cap \mathrm{FIRST}_k(\alpha\delta_2\gamma') = \emptyset$$

is used. Thus, in the case of LP(k) grammars it is not necessary to consider the terminal string which can be derived from the longest common prefix α of the right-hand sides of two distinct productions $A \to \alpha\delta_1$ and $A \to \alpha\delta_2$.

In [128] we have tried to characterize LP(k) grammars by saying that if

$$S \overset{*}{\underset{L}{\Rightarrow}} wA\gamma$$

and $A \to \alpha\delta_1$, $A \to \alpha\delta_2$ are two distinct productions such that α is the longest common prefix of $\alpha\delta_1$ and $\alpha\delta_2$, then

$$\mathrm{FIRST}_k(\delta_1\gamma) \cap \mathrm{FIRST}_k(\delta_2\gamma) = \emptyset.$$

This seems to be the straightforward generalization of the LL(k) definition. However, it is not what we want since such a characterization allows ambiguous grammars. This can be seen as follows. Consider the grammar with productions

$$S \to Ac \mid Aac$$
$$A \to a \mid aa$$

This grammar is ambiguous. Moreover, we have

(i) $S \overset{*}{\underset{L}{\Rightarrow}} S$, $S \to Ac \mid Aac$ and $\mathrm{FIRST}_2(c) \cap \mathrm{FIRST}_2(ac) = \emptyset$.

(ii) $S \overset{*}{\underset{L}{\Rightarrow}} Ac$, $A \to a \mid aa$ and $\mathrm{FIRST}_2(c) \cap \mathrm{FIRST}_2(ac) = \emptyset$.

(iii) $S \overset{*}{\underset{L}{\Rightarrow}} Aac$, $A \to a \mid aa$ and $\mathrm{FIRST}_2(ac) \cap \mathrm{FIRST}_2(aac) = \emptyset$.

Hence, the condition which is given above is satisfied. However, this grammar does not satisfy Definition 12.3 since we have productions $A \to a$ and $A \to aa$ and derivations

$$S \overset{*}{\underset{L}{\Rightarrow}} Ac \underset{L}{\Rightarrow} aac$$

and

$$S \overset{*}{\underset{L}{\Rightarrow}} Aac \underset{L}{\Rightarrow} aac$$

while

$$\text{FIRST}_k(ac) \cap \text{FIRST}_k(ac) \neq \emptyset$$

for any $k \geq 0$.

The class of strong LP(k) grammars is now defined by demanding that

$$\text{FIRST}_k(\delta_1 \text{ FOLLOW}_k(A)) \cap \text{FIRST}_k(\delta_2 \text{ FOLLOW}_k(A)) = \emptyset$$

for any pair of distinct productions $A \to \alpha\delta_1$ and $A \to \alpha\delta_2$, where α is the longest common prefix of $\alpha\delta_1$ and $\alpha\delta_2$.

We consider the possibility of obtaining a similar characterization for LP(k) grammars as is displayed in Lemma 12.1 for LL(k) grammars. Therefore it is necessary to generalize two results for simple chain grammars.

<u>LEMMA 12.3.</u> Let $G = (N,\Sigma,P,S)$ be an LP(k) grammar, $k \geq 0$. For any w, w_1, $w_2 \in \Sigma^*$ and μ, ω, $\omega' \in V^*$, if $S \overset{*}{\underset{L}{\Rightarrow}} w\mu\omega$, $S \overset{*}{\underset{L}{\Rightarrow}} w\mu\omega'$, $\mu \overset{*}{\underset{L}{\Rightarrow}} w_1$ and $\mu \overset{*}{\underset{L}{\Rightarrow}} w_1w_2$ with $w_2 \neq \varepsilon$, then $\text{FIRST}_k(\omega) \cap \text{FIRST}_k(w_2\omega) = \emptyset$.

Proof. The proof is by induction on the lengths of the derivations from μ to w_1 and from μ to w_1w_2.

Basis. Consider two derivations of length 1 which can be used to obtain w_1 and w_1w_2 from $\mu \in V^+$. The case in which one derivation is of length 0 and the other is of length 1 can not occur. If $\mu \underset{L}{\Rightarrow} w_1$ and $\mu \underset{L}{\Rightarrow} w_1w_2$ then there exist a nonterminal $C \in N$ and strings w', w'', z_1, $z_2 \in \Sigma^*$ such that

$$\mu = w'Cw'' \underset{L}{\Rightarrow} w'z_1w'' = w_1$$

and

$$\mu = w'Cw'' \underset{L}{\Rightarrow} w'z_2w'' = w_1w_2.$$

It follows that z_1 is a proper prefix of z_2. We write $z_2 = z_1z_2'$. Hence, we have productions $C \to z_1$ and $C \to z_1z_2'$ and derivations $S \overset{*}{\underset{L}{\Rightarrow}} ww'Cw''\omega$ and $S \overset{*}{\underset{L}{\Rightarrow}} ww'Cw''\omega'$. Since G is LP(k) we have

$$\text{FIRST}_k(w''\omega) \cap \text{FIRST}_k(z_2'w''\omega') = \emptyset.$$

Moreover, since w'' is a prefix of $z_2'w''$ such that $w''w_2 = z_2'w''$, it follows that

$$\text{FIRST}_k(\omega) \cap \text{FIRST}_k(w_2\omega') = \emptyset,$$

which had to be proved.

Induction. Assume for all $\mu \in V^+$ and derivations $\mu \overset{*}{\underset{L}{\Rightarrow}} w_1$ and $\mu \overset{*}{\underset{L}{\Rightarrow}} w_1w_2$ with lengths less than n, we have

$$\mathrm{FIRST}_k(\omega) \cap \mathrm{FIRST}_k(w_2\omega') = \emptyset.$$

Now consider derivations $\mu \overset{*}{\underset{L}{\Rightarrow}} w_1$ and $\mu \overset{*}{\underset{L}{\Rightarrow}} w_1w_2$ with lengths less than or equal to n. Then there exist $C \in N$, α, ρ, δ_1, $\delta_2 \in V^*$ and $w' \in \Sigma^*$ such that $\delta_1 \neq \delta_2$ and α is the longest common prefix of $\alpha\delta_1$ and $\alpha\delta_2$ and

$$\mu \overset{*}{\underset{L}{\Rightarrow}} w'C\rho \underset{L}{\Rightarrow} w'\alpha\delta_1\rho \overset{*}{\underset{L}{\Rightarrow}} w_1$$

and

$$\mu \overset{*}{\underset{L}{\Rightarrow}} w'C\rho \underset{L}{\Rightarrow} w'\alpha\delta_2 \ \overset{*}{\underset{L}{\Rightarrow}} w_1w_2$$

where $w'C\rho$ is the last left sentential form which these two derivations have in common. Now consider the following two derivations:

$$\alpha\delta_1\rho\omega \overset{*}{\underset{L}{\Rightarrow}} w_1\omega \qquad (1)$$

and

$$\alpha\delta_2\rho\omega' \overset{*}{\underset{L}{\Rightarrow}} w_1w_2\omega' \qquad (2)$$

Suppose that both in (1) and in (2) we have $\alpha \overset{*}{\underset{L}{\Rightarrow}} u_1$, for some $u_1 \in \Sigma^*$. Hence, we can write $w_1 = u_1v_1$, where $v_1 \in \Sigma^*$. Since G is LP(k) it follows that

$$\mathrm{FIRST}_k(\delta_1\rho\omega) \cap \mathrm{FIRST}_k(\delta_2\rho\omega') = \emptyset$$

and we can conclude that

$$\mathrm{FIRST}_k(v_1\omega) \cap \mathrm{FIRST}_k(v_1w_2\omega') = \emptyset.$$

Thus,

$$\mathrm{FIRST}_k(\omega) \cap \mathrm{FIRST}_k(w_2\omega') = \emptyset$$

which had to be proved. Now suppose that $\alpha \overset{*}{\underset{L}{\Rightarrow}} u_1$ in derivation (1) and $\alpha \overset{*}{\underset{L}{\Rightarrow}} u_1u_2$ in derivation (2), with $u_2 \neq \varepsilon$. From the induction hypothesis we can conclude that

$$\mathrm{FIRST}_k(\delta_1\rho\omega) \cap \mathrm{FIRST}_k(u_2\delta_2\rho\omega') = \emptyset.$$

We can write $w_1 = u_1 v_1$, for some $v_1 \in \Sigma^*$. It follows that

$$\mathrm{FIRST}_k(v_1\omega) \cap \mathrm{FIRST}_k(v_1 w_2 \omega') = \emptyset$$

and therefore

$$\mathrm{FIRST}_k(\omega) \cap \mathrm{FIRST}_k(w_2\omega') = \emptyset$$

which had to be proved. The symmetric case with $\alpha \overset{*}{\underset{L}{\Rightarrow}} u_1u_2$ in (1) and $\alpha \overset{*}{\underset{L}{\Rightarrow}} u_1$ in (2) can be treated similarly and therefore it is omitted. This concludes the proof of Lemma 12.3. □

Notice that Lemma 12.3 can be considered as a generalization of Theorem 11.1. We can also obtain an analogue for Theorem 11.3.

LEMMA 12.4. Let $G = (N,\Sigma,P,S)$ be an LP(k) grammar, $k \geq 0$. For any $n \geq 0$, $X, Y \in V$ with $X \neq Y$ and $\alpha, \varphi, \psi \in V^*$, if $S \overset{n}{\underset{L}{\Rightarrow}} \alpha X\varphi$ and $S \overset{n}{\underset{L}{\Rightarrow}} \alpha Y\psi$, then $\mathrm{FIRST}_k(X\varphi) \cap \mathrm{FIRST}_k(Y\psi) = \emptyset$.

Proof. We prove the slightly more general result that if $S \overset{*}{\underset{L}{\Rightarrow}} w\mu\omega$ and $S \overset{*}{\underset{L}{\Rightarrow}} w\mu\omega'$, where $w \in \Sigma^*$, and $\mu, \omega, \omega' \in V^*$, then for any $n \geq 0$, $X, Y \in V$ with $X \neq Y$ and $\alpha, \varphi, \psi \in V^*$, if $\mu \overset{n}{\underset{L}{\Rightarrow}} \alpha X\varphi$ and $\mu \overset{n}{\underset{L}{\Rightarrow}} \alpha Y\psi$, then $\mathrm{FIRST}_k(X\varphi\omega) \cap \mathrm{FIRST}_k(Y\psi\omega') = \emptyset$. The proof is done by induction on n.

Basis. Assume that $\mu \overset{1}{\underset{L}{\Rightarrow}} \alpha X\varphi$ and $\mu \overset{1}{\underset{L}{\Rightarrow}} \alpha Y\psi$. We can write $\mu = vC\rho$ for some $v \in \Sigma^*$, $C \in N$ and $\rho \in V^*$. Then there exist productions $C \to \gamma\delta_1$ and $C \to \gamma\delta_2$, where $\delta_1 \neq \delta_2$, $\gamma, \delta_1, \delta_2 \in V^*$ and γ is the longest common prefix of $\gamma\delta_1$ and $\gamma\delta_2$. Since G is LP(k) we have that

$$\mathrm{FIRST}_k(\delta_1\rho\omega) \cap \mathrm{FIRST}_k(\delta_2\rho\omega') = \emptyset.$$

There exists a prefix β of $\delta_1\rho\omega$ and of $\delta_2\rho\omega'$ such that $v\gamma\beta = \alpha$, $\beta X\varphi\omega = \delta_1\rho\omega$ and $\beta Y\psi\omega' = \delta_2\rho\omega'$. It follows that

$$\mathrm{FIRST}_k(X\varphi\omega) \cap \mathrm{FIRST}_k(Y\psi\omega') = \emptyset.$$

Induction. Let $\mu \overset{n}{\underset{L}{\Rightarrow}} \alpha X\varphi$ and $\mu \overset{n}{\underset{L}{\Rightarrow}} \alpha Y\psi$, where $X \neq Y$ and assume the property holds for all $\mu \in V^*$ and leftmost derivations with length less than n. Then there exist $v \in \Sigma^*$, $\gamma, \delta_1, \delta_2, \rho \in V^*$, $C \in N$ and productions $C \to \gamma\delta_1$, $C \to \gamma\delta_2$ in P where γ is the longest common prefix of $\gamma\delta_1$ and $\gamma\delta_2$, such that

$$\mu \overset{k}{\underset{L}{\Rightarrow}} vC\rho \underset{L}{\Rightarrow} v\gamma\delta_1\rho \overset{m}{\underset{L}{\Rightarrow}} \alpha X\varphi \qquad (1)$$

and

$$\mu \overset{k}{\underset{L}{\Rightarrow}} vC\rho \underset{L}{\Rightarrow} v\gamma\delta_2\rho \overset{m}{\underset{L}{\Rightarrow}} \alpha Y\psi \qquad (2)$$

with n = k + m + 1. Now consider the following possibilities:

(i) $v\gamma \overset{m}{\underset{L}{\Rightarrow}} \alpha X\varphi'$ in (1), with $\varphi'\delta_1\rho = \varphi$ and $v\gamma \overset{*}{\underset{L}{\Rightarrow}} \alpha'$ in (2), such that α can be written as $\alpha'\alpha''$ for $\alpha', \alpha'' \in V^*$. It follows from Lemma 12.3 that

$$\text{FIRST}_k(\alpha''X\varphi\omega) \cap \text{FIRST}_k(\alpha''Y\psi\omega') = \emptyset.$$

Hence,

$$\text{FIRST}_k(X\varphi\omega) \cap \text{FIRST}_k(Y\psi\omega') = \emptyset.$$

The symmetric case with $v\gamma \overset{*}{\underset{L}{\Rightarrow}} \alpha'$ in (1) and $v\gamma \overset{m}{\underset{L}{\Rightarrow}} \alpha Y\psi'$ in (2) can be treated similarly and therefore it is omitted.

(ii) $v\gamma \overset{m}{\underset{L}{\Rightarrow}} \alpha X\varphi'$ in (1), with $\varphi'\delta_1\rho = \varphi$
and
$v\gamma \overset{m}{\underset{L}{\Rightarrow}} \alpha Y\psi'$ in (2), with $\psi'\delta_2\rho = \psi$.
Since $m < n$, we may conclude that

$$\text{FIRST}_k(X\varphi'\delta_1\rho\omega) \cap \text{FIRST}_k(Y\psi'\delta_2\rho\omega') = \emptyset$$

that is,

$$\text{FIRST}_k(X\varphi\omega) \cap \text{FIRST}_k(Y\psi\omega') = \emptyset.$$

(iii) $v\gamma \overset{*}{\underset{L}{\Rightarrow}} \alpha_1$ in (1), with $\alpha = \alpha_1\alpha_2$ for $\alpha_1, \alpha_2 \in V^*$
and
$v\gamma \overset{*}{\underset{L}{\Rightarrow}} \alpha_1'$ in (2), with $\alpha = \alpha_1'\alpha_2'$ for $\alpha_1', \alpha_2' \in V^*$.

If $\alpha_1 \neq \alpha_1'$, then α_1 is a prefix of α_1' or conversely. With the same type of argument as used above it can again be shown that the desired property holds. If $\alpha_1 = \alpha_1'$, then there exists $\alpha'' \in V^*$ such that $\alpha_1\alpha'' = \alpha_1'\alpha'' = \alpha$ and

$$\delta_1\rho \overset{*}{\underset{L}{\Rightarrow}} \alpha''X\varphi \qquad \text{in (1)}$$

and

$$\delta_2\rho \overset{*}{\underset{L}{\Rightarrow}} \alpha''Y\psi \qquad \text{in (2)}.$$

However, since G is LP(k) and γ is the longest common prefix of $\gamma\delta_1$ and $\gamma\delta_2$, it follows that

$$FIRST_k(\delta_1\rho\omega) \cap FIRST_k(\delta_2\rho\omega') = \emptyset.$$

Therefore,

$$FIRST_k(\alpha''X\varphi) \cap FIRST_k(\alpha''Y\psi) = \emptyset$$

and it follows that

$$FIRST_k(X\varphi) \cap FIRST_k(Y\psi) = \emptyset.$$

This concludes the induction proof. For $w = \omega = \omega' = \varepsilon$ and $\mu = S$, we obtain the result which is mentioned in Lemma 12.4. □

Now we are sufficiently prepared to present the following theorem.

THEOREM 12.1. Let $k \geq 0$ and let $G = (N,\Sigma,P,S)$ be an LP(k) grammar. For any $n \geq 0$, $w \in \Sigma^*$, $A, A' \in N$, $\alpha,\gamma,\gamma',\delta_1, \delta_2 \in V^*$ such that $\delta_1 \neq \delta_2$ and α is the longest common prefix of $\alpha\delta_1$ and $\alpha\delta_2$, the conditions

$$S \overset{n}{\underset{L}{\Rightarrow}} wA\gamma \underset{L}{\Rightarrow} w\alpha\delta_1\gamma$$

and

$$S \overset{n}{\underset{L}{\Rightarrow}} wA'\gamma' \underset{L}{\Rightarrow} w\alpha\delta_2\gamma'$$

always imply that

$$FIRST_k(\delta_1\gamma) \cap FIRST_k(\delta_2\gamma') = \emptyset.$$

Proof. If $A = A'$, then the theorem is only a restricted version of the LP(k) definition. If $A \neq A'$, then it follows from Lemma 12.4 that

$$FIRST_k(A\gamma) \cap FIRST_k(A'\gamma') = \emptyset.$$

Hence,

$$FIRST_k(\alpha\delta_1\gamma) \cap FIRST_k(\alpha\delta_2\gamma') = \emptyset$$

and it follows that

$$FIRST_k(\delta_1\gamma) \cap FIRST_k(\delta_2\gamma') = \emptyset$$

which had to be proved. □

Clearly, with this theorem in mind we can again consider Figure 12.1. Notice that in Lemma 12.1 we have changed the LL(k) definition (in which we use the condition $S \overset{*}{\underset{L}{\Rightarrow}} wA\gamma$) into a characterization with $S \overset{n}{\underset{L}{\Rightarrow}} wA\gamma$ and $S \overset{n}{\underset{L}{\Rightarrow}} wA'\gamma'$. Also in Theorem 12.1 for LP(k) grammars we have used a superscript n. It is rather inviting to omit n from the derivations. However, consider the following LL(0) grammar with productions

$S \to aAb$

$A \to Bc$

$B \to a$

Here we have derivations

$$S \overset{1}{\underset{L}{\Rightarrow}} aAb \underset{L}{\Rightarrow} aBcb$$

and

$$S \overset{2}{\underset{L}{\Rightarrow}} aBcb \underset{L}{\Rightarrow} aacb$$

while

$$FIRST_k(Bcb) \cap FIRST_k(acb) \neq \emptyset$$

for any $k \geq 0$. It follows that we can not omit superscript n from the derivations in Lemma 12.1 and in Theorem 12.1.

<u>THEOREM 12.2.</u> Every LL(k) grammar is an LP(k) grammar, $k \geq 0$.

Proof. Assume that a grammar $G = (N,\Sigma,P,S)$ is LL(k) but not LP(k). Then there exist a terminal string w, a nonterminal A and strings $\alpha,\gamma,\gamma',\delta_1$ and δ_2 in V^* such that $A \to \alpha\delta_1$ and $A \to \alpha\delta_2$ are two distinct productions in P, with α is the longest common prefix of $\alpha\delta_1$ and $\alpha\delta_2$, such that

$$S \overset{*}{\underset{L}{\Rightarrow}} wA\gamma \underset{L}{\Rightarrow} w\alpha\delta_1\gamma$$

$$S \overset{*}{\underset{L}{\Rightarrow}} wA\gamma' \underset{L}{\Rightarrow} w\alpha\delta_2\gamma'$$

and

$$FIRST_k(\delta_1\gamma) \cap FIRST_k(\delta_2\gamma') \neq \emptyset.$$

It follows that

$$FIRST_k(\alpha\delta_1\gamma) \cap FIRST_k(\alpha\delta_2\gamma') \neq \emptyset.$$

It is straightforward to verify that in the case of LL(k) grammars we have that $\gamma = \gamma'$. Hence, we obtain a contradiction with the LL(k) definition. Therefore we must conclude that G is also LP(k). □

The definition of LP(k) grammars can be considered as a generalization with 'look-ahead' of the definition of the simple chain and left part grammars of Chapter 11. The following corollary is an immediate consequence of the definitions.

COROLLARY 12.1. A grammar $G = (N,\Sigma,P,S)$ is a simple chain grammar if and only if P is prefix-free and G is an ε-free LP(1) grammar.

Context-free grammar G with productions

$S \to a$
$S \to ab$

is an example of a grammar which is not a simple chain grammar. However, grammar G is LP(1).

Since there exist simple chain grammars which are not LL(k) for any k (cf. Example 11.2) we conclude that the class of LL(k) grammars is properly contained in the class of LP(k) grammars.

Just as in the case of LL(k) grammars one may conclude that if k = 0, then the language of an LP(k) grammar does exist of one element only.

The following two theorems are also immediate consequences of the LP(k) definition. The proofs are analogous to corresponding proofs for the LL(k) case and they are slight generalizations of corresponding proofs for simple chain grammars. Notice, once more, that the grammars under consideration are assumed to be reduced.

THEOREM 12.3. Each LP(k) grammar is unambiguous.

Proof. We show that each $w \in L(G)$, where G is an LP(k) grammar, has exactly one leftmost derivation from S. Suppose that $S \overset{*}{\underset{L}{\Rightarrow}} w$ by at least two leftmost derivations. We can write

$$S \overset{*}{\underset{L}{\Rightarrow}} uA\omega \underset{L}{\Rightarrow} u\alpha\delta_1\omega \overset{*}{\underset{L}{\Rightarrow}} uv = w \qquad (*)$$

and

$$S \overset{*}{\underset{L}{\Rightarrow}} uA\omega \underset{L}{\Rightarrow} u\alpha\delta_2\omega \overset{*}{\underset{L}{\Rightarrow}} uv = w \qquad (**)$$

where $u, v \in \Sigma^*$, $A \in N$, $\alpha,\delta_1,\delta_2, \omega \in V^*$ and α is the longest common prefix of the distinct strings $\alpha\delta_1$ and $\alpha\delta_2$.

Assume that in (*) we have used $\alpha \overset{*}{\underset{L}{\Rightarrow}} u_1$, $\delta_1 \overset{*}{\underset{L}{\Rightarrow}} x$ and $\omega \overset{*}{\underset{L}{\Rightarrow}} v_1$ and in (**) we have used $\alpha \overset{*}{\underset{L}{\Rightarrow}} u_2$, $\delta_2 \overset{*}{\underset{L}{\Rightarrow}} y$ and $\omega \overset{*}{\underset{L}{\Rightarrow}} v_2$, such that $u_1xv_1 = u_2yv_2 = v$. Since $k : xv_1 \neq k : yv_2$ we can not have $u_1 = u_2$, If u_1 is a proper prefix of u_2 (or the symmetric case which we omit) and we write $u_2 = u_1u_1'$ then, since $k : u_1'yv_2 = k : xv_1$, we have that α does not satisfy Lemma 12.3. We must conclude that G is unambiguous. □

<u>THEOREM 12.4.</u> LP(k) grammars are not left recursive.

Proof. The proof is a straightforward adaptation of the corresponding proof for LL(k) grammars. □

Clearly, as we did in Chapter 11 for simple chain grammars, we now can obtain properties for the leftmost and rightmost derivations of LP(k) grammars. We will, however, turn our attention to transformations of LP(k) grammars. We shall show that the LP(k) grammars are exactly those grammars which can be transformed into LL(k) grammars by left factoring the grammar until it has no two productions of the form $A \to \alpha\varphi$ and $A \to \alpha\psi$ with $\alpha \neq \varepsilon$.

The definitions of LL(k) and LP(k) grammars immediately imply the following theorem.

<u>THEOREM 12.5.</u> A left factored grammar is LL(k) if and only if it is LP(k).

Proof. Trivial. □

The process of left factoring consists of consecutively replacing productions of the form $A \to \alpha\varphi$ and $A \to \alpha\psi$, where $\alpha \neq \varepsilon$ and α is the longest common prefix of $\alpha\varphi$ and $\alpha\psi$, by the productions

$$A \to \alpha H$$
$$H \to \varphi$$
$$H \to \psi$$

where H is a newly introduced nonterminal symbol, until the grammar is left factored. Clearly, this transformation preserves the original language.

<u>THEOREM 12.6.</u> The grammar obtained by the left factoring process is LL(k) if and only if the original grammar is LP(k).

Proof. By Theorem 12.5 it is sufficient to show that the process of left factoring does not affect the LP(k) property and that this process can not produce an LP(k) grammar from a non-LP(k) grammar. It is clear from the definition that this is true as regards one individual step in the left factoring process. Since the whole process is just a consecutive sequence of these individual steps, we thus conclude the theorem.

<u>COROLLARY 12.2.</u> The families of LP(k) and LL(k) languages coincide.

As we already showed in section 10.1, if we have productions i. $A \rightarrow \alpha\varphi$ and j. $A \rightarrow \alpha\psi$ and we define

$$\begin{array}{ll} A \rightarrow \alpha H & \langle \varepsilon \rangle \\ H \rightarrow \varphi & \langle i \rangle \\ H \rightarrow \psi & \langle j \rangle \end{array}$$

then it will also be clear that the newly obtained left factored grammar right covers the original grammar. Moreover, also shown in section 10.1 and a consequence of Theorem 9.1, top-down parsing of LL-grammars can be done in such a way that right parses are obtained and therefore this right cover result is not only of theoretical value.

It is also possible to obtain an LL(k) grammar which left-to-right covers the original LP(k) grammar.

<u>THEOREM 12.7.</u> Each LP(k) grammar can be left-to-right covered by an LL(k) grammar.

Proof. Let $G_1 = (N_1,\Sigma,P_1,S)$ be an LP(k) grammar. Define $G_1' = (N_1',\Sigma,P_1',S)$ with

$$N_1' = N_1 \cup \{[A\alpha] \mid A \rightarrow \alpha \text{ is in } P_1\}$$

and

$$P_1' = \{A \rightarrow \alpha[A\alpha] \mid A \rightarrow \alpha \text{ is in } P_1\} \cup \{[A\alpha] \rightarrow \varepsilon \mid A \rightarrow \alpha \text{ is in } P_1\}.$$

Clearly, G_1' is LP(k) if and only if G_1 is LP(k) and the grammar which is obtained by the left factoring process from G_1' is LL(k) if and only if any grammar obtained by the left factoring process from G_1 is LL(k). Hence, if $G_2 = (N_2,\Sigma,P_2,S)$ is the grammar which is obtained by the left factoring process from G_1', then G_2 is LL(k).

Now define a homomorphism $\psi_1 : P_1'^* \rightarrow P_1^*$ such that

$$\psi_1([A\alpha] \rightarrow \varepsilon) = A \rightarrow \alpha$$

and

$$\psi_1(A \rightarrow \alpha) = \varepsilon.$$

Clearly, $G_1'[\ell/\bar{r}]G_1$ (cf. Lemma 4.4) where the cover is supported by the productions of the form $[A\alpha] \to \varepsilon$. These productions remain unchanged in the left factoring process and, moreover, this process does not affect the order in which these productions appear in a left parse. Therefore, if we define $\psi_2 : P_2^* \to P_1^*$ such that

$$\psi_2([A\alpha] \to \varepsilon) = A \to \alpha$$

and

$$\psi_2(C \to \gamma) = \varepsilon$$

where $C \notin N_1' - N_1$, then we can conclude that G_2 left-to-right covers grammar G_1 with respect to homomorphism ψ_2. □

The next class of grammars which we want to consider is the class of LC(k) or left corner grammars. There are two ways to characterize LC(k) grammars. The first definition we present makes use of rightmost derivations. The second, original, definition uses leftmost derivations.

In order to present the first characterization we recall the definition of an LR(k) grammar as it was presented in section 8.2.

A grammar $G = (N,\Sigma,P,S)$ is said to be an LR(k) grammar if $S \overset{+}{\underset{R}{\Rightarrow}} S$ is not possible in G and for each w, w', $x \in \Sigma^*$; $\gamma,\alpha,\alpha',\beta$ and β' in V^* and $A,A' \in N$, if

(i) $S \overset{*}{\underset{R}{\Rightarrow}} \alpha Aw \underset{R}{\Rightarrow} \alpha\beta w$ and

(ii) $S \overset{*}{\underset{R}{\Rightarrow}} \alpha'A'x \underset{R}{\Rightarrow} \alpha'\beta'x = \alpha\beta w'$ and

(iii) $k : w = k : w'$
then $A \to \beta = A' \to \beta'$ and $|\alpha\beta| = |\alpha'\beta'|$.

An equivalent definition is obtained if we conclude from (i), (ii) and (iii) that $\alpha A = \alpha'A'$ and $x = w'$. Moreover, it is useful to say that a fixed production $A \to \beta$ of CFG G *satisfies* the LR(k) condition if, whenever we have derivations (i) and (ii), then $k : w = k : w'$ implies $\alpha A = \alpha'A'$ and $x = w'$. We use the notation $\underline{\alpha}\beta \overset{*}{\underset{R}{\Rightarrow}} \underline{\alpha}\gamma$ or $\beta\underline{\alpha} \overset{*}{\underset{L}{\Rightarrow}} \gamma\underline{\alpha}$ to denote that in the specific derivations $\alpha\beta \overset{*}{\underset{R}{\Rightarrow}} \alpha\gamma$ and $\beta\alpha \overset{*}{\underset{L}{\Rightarrow}} \gamma\alpha$ which are considered, respectively, the displayed string α is not rewritten.

<u>DEFINITION 12.4.</u> A CFG $G = (N,\Sigma,P,S)$ is said to be an LC(k) *grammar* if $S \overset{+}{\underset{R}{\Rightarrow}} S$ is not possible in G, each ε-production of G satisfies the LR(k) condition and if for each $w,w',y,y' \in \Sigma^*$; $\alpha,\alpha',\alpha'',\beta,\gamma \in V^*$; $X \in V$; $A,A' \in N$ and production $A \to X\beta$ in P, the conditions

(i) $S \overset{*}{\underset{R}{\Rightarrow}} \alpha A w \underset{R}{\Rightarrow} \underline{\alpha X}\beta w \overset{*}{\underset{R}{\Rightarrow}} \underline{\alpha X}yw$

(ii) $S \overset{*}{\underset{R}{\Rightarrow}} \alpha' A' w' \underset{R}{\Rightarrow} \underline{\alpha'\alpha'' X}\gamma w' \overset{*}{\underset{R}{\Rightarrow}} \alpha'\alpha'' X y' w'$

(iii) $\alpha'\alpha'' = \alpha$ and $k : yw = k : y'w'$, always imply that $\alpha A = \alpha' A'$ and $\beta = \gamma$.

We have included the condition that $S \overset{+}{\underset{R}{\Rightarrow}} S$ is not possible for an LC(k) grammar. Otherwise, the following ambiguous grammar with productions

$$S \rightarrow S \mid a$$

is to be called LC(0). Another possibility would have been to extend the grammar by adding an 'initial production' $S' \rightarrow \bot S$, with $\bot$ is a symbol not in V and S' is a newly introduced start symbol. This latter method has been used in [157]. We have, in accordance with our definition of LR(k) grammars, excluded the possibility $S \overset{+}{\underset{R}{\Rightarrow}} S$ from the definition of LC(k) grammars.

In Geller and Harrison [40] the following context-free grammar G with productions

$$S \rightarrow Sa \mid a$$

is given as an example to show that there exist grammars which are LR(0) according to the LR(k) definition which is used here, but which are not LR(0) according to the definition in Aho and Ullman [3]. Moreover, it follows easily that G is not LR(0), PLR(0) or LC(0) according to the definitions which are given in Soisalon-Soininen and Ukkonen [157]. However, the grammar G is LC(0), PLR(0) and LR(0) according to the definitions which are used in this chapter.

We now want to show that any LC(k) grammar is an LR(k) grammar. We use the following lemma which tells us when a grammar is not LR(k).

<u>LEMMA 12.5.</u> Let $G = (N,\Sigma,P,S)$ be a (reduced) CFG such that $S \overset{+}{\underset{R}{\Rightarrow}} S$ is impossible in G. G is not LR(k) if and only if there exist $w,w',x \in \Sigma^*$; $A,A' \in N$; $\gamma',\gamma,\alpha,\alpha',\beta,\beta' \in V^*$ such that

(i) $S \overset{*}{\underset{R}{\Rightarrow}} \alpha A w \underset{R}{\Rightarrow} \alpha\beta w$,

(ii) $S \overset{*}{\underset{R}{\Rightarrow}} \alpha' A' x \underset{R}{\Rightarrow} \alpha'\beta' x = \alpha\beta w'$,

(iii) $k : w = k : w'$, and

(iv) $\alpha A \neq \alpha' A'$ or $x \neq w'$, with

(v) $|\alpha'\beta'| \geq |\alpha\beta|$.

Proof. This lemma is a slight modification of Lemma 2.5 of Geller and Harrison [40].

THEOREM 12.8. Every LC(k) grammar is an LR(k) grammar.

Proof. Assume that an LC(k) grammar G = (N,Σ,P,S) is not LR(k). Then there exist derivations (cf. Lemma 12.5)

(i) $S \overset{*}{\underset{R}{\Rightarrow}} \alpha A w \underset{R}{\Rightarrow} \alpha\beta w$,

(ii) $S \overset{*}{\underset{R}{\Rightarrow}} \alpha' A' x \underset{R}{\Rightarrow} \alpha'\beta' x = \alpha\beta w'$

such that $k : w = k : w'$, $|\alpha'\beta'| \geq |\alpha\beta|$, and $\alpha A \neq \alpha' A'$ or $x \neq w'$. Notice, that due to the definition of LC(k) grammars we do no have to consider the possibility that the production $A \to \beta$ which is displayed in (i) is an ε-production. Moreover, since (i) and (ii) can be reversed, we do not have to consider the possibility $\beta' \neq \varepsilon$. Hence, we may assume $\beta \neq \varepsilon$ and $\beta' \neq \varepsilon$. Since $|\alpha'\beta'| \geq |\alpha\beta|$ we can distinguish the three cases depicted in Figure 12.3.

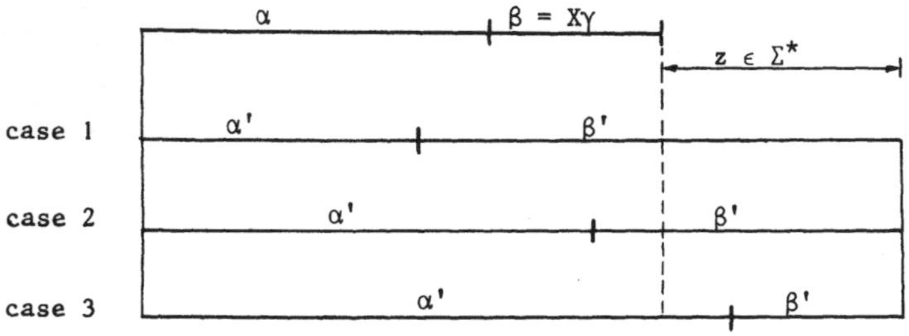

Figure 12.3. Three cases for Theorem 12.8.

It is straightforward to show that each of these three cases violates the conditions of an LC(k) grammar. □

This inclusion of LC(k) grammars in LR(k) grammars is proper. Context-free grammar G with productions

$S \to aB \mid aC$

$B \to aB \mid b$

$C \to aC \mid c$

is a grammar which is LR(0) while G is not, for any $k \geq 0$, LC(k).

In the original definition of LC(k) grammars (Rosenkrantz and Lewis [143]) conditions are imposed on the leftmost derivations of a grammar. As mentioned in [155,

157], in the original definition the look-ahead is used in a slightly different way since distinction is made between the cases that the left corner of a production is a terminal or a nonterminal.

THEOREM 12.9. Every LL(k) grammar is an LC(k) grammar.

Proof. See Soisalon-Soininen [155]. Although our definition of an LC(k) grammar does not use an 'initial production' $S' \to \bot S$ it can be easily seen that the proof in [155] can be used for the case that our definition is used. □

We have a short discussion on the original definition of LC(k) grammars. If we use the abbreviation LC_{SU} to denote LC-grammars according to Soisalon-Soininen and Ukkonen (cf. Definition 12.3) and LC_{RL} to denote LC-grammars according to Rosenkrantz and Lewis, then it can be shown that there exist $LC_{SU}(k)$ grammars which are $LC_{RL}(k+1)$ but not $LC_{RL}(k)$.

In [100] and in a revised form in [143] a method is presented which transforms $LC_{RL}(k)$ grammars into LL(k) grammars. A rigorous proof that the method indeed does what it is supposed to do is not available. However, such a proof has been given for the following class of grammars which can be transformed into LL(k) grammars.

DEFINITION 12.5. A CFG $G = (N,\Sigma,P,S)$ is said to be a PLR(k) *grammar* if G is LR(k) and if for each $w,w',y,y' \in \Sigma^*$; $\alpha,\alpha',\alpha'',\beta,\gamma \in V^*$; $X \in V$; $A,A' \in N$ and production $A \to X\beta$ in P, the conditions

(i) $S \overset{*}{\underset{R}{\Rightarrow}} \alpha Aw \underset{R}{\Rightarrow} \underline{\alpha X\beta}w \overset{*}{\underset{R}{\Rightarrow}} \underline{\alpha X}yw$

(ii) $S \overset{*}{\underset{R}{\Rightarrow}} \alpha'A'w' \underset{R}{\Rightarrow} \underline{\alpha'\alpha''X\gamma}w' \overset{*}{\underset{R}{\Rightarrow}} \underline{\alpha'\alpha''X}y'w'$

(iii) $\alpha'\alpha'' = \alpha$ and $k : yw = k : y'w'$

always imply that $\alpha A = \alpha'A'$.

Notice that any LL(k) grammar is also LC(k) (Theorem 12.9), any LC(k) grammar is PLR(k) (cf. Definition 12.4 and 12.5 and Theorem 12.8) and, by definition, any PLR(k) grammar is also an LR(k) grammar. These inclusions are proper (cf.[157]).

Theorem 12.5 has the following analogue.

THEOREM 12.10. A left factored grammar is LC(k) if and only if it is PLR(k).

Proof. See [157]. □

Moreover, there is an analogue for Theorem 12.6.

THEOREM 12.11. The grammar obtained by the left factoring process is LC(k) if and only if the original grammar is PLR(k).

Proof. See [157, p. 349]. □

Maybe it is not yet clear that every LP(k) grammar is also PLR(k). This can be seen as follows.

THEOREM 12.12. Every LP(k) grammar is a PLR(k) grammar.

Proof. Any LP(k) grammar can be made LL(k) by left factoring (Theorem 12.6). Since LL(k) grammars are also LC(k) grammars we can say that any LP(k) grammar can be made LC(k) by left factoring. It follows from Theorem 12.11 that every LP(k) grammar is also PLR(k). □

Context-free grammar G with productions

$S \to aBc$
$S \to aBd$
$B \to aB$
$B \to c$

is a context-free grammar which is LP(1). However, there does not exist $k \geq 0$ such that G is LC(k). Since there exist LC(k) grammars which are left recursive and, by Theorem 12.4 LP(k) grammars can not be left recursive we conclude that the classes of LP(k) and LC(k) grammars are incomparable. Hence, we have the situation displayed in Figure 12.4.

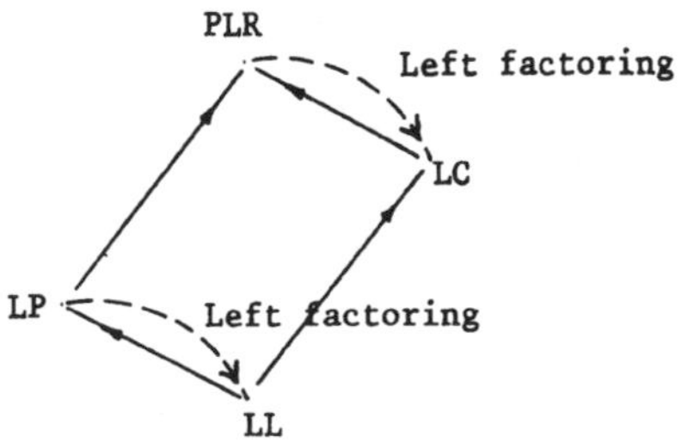

Figure 12.4. Inclusion diagram.

In this figure we have also displayed the role of the left factoring process. The reader is asked to recall the cover properties of this transformation.

Soisalon-Soininen and Ukkonen [157] present a transformation τ from PLR(k) grammars to LL(k) grammars. It is necessary for this transformation to provide the grammar with an 'initial production' $S' \to \bot S$. If we use the notation $\tau(G)$ to denote the transformed grammar, then the following result can be shown.

THEOREM 12.13. Let $k > 0$. A grammar G is PLR(k) if and only if $\tau(G)$ is LL(k).

Proof. See [157]. □

Moreover, it is shown in [157] that transformation τ has the following property.

THEOREM 12.14. Every PLR(k) grammar G can be transformed to an LL(k) grammar $\tau(G)$ such that $\tau(G)[\ell/\bar{r}]G$ and $\tau(G)[\bar{r}/\bar{r}]G$.

Proof. The proof that $\tau(G)[\ell/\bar{r}]G$ can be found in [157]. The cover-homomorphism ψ which is defined to show that $\tau(G)[\ell/\bar{r}]G$ is such that, for each $i \in \Delta_{\tau(G)}$, $\psi(i) \neq \varepsilon$ only if the production with label i is an ε-production. It follows from Lemma 4.3 that $\tau(G)[\bar{r}/\bar{r}]G$. □

In summary, if we use the notation τ_{LF} for the left factoring process and τ_{SU} for the transformation of Soisalon-Soininen and Ukkonen [157], then:

(i) $\tau_{LF}(LP) \subseteq LL$

$\tau_{LF}^{-1}(LL) = LP$

(ii) $\tau_{LF}(PLR) \subseteq LC$

$\tau_{LF}^{-1}(LC) = PLR$

(iii) $\tau_{SU}(PLR) \subseteq LL$

$\tau_{SU}^{-1}(LL) = PLR$

and, if we consider a specific amount of look-ahead k,

(iv) $\tau_{SU}(PLR(k)) \subseteq LL(k),\ k > 0$

$\tau_{SU}(PLR(0)) \subseteq LL(1)$

$\tau_{SU}^{-1}(LL(k)) = PLR(k),\ k \geq 0.$

This section is concluded with a note on Table XIII and a general note on the possibility to transform grammars to LL(k) grammars.

Note 1. In Table XIII we have that for LP(k) and for LR(k) grammars the production $A \to X_1 \ldots X_p$ is recognized with certainty after seeing k symbols of look-ahead of the string z. However, for LP(k) grammars we need this look-ahead only to distinguish productions of the form $A \to \alpha$ and $A \to \alpha\beta$ with $\beta \neq \varepsilon$. If the set of productions is prefix-free (i.e., if $A \to \alpha$ and $A \to \alpha\beta$ in P, then $\beta = \varepsilon$) then it is only necessary to consider k symbols of the terminal string which is obtained from X_p in order to be able to recognize the production $A \to X_1 \ldots X_p$. Notice that this remark is of the same type as the remark which was made on Chomsky normal form in section 12.2. That is, due to a special form of the productions it is possible to modify a parsing strategy.

Note 2. In Hammer [56] there is a thorough discussion on 'k-transformable' grammars. The class of k-transformable grammars is a subclass of the class of LR(k) grammars. Each k-transformable grammar can be transformed to an LL(k) grammar in such a way that a left-to-right cover is obtained. There is an interesting conjecture in [56] concerning this transformation. This conjecture, which is attributed to R.E. Stearns, says that for any CFG G, if there is some LL(k) grammar which is as useful for parsing as G then that grammar can be found by application of this transformation. 'As useful' means e.g. that a left-to-right cover can be defined. In [56] it is shown that the LC(k) grammars are k-transformable. In [155] it is mentioned that the PLR(k) grammars are k-transformable.

12.4. PARSING STRATEGIES REVISITED: A SURVEY OF RECENT RESEARCH

In the preceeding sections we have distinguished between two main techniques for recognizing a production during the parsing process. The first technique assumes that each production has a position in its righthand side where the whole production should be recognized. The second technique distinguishes between recognition of the lefthand side of a production and recognition of the whole production. The first technique leads to definitions of LL-, LC- and LR-grammars. The second technique gives rise to definitions of PLC-, LP- and PLR-grammars.

Other approaches, which give rise to new classes of grammars, are possible. Ukkonen [162,166] considers a slight extension of the definition of PLR(k) grammars. Due to this extension the class of corresponding languages is not the class of LL(k) languages but the class of deterministic languages.

Consider again Figure 12.1. The LL-, PLC-, LP-, LC- and PLR-grammars have in common that for each of their productions the lefthand side is recognized before the recognition of the righthand side. However, for these classes of grammars it is not only the lefthand side A which is certainly known after scanning k : yz but also symbol X_1 is known as being the left corner of the next production which is going to be recognized. Hence, here we see the possibility to introduce a new parsing strategy in which we distinguish the recognition of the left corner (or a generalized left corner) from the recognition of the complete production. This has been done in the definition of 'weak' PLR(k) grammars. It is required that each left corner of a non-ε-production can be recognized with certainty after scanning at most k terminal symbols of string yz in Figure 12.1. The definition follows below.

<u>DEFINITION 12.6.</u> A grammar $G = (N,\Sigma,P,S)$ is said to be *weak* PLR(k) if it is LR(k) and if for each $\alpha,\alpha',\alpha'',\beta,\gamma \in V^*$; $w,w',y,y' \in \Sigma^*$; $A,A' \in N$, $X \in V$ and for each production $A \to X\beta$, the conditions

(i) $S \overset{*}{\underset{R}{\Rightarrow}} \alpha Aw \underset{R}{\Rightarrow} \underline{\alpha X}\beta w \overset{*}{\underset{R}{\Rightarrow}} \underline{\alpha X}yw$

(ii) $S \overset{*}{\underset{R}{\Rightarrow}} \alpha'A'w' \underset{R}{\Rightarrow} \underline{\alpha'\alpha''X}\gamma w' \overset{*}{\underset{R}{\Rightarrow}} \underline{\alpha'\alpha''X}y'w'$

(iii) $\alpha'\alpha'' = \alpha$ and $k : yw = k : y'w'$

always imply that $\alpha = \alpha'$.

It is intuitively clear that every LR(k) grammar such that the length of each righthand side of the productions is less than or equal to two is weak PLR(k). It follows (cf. [166]) that any LR(k) grammar G can be transformed to a weak PLR(k) grammar G'. This can be seen as follows. Every production i. $A \to X_1X_2\ldots X_p$ of G such that $|X_1X_2\ldots X_p| \leq 2$ is also a production of G'. If $|X_1X_2\ldots X_p| > 2$, then add the productions

$$A \to X_1[X_2\ldots X_p] \quad \langle i\rangle$$
$$[X_2\ldots X_p] \to X_2[X_3\ldots X_p] \quad \langle\varepsilon\rangle$$
$$\vdots$$
$$[X_{p-1}X_p] \to X_{p-1}X_p \quad \langle\varepsilon\rangle$$

to P'. Clearly, in this case a right cover homomorphism can be defined.

There is another consequence of this definition. In general we can not recognize the lefthand side of a production of a weak PLR(k) grammar before we have seen the next k terminal symbols after the yield of this lefthand side. That is, in Figure 12.1, after we have seen k : z. However, once we have recognized a left corner then in general not all the nonterminal symbols in N will deserve consideration for being a lefthand side of the production. That is, once we have recognized the left corner X of a production then we know that the lefthand side of the production is in the set $\{A \mid A \rightarrow X\alpha$ in P, for some $\alpha \in V^*\}$. These sets form a so-called weak partition of the set of nonterminal symbols. That is, a family of nonempty subsets of N is called a *weak partition* of N if for each element $A \in N$ there is a subset in this family which contains A. Notice that in the usual definition of a partition we have also the condition that the subsets are pairwise disjoint. For weak partitions we will use the same notation as for partitions. Hence, if π is a weak partition of a set V, then we write $x \equiv y \pmod{\pi}$ if x and y are in the same subset of the weak partition π. Notice that for a weak partition we do not necessarily have that $x \equiv y$ and $y \equiv z$ implies that $x \equiv z$.

Recently various classes of grammars have been introduced for which a (weak) partition of the set V of grammar symbols plays an essential role. Clearly, in Chapter 8 we have already given a definition of such a class of grammars, viz. the strict deterministic grammars. We recall this definition since we want to generalize it.

A grammar $G = (N,\Sigma,P,S)$ is said to be a strict deterministic grammar if there exists a partition π of V such that

(i) $\Sigma \in \pi$,

(ii) For any $A,A' \in N$ and $\alpha,\beta,\beta' \in V^*$, if $A \rightarrow \alpha\beta$, $A' \rightarrow \alpha\beta'$ and $A \equiv A' \pmod{\pi}$, then either

(a) both $\beta,\beta' \neq \varepsilon$ and $1 : \beta \equiv 1 : \beta' \pmod{\pi}$, or

(b) $\beta = \beta' = \varepsilon$ and $A = A'$.

In Harrison and Havel [60] some remarks on the parsing procedure for strict deterministic grammars are given. The strategy can be explained by specifying a 'working set' which consists of the nodes of the parse tree that are currently under processing. The nodes enter this set in a top-down order and the nodes exit from the working set in a bottom-up order.

In Friede [36,37] a definition for strict deterministic grammars with look-ahead is given. We use the name strong SD(k) to denote these grammars.

<u>DEFINITION 12.7.</u> A CFG $G = (N,\Sigma,P,S)$ is said to be a *strong* SD(k) grammar for some $k \geq 0$, if there exists a partition π of V such that

(i) $\Sigma \in \pi$,

(ii) For any $A,A' \in N$ and $\alpha,\beta,\beta' \in V^*$, if $A \rightarrow \alpha\beta$, $A' \rightarrow \alpha\beta'$ are productions in P, $A \equiv A' \pmod{\pi}$ and

$$FIRST_k(\beta\ FOLLOW_k(A)) \cap FIRST_k(\beta'\ FOLLOW_k(A')) \neq \emptyset$$

then either

(a) both $\beta, \beta' \neq \varepsilon$ and $1 : \beta \equiv 1 : \beta' \pmod{\pi}$, or

(b) $\beta = \beta' = \varepsilon$ and $A = A'$.

We will present the relations between the classes of grammars which have been defined in section 12.3 and those which will be defined here. We start with the strong LP(k) grammars and we show that any strong LP(k) grammar is a strong SD(k) grammar, with that also accomplishing the inclusion of the class of strong LL(k) grammars in the class of strong SD(k) grammars.

THEOREM 12.15. For any $k \geq 0$, if G is a strong LP(k) grammar then G is a strong SD(k) grammar.

Proof. Let $G = (N,\Sigma,P,S)$ be a strong LP(k) grammar. Define a partition π of V by

$$\pi = \{\{A\} \mid A \in N\} \cup \{\Sigma\}.$$

We prove that π satisfies the conditions of Definition 12.7. Consider two productions $A \to \alpha\beta$ and $A \to \alpha\beta'$. If $\beta = \beta'$ then the conditions are trivially satisfied. Otherwise, if α is not the longest common prefix of $\alpha\beta$ and $\alpha\beta'$, then both $\beta \neq \varepsilon$, $\beta' \neq \varepsilon$ and $1 : \beta = 1 : \beta'$, whence $1 : \beta \equiv 1 : \beta' \pmod{\pi}$. If α is the longest common prefix of $\alpha\beta$ and $\alpha\beta'$, then by definition of a strong LP(k) grammar we have that

$$\mathrm{FIRST}_k(\beta\ \mathrm{FOLLOW}_k(A)) \cap \mathrm{FIRST}_k(\beta'\ \mathrm{FOLLOW}_k(A)) = \emptyset.$$

Therefore, any strong LP(k) grammar is also a strong SD(k) grammar. □

However, and therefore we have used the name strong SD(k), it is not the case that every LL(k) or LP(k) grammar is SD(k). Consider the following LL(2) grammar with productions

$S \to aAa$

$S \to bAba$

$A \to b$

$A \to \varepsilon$

If we follow the definition of a strong SD(k) grammar, then we see that for the productions $A \to b$ and $A \to \varepsilon$ we have $A \equiv A$ and

$$ba \in \mathrm{FIRST}_2(b\ \mathrm{FOLLOW}_2(A)) \cap \mathrm{FIRST}_2(\varepsilon\ \mathrm{FOLLOW}_2(A))$$

and the conditions (a) and (b) are not satisfied.

Pittl [132] introduced another generalization of the class of strict deterministic grammars. However, instead of a partition of V, a weak partition of the set

$$M_k(G) = \{(A,u) \mid A \in N \text{ and } u \in FOLLOW_k(A)\}$$

is defined.

<u>DEFINITION 12.8.</u> Let $G = (N,\Sigma,P,S)$ be a CFG, let $k \geq 0$ and let π be a weak partition of $M_k(G)$. Then π is called *admissible* if for any (A,u), $(A',u') \in M_k(G)$, with α,β, $\beta' \in V^*$, if $A \rightarrow \alpha\beta$ and $A' \rightarrow \alpha\beta'$ are in P and $(A,u) \equiv (A',u') (\text{mod } \pi)$, then

$$FIRST_k(\beta u) \cap FIRST_k(\beta' u') \neq \emptyset$$

implies that either

(i) $1 : \beta \in \Sigma$ and $1 : \beta' \in \Sigma$, or

(ii) $\beta = C\gamma$, $\beta' = C'\gamma'$ for some $C,C' \in N$, $\gamma,\gamma' \in V^*$ and $(C,Z) \equiv (C',z') (\text{mod } \pi)$ for all $z \in FIRST_k(\gamma u)$, $z' \in FIRST_k(\gamma' u')$, or

(iii) $\beta = \beta' = \varepsilon$ and $A = A'$.

In Pittl [132] this definition is obtained as the result of his efforts to give a simple characterization of a class of grammars which had only been defined, until then, in a rather obscure way. In the framework of this chapter we prefer to use the name weak SD(k) grammars for grammars which have an admissible partition.

<u>DEFINITION 12.9.</u> Let $k \geq 0$. A grammar $G = (N,\Sigma,P,S)$ is said to be a *weak* SD(k) grammar if there exists an admissible partition of $M_k(G)$.

The classes of strict deterministic grammars, strong SD(0) grammars and weak SD(0) grammars coincide. The adjectives strong and weak are justified as follows.

<u>THEOREM 12.16.</u> Let $k \geq 0$. If CFG G is a strong SD(k) grammar then G is a weak SD(k) grammar.

Proof. Assume that $G = (N,\Sigma,P,S)$ is a strong SD(k) grammar with a partition π of V which satisfies Definition 12.7. Define π_a, an admissible partition of $M_k(G)$ in the following way. For any (A,u), $(A',u') \in M_k(G)$, define

$$(A,u) \equiv (A',u') \quad (\text{mod } \pi_a)$$

if and only if

$A \equiv A' \pmod{\pi}$.

Clearly, π_a is a partition of $M_k(G)$. Reflexivity, symmetry and transitivity are trivially satisfied since π is a partition of V. Moreover, π_a is admissible. This can be seen as follows. Let (A,u), $(A'u') \in M_k(G)$ and let $A \to \alpha\beta$, $A \to \alpha\beta' \in P$, for some $\alpha,\beta,\beta' \in V^*$. If $(A,u) \equiv (A',u') \pmod{\pi_a}$ and

$$FIRST_k(\beta u) \cap FIRST_k(\beta' u') \neq \emptyset,$$

then also

$$FIRST_k(\beta\ FOLLOW_k(A)) \cap FIRST_k(\beta'\ FOLLOW_k(A)) \neq \emptyset$$

and it follows from Definition 12.7 that we can have the following two cases:

(1) $\beta,\beta' \neq \varepsilon$ and $1 : \beta \equiv 1 : \beta' \pmod{\pi}$. Hence, $1 : \beta \in \Sigma$ and $1 : \beta' \in \Sigma$ or $\beta = C\gamma$ and $\beta' = C'\gamma'$ for some $C,C' \in N$, $\gamma,\gamma' \in V^*$ and $C \equiv C' \pmod{\pi}$. In the latter case, if $z \in FIRST_k(\gamma u)$ and $z' \in FIRST_k(\gamma' u')$, then $z \in FOLLOW_k(C)$ and $z' \in FOLLOW_k(C')$ and it follows from the definition of π_a that $(C,z) \equiv (C',z') \pmod{\pi_a}$.

(2) $\beta = \beta' = \varepsilon$ and $A = A'$.

Hence, any strong SD(k) grammar is a weak SD(k) grammar. □

We emphasize that the admissible partition π_a which is defined in Theorem 12.16 is a partition (without the adjective *weak*) of $M_k(G)$. The question can be raised whether each weak SD(k) grammar with an admissible partition π_a which is in fact a partition of $M_k(G)$ is a strong SD(k) grammar. However, this is not the case. The intuitive reason is that for strong SD(k) grammars the look-ahead is not used in a 'context-dependent' way. That is, for strong SD(k) grammars there exist situations in which nonterminal symbols are forced to be equivalent due to some look-ahead which can only appear in other situations.

Our LL(2) example grammar with productions

$S \to aAa$

$S \to bAba$

$A \to b$

$A \to \varepsilon$

is a grammar which is not strong SD(k) but it is weak SD(2) for the partition

$$\pi_a = \{\{(S,\varepsilon)\}, \{(A,a)\}, \{(A,ba)\}$$

of $M_2(G)$. In [132] an example of a grammar G can be found which is weak SD(k) and for which only a weak partition of $M_k(G)$ can be found. Therefore it is possible to define a proper subclass of the class of weak SD(k) grammars which properly includes the class of strong SD(k) grammars and which is defined by the restriction that the admissible partition should be a partition of $M_k(G)$. We will not investigate this class of grammars here.

Next we show that any LP(k) grammar is a weak SD(k) grammar, with that also accomplishing the inclusion of the class of LL(k) grammars in the class of weak SD(k) grammars. A few preliminaries are needed.
Let $G = (N,\Sigma,P,S)$ be a CFG and let $k \geq 0$. For any $A \in N$, define

$$\sigma LL_k(A) = \{L \mid L = FIRST_k(\alpha) \text{ for some } \alpha \in V^* \text{ and } w \in \Sigma^* \text{ such that } S \overset{*}{\underset{L}{\Rightarrow}} wA\alpha\}$$

and define

$$\sigma LP_k(A) = \{L \mid L = \bigcup_i FIRST_k(\alpha_i) \text{ for some } w \in \Sigma^* \text{ such that } S \overset{*}{\underset{L}{\Rightarrow}} wA\alpha_i,\ \alpha_i \in V^*\}.$$

Notice that, due to Lemma 12.1, for LL(k) grammars both sets coincide. In Aho and Ullman [3] the sets $\sigma LL_k(A)$ are used for LL(k) testing.

<u>THEOREM 12.17.</u> For any $k \geq 0$, if G is an LP(k) grammar then G is a weak SD(k) grammar.

Proof. Let $G = (N,\Sigma,P,S)$ be an LP(k) grammar. Define a weak partition π of $M_k(G)$ as follows. For any (A,u), $(A,u') \in M_k(G)$ define $(A,u) \equiv (A,u') \pmod{\pi}$ if and only if there exists a set $L \in \sigma LP_k(A)$ such that $u, u' \in L$. Clearly, in this way a weak partition of $M_k(G)$ is defined. We show that π is an admissible partition. Let (A,u), $(A,u') \in M_k(G)$ such that $(A,u) \equiv (A,u') \pmod{\pi}$. Then we know that there exist leftmost derivations

$$S \overset{*}{\underset{L}{\Rightarrow}} wA\omega$$

and

$$S \overset{*}{\underset{L}{\Rightarrow}} wA\omega'$$

such that $u \in FIRST_k(\omega)$ and $u' \in FIRST_k(\omega')$. Let, for some $\alpha,\beta,\beta' \in V^*$, the productions $A \to \alpha\beta$ and $A \to \alpha\beta'$ be in P.

Suppose $\beta \neq \beta'$ and α is the longest common prefix of $\alpha\beta$ and $\alpha\beta'$. Since G is LP(k) we have that

$$FIRST_k(\beta u) \cap FIRST_k(\beta' u') = \emptyset.$$

Suppose $\beta \neq \beta'$ and α is not the longest common prefix of $\alpha\beta$ and $\alpha\beta'$. Then

$1 : \beta = 1 : \beta'$ and either $1 : \beta \in \Sigma$ and $1 : \beta' \in \Sigma$ or $\beta = C\gamma$ and $\beta' = C\gamma'$ for some $C, C' \in N$, $\gamma, \gamma' \in V^*$. Since there exist derivations

$$S \overset{*}{\underset{L}{\Rightarrow}} w'C\gamma\omega$$

and

$$S \overset{*}{\underset{L}{\Rightarrow}} w'C\gamma'\omega'$$

for some $w' \in \Sigma^*$, we may conclude that for all $z \in FIRST_k(\gamma u)$ and $z' \in FIRST_k(\gamma' u')$ we have that $(C,z) \equiv (C,z') \pmod{\pi}$.

It remains to verify that if $\beta = \beta'$ then the conditions of an admissible partition are also satisfied. If $\beta = \beta'$ and $\beta \neq \varepsilon$, then we have exactly the situation $(1 : \beta = 1 : \beta')$ which was described above. If $\beta = \beta' = \varepsilon$ then condition (iii) of the implication is trivially satisfied.

This concludes the proof that π is an admissible partition and therefore grammar G is a weak SD(k) grammar. □

We are now in a position to present the inclusion diagram of Figure 12.5. The drawn lines in this figure denote proper inclusions. The interrupted line denotes a conjecture. That is, we conjecture that any weak SD(k) grammar is a weak PLR(k) grammar. Because LC(k) grammars can be left recursive and weak SD(k) grammars can not be left recursive (cf. Pittl [132]) we can not have the inclusion of the class of LC (or PLR) grammars in the class of weak SD grammars.

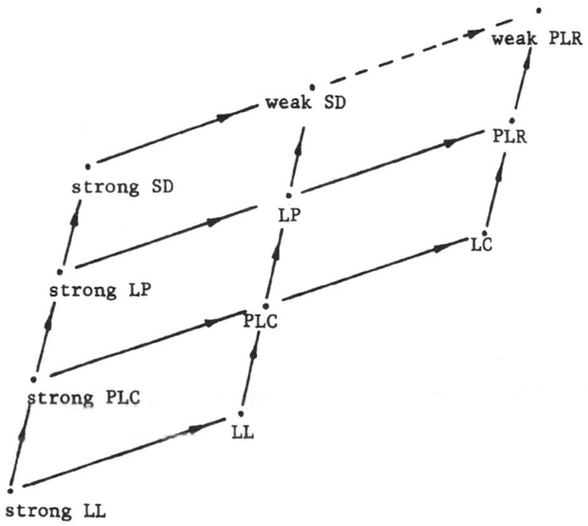

Figure 12.5. Inclusion diagram.

We conclude this section with some notes on possible future research. Moura (cf. [113]) has announced results and transformations which deal with the relationships between the classes of LR(k), weak SD(k) and strong SD(k) grammars. Ukkonen [162] has presented a transformation from weak PLR(0) grammars to strict deterministic grammars. The question arises whether this transformation can be used for weak PLR(k) grammars. Unfortunately the transformation is rather complicated. It would be useful if we had more insight in the class of k-transformable grammars (cf. Hammer [56]). No formal proof is available for the inclusion of the class of PLR(k) grammars in the class of k-transformable grammars. Moreover, is every k-transformable grammar a weak PLR(k) grammar ?

Schlichtiger [147,148] has introduced the class of 'partitioned chain grammars'. Partitioned chain grammars are defined with the help of chains (cf. Definition 5.1.) and a partition of the set of nonterminal symbols. Schlichtiger uses the names PC(k) (partitioned chain) grammars and EPC(k) (extended PC(k)) grammars. In the framework of this chapter and, moreover, to avoid confusion with the extended context-free grammars, it would be better to use the names strong PC(k) grammars and PC(k) grammars. In [148] relationships between the partitioned chain grammars and the PLR(k) grammars are mentioned. Moreover, it is mentioned that the class of PC(k) grammars (which we prefer to call strong PC(k) grammars) properly includes the class of strong SD(k) grammars.

It is our belief that the classes of grammars which have been mentioned in this chapter can be put together in a framework and in an inclusion diagram in which the relationships and the parsing strategies can be shown in a rather natural way.

BIBLIOGRAPHY

CONTEXT-FREE GRAMMARS:

COVERS, NORMAL FORMS, AND PARSING

[1] AHO, A.V. & S.C. JOHNSON, LR parsing, Computing Surveys 6 (1974), 99-124.

[2] AHO, A.V., S.C. JOHNSON & J.D. ULLMAN, Deterministic parsing of ambiguous grammars, Comm. ACM 18 (1975), 441-452.

[3] AHO, A.V. & J.D. ULLMAN, The Theory of Parsing, Translation and Compiling, Vols. 1 and 2, Prentice Hall, Englewood Cliffs, N.J., 1972 and 1973.

[4] AHO, A.V. & J.D. ULLMAN, Principles of Compiler Design, Addison-Wesley, Reading, Mass., 1977.

[5] ANDERSON, S.O., Eliminating left recursion in attribute grammars, manuscript, Heriot-Watt University, Edinburgh.

[6] ANDERSON, T., J. EVE & J.J. HORNING, Efficient LR(1) parsers, Acta Informatica 2 (1973), 12-39.

[7] ARBIB, M.A. & E.G. MANES, Arrows, Structures and Functors: The Categorical Imperative, Academic Press, New York, 1975.

[8] BACKHOUSE, R.C., Syntax of Programming Languages: Theory and Practice, Prentice Hall International, London, 1979.

[9] BAKER, B.S., Generalized syntax directed translation, tree transducers and linear space, SIAM J. of Comput. 7 (1978), 376-391.

[10] BEATTY, J.C., Iteration theorems for the LL(k) languages, Ph.D. Thesis, Lawrence Livermore Laboratory, University of California, Livermore, 1977.

[11] BEATTY, J.C., Two iteration theorems for the LL(k) languages, report, Lawrence Livermore Laboratory, University of California, Livermore, 1978.

[12] BENSON, D.B., The basic algebraic structures in categories of derivations, Information and Control 28 (1975), 1-29.

[13] BENSON, D.B., Some preservation properties of normal form grammars, SIAM J. of Comput. 6 (1977), 381-402.

[14] BERTSCH, E., An observation on relative parsing time, J. Assoc. Comput. Mach. 22 (1975), 493-498.

[15] BOCHMANN, G.V., Semantic equivalence of covering attribute grammars, Int. J. of Computer and Information Sciences 8 (1979), 523-540.

[16] BOCHMANN, G.V. & P. WARD, Compiler writing system for attribute grammars, Computer Journal 21 (1978), 144-148.

[17] BROSGOL, B.M., Deterministic translation grammars, Ph.D. Thesis, TR-3-74, Harvard University, Cambridge.

[18] BROSGOL, B.M., Deterministic translation grammars, Proc. Eight Princeton Conf. on Information Sciences and Systems 1974, 300-306.

[19] CHO, Y.E., Simple left corner grammars, Proc. Seventh Princeton Conf. on Information Sciences and Systems 1973, 557-557.

[20] COLMERAUER, A., Total precedence relations, J. Assoc. Comput. Mach. 17 (1970), 14-30.

[21] CREMERS, A.B. & S. GINSBURG, Context-free grammar forms, J. Comput. System Sci. 11 (1975), 86-117.

[22] CULIK II, K., Contribution to deterministic top-down analysis of context-free languages, Kybernetika 4 (1968), 422-431.

[23] CULIK II, K. & R.S. COHEN, LR-regular grammars - an extension of LR(k) grammars, J. Comput. System Sci. 7 (1973), 66-96.

[24] DEMERS, A.J., Generalized left corner parsing, Conf. Record of the Fourth ACM Symp. on Principles of Programming Languages 1977, 170-182.

[25] DeREMER, F.L., Simple LR(k) grammars, Comm. ACM 14 (1971), 453-460.

[26] DeREMER, F.L., Extended LR(k) grammars and their parsers, University of California, Santa Cruz, 1970.

[27] DeREMER, F.L. & T.J. PENNELLO, Efficient computation of LALR(1) look-ahead sets, SIGPLAN Notices 14, Nr. 8, August 1979, 176-187.

[28] DRUSEIKIS, F.C., SLR(1) parser generator, Dept. of Computer Science, University of Arizona, 1975.

[29] EARLEY, J., Ambiguity and precedence in syntax description, Acta Informatica 4 (1975), 183-192.

[30] FELDMAN, J. & D. GRIES, Translator writing systems, Comm. ACM 11 (1968), 77-108.

[31] FISHER, G.A. & M. WEBER, LALR(1) parsing for languages without reserved words, SIGPLAN Notices 14, Nr. 11, November 1979, 26-30.

[32] FLOYD, R.W., Syntactic analysis and operator precedence, J. Assoc. Comput. Mach. 10 (1963), 316-333.

[33] FLOYD, R.W., Bounded context syntactic analysis, Comm. ACM 7 (1964), 62-67.

[34] FOSTER, J.M., A syntax improving program, Computer Journal 11 (1968), 31-34.

[35] FOSTER, J.M., Automatic Syntactic Analysis, Macdonald, London, 1970.

[36] FRIEDE, D., Partitioned LL(k) grammars, in: Automata, Languages and Programming, H.A. Maurer (ed.), Lect. Notes in Comp. Sci. 71 (Springer, Berlin, 1979), 245-255.

[37] FRIEDE, D., Transition diagrams and strict deterministic grammars, 4th GI Conf. on Theoretical Computer Science, K. Weihrauch (ed.), Lect. Notes in Comp. Sci. 67 (Springer, Berlin, 1979), 113-123.

[38] GELLER, M.M., S.L. GRAHAM & M.A. HARRISON, Production prefix parsing, in: Automata, Languages and Programming, J. Loeckx (ed.), Lect. Notes in Comp. Sci. 14 (Springer, Berlin, 1974), 232-241.

[39] GELLER, M.M. & M.A. HARRISON, Strict deterministic versus LR(0) parsing, Conf. Record of the ACM Symp. on Principles of Programming Languages 1973, 22-32.

[40] GELLER, M.M. & M.A. HARRISON, On LR(k) grammars and languages, Theoret. Comput. Sci. 4 (1977), 245-276.

[41] GELLER, M.M. & M.A. HARRISON, Characteristic parsing: A framework for producing compact deterministic parsers, J. Comput. System Sci. 14 (1977), 265-345.

[42] GELLER, M.M., M.A. HARRISON & I.M. HAVEL, Normal forms of deterministic grammars, Discrete Mathematics 16 (1976), 313-322.

[43] GINSBURG, S. & M.A. HARRISON, Bracketed context-free languages, J. Comput. System Sci. 1 (1967), 1-23.

[44] GINSBURG, S., B. LEONG, O. MAYER & D. WOTSCHKE, On strict interpretations of grammar forms, Math. Systems Theory 12 (1979), 233-252.

[45] GOGUEN, J.A., J.W. THATCHER, E.G. WAGNER & J.B. WRIGHT, A junction between computer science and category theory I (part 1), IBM research report RC 4526, 1973.

[46] GRAHAM, S.L., On bounded right context languages and grammars, SIAM J. of Comput. 3 (1974), 224-254.

[47] GRAHAM, S.L., C.B. HALEY & W.N. JOY, Practical LR error recovery, SIGPLAN Notices 14, Nr. 8, August 1979, 168-175.

[48] GRAY, J.N. & M.A. HARRISON, Single pass precedence analysis, IEEE Conf. Record of 10th Annual Sympos. on Switching and Automata Theory 1969, 106-117.

[49] GRAY, J.N. & M.A. HARRISON, On the covering and reduction problems for context-free grammars, J. Assoc. Comput. Mach. 19 (1972), 385-395.

[50] GREIBACH, S.A., A new normal form theorem for context-free phrase structure grammars, J. Assoc. Comput. Mach. 12 (1965), 42-52.

[51] GREIBACH, S.A., Formal parsing systems, Comm. ACM 7 (1964), 499-504.

[52] GREIBACH, S.A., Erasable context-free languages, Information and Control 29 (1975), 301-326.

[53] GRIFFITHS, T.V. & S.R. PETRICK, On the relative efficiencies of context-free grammar recognizers, Comm. ACM 8 (1965), 289-300.

[54] GRIFFITHS, T.V. & S.R. PETRICK, Top-down versus bottom-up analysis, Proc. IFIP Congress 68, North Holland, Amsterdam, 1969, 437-443.

[55] HAMMER, M., A new grammatical transformation into LL(k) form, Conf. Record of the 6th Annual ACM Sympos. on Theory of Computing 1974, 266-275.

[56] HAMMER, M., A new grammatical transformation into deterministic top-down form, MAC TR-119, Ph.D. Thesis, Massachusetts Institute of Technology, 1974.

[57] HARRISON, M.A., On covers and precedence analysis, G.I.-3. Jahrestagung, W. Brauer (ed.), Lect. Notes in Comp. Sci. 1 (Springer, Berlin, 1973), 2-17.

[58] HARRISON, M.A., Introduction to Formal Language Theory, Addison-Wesley, Reading, Mass., 1978.

[59] HARRISON, M.A. & I.M. HAVEL, Strict deterministic grammars, J. Comput. System Sci. 7 (1973), 237-277.

[60] HARRISON, M.A. & I.M. HAVEL, On the parsing of deterministic languages, J. Assoc. Comput. Mach. 21 (1974), 525-548.

[61] HARRISON, M.A. & I.M. HAVEL, Real-time strict deterministic languages, SIAM J. of Comput. 1 (1972), 333-349.

[62] HEILBRUNNER, S., On the definition of ELR(k) and ELL(k) grammars, Acta Informatica 11 (1979), 169-176.

[63] HOTZ, G., Eine Algebraisierung des Synthese-problems von Schaltkreisen, Elektr. Informationsverarbeitung und Kybernetik (EIK) 1 (1965), 185-205 and 209-231.

[64] HOTZ, G., Eindeutigkeit und Mehrdeutigkeit formaler Sprachen, Elektr. Informationsverarbeitung und Kybernetik (EIK) 2 (1966), 235-246.

[65] HOTZ, G., Strukturelle Verwandschaften von Semi-Thue Systemen, in: Category Theory Applied to Computation and Control, E.G. Manes (ed.), Lect. Notes in Comp. Sci. 25 (Springer, Berlin, 1975), 174-179.

[66] HOTZ, G., Normal-form transformations of context-free grammars, Acta Cybernetica 4 (1978), 65-84.

[67] HOTZ, G. & V. CLAUS, Automatentheorie und formale Sprachen, B.I.-Hochschulskripten, Bibliographisches Institut, Mannheim, 1972.

[68] HOTZ, G. & R.J. ROSS, LL(k)- und LR(k)-Invarianz von kontextfreien Grammatiken unter einer Transformation auf Greibach-Normalform, Elektr. Informationsverarbeitung und Kybernetik (EIK) 15 (1979), 73-86.

[69] HUNT III, H.B. & D.J. ROSENKRANTZ, Complexity of grammatical similarity relations, Proc. of the Conf. on Theoretical Computer Science, Waterloo 1977, 139-145.

[70] HUNT III, H.B. & D.J. ROSENKRANTZ, Efficient algorithms for structural similarity of grammars, Conf. Record of the Seventh ACM Symp. on Principles of Programming Languages 1980, 213-219.

[71] HUNT III, H.B., D.J. ROSENKRANTZ & T.G. SZYMANSKI, The covering problem for linear context-free grammars, Theoret. Comput. Sci. 2 (1976), 361-382.

[72] HUNT III, H.B., D.J. ROSENKRANTZ & T.G. SZYMANSKI, On the equivalence, containment and covering problems for the regular and context-free languages, J. Comput. System Sci. 12 (1976), 222-268.

[73] JARZABEK, S. & T. KRAWCZYK, LL-regular grammars, Info. Proc. Letters 4 (1975), 31-37.

[74] JOHNSON, S.C., Yacc-yet another compiler-compiler, CSTR 32, Bell Laboratories 1975 (see also UNIX programmer's manual, January 1979).

[75] JOLIAT, M.L., The BIGLALR parser generator system, Bell-Northern Research Ltd., report (613) 596-3293, January 1975.

[76] KNUTH, D.E., On the translation of languages from left to right, Information and Control 8 (1965), 607-639.

[77] KNUTH, D.E., A characterization of parenthesis languages, Information and Control 11 (1967), 269-289.

[78] KNUTH, D.E., Semantics of context-free languages, Math. Systems Theory 2 (1968), 127-145.

[79] KNUTH, D.E., Top-down syntax analysis, Acta Informatica 1 (1971), 79-110.

[80] KORENJAK, A.J. & J.E. HOPCROFT, Simple deterministic languages, IEEE Conf. Record of 7th Annual Sympos. on Switching and Automata Theory 1966, 34-46.

[81] KRAL, J., Syntax directed compiling and the problem of grammatical covering, Acta Polytech. Prace CVUT 4 (1977), 39-52.

[82] KRAL, J., Bottom-up versus top-down syntax analysis revised, Research report UVT 10-11/74, Technical University of Prague, 1974.

[83] KRAL, J. & J. DEMNER, A note on the number of states of DeRemer's recognizer, Info. Proc. Letters 2 (1973), 22-23.

[84] KRAL, J. & J. DEMNER, Semi-top-down syntactic analysis, Research report UVT 6/73/M, Technical University of Prague, 1973.

[85] KRETINSKY, M., Semi-top-down syntax analysis of precedence grammars, Scripta Fac. Sci. Natur. UJEP Brunensis Math. 8 (1978), 1-11.

[86] KRON, H.H., H.J. HOFFMANN & G. WINKLER, On a SLR(k) based parser system which accepts non-LR(k) grammars, G.I.-4. Jahrestagung, D. Siefkes (ed.), Lect. Notes in Comp. Sci. 26 (Springer, Berlin, 1975), 214-223.

[87] KUNO, S., The augmented predictive analyzer for context-free languages - Its relative efficiency, Comm. ACM 9 (1966), 810-823.

[88] KUO-CHUNG TAI, Non canonical SLR(1) grammars, ACM Transactions on Progr. Languages and Systems 1 (1979), 295-320.

[89] KURKI-SUONIO, R., On top-to-bottom recognition and left recursion, Comm. ACM 9 (1966), 527-528.

[90] KURKI-SUONIO, R., Notes on top-down languages, BIT 9 (1969), 225-238.

[91] KURODA, S.Y., A topological study of phrase structure languages, Information and Control 30 (1976), 307-379.

[92] LALONDE, W.R., Regular right part grammars and their parsers, Comm. ACM 20 (1977), 731-741.

[93] LALONDE, W.R., Constructing LR parsers for regular right part grammars, Acta Informatica 11 (1979), 177-193.

[94] LALONDE, W.R., E.S. LEE & J.J. HORNING, An LALR(k) parser generator, Proc. IFIP Congress 71, North Holland, Amsterdam, 1972, 513-518.

[95] LECARME, O. & G.V. BOCHMANN, A (truly) usable and portable compiler writing system, Proc. IFIP Congress 74, North Holland, Amsterdam, 1974, 218-221.

[96] LEWI, J., K. DeVLAMINCK, J. HUENS & M. HUYBRECHTS, The ELL(1) parser generator and the error recovery mechanism, Acta Informatica 10 (1978), 209-228.

[97] LEWI, J., K. DeVLAMINCK, J. HUENS & M. HUYBRECHTS, Project LILA: The ELL(1) generator of LILA; an introduction, Proceedings of the Int. Computing Symposium 1977, Liège, Belgium, 237-251.

[98] LEWI, J., K. DeVLAMINCK, J. HUENS & P. MERTENS, SLS/1: A translator writing system, G.I.-5. Jahrestagung, J. Mühlbacher (ed.), Lect. Notes in Comp. Sci. 34 (Springer, Berlin, 1975), 627-641.

[99] LEWIS II, P.M., D.J. ROSENKRANTZ & R.E. STEARNS, Attributed translations, J. Comput. System Sci. 9 (1974), 279-307.

[100] LEWIS II, P.M., D.J. ROSENKRANTZ & R.E. STEARNS, Compiler Design Theory, Addison-Wesley, Reading, Mass., 1976.

[101] LEWIS II, P.M. & R.E. STEARNS, Syntax-directed transduction, J. Assoc. Comput. Mach. 15 (1968), 465-488.

[102] LOMET, D.B., A formalization of transition diagram systems, J. Assoc. Comput. Mach. 20 (1973), 235-257.

[103] MACLANE, S., Categories for the working Mathematician, Springer-Verlag, New York, 1971.

[104] MADSEN, M. & N.D. JONES, Letting the attributes influence the parsing, paper presented at a Workshop on Semantics-Directed Compiler Generation, Aarhus, 1980.

[105] MADSEN, O.L. & B.B. KRISTENSEN, LR-parsing of extended context-free grammars, Acta Informatica 7 (1976), 61-73.

[106] MAYER, O., Syntaxanalyse, Bibliographisches Institut, Mannheim, 1978.

[107] McNAUGHTON, R., Parenthesis grammars, J. Assoc. Comput. Mach. 14 (1967), 490-500.

[108] MICKUNAS, M.D., On the complete covering problem for LR(k) grammars, J. Assoc. Comput. Mach. 23 (1976), 17-30.

[109] MICKUNAS, M.D., R.L. LANCASTER & V.B. SCHNEIDER, Transforming LR(k) grammars to LR(1), SLR(1) and (1,1) bounded right-context grammars, J. Assoc. Comput. Mach. 23 (1976), 511-533.

[110] MICKUNAS, M.D. & V.B. SCHNEIDER, On the ability to cover LR(k) grammars with LR(1), SLR(1) and (1,1) bounded-context grammars, IEEE Conf. Record of 14th Annual Sympos. on Switching and Automata Theory 1973, 109-121.

[111] MICKUNAS, M.D. & V.B. SCHNEIDER, A parser generating system for constructing compressed compilers, Comm. ACM 16 (1973), 669-676.

[112] MILTON, D.R., L.W. KIRCHHOFF & B.R. ROWLAND, An ALL(1) compiler generator, SIGPLAN Notices 14, August 1979, 152-157.

[113] MOURA, A., Syntactic equivalence of grammar classes, Ph.D. Thesis, in preparation.

[114] NIJHOLT, A., On the parsing of LL-regular grammars, in: Mathematical Foundations of Computer Science, A. Mazurkiewicz (ed.), Lect. Notes in Comp. Sci. 45 (Springer, Berlin, 1976), 446-452.

[115] NIJHOLT, A., On the covering of left-recursive grammars, Conf. Record of the Fourth ACM Symp. on Principles of Programming Languages 1977, 86-96.

[116] NIJHOLT, A., On the covering of parsable grammars, J. Comput. System Sci. 15 (1977), 99-110.

[117] NIJHOLT, A., Cover results and normal forms, in: Mathematical Foundations of Computer Science, J. Gruska (ed.), Lect. Notes in Comp. Sci. 53 (Springer, Berlin, 1977), 420-429.

[118] NIJHOLT, A., On the parsing and covering of simple chain grammars, in: Automata, Languages and Programming, G. Ausiello and C. Böhm (eds.), Lect. Notes in Comp. Sci. 62 (Springer, Berlin, 1978), 330-344.

[119] NIJHOLT, A., A left part theorem for grammatical trees, Discrete Mathematics 25 (1979), 51-64.

[120] NIJHOLT, A., Grammar functors and covers: From non-left-recursive to Greibach normal form grammars, BIT 19 (1979), 73-78.

[121] NIJHOLT, A., From left regular to Greibach normal form grammars, Info. Proc. Letters 9 (1979), 51-55.

[122] NIJHOLT, A., Simple chain grammars and languages, Theoret. Comput. Sci. 9 (1979), 287-309.

[123] NIJHOLT, A., Strict deterministic grammars and Greibach normal form, Elektr. Informationsverarbeitung und Kybernetik (EIK) 15 (1979), 395-401.

[124] NIJHOLT, A., Structure preserving transformations on non-left-recursive grammars, in: Automata, Languages and Programming, H.A. Maurer (ed.), Lect. Notes in Comp. Sci. 71 (Springer, Berlin, 1979), 446-459.

[125] NIJHOLT, A., Over ontleden en grammaticale equivalentie-relaties, in: Coll. Capita Implementatie van Programmeertalen, J.C. van Vliet (ed.), MC-Syllabus 42, Mathematisch Centrum, Amsterdam, 1980, 47-72.

[126] NIJHOLT, A., LL-regular grammars, Int. J. of Computer Mathematics 8 (1980), to appear.

[127] NIJHOLT, A., A survey of normal form covers for context-free grammars, Acta Informatica, to appear.

[128] NIJHOLT, A. & E. SOISALON-SOININEN, Ch(k) grammars - A characterization of LL(k) languages, in: Mathematical Foundations of Computer Science, J. Becvár (ed.), Lect. Notes in Comp. Sci.74 (Springer, Berlin, 1979), 390-397.

[129] PAULL, M.C. & S.H. UNGER, Structural equivalence of context-free grammars, J. Comput. System Sci. 2 (1968), 427-463.

[130] PAULL, M.C. & S.H. UNGER, Structural equivalence and LL-k grammars, IEEE Conf. Record of 9th Annual Sympos. on Switching and Automata Theory 1968, 160-175.

[131] PITTL, J., On two subclasses of real-time grammars, in: Mathematical Foundations of Computer Science, J. Winkowski (ed.), Lect. Notes in Comp. Sci. 64 (Springer, Berlin, 1978), 426-435.

[132] PITTL, J., On LLP(k) grammars and parsers, Theoret. Comput. Sci., to appear.

[133] POPLAWSKI, D.A., On LL-regular grammars, J. Comput. System Sci. 18 (1979), 218-227.

[134] PRATHER, R.E., Minimal solutions of Paull-Unger problems, Math. Systems Theory 3 (1969), 76-85.

[135] RAIHA, K.-J., On attribute grammars and their use in a compiler writing system, Report A-1977-4, Dept. of Computer Science, University of Helsinki.

[136] RAIHA, K.-J. & M. SAARINEN, Developments in compiler writing systems, G.I.-6. Jahrestagung, E.J. Neuhold (ed.), Informatik Fachberichte 5 (Springer, Berlin, 1976), 164-178.

[137] RAIHA, K.-J., M. SAARINEN, E. SOISALON-SOININEN, M. TIENARI, The compiler writing system HLP, Report A-1978-2, Dept. of Computer Science, University of Helsinki.

[138] RECHENBERG, P., Sackgassenfreie Syntaxanalyse, Elektronische Rechenanlagen 3/4 (1973), 119-125 and 170-176.

[139] REICHARDT, J., Analysierbarkeit und Normalformen Transformation kontextfreier Grammatiken, TI 179, Technische Hochschule Darmstadt, 1979.

[140] REYNOLDS, J.C., Grammatical covering, Argonne National Laboratory, T.M. 96, 1968.

[141] REYNOLDS, J.C. & R. HASKELL, Grammatical coverings, unpublished manuscript, 1970.

[142] ROSENKRANTZ, D.J., Matrix equations and normal forms for context-free grammars, J. Assoc. Comput. Mach. 14 (1967), 501-507.

[143] ROSENKRANTZ, D.J. & P.M. LEWIS II, Deterministic left-corner parsing, IEEE Conf. Record of 11th Annual Sympos. on Switching and Automata Theory 1970, 139-152.

[144] ROSENKRANTZ, D.J. & R.E. STEARNS, Properties of deterministic top-down grammars, Information and Control 17 (1970), 226-256.

[145] RUZICKA, P., Local disambiguating transformations, in: Mathematical Foundations of Computer Science, J. Becvâr (ed.), Lect. Notes in Comp. Sci. 32 (Springer, Berlin, 1975), 399-404.

[146] SCHEPEN, H.I., Equivalentie van kontekstvrije grammatica's, afstudeerverslag T.H.-Delft, 1973.

[147] SCHLICHTIGER, P., Kettengrammatiken: Ein Konzept zur Definition handhabbarer Grammatikklassen met effizientem Analyseverhalten, Ph.D. Thesis, University of Kaiserslautern, 1979.

[148] SCHLICHTIGER, P., Partitioned chain grammars, in: Automata, Languages and Programming, J.W. de Bakker and J. v. Leeuwen (eds.), Lect. Notes in Comp. Sci., to appear.

[149] SCHLICHTIGER, P., On the parsing of partitioned chain grammars, Interner Bericht Nr. 21/79, University of Kaiserslautern, 1979.

[150] SCHLICHTIGER, P., On how to construct efficiently parsable grammars, Interner Bericht Nr. 22/80, University of Kaiserslautern, 1980.

[151] SCHNORR, C.P., Transformational classes of grammars, Information and Control 14 (1969), 252-277.

[152] SEBESTA, R.W. & N.D. JONES, Parsers for indexed grammars, Int. J. of Computer and Information Sciences 7 (1978), 345-359.

[153] SIPPU, S. & E. SOISALON-SOININEN, On defining error recovery in context-free parsing, in: Automata, Languages and Programming, A. Salomaa and M. Steinby (eds.), Lect. Notes in Comp. Sci. 52 (Springer, Berlin, 1977), 492-503.

[154] SIPPU, S. & E. SOISALON-SOININEN, A scheme for LR(k) parsing with error recovery, Int. J. of Computer Mathematics, to appear.

[155] SOISALON-SOININEN, E., Characterization of LL(k) languages by restricted LR(k) grammars, Ph.D. Thesis, Report A-1977-3, Dept. of Computer Science, University of Helsinki.

[156] SOISALON-SOININEN, E., On the covering problem for left-recursive grammars, Theoret. Comput. Sci. 8 (1979), 1-12.

[157] SOISALON-SOININEN, E. & E. UKKONEN, A method for transforming grammars into LL(k) form, Acta Informatica 12 (1979), 339-369.

[158] STEARNS, R.E., Deterministic top-down parsing, Proc. Fifth Princeton Conf. on Information Sciences and Systems 1971, 182-188.

[159] SZYMANSKI, T.G. & J.H. WILLIAMS, Noncanonical extensions of bottom-up parsing techniques, SIAM J. of Comput. 5 (1976), 231-250.

[160] TANIGUCHI, K. & T. KASAMI, Reduction of context-free grammars, Information and Control 17 (1970), 92-108.

[161] THOMPSON, D.H., The design and implementation of an advanced LALR parse table construct, UT-CSRG-79 (1977), University of Toronto.

[162] UKKONEN, E., Transformations to produce certain covering grammars, in: Mathematical Foundations of Computer Science, J. Winkowski (ed.), Lect. Notes in Comp. Sci. 64 (Springer, Berlin, 1978), 516-525.

[163] UKKONEN, E., Remarks on the nonexistence of some covering grammars, 4th G.I. Conf. on Theoretical Computer Science, K. Weihrauch (ed.), Lect. Notes in Comp. Sci. 67 (Springer, Berlin, 1979), 298-309.

[164] UKKONEN, E., The nonexistence of some covering context-free grammars, Info. Proc. Letters 8 (1978), 187-192.

[165] UKKONEN, E., Notes on grammatical covering by context-free grammars in normal forms, unpublished manuscript, 1979.

[166] UKKONEN, E., A modification of the LR(k) method for constructing compact bottom-up parsers, in: Automata, Languages and Programming, H.A. Maurer (ed.), Lect. Notes in Comp. Sci. 71 (Springer, Berlin, 1979), 646-658.

[167] WALTERS, D.A., Deterministic context-sensitive languages, Information and Control 17 (1970), 14-61.

[168] WHARTON, R.M., Resolution of ambiguity in parsing, Acta Informatica 6 (1976), 387-395.

[169] WILLIAMS, J.H., Bounded context parsable grammars, Information and Control 28 (1975), 314-334.

[170] WIRTH, N. & H. WEBER, Euler: A generalization of ALGOL and its formal definition:Parts I and II, Comm. ACM 9 (1966), 13-25 and 89-99.

[171] WOOD, D., The normal form theorem - another proof, Computer Journal 12 (1969), 139-147.

[172] WOOD, D., A generalized normal form theorem for context-free grammars, Computer Journal 13 (1970), 272-277.

[173] WOOD, D., The theory of left factored languages, Computer Journal 12 (1969), 349-356 and 13 (1970), 55-62.

[174] WOOD, D., A note on top-down deterministic languages, BIT 9 (1969), 387-399.

[175] WOOD, D., Lecture Notes on top-down syntax analysis, TR-78-CS-12, McMaster University, Hamilton, 1978.

[176] WOOD, D., Bibliography of grammatical similarity, EATCS-Bulletin 5, June 1978, 15-22.

[177] (added in proof) LAUFKÖTTER, F., Überdeckung kontextfreier Grammatiken,

insbesondere ε-freie Überdeckungen, Diplomarbeit, Techn. Hochschule Aachen, Dezember 1979.

INDEX

acceptance 10
ADJ 12
admissible partition 234
Aho, A.V. 5,7,9,20,24,34,35,48,51,101, 103,105,111,114,117,140,193,225, 236
almost-GNF 67,151
almost-standard 2-form 157
alphabet 5
ambiguous 6
AME 80
Anderson, S.O. 3,48
Anderson, T. 3
Arbib, M.A. 12
attribute grammar 30
automaton
  deterministic pushdown 105
  pushdown 9

Baker, B.S. 32
Beatty, J.C. 100,195
Benson, D.B. 3,5,12,28,48,51,54
Bertsch, E. 3,30
Bochmann, G.V. 3,31,104
bottom-up parsing 25,100
bounded right context grammars 101
bracketed context-free grammars 7,24
Brosgol, B.M. 3,25,49,102,117,208

category 12
CFG, see context-free grammar
CFL, see context-free language
chain 55
  -independent 172
  -k grammar 208
Ch(k) grammar 208
Cho, Y.E. 208
Chomsky normal form 210
Claus, V. 12,30
closure
  transitive-reflexive 6
  transitive-irreflexive 6
Cohen, R.S. 19,102
Colmerauer, A. 19,33,102
compiler-compiler 98
compiler writing system 98
complete cover 20
complexity 47
composition of morphisms 12
concatenation 5
configuration 9,10
context-free
  grammar 5
  language 6
corner
  extended left 25
  generalized left 25
  left 25
cover
  complete 20
  f-to-h 18
  left 26
  left-to-right 26
  right 26
  right-to-left 26
  weak 19
cover homomorphism 16
  faithful 16
  fine 20
  partial 16

proper 16
total 16
very fine 20
cover-table for
context-free grammars 82
LL-grammars 138
LR-grammars 169
regular grammars 93
strict deterministic grammars 163
Cremers, A.B. 3,30
Culik II, K. 19,100,102
cycle-free 8

degree of
ambiguity 7
a strict deterministic grammar 181
Demers, A.J. 24,102,208,209
Demner, J. 102,171
DeRemer, F.L. 33,101,102,105,171
derivation 6
leftmost 6
rightmost 6
derivation tree 7
derive relation 6
deterministic
bottom-up parsing 25,100
context-free language 106
finite transducer 106
left part parsing 196
pushdown automaton 105
pushdown transducer 106
top-down parsing 25,99
DPDA, see deterministic pushdown automaton
DPDT, see deterministic pushdown transducer
Druseikis, F.C. 105

Earley, J. 103
ε-free 8
elimination of
ε-rules 45
left recursion 48
single productions 41
empty set 5
empty string 5
equivalence
strong 7
structural 7
weak 7
Euler 19
extended
context-free grammar 58,102
left corner grammar 25
LL(k) grammar 102,104
LR(k) grammar 102
PC(k) grammar 238
Eve, J. 3

faithful
cover 16
functor 29
Feldman, J. 98,103
final state 9
fine cover homomorphism 20
FIRST function 6
$FIRST_k$ function 6
Fisher, G.A. 105
f-to-h cover 18
f_G-parsable grammar 113
f_G-parse 14
Floyd, R.W. 33
$FOLLOW_k$ function 212
Foster, J.M. 34,35,48,49,84,100,103
Friede, D. 232
frontier of a tree 7,191

Geller, M.M. 33,51,101,102,106,107,147,171,183,196,225,226
generalized left corner 25
generalized SDTS 32
Ginsburg, S. 3,7,24,29,30

GNF 8
$\overline{GNF}$ 8
Graham, S.L. 33,105,171,196
grammar (see also context-free grammar)
  cycle-free 8
  ε-free 8
  left recursive 8
  non-left-recursive 8
  non-right-recursive 8
  proper 8
  reduced 8
grammar functor 28
  externally fixed 28
  externally full 29
  faithful 29
  full 29
grammatical tree 191
Gray, J.N. 2,19,29,33,34,35,36,48,94,
    102
Greibach, S.A. 34,48
Greibach normal form 8,206
Griffiths, T.V. 34,83
Gries, D. 98,103
Goguen, J.A. 12

Haley, C.B. 105
Hammer, M. 33,100,208,230,238
handle 100
Harrison, M.A. 2,5,7,19,24,29,33,34,35,
    36,47,48,51,94,101,102,105,106,107,
    108,111,119,142,147,171,181,183,
    189,191,195,196,225,226,232
Haskell, R. 29
Havel, I.M. 51,101,107,108,111,119,142,
    147,172,181,189,191,195,232
Heilbrunner, S. 58,102
Hoffmann, H.J. 105
homomorphism 5
  cover 16
  fine 20
  parse 15
  partial cover 16
  partial parse 15
  very fine 20
Hopcroft, J.E. 108,171
Horning, J.J. 3,104
Hotz, G. 1,2,3,12,30,48,206
Hunt III, H.B. 3,20,29,30,33,100

identity 13
identity homomorphism 18,19
immediate descendancy 190
initial
  configuration 10,197
  production 225
  state 9
injective 15
input grammar 9
input symbol 9
invertible 181
iteration theorem 195

Jarzabek, S. 102
Johnson, S.C. 101,103,104,105,114,206
Joliat, M.L. 104
Jones, N.D. 102,104
Joy, W.N. 105

Kasami, T. 30
Kirchhoff, L.W. 104
Knuth, D.E. 3,30,33,101
Korenjak, A.J. 108,171
Kral, J. 102,171,189
Krawczyk, T. 102
Kretinsky, M. 102
Kristensen, B.B. 102
Kron, H.H. 105
k-transformable grammar 230,238
Kuno, S. 24,33,34,48,49,84
Kuo-Chung Tai 102
Kurki-Suonio, R. 24,34,48,49,84
Kuroda, S.Y. 30

label 5,191
LaLonde, W.R. 102,104
LALR(1) grammar 101
Lancaster, R.L. 104,105
language, see context-free language
lattice 28,150
Laufkötter, F. 47
LC(k) grammar 209,224
LeCarme, O. 104
Lee, E.S. 104
left
  cover 26
  factored form 8,139,222
  factoring 139,186,222
  parse relation 18
  parsable grammar 113
  recursive grammar 8
  recursive nonterminal 8
  regular grammar 8,85
left corner 25
  grammar, see LC(k) grammar
  parsable grammar 113
  parse 22
lefthand side of a production 5
leftmost derivation 6
left part 191
  grammar 192
  parsable grammar 113
  parse 25,26
  property 192
  theorem 189
  transformation 56
left-right order 190
left sentential form 7
left-to-right cover 26
length of a
  derivation 6
  string 5
letter 5
Leong, B. 3
Lewi, J. 102,104,105
Lewis II, P.M. 5,25,33,48,100,102,
  111,112,139,207,226,227
LL(k) grammar 100,109,127,208,211
LL-regular grammar 102
Lomet, D.B. 147
LP(k) grammar 208,213
LR-regular grammar 102

MacLane, S. 12
Madsen, M. 104
Madsen, O.L. 102
Manes, E.G. 12
Mayer, O. 3
McNaughton, R. 7,24,30
Mickunas, M.D. 104,105
Milton, D.R. 104
minimal strict partition 107
morphism 12
Moura, A. 164,238
move 9,10
mutually chain-independent 173

NLR 8
non-left-recursive grammar 8
non-right-recursive grammar 8
nonterminal symbol 5,9
NRR 8
normal form
  (see Chomsky normal form)
  (see Greibach normal form)
number of a production 5
Nijholt, A. 19,25,36,48,51,84,100,
  102,105,117,147,171,207,208

object 12
output grammar 9
output symbol 9,10

parenthesis grammar 7,24
parse
  homomorphism 15,16

relation 14
tree 7,191
parser 112
partial parse homomorphism 15
partial cover homomorphism 16
partition 107,232
partitioned chain grammar 238
Paull, M.C. 29,30,33,100
PC(k) grammar 238
PDA, see pushdown automaton
PDT, see pushdown transducer
Pennello, T.J. 105
Petrick, S.R. 34,83
Pittl, J. 108,212
PLC(k) grammar 208,213
PLR(k) grammar 209,227
pushdown automaton 9
pushdown list symbol 9
pushdown transducer 10
Poplawski, D.A. 102
Prather, R.E. 30
prefix-free 55,107,175
production 5
production directed parse relation 21, 102
production map 20
proper context-free grammar 8
properly injective 15
properly surjective 16
proper parse relation 14

quasi-GNF 8
quasi Greibach normal form 8

Räihä, K.-J. 103,104
real-time strict deterministic grammar 108
Rechenberg, P. 208
reduced grammar 8
regular grammar 8,85
Reichardt, J. 48,184,210
representation 45,127
Reuvecamp, Carla *iv*
reverse of a string 5
Reynolds, J.C. 29,34
right cover 26
righthand side of a production 5
rightmost derivation 6
right parsable grammar 113
right parse relation 18
right regular grammar 8,85
right sentential form 7
right-to-left cover 26
root label 191
Rosenkrantz, D.J. 3,5,20,25,29,30,33, 34,48,51,87,100,102,109,112,139, 140,207,226,227
Ross, R.J. 3
Rowland, B.R. 104
rule alternative 5
Ruzicka, P. 103

Saarinen, M. 103
Schepen, H.I. 30
Schlichtiger, P. 184,238
Schneider, V.B. 104,105
Schnorr, C.P. 12,30
Sebesta, R.W. 102
semantic actions 24
semantically unambiguous 9,11
sentential form 7
simple
chain grammar 23,171,172,221
deterministic grammar 30,108
DPDT 197
f_G-parsable 198
LR(1) grammar 101
SDTS 9
syntax directed translation scheme 9
single production 7,41
SLR(1), see simple LR(1) grammar
Sippu, S. 105

Soisalon-Soininen, E. 33,48,49,84, 100,105,112,207,208,225,227,229
sparse parse relation 20
standard construction 11,119
standard form 8
standard 2-form 8
standard observation 12
start symbol 5,9
state symbol 9
Stearns, R.E. 5,33,35,48,51,100,102, 109,111,139,140,230
srict deterministic grammar 101,107, 141
strict ε-production 127
strict partition 107
strong
  equivalence 7
  LL(k) grammar 109,140,212
  LP(k) grammar 215
  PC(k) grammar 238
  PLC(k) grammar 213
  SD(k) grammar 232
structural equivalence 7,30
structurally isomorphic 30,190
surjective 15
symbol 5
symmetry 40
syntax category 12
syntax directed parse relation 21
Szymanski, T.G. 19,20,30,102

Taniguchi, K. 30
terminal symbol 5
Thatcher, J.W. 12
Thompson, D.H. 102,105
top-down parsing 25,99
transitivity
  of covers 38
  partition 38,121
  relation 38,121
translation 9,11

Ukkonen, E. 19,48,78,80,100,102,207, 208,225,227,229,230,238
Ullman, J.D. 5,7,9,20,24,34,35,48,51, 101,103,105,111,114,117,140,193, 225,236
unambiguous grammar 6
unambiguous parse relation 113
Unger, S.H. 29,30,33,100
uniform grammar 108,150
useless symbol 7

valid DPDT 112
valid simple DPDT 198
very fine cover homomorphism 20

Wagner, E.G. 12
Walters, D.A. 102
Ward, P. 104
weak
  cover 19
  equivalence 7
  partition 232
  PLR(k) grammar 231
  SD(k) grammar 234
Weber, H. 30
Weber, M. 105
Wharton, R.H. 103
Williams, J.H. 19,33,102
Winkler, G. 105
Wirth, N. 33
Wood, D. 48,100,207
word 5
Wotschke, D. 3
Wright, J.B. 12

Yacc 104,206

Vol. 49: Interactive Systems. Proceedings 1976. Edited by A. Blaser and C. Hackl. VI, 380 pages. 1976.

Vol. 50: A. C. Hartmann, A Concurrent Pascal Compiler for Minicomputers. VI, 119 pages. 1977.

Vol. 51: B. S. Garbow, Matrix Eigensystem Routines – Eispack Guide Extension. VIII, 343 pages. 1977.

Vol. 52: Automata, Languages and Programming. Fourth Colloquium, University of Turku, July 1977. Edited by A. Salomaa and M. Steinby. X, 569 pages. 1977.

Vol. 53: Mathematical Foundations of Computer Science. Proceedings 1977. Edited by J. Gruska. XII, 608 pages. 1977.

Vol. 54: Design and Implementation of Programming Languages. Proceedings 1976. Edited by J. H. Williams and D. A. Fisher. X, 496 pages. 1977.

Vol. 55: A. Gerbier, Mes premières constructions de programmes. XII, 256 pages. 1977.

Vol. 56: Fundamentals of Computation Theory. Proceedings 1977. Edited by M. Karpiński. XII, 542 pages. 1977.

Vol. 57: Portability of Numerical Software. Proceedings 1976. Edited by W. Cowell. VIII, 539 pages. 1977.

Vol. 58: M. J. O'Donnell, Computing in Systems Described by Equations. XIV, 111 pages. 1977.

Vol. 59: E. Hill, Jr., A Comparative Study of Very Large Data Bases. X, 140 pages. 1978.

Vol. 60: Operating Systems, An Advanced Course. Edited by R. Bayer, R. M. Graham, and G. Seegmüller. X, 593 pages. 1978.

Vol. 61: The Vienna Development Method: The Meta-Language. Edited by D. Bjørner and C. B. Jones. XVIII, 382 pages. 1978.

Vol. 62: Automata, Languages and Programming. Proceedings 1978. Edited by G. Ausiello and C. Böhm. VIII, 508 pages. 1978.

Vol. 63: Natural Language Communication with Computers. Edited by Leonard Bolc. VI, 292 pages. 1978.

Vol. 64: Mathematical Foundations of Computer Science. Proceedings 1978. Edited by J. Winkowski. X, 551 pages. 1978.

Vol. 65: Information Systems Methodology, Proceedings, 1978. Edited by G. Bracchi and P. C. Lockemann. XII, 696 pages. 1978.

Vol. 66: N. D. Jones and S. S. Muchnick, TEMPO: A Unified Treatment of Binding Time and Parameter Passing Concepts in Programming Languages. IX, 118 pages. 1978.

Vol. 67: Theoretical Computer Science, 4th GI Conference, Aachen, March 1979. Edited by K. Weihrauch. VII, 324 pages. 1979.

Vol. 68: D. Harel, First-Order Dynamic Logic. X, 133 pages. 1979.

Vol. 69: Program Construction. International Summer School. Edited by F. L. Bauer and M. Broy. VII, 651 pages. 1979.

Vol. 70: Semantics of Concurrent Computation. Proceedings 1979. Edited by G. Kahn. VI, 368 pages. 1979.

Vol. 71: Automata, Languages and Programming. Proceedings 1979. Edited by H. A. Maurer. IX, 684 pages. 1979.

Vol. 72: Symbolic and Algebraic Computation. Proceedings 1979. Edited by E. W. Ng. XV, 557 pages. 1979.

Vol. 73: Graph-Grammars and Their Application to Computer Science and Biology. Proceedings 1978. Edited by V. Claus, H. Ehrig and G. Rozenberg. VII, 477 pages. 1979.

Vol. 74: Mathematical Foundations of Computer Science. Proceedings 1979. Edited by J. Bečvář. IX, 580 pages. 1979.

Vol. 75: Mathematical Studies of Information Processing. Proceedings 1978. Edited by E. K. Blum, M. Paul and S. Takasu. VIII, 629 pages. 1979.

Vol. 76: Codes for Boundary-Value Problems in Ordinary Differential Equations. Proceedings 1978. Edited by B. Childs et al. VIII, 388 pages. 1979.

Vol. 77: G. V. Bochmann, Architecture of Distributed Computer Systems. VIII, 238 pages. 1979.

Vol. 78: M. Gordon, R. Milner and C. Wadsworth, Edinburgh LCF. VIII, 159 pages. 1979.

Vol. 79: Language Design and Programming Methodology. Proceedings, 1979. Edited by J. Tobias. IX, 255 pages. 1980.

Vol. 80: Pictorial Information Systems. Edited by S. K. Chang and K. S. Fu. IX, 445 pages. 1980.

Vol. 81: Data Base Techniques for Pictorial Applications. Proceedings, 1979. Edited by A. Blaser. XI, 599 pages. 1980.

Vol. 82: J. G. Sanderson, A Relational Theory of Computing. VI, 147 pages. 1980.

Vol. 83: International Symposium Programming. Proceedings, 1980. Edited by B. Robinet. VII, 341 pages. 1980.

Vol. 84: Net Theory and Applications. Proceedings, 1979. Edited by W. Brauer. XIII, 537 Seiten. 1980.

Vol. 85: Automata, Languages and Programming. Proceedings, 1980. Edited by J. de Bakker and J. van Leeuwen. VIII, 671 pages. 1980.

Vol. 86: Abstract Software Specifications. Proceedings, 1979. Edited by D. Bjørner. XIII, 567 pages. 1980

Vol. 87: 5th Conference on Automated Deduction. Proceedings, 1980. Edited by W. Bibel and R. Kowalski. VII, 385 pages. 1980.

Vol. 88: Mathematical Foundations of Computer Science 1980. Proceedings, 1980. Edited by P. Dembiński. VIII, 723 pages. 1980.

Vol. 89: Computer Aided Design - Modelling, Systems Engineering, CAD-Systems. Proceedings, 1980. Edited by J. Encarnacao. XIV, 461 pages. 1980.

Vol. 90: D. M. Sandford, Using Sophisticated Models in Resolution Theorem Proving.
XI, 239 pages. 1980

Vol. 91: D. Wood, Grammar and L Forms: An Introduction. IX, 314 pages. 1980.

Vol. 92: R. Milner, A Calculus of Communication Systems. VI, 171 pages. 1980.

Vol. 93: A. Nijholt, Context-Free Grammars: Covers, Normal Forms, and Parsing. VII, 253 pages. 1980.

Printed in the United States
by Baker & Taylor Publisher Services